A SURVEY OF PRIMITIVE MONEY

1. *Sapi sapi*, Trobriands, p. 172
2. *Sapi sapi*, New Guinea, p. 172
3, 4. Trade beads, Uganda, p. 99

5. Trade beads, Ujiji, p. 102
6. " Aggry " beads, West Africa, p. 39
7. Chevron bead, Africa, p. 39
8. " Aggry " bead, Gold Coast, p. 39

A Survey of
Primitive Money

THE BEGINNING OF CURRENCY

by

A. HINGSTON QUIGGIN

with an introduction by
A. C. HADDON

METHUEN & CO LTD
36 ESSEX STREET · STRAND · WC2

First published 1949
Reprinted with corrections 1963
Type set by Butler & Tanner Ltd
Reprinted lithographically in Great Britain
by John Dickens & Co Ltd Northampton
Catalogue No 2/3978/10
1.2

TO

H. F. BIRD

WHO COULD AND SHOULD
HAVE WRITTEN THIS BOOK

INTRODUCTION

By A. C. HADDON

MANY years ago Sir William Ridgeway and I were collecting examples of 'primitive money'. Sir William approached the subject from the side of classical archaeology, but he was no mere classicist or archaeologist, as he had a considerable knowledge of various aspects of ethnology and was keen to apply the data of ethnology to the elucidation of classical and archaeological problems. These wide interests were manifest in his writings and not least in his *Origin of Metallic Currency*, 1892. In this stimulating book he presented views new and old, for, as in all he said and did, he markedly had the courage of his convictions, and was not afraid of making suggestions which, though often discredited by his colleagues, had a queer habit of being more or less verified in the end. The *Origin* marked a distinct advance in the study of comparative currency and laid a foundation upon which others could build.

On the other hand, I approached the subject from the opposite side. As early as 1888 I was interested in the trading operations of the Torres Straits islanders and in their media of exchange. In later years I began to collect specimens of primitive currency from various parts of the world, and Ridgeway and I exchanged duplicates.

Sir Richard Temple in his paper read to the Anthropological Institute in London in 1899 was the first to review the whole world, and propose a classification of the material, though *La science sociale* had already published several of the articles which appeared in book form in Babelon's *Origines de la monnaie* in 1897. Schurtz (*Grundriss einer Entstehungsgeschichte des Geldes*, 1898) attacked the theory of exchanges ; Thilenius ('Primitives Geld', 1921) and Regling (in Ebert's *Reallexikon der Vorgeschichte*, 1926) added comprehensive reviews of the material, which Montandon (*Traité d'ethnologie culturelle*, 1934) expanded and plotted on a map.

But the material is constantly accumulating. There are innumerable accounts by missionaries, administrators and field-ethnologists concerning local types of currency and native trading which afford valuable data, and in a few cases throw light upon the social, economic and even ethical aspects of the accumulation of wealth and its distribution.

Cambridge has been particularly fortunate in her field-ethnologists, and, perhaps partly owing to the well-known interest of both Sir William Ridgeway and myself in the subject, has obtained an unusually large collection of primitive currency. I have much pleasure in taking this opportunity to express my cordial appreciation of the honorary work done in the University Museum of Archaeology and Ethnology by Mr. H. F. Bird, M.A. Besides cataloguing numerous collections and other assistance he has devoted years of patient labour to arranging the specimens of primitive currency and to garnering all the published and unpublished information available to him on the subject.

It is full time that these scattered records should be collated for the use of students, and we have to thank Mrs. Quiggin for having accomplished this task. Not only has she done this, but she has studied in many museums in England, on the continent of Europe, in Africa, in Canada and the United States of America. This has enabled her to gain a first-hand knowledge of the actual specimens about which others have written, and also to add unpublished examples to those already available for study. In the course of her studies Mrs. Quiggin has found herself unable to agree with various theories concerning the origin of money, and she offers a fresh interpretation for the consideration of students. This suggestion is the result of a careful weighing of the evidence and it provides an explanation which is, to my mind, more satisfactory than those which have preceded it.

A. C. H.

AUTHOR'S PREFACE

WHEN the yearly output of books in Great Britain alone used to average some 16,000, of which barely a third consisted of fiction, it is surprising that there can be any subject of human interest still undescribed. But there is, as yet, no general survey of the stages which preceded the use of coins as the medium of exchange, and of the objects that coins displaced, objects which for want of a better name are here called Primitive Money.

Many books have been written about the obsolete currencies of different countries, especially about those of the ancient civilizations of the Orient, where money has been in use for hundreds if not thousands of years ; papers have from time to time appeared in scientific journals, and occasionally in more popular form, describing different objects used as currency and the methods in which they are (more commonly were) employed ; collections of currency, consisting of shells, beads, hoes, spears and other picturesque types are exhibited in museums ; and there are abundant references in ethnographical literature and in books of travel. But there is no general book on the subject ; there is scarcely an adequately descriptive catalogue of a comprehensive collection.[1]

The eleventh edition of the *Encyclopaedia Britannica* (1910) though it had a separate article on ' Shell-money ' paid no attention to primitive currency beyond quotations from Tylor and a brief review of ' substitutes for money ', and the bibliography contained no further references.

The fifteenth edition (1929) has a separate article on ' Currency, Primitive ', with a short bibliography and a cross-reference to ' Trade, Primitive ', by the same able pen. The author, however, limits himself so severely by precise terminology that he rejects all objects that cannot be proved to have attained the high standard of his definition. Such rigidity would eliminate most of the objects labelled

---

[1] Professor Henry Balfour's descriptive catalogue of the Pitt Rivers Collection, Oxford, was eagerly awaited. But while this book was in the making the news of his death destroyed our hopes. I take this opportunity of recording my gratitude for his kindly help.

' Currency ' in museum collections. And it is museum collections, and especially the one in the Museum of Archaeology and Ethnology at Cambridge, that provided the inspiration and much of the material for this book.

The problems entangled in the subject of primitive money and the beginnings of currency are many and varied, and the earlier solutions were based more on literary evidence than on museum specimens. This attempt at disentanglement is based on a display of all the material evidence, an examination of it without prejudice, with such deductions as appear to be justified.

The material evidence is provided for others by the numerous illustrations, without which the letterpress would have little value. Most of the photographs of the Cambridge Collection owe their excellence to the skill and care of Mr. Strickland or of Mr. Tams ; many were collected by Sir William Ridgeway or by Mr. Bird ; many are loans, acknowledgements of which will be found on p. xxi. The maps and diagrams were drawn for me by D. Baldwin at the Cambridge Geography School and by my sons. The maps include all place-names mentioned in the text, and those who have worked on similar lines will appreciate the advantage of having a draughtsman at hand, ready, up to the last moment before going to press, to add, alter or eliminate a name.

May I here record in permanent form my gratitude to Mrs. Daphne Kennett for her skill, and also for her scrupulous care and unceasing patience, in the reproduction of more than 150 examples.[1] These were specially chosen to provide a sure basis for present and, it is hoped, for future discussion. Had author and artist had their way, all would have been in colour, or at least in wash, but this would have raised the price of the book far beyond the reach of those students for whom it is intended. For it is hoped that by co-ordinating a vast amount of fragmentary evidence, by sifting contradictory accounts and collecting the results into a handy volume, some service may be rendered to other ethnographical, sociological or economic students working in adjoining fields.

[1] The life-like sketch of the man with the copper on p. 302 was kindly made for me by Miss Helen Cabot of the Museum of Natural History, New York.

R. S. Poole, Professor of Archaeology at University College, London, declared that

To be a great general numismatist is beyond the powers of one man. Some may know Greek and Latin enough, with such mastery of English, German and Italian as the modern commentaries demand, to begin the study of Greek and Roman money. Those who would enter the vast field of Oriental numismatics must be fortified with Arabic, Hebrew, Sanskrit and Persian, besides adding Spanish and Russian to the other languages still necessary for their work. Even they must pause beneath the Himalayas not dare to cross the Golden Chersonese unless they are prepared to master the uncouth languages and intricate characters of the further East (pp. 1–2, 1892).

One might add that to attempt the study of the general prehistory of numismatics is beyond the powers of one man, save of the type that rushes in where angels fear to tread, especially where the study necessitates some acquaintance with the human history of the whole world. But Fortune favours the bold ; so too does the expert, whether ethnologist, archaeologist or numismatist, and here follows a short list of benefactors. The complete list of names and services rendered would fill many pages, so although it may appear invidious and ungrateful to make a selection, only those who have read and criticized the main sections are mentioned here.

Dr. A. B. Cook, the ' onlie begetter ' of the book, read through the chapter on Europe and he, Mrs. Hutton and Mr. C. T. Seltman are responsible for many emendations. Dr. A. C. Haddon, while specially criticizing the sections on Oceania, gave generous help, counsel and encouragement throughout, and the introduction (pp. vii and viii) was the last he wrote before his death. Mr. J. Driberg, besides criticizing the introductory chapters, made valuable suggestions in the sections on Africa. Professor E. H. Minns materially improved the section on China and so did Mr. J. I'a. Bromwich of St. John's. Dr. R. B. Whitehead corrected and amended the section on India ; Dr. W. W. Skeat, the Malay Peninsula ; Mr. J. C. Swayne, Borneo ; Dr. R. le May, Siam ; Mr. W. E. Armstrong, Rossel Island, and Mr. J. Layard, the New Hebrides. Mr. G. Shove gave advice on economic problems as also did Mr. E. Dale.

To all of these fairy godfathers and to many more, in this country (especially in the British Museum, the Horniman Museum and the Pitt Rivers), on the Continent (especially in Tervueren, Hamburg, Berlin and Vienna), in Africa (especially at Livingstone, Bulawayo, East London and Cape Town), in Canada (especially Toronto), in the United States (especially in Buffalo, Chicago, Washington and New York), who so generously allowed their special knowledge to be shared, and were so patient in answering questions, I record my gratitude and my consciousness of a debt that can never be repaid.

E. & O.E.

In official communications the above letters are familiar. The author alone is responsible for E. & O. in the following pages. The omissions are many, due to ignorance and lack of information : the errata are probably more, due to the same misfortunes. All corrections and additions will be welcomed.

A. H. Q.

CONTENTS

TEXT ILLUSTRATIONS

2

PLATES

MAPS
(*at end*)

ACKNOWLEDGEMENTS

GRATEFUL acknowledgement is made to the following:

W. R. Ridgeway and the Cambridge University Press, for illustrations from *Origin of Metallic Currency* (1892)	Figs. 26, 81, 82, 120-2, 124-6, 129
A. C. Haddon and the Cambridge University Press, for an illustration from *Torres Straits Reports*, Vol. IV (1912)	Fig. 79
The Trustees of the Royal Ontario Museum, Toronto	Pl. 2, Fig. 5; Pl. 3, Fig. 1
The Rev. K. Smith, for an illustration from *Yakusu* (published by Marshall Bros.)	Pl. 3, Fig. 4
Templeton Crocker	Pl. 6
The Trustees of the Australian Museum, Sydney	Pl. 7, Fig. 1
The Trustees of the British Museum	Pl. 9; Pl. 23, Fig. 2; Pl. 28, Fig. 1
The Trustees of the Dresden Museum	Pl. 10, Fig. 1
Beatrice Blackwood and the Clarendon Press, Oxford, for an illustration from *Both Sides of Buka Passage*	Pl. 10, Figs. 2-5
The Trustees of the Hamburg Museum	Pl. 11
G. Bushnell	Pl. 12, Fig. 1
C. G. Seligman, for a photograph and an illustration from *The Melanesians of British New Guinea* (published by the Cambridge University Press)	Pl. 13, Fig. 1; Pl. 14
The Trustees of the Field Museum of Natural History, Chicago	Pl. 15
The Trustees of the Smithsonian Institute, U.S. National Museum, Washington	Pls. 29, 31, 32
W. E. Armstrong; Cambridge University Press, and Royal Anthropological Institute, for an illustration from *Man* and *Rossel Island*	Pl. 18

xxi

Chapter I

DEFINITIONS

Th' intrinsic value of a thing
Is just as much as it will bring.
HUDIBRAS

EVERYONE, except an economist, knows what ' money ' means, and even an economist can describe it in the course of a chapter or so, but it is impossible to define with rigid outlines. It emerges dimly from objects of presentation or exchange, and shades imperceptibly into recognizable monetary forms with uncertain boundaries on either hand, and much of the material of this book hovers on the borders.

The *O.E.D.* definition of *money* as ' current coin ' is too narrow for a student of economics or of sociology, and would exclude almost all of the primitive money which is dealt with here. The definition of *currency*, ' that which is current as a medium of exchange ' includes the entire range from coconuts, cattle, or even sisters, to bank-notes ; so some limits must be set and Temple's threefold classification of ' barter ', ' currency ' and ' money ' supplied a useful scheme for sorting the heterogeneous mass of material to which he was among the first to draw attention at the Anthropological Institute in London in 1899.

Barter is exchange of possessions pure and simple. I exchange today my grain for your fruit and tomorrow my adze for your knife ; that is barter. But when our daily transactions become so far complicated as to require some other article in common domestic use to be interposed between the grain and the fruit, and between the adze and the knife, i.e. a medium between the articles bartered, we have set up a currency and a medium of exchange. Thus : you and I and the rest of our tribe have all got coconuts in varying quantities, and can find a use for them every day. I want fruit and you want grain, but instead of exchanging my grain for your fruit, I give you six pairs of coconuts for the fruit I want, and later on you come to me and give me five pairs of coconuts for the corn you want. Here we are bartering through a medium and coconuts are our currency. When we become a little more civilized and proceed to make purely conventional articles, usable only as a medium of exchange, we have set up a system of money. For currency consists of articles real or imaginary, used for account, i.e. for measuring the relative values of different articles of use. So many coconuts make one knife ; so many coconuts make one adze. Whereas money consists of tokens convertible into property. So many imitation spear heads can buy an adze ; so many can buy an axe.

He sums up his definitions thus :

Barter is the exchange of one article for another ; currency implies exchange through a medium ; money that the medium is a token.

This threefold division, although unacceptable to modern economists, makes a useful foundation for classification, and Temple fitted his examples into its framework. But it is easy to see its defects. For example, lumps or bars of metal can be used for barter, as currency and as money. A gold ring may be worn in the nose, or appear in a collection of Greek coins. Brick tea, weighed and stamped like a coin, may be crumbled and drunk. Salt may be a condiment or a dowry. Strings of shell disks may be merely ornaments in one island, and objects of barter, currency or tokens of value in another. Trade beads, primarily used for barter, develop through ' currency ' into ' money '; and cowries have passed through the same stages of evolution and back again into ornament without any money value. And it is the borderline cases that throw most light on the evolution of money and interesting sidelights on human societies as well.

For the two parties in a transaction may themselves stand in different categories. The trader may consider that he is paying current money when he buys a fowl for ten lengths of brass wire ; while the seller regards the exchange as ' mere barter '.

Commerce among the Baluba in the Belgian Congo gives a simple example. A man has something to sell. He squats down somewhere—anywhere—where a client may be expected, with his merchandise in front of him.

L'amateur passe—s'arrête—Eh, cette mesure de sel, combien ?—Dix perles—Discussion—Accord—On troque, pas de formalité, c'est tout (Colle, 1913, p. 790).

Are the beads used in barter, as currency, or are they ' money ' ?

An illustration may be taken from Uganda to show how an object can be at the same time currency or money, a religious symbol or a mere ornament. The Acholi being received as catechumens at the Roman Catholic Mission were given metal crosses as signs of conversion. With these they used to hurry away to the Didinga and exchange a cross for a goat. They returned later and entered as catechumens again. The crosses were religious symbols ; but to the Acholi they represented money ; they were tokens with which they could purchase goats ; while the Didinga received the crosses as ornaments and wore them in their head-dresses (J. H. Driberg).[1]

Our conception of money and the practice of buying and selling for the purpose of acquiring it for personal enrichment are seldom met with among the simpler societies. ' Primitive money ' is often indistinguishable from barterable goods, and when it is amassed it is more for social or religious than for commercial ends. If ' money-substitute ' (Geldsurrogat) were not too cumbrous a term it would be used in place of ' money ' throughout this book.

[1] A name without literary reference indicates that the information was supplied personally.

A useful dissection was made by Thilenius (1921, pp. 11 *ff.*) who distinguishes between *Nutzgeld* and *Zeichengeld*, between useful objects used in exchange ('Temple's ' barter ' stage) and objects of conventional form, practically useless, mere tokens of value (' currency ' or ' money '). Petri (1936, pp. 192–3) goes further. All objects in the *Nutzgeld* group are, he claims, not *Geld* in its true sense. True *Geld* or money has not only mercantile but also social significance, which latter is absent in merely useful objects. For example, in the South Seas, pigs, turmeric, red ochre, axe blades, arrows and spears are well established exchange articles in interinsular trade. This is only *Nutzgeld*. If we turn to strings of shell disks, pieces of mother of pearl shell, arm-rings or mats as recognized standards of value with social significance in a community, we have to do with *Zeichengeld*.

But ' social significance ' is a vague term, and in sorting out material in a museum it is difficult to discover a dividing line between the two classes. Shells are merely shells on one island, but are used in trade exchange with another, where they form the currency. Mats are used in barter, but some, acquiring dignity with age, or prestige with travel or special use, develop into a recognized currency. Spears and hoes in Africa, like knives and hoes in China, pass readily from *Nutzgeld* to *Zeichengeld*, and, in Africa, pass as easily back again. It is still more difficult to classify the varied ornaments which those who study the South Seas alone may well believe to be the basis of all primitive money. Is a string of shell-money no longer currency when you wear it round your neck ? Is a sovereign no longer money when dangled on your watchchain ?

In short (to quote Chase, 1938, p. 197):

Neither you nor I nor anyone else knows what ' money ' means or how it works. We know what it means where and when we use it, for here we are performing little personal operations. But its general laws, if any, are unknown to even the wisest banker or the profoundest economist.

Both banker and economist would probably agree, however, upon certain fundamental characteristics, which have been fixed since the time of Aristotle : portability, durability, divisibility and distinction. Among the humbler folk with whom this book deals there is an intangible essential which is more important than these four qualities and far more difficult to define. It is a quality or intrinsic virtue acquired by reputation, association or use, something akin to *mana* in Oceania, to what is often loosely called ' fetish ' in Africa or ' luck ' with us (*cf.* Laum, 1924 *passim*). This makes such objects so desirable that they ' pass for money '. A general survey of such objects and of the local attitude towards them provides a necessary foundation for the study of the origin and evolution of money.

It is therefore with the practical and objective, not the theoretical aspect of money, that we are here concerned. For our present purpose the term money will be restricted to such forms as serve the threefold function of a recognized medium of exchange, a standard of value and a symbol of wealth. Whether the object so employed is of intrinsic value, like a golden sovereign, or none, like a five-pound note, i.e. ' full-bodied money ' or ' token-money ', is of minor importance. Axes and spears, mill-stones or beetle-legs, beads, shells, teeth or gold rings are money if they behave as such. If they fail in any of these three essentials they may be called currency (a recognized medium of exchange [1] or standard of value) or they may (like much so-called primitive money) be merely evidence of wealth. Wealth also needs interpretation, for in this connexion it is less concerned with the possession of objects of value, than with the power or prestige associated with them. But terminological exactitude cannot be enforced where evidence of function is so lamentably difficult to obtain. Perhaps (to quote Chase again, 1938, p. 198) : ' the most important thing about money is the human willingness to accept it ', and the following chapters are concerned with such objects as are or have been accepted by peoples before the introduction of a system of coined money.

And here, at the outset of our investigation, it must frankly be admitted that many objects are called ' currency ' which are never current. They may serve as standards of value or as symbols of wealth, two of the functions of money, but they are never used in ordinary trading. They pass from hand to hand, or from group to group, in important transactions, and play a large part in gift-exchange and in ' bride-price ' [2] but they cannot be termed currency, still less, money, in their proper senses. Unfortunately it is too late now to discover actual or ' ceremonial ' [3] use of many of these objects. All that can be done is to collect what information is still

---

[1] The term ' medium of exchange ' is far too loosely used. With us money can be used to buy anything from daily bread to a motor-car, and indirectly the same money can buy titles and even wives. But with primitive forms of money there is rarely universal use. One kind will buy food ; another is necessary for a canoe ; while still another may be essential in secret societies or in marriage payments.

[2] The incorrect term ' bride-price ' is here used as no satisfactory substitute has so far been generally accepted. ' Bride-wealth ', ' bride-compensation ', ' marriage-insurance ', ' dower ', ' settlement ', ' indemnity ', ' earnest ', ' equilibrium-guarantee ' all have their supporters—and critics. So it seems best to retain the earlier word, placing it within inverted commas to indicate ' so-called ', though no one who reads this book is likely to be misled into thinking that either ' bride-price ' or marriage by purchase necessarily imply commercial buying and selling. Cf. discussions in Man, 1929–31.

[3] ' Ceremonial '. For the significance of this term cf. Malinowski, 1922, pp. 89–90.

available as a basis, and leave deductions to more experienced workers in the field.

> Every book on economics [says Burns, 1927, p. 1] introduces the reader to the subject of money by way of an account of the trials and troubles of life in a community where unorganized barter is the only method of exchange. A community without a medium of exchange or a unit of value has, however, never been found and the stage is one imagined for simplicity of exposition of the merits of money—it must not be taken seriously.

This is a stage however which *must* be taken seriously in the following pages, many of which are devoted to the study of communities all over the world ' without a medium of exchange or a unit of value '.

Rajah Brooke gives a picture of the Land Dyak in a Borneo bazaar.

> He has no conception of the use of a circulating medium. He may be seen wandering in the bazaar with a .ball of beeswax in his hand for days together because he cannot find anyone willing to take it for the exact article he requires. This article may not be more than a tenth of the value of the beeswax, but he would not sell it for money and then buy what he wants. From the first he had the particular article in his mind's eye and worked for the identical ball of beeswax with which and nothing else to purchase it (Ling Roth, 1896, II, p. 231).

Beeswax is, however, a recognized form of currency in Borneo (p. 259) and a better example of the inconvenience of barter may be found nearer home.

A witness before the Inquiry of Framework Knitters in 1845 stated as follows :

> When Saturday night came I had to turn out with a certain quantity of meat and candles or tobacco or ale or whatever I had drawn in wages to dispose of at a serious loss. I used to take a can of ale to the barber to get shaved with, and a can of ale to the sweep to sweep my chimney. I was in good receipt of wages and in company with my neighbours used to take in a newspaper, and I was obliged to take a pound of candles at sevenpence and leave it for the newspaper, the price of which was fourpence halfpenny. I used to take my beef at sevenpence a pound and sell it to the coal woman that I had my coals from, for fivepence, and any bit of sugar or tea or anything of the kind that my employer did not sell, I used to get from the grocer by swapping soap or starch (Knowles, 1922, p. 88).

Such inconveniences are avoided in simpler societies by elaborate customs of credit, deferred payments or payment by services. Wealth sometimes appears to consist in the amassing of goods or obligations by one man, so that the entire community is dependent on him, sometimes by his lavish distributions, so that all are in his debt. But it would be hard to find any among the simpler societies consciously troubled by the inconveniences of barter, and money is usually the introduction of the trader and troubles from outside.

The absence of any medium of exchange or unit of value in Australia, Polynesia, and the greater part of the Americas will be discussed later. The absence in Africa [1] added greatly to the trials and troubles of explorers. Stanley recalls how in Zanzibar, in 1871, he tossed on his bed at night, asking himself how much cloth, how many beads, how much wire would be needed ; and much worse, how many carriers for all these loads. And he finally started off in his search for Livingstone with an equipment in cloth, beads and wire weighing sixty tons and a total number in his expedition of 200 men.

But unfortunately for the explorer and for the trader, the cloth, beads and brass wire are not yet currency. They have only an unorganized bartering value, and local preferences or prejudices may give them fictitious values or render them worthless lumber. When cowries were first brought into Uganda, two would purchase a woman ; a generation later it took 2,000 or 3,000 to purchase even a male slave. One district in the Congo will accept only blue beads,[2] another, red ; here a short length of wire is accepted, there, rejected ; and a whole cargo of *manillas* may be left on a trader's hands, owing to some deviation from the standard.

Cameron's experiences travelling across Africa from east to west illustrate these difficulties. He, like Stanley, started off with the usual assortment of trade beads and trade goods, but found, on crossing Lake Tanganyika, that the beads were no longer currency, and he had to lay in a stock of copper crosses. When he reached Nyangwe on the Lualaba, an important market town, where he was expecting to buy a canoe and continue his journey, nothing was accepted save slaves, goats and cowries. Here he was delayed for weeks unable to trade. He tried to buy cowries at the extortionate rate of the equivalent of 3d. or 4d. a piece, and collected the price of a canoe. But the chief would not sell. He explained that as the shells would all be appropriated by his wives for decorations, the canoe would be a dead loss to him, as the wives, however lavishly decorated with cowries, would not feed or look after him any the better. Cameron offered double the value of the canoe in cowries saying that the wives could not possibly wear them all. But No, that was not the only disadvantage of cowries compared with livestock. The shells would lie idle, while the slaves or goats as soon as they were bought started reproductive work and soon repaid their purchase money (1877, II, p. 7).

[1] The most conspicuous examples of trading communities with established markets and no currency are described by Barth in Bornu (1858, II, pp. 310 ff.).
[2] For a missionary gamble in large blue beads, making £16 10s. out of 2s. 9d. worth, see Bentley's entertaining account (1900 II, p. 21).

The stages which preceded the use of money throw light on its early history. Writers on its origin and evolution have paid exaggerated attention to the influence of trade, which, though doubtless the chief stimulus in its subsequent development, was possibly absent, or at any rate negligible, at its birth. There are earlier human institutions than trading, and among the earliest are marriage and blood-revenge. It would be extravagant to claim that ' brideprice ' and wergeld brought currency into existence, but they certainly established standards of value and regularized certain media of exchange, which are two of the three main functions of money as defined above.

It is a custom almost as universal as marriage itself that among the less-civilized societies a man has in some way or other to give compensation for his bride, either by exchange, by services rendered or by transfer of property (Westermarck, 1891, p. 390).

Among the simpler societies, where property is insignificant, gifts at marriage are also insignificant or non-essential, although even among the Eskimo or the aborigines of Australia, where wedding ceremonies are reduced to a minimum, the man is commonly expected to give presents to his future father-in-law. And among the Tikopians, by whom money is ignored, and pennies given in exchange for coconuts or bananas, thrown away as ' useless bits of iron ', the ' payment for the woman ' consists of certain conventional presents of wooden bowls and rolls of sinnet, ' a formal equivalent to her family for the loss of her services ' (Firth, 1936, pp. 6, 551–2). Examples may be found all over the world.   Among the ancient as among the modern Semites, in the Vedic texts as in Homer, in Babylonia, China and Japan, Africa, Melanesia, Polynesia or the New World, the giving of presents and/or extortion of payments appear (with few exceptions) as essential features of the marriage rites : and whether reminiscent of ' bride-price ' or of dower, wedding presents are universally considered an essential feature of the ceremony in civilized communities at the present day.   There can be no uniformity in a world-wide custom such as this, dating from the beginning of human history ; but certain characteristic features can generally be recognized. The wedding presents or payments tend to become conventionalized or symbolic, and hence preserve antiquated forms even when coins are in ordinary commercial use.   This accounts for much of the ' primitive money ' found in museums at the present day.   Also, there is, in less advanced societies, a tendency to regard the presents or payments made by the bridegroom or his kin, as the equivalent of the value of the woman, and they fluctuate with the position and attractions of the bride and the bargaining powers of her relatives.   Thus recognized media of exchange and standards of value are established.

When objects formerly used as money are still used in marriage-payments it is usual to say that these archaic forms ' survive in bride-price '; but they represent a pre-currency origin, as well as a post-currency survival, and the ease with which cash payments are now substituted shows the part they take in the story of the evolution of money.

' Bride-price ' and ' blood-price ' have much in common—the payment represents an indemnity. (*Cf.* Radcliffe-Brown, 1929.)

Blood feud in primitive form demands life for life; as society grows less bloodthirsty the demand is whittled down into a system of payments made to the injured party, or if he is beyond repair, to his kinsfolk. This wergeld, like ' bride-price ', is often the occasion of prolonged controversy and perhaps further casualties, but usually, as with the latter, there is a definite scale of values. In India the *vairan* or wergeld was in cows, a 100 for a man, whether he was insulted, wounded or murdered, and 100 cows was also the average ' bride-price '. In Scandinavia a silver ring was the equivalent of a thrall, 100 rings or 100 head of cattle of a freeman. In Ireland the *eric* consisted of cattle or slaves, the clan chief being reckoned at 180 cows and a slave at 3 or 4, and a pound of silver. Or a slave's freedom might be bought for a gold ring. In Scotland in the 12th century the worth of the king's person was valued at 1,000 cows, down to the villein at 10. In ancient Arabia, the ransom of a murder was 100 camels for the death of a freeman (*cf.* Hastings, 1908).

An example of a people with no currency, yet with definite scales of prices for wives and for blood-money may be taken from Kenya. The Mkamba of the Kitui district, between the Athi and the Tana rivers, are cattle-keepers and the cattle are all-important.

> To a Mkamba his greatest pride and joy are his cattle, nothing else has the same value in his eyes. . . . Even a wife is a second consideration to these, for after all she is only valued as a portion of the herd.

Cattle here include cows, sheep and goats, about 30 of the latter being equal to a cow. A cow is rarely parted with, save for wife purchase, and the slaughter of one, even to avert starvation, is inconceivable. The main use of goats and sheep, on the contrary, is for presents, sacrifices and trading.

The average scale for injuries is high. For the loss of a finger, one bull and one goat, for two fingers you pay double. For a leg, a bull and a cow, and the same for the loss of an eye. Accidental killing costs 7 cows and a bull for a man and 4 cows and a bull for a woman.

To an onlooker it certainly appears as if the Mkamba wife is bought and sold, or even traded as a piece of goods. Many men invest all their capital in wives, considering them more profitable even than cattle, so a wealthy man may have 6 to 10, and chiefs 20 to 40. The average ' price ' is 3 or 4 cows and a bull, but naturally a father will get as much as he can, though he may later regret his greed, if the girl runs away, for every ' present ' has then to be returned (Dundas, 1913, pp. 501, 519).

The Dinka of the Upper Nile have a definite scale of compensations. The killing of a man is still assessed nominally at 100 cows, though considerably less will usually be accepted. An injury to the head is reckoned at one cow calf ; to an arm (more serious) one cow ; to a leg (still more crippling) 5 cows ; 8 or 10 cows (the average ' bride-price ' among the Dinka) is the usual compensation for the killing of a woman or a girl. Not that she is worth less. It is rather a tribute to her value to the community. No Dinka would harm a cow—how much less a woman who is worth many cows. So it must have been an accident, and manslaughter usually costs less than murder.

There are many other ceremonial occasions which had their share, together with ' bride-price ' and wergeld bargaining, in attaching a conventional value to certain objects. The cementing of blood-brotherhood and the upward steps in various societies necessitate presents or payments, and the objects used, if not already currency, are hovering on the verge.

Two final illustrations may be taken from ceremonies connected with the settling of accounts at peace celebrations marking the end of hostilities in New Guinea and in Borneo.

It is unwise [says Seligman, 1910, p. 544] to reconstruct primitive society from what can be seen among ' unrisen ' communities of the present day, but it is safe to say that Melanesia gives no support to the theory that primitive man lived in a state of peace and amity with his neighbours. On the contrary, raiding and warfare appear to be the rule rather than the exception ; each group carried on a traditional feud with some other group, and tallies of murders were carefully counted on each side, which only awaited an opportunity for revenge. When one or both sides felt that they had had enough of it, a peace-making ceremony was formally proposed by one or the other, and, if accepted, there was a large amount of present-giving.

Among the ' presents ' at the peace-making between the Wagawaga and Maivara (Milne Bay, at the eastern end of New Guinea) a few years ago were included 15 pairs of *toia* arm-shells, 9 strings of *sapisapi* shell disks, including *bagi* and *samakupa* (Pls. 13 and 14), 4 shell nose ornaments, besides boars' tusk ornaments and pigs.[1]

Furness (1902, p. 98) describes a peace-making ceremony in Borneo, when settlement was being made and compensations for

[1] The significance of the list is seen on pp. 172 ff.

killings were arranged. ' There must always be a palpable exchange of beads, highly prized jars, brass gongs, &c., as an indemnity.' The claim in this case was 5 bronze *tawak* gongs, and 5 smaller ones, totalling about 300 Mexican dollars altogether. But a compromise was made for one *tawak* gong and one smaller one and one of the exorbitantly valued *luku sekala* beads. These objects may all be called ' presents '. It is noteworthy that they all also serve as currency (see pp. 257 *ff.*).

Chapter II

PRE-CURRENCY STAGES

Friendships, like teeth, may be cemented with gold

SOMEWHERE in between the insignificant giving of presents and recognized money transactions there are two customs of world-wide, though sporadic distribution, ' silent trade ' and ' gift-exchange '.

Silent trade has been reported from Northern Europe, from the East (India, Ceylon, East Indies), New Guinea and the New Hebrides, but its greatest extension is in Africa, where it was noted by Herodotus and may be met with at the present day (Grierson, 1903 ; Firth, 1929).

When the little pygmy hunter, having made his kill, is gorged to satiety, he takes what is over of the meat, and in the darkness of the night hangs it to a branch of a tree at the entrance of the village. In the morning the villagers cut off what they want, and hang up in return maize, manioc or yams of equal value. This is honestly calculated, for the pygmies who will come in the course of the night to fetch their due, will not submit to trickery, and their little poisoned arrows have an unpleasant way of tickling the sides of the villagers who have omitted to pay a fair price (Torday, *Causeries congolaises*, p. 176).

A recent example may be taken from Northern Rhodesia. The Awatwa (Abatwa), living in the Great Lukanga Swamp to the west of Broken Hill, carry on a ' silent trade ' in exchanging their fish for grain.

The chief produce of the swamp is fish, for which there is a considerable demand on shore. A party of people would come from an inland village with corn, which they deposited near the edge of the swamp during the daytime ; they then returned to their villages or if they had come from some distance, into the timber where they were camping. During the night the Awatwa having heard of their arrival, would journey to the edge in their canoes, taking with them dried fish, which they left in exchange for the corn, the latter being taken back with them into the swamp. The inland people then returned in the morning and removed the fish, neither party to the transaction having seen the other (Moubray, 1912, p. 58).

Moubray adds : ' This was the method of trading in unsettled times, but with the arrival of law and order and the cessation of raids, there is more peaceful and trustful intercourse between the groups.'

Miss Kingsley's example from West Africa may be noted as showing an ingenious mixture of the primitive method of ' silent trade ' and up-to-date shop-keeping with modern coins.

I have often seen on market roads . . . a little space cleared by the wayside, and neatly laid with plantain leaves, whereon were very tidily arranged various little articles for sale—a few kola nuts, leaves of tobacco, cakes of salt, a few heads of maize, or a pile of yams or sweet potatoes. Against each class of articles so many cowrie shells or beans are placed, and, always hanging from a branch above or sedately sitting in the middle of the shop, a little fetish. The number of cowrie shells or beans indicate the price of the individual articles in the various heaps and the little fetish is there to see that anyone who does not place in the stead of the articles their proper price or who meddles with the till shall swell up and burst (1899, pp. 248–9).

Miss Kingsley adds later :

In the cases of silent trade that I have seen, no doubt it was done mostly for convenience, one person being thereby enabled to have several shops open at but little working expense, but I have seen it employed as a method of trading between tribes at war with each other (p. 349).

Silent trade, therefore, does not exclude the use of money, although from its distribution it appears to be mainly confined to the hunting and collecting peoples, who, having little or no barterable property of their own, have no organization for exchange. It is obviously the most convenient method for peoples of different cultural levels, mutually hostile or mutually unintelligible.[1]

Montandon claims that ' silent trade based on fear ' is the prelude to ' the market based on confidence ' (1934, pp. 615-16), but it is impossible to prove that silent trade was ever more than a local development to suit local needs.

Barter, in spite of the inconveniences visible from a superior standpoint, does not necessarily produce a medium of exchange. ' The sad state of the hungry hatter, unable in the days of barter to get meat, because the butcher wants not hats but boots, is a commonplace of the economic textbooks,' wrote Withers (1937, p. 9), and the same textbooks picture a ' primitive state of society ' in which a man is unable to decide between exchanging his cow for an ornament, twelve sheep or a carpet. If instead of introducing hypothetical hatters and butchers and carpets into primitive societies, attention is turned to what is happening at the present day among the less-advanced peoples, a clearer idea can be obtained of the process of evolution, with the possible discovery of the reason why certain objects become ' money ' while others with equal claims do not.

The objects that are the nearest approach to money-substitutes may be seen to have acquired their functions by their use, not in barter, but in social ceremony. A certain standard of value is fixed by their special use in ' bride-price ' or in wergeld, as already discussed. Their more general use is in present-giving.

[1] Landtman (1927, pp. 216–17) gives examples of almost silent trading between friendly neighbours in New Guinea, a measure of secrecy being necessary, especially for the transfer of valuables.

The custom of present-giving or gift-exchange of a more or less ceremonial character is found among civilized and uncivilized peoples all over the world. This exchange may be entirely distinct from barter ; it may be incorporated in it ; and it may be an essential feature in a trade complex, and evolve money in the process.

Illustrations may be seen in the Andaman Islands and New Zealand, where there is no native currency ; elaborated in the Fijian *solevu* or North American potlatch, where ideas of money are emerging ; while the process of presents-developing-into-money is visible in the canoe trade of Torres Straits or the *hiri* and *kula* voyages of New Guinea.

Radcliffe-Brown, describing the prearranged meetings of two or more communities of the Andaman Islanders during the fine season, says (1922, pp. 83–4) :

> Visitors would bring with them various objects such as bows, arrows, adzes, baskets, nets, red paint, white clay and so on. These were given by the visitors to their hosts, and other presents were received in return. Although the natives themselves regarded the objects thus given as being presents, yet when a man gave a present to another, he expected that he would receive something of equal value in return, and would be very angry if the return present did not come up to his expectations. A man would sometimes mention in giving his present that he would like some particular object in exchange, but this was the exception and not the rule, and the process cannot be spoken of as barter. . . . When the meeting was between inland and coast-dwelling communities the exchange was to the advantage of the inlanders, who thus obtained coast products, but otherwise since every tribe was self-supporting, there was nothing more in it than an exchange of presents, the easiest way of testifying friendship—so the Andamanese regarded it. The exchange of presents did not serve the same purpose as trade and barter in more developed communities.

Firth (1929, Chap. XII) has made a special study of the gift-exchange among the Maori. He concludes that the custom developed as a sign of goodwill and was fostered and encouraged, as liberality and generosity are always encouraged in primitive societies, to promote social harmony. For the purposes of gift-exchange, all articles, food, clothing and ornaments had their potential exchange value. Conspicuous among these were the *harakeke* cloaks of New Zealand flax (*Phormium tenax*) and the nephrite ('greenstone') weapons or ornaments, and it is these last which so nearly developed into money that they have been so described by Europeans and even by the Maori themselves. Nephrite (*pounamu*) was, however, never a common measure of values, nor was it used as a medium of exchange in trading transactions. When traders first arrived at the islands, this native custom of gift-exchange was a good preparation for barter ; fish, flax, mats and weapons, potatoes and timber were bartered for European goods, tools, shirts and the popular mirrors and beads. In some parts it was the custom for the natives to place hundreds of baskets of potatoes in a row; the purchaser then went along and placed a stick of tobacco and a farthing on each, an equivalent which gave complete satisfaction (quoted by Firth, p. 452). Here was a sudden jump characteristic of so much of the Pacific area, as of Africa, from barter with no medium of exchange to the use of money; with tobacco as a form of currency or *Nutzgeld* in between.

Firth points out the essential distinction between gift-exchange and barter. In the former no bargaining ever upset the proceedings. Such was not *tika* (correct), though the recipient was bound, as he valued his name and reputation, to make adequate repayment, and usually tried to give back more than he received, to enhance his own prestige. 'The desire to obtain fame by being liberal strove with the wish to have the economic advantage.'

The enhancement of prestige, either personal or tribal, appears as the main motive of the keen rivalry of the potlatch[1] of the North-West Coast of America.

Hill-Tout describes the potlatch as

a most ingeniously devised system peculiar to the North-West tribes of America for acquiring social prestige and influence and at the same time laying up a provision for the future. By a well-understood rule, which is observed with a greater punctiliousness than any observance among ourselves, every recipient of a gift at a potlatch gathering is bound in honour to return another of double value to the donor or his legal heirs at some future time.

The property usually distributed consists in the main of skins, horses, personal clothing, blankets, guns, canoes, and since the advent of the dollar, money. On one historic occasion presents to the value of $15,000 are known to have been distributed, chiefly in the form of blankets, the old-time measure of wealth (1907, pp. 155-6).

The intricate system of present-giving among the Kwakiutl of Vancouver Island is described by Boas.

When a boy is about to take his third name, at the age of 10 or 12, he borrows blankets from other members of his clan or tribe for distribution. In any future distribution of blankets [2] he will receive a generous share, but all debts have to be repaid. He can lend his blankets out at 100 per cent interest—the loan may not be refused without loss of prestige—and in this way he can amass a fortune.

Possession of wealth is considered honourable, and it is the endeavour of each Indian to acquire a fortune. But it is not as much the possession of wealth as the ability to give great festivals which makes wealth a desirable object. . . . As the boy acquires his name and man's estate by means of

---

[1] Potlatch = a gift, in Chinook; *cf.* Halliday, 1935, p. 5.
[2] Nowadays the blanket, the unit of value, is here a cheap woollen one, valued at 50 cents.

a distribution of property which will in course of time revert to him with interest, the man's name acquires greater weight in the councils of the tribe and greater renown among the whole people, as he is able to distribute more and more property at each successive festival. Therefore boys and men are vying with each other in the arrangement of great distributions of property. Boys of different clans are pitted against each other by their elders, and each is exhorted to do his utmost to outdo his rival.

Formerly acts of bravery counted as well as distribution of property, but nowadays the Indians say ' rivals fight with property only ' (1895, pp. 341–58 ; cf. also Mead, 1937, Chap. VI).

The acquisition of credit and prestige by present-giving or exchange is more intricate still in connexion with the famous ' coppers ' (cf. pp. 301 ff.). These are sold for blankets with elaborate ceremonial, the greater the number of blankets given in exchange—and these may be thousands—the greater the renown acquired.

This manipulation of wealth on the North-West Coast is clearly enough in many ways a parody on our own economic arrangements [says Miss Benedict (1935, pp. 184, 188)]. These tribes did not use wealth to get for themselves an equivalent value.in economic goods, but as counters of fixed value in a game they played to win. They saw life as a ladder of which the rungs were the titular names with the owned prerogatives that were vested in them. Each new step on the ladder called for the distribution of great amounts of wealth which nevertheless were returned with usury to make possible the next elevation to which the climber might aspire. Goods passed from hand to hand like bank-notes.

The same technique was used in the ' bride-price ', which was bid up and up, as in the case of the purchase of a copper. The bridegroom and his supporters went to the house of the father of the bride laden with gifts. Contributions were made ' to lift the bride from the floor ' or ' to make a seat for the bride '. More and more blankets were counted out to overpower the family of the father-in-law, and to show the greatness of the bridegroom. Among the Kwakiutl the gifts must be returned later, with interest. There are payments due on the birth of a child, not only in blankets, but in names and prerogatives, to be passed on to heirs. There are also conventional gifts of boxes, dishes, spoons, kettles, bracelets and coppers. These will be met again later on (Chap. IX).

The Fijian *solevu* (or Great Presentation) contains many features of the potlatch, though its main purpose is bartering varied and strictly localized commodities. No tribe, however wide its territory, could be entirely self-supporting, and exchange was therefore a necessity.

Salt came only from the salt pans in the mangrove swamps ; cooking pots from the clay-pits on outlying islands ; the painting of *gnatu* [bark-cloth] was an art peculiar to a few ; the carving of bowls and the building of canoes were the craft of the carpenter clans and no other. The comfort if not the existence of a tribe depended on barter, and the form of barter devised by the Fijians accorded exactly with their passion for formal ceremonial (Thomson, 1908, pp. 280 *ff.*).

The *solevu* is the formal presentation of property by one clan or sept to another. The ceremonial was much the same whenever merchandise had to pass, whether in tribute, reward or free exchange between equals. Thomson gives the following example (p. 281):

A tribe that owned saltpans, such as those at Nandi Bay, wanted mats. It would send a formal messengei to one of the islands of Yasawa, asking permission to bring them a *solevu* of salt. Yasawa accepted. The *solevu* took place, both donors and recipients preserving a very accurate remembrance of the value of the present. After some months, or even years, Yasawa, having plaited a store of mats equivalent to their estimate of the value of the salt, would propose to return the *solevu* and the score would be wiped off. If they seemed to hang fire, deft hints would be conveyed to them that they were fast becoming a by-word on the Nandi coast.

If their offerings were less than was expected of them, the ceremonial would lose nothing of its correctness. The speeches would be as complimentary, the hand-clapping as hearty, but they would be made to hang their heads with shame when they heard the caustic epigrams current at Nandi at their expense. With the arrival of the trader, the need for the *solevu* vanished, and the native products, salt, mats, pots, bark-cloth or wooden bowls were estimated according to their value in calico or in money.

The spirit of the potlatch and rivalry in ceremonial gift-exchanges, mainly of food at feasts, are found among the Torres Straits Islanders (Haddon, Vol. IV, 1912, pp. 310-11 and VI, 1908, pp. 186-7).

There seems to be a great tendency on the part of the natives to give presents, but always with the expectation of receiving at least an equivalent in exchange.

Such presents would include useful objects such as dugong harpoons, bows and arrows or canoe balers, but are chiefly ornamental, arm-rings, necklaces or chest pendants of shell. Some of these become recognized as standard values, and standard articles of exchange for certain goods, an early stage in the development of a recognized currency.

In the remarkable canoe trade ' presents '[1] play an essential part. A Murray Islander (of the Eastern group) [2] who wants a canoe gives

[1] Landtman, describing the canoe trade from the Fly River end, emphasizes the point that there is no clearly marked difference here between actual commerce and the exchange of friendly presents (1927, p. 215).

[2] The canoe trade of the Western Islands is more complicated, as each island has its price, paid in dugong harpoons, shells and shell ornaments, with additional ' presents ' for intermediaies all along the route (Vol. V, 1904, pp. 296-7).

the trader a fine shell armlet *wauri* (Fig. 77) which is the recognized price (*cf.* p. 181). The traders start out on their voyage with various added presents, shell ornaments as well as food, intended for the middlemen. For the transaction is from island to island, all the way to the estuary of the Fly River on the mainland of New Guinea, where the large canoes come from. The traders may travel merely to the nearest island, give the order, leave the purchase gifts and return, while others carry the trade a stage farther. Eventually the canoe is purchased in exchange for the arm-ring ; but additional ' presents ' such as cassowary feathers, bird of paradise plumes, dogs' tooth or other necklaces, or boars' tusks are added by the vendor and by the intermediaries as it is conveyed to its final destination.

Haddon concludes that ' probably a mental record is kept of the source and destination of every object and doubtless in the long run [and canoe purchase may spread over several years] everyone is more or less satisfied ' (Vol. VI, 1908, p. 187). He emphasizes the significance of present-giving. Exchange of ornaments makes for peaceful relations and there is a great love of exchange for its own sake, regardless of utility. It serves as an effective protection to normal trade in an area full of fear of malevolent magic, of suspicion and potential hostility.

Certain of the articles considered as ' presents ' acquired conventionally recognized values. A canoe, a dugong harpoon, a *wauri* shell armlet, a necklace of olive shells (Fig. 78) or dogs' teeth were all about equal, and were regarded as the exchange value of a wife. The *dibidibi* chest ornaments (Fig. 79) were of less value ; they were used more often in barter, and ' served as a kind of currency '. Ten or twelve *dibidibi* of fair size would be equal to a large shell armlet (*wauri*), a canoe, a dugong harpoon or a wife (see pp. 180 *ff.*).

The value of these articles depends chiefly on their being special products of their respective areas. Canoes could only be obtained from the Fly River. Dugong harpoons were a speciality of the two islands Muralug or Mabuiag (each thought its own the best). The best *Conus* shells were found on the Warrior Reef, so the neighbouring islands had the finest armlets and chest ornaments. Mother-of-pearl shell, occurring everywhere, though everywhere prized, did not acquire such definite exchange value. Neither did any of these objects develop into currency. The white trader upset native economy by the introduction of objects that were desired by all. In MacGillivray's time (1848) a knife or a glass bottle was considered a sufficient price for a wife in Muralug, and calico is now the chief ' present ' in canoe-trading (Haddon, 1904, p. 231).

The *hiri* trading voyages of New Guinea show the same combination of barter and present-giving, out of which certain objects appear to emerge as currency. The chief stimulus here is provided by the

pottery industry of Port Moresby. Every year, at the end of Sep-
tember or beginning of October, at the end of the south-east trade
wind season, a fleet of large sailing canoes, *lakatoi*, sets out from the
neighbourhood of Port Moresby to the estuaries and rivers of the
Papuan Gulf. The canoes are laden with pots carefully packed in
dry banana leaves, and certain articles of value are taken also, and
these are bartered for sago with which the boats return with the
the north-east monsoon, about three months later.

The special ornaments taken on these voyages are the shell arm-
rings *toia*; pearl-shell crescents, *mairi*; necklaces made of *Nassa*
shells, *tautau*; or dogs' teeth, *dodoma*.[1]

Other ornaments or articles of value may be added (especially
the artificially deformed boars' tusks), but these four are more than
mere ornaments, and they have their special significance and market
value. When the boats reach the Gulf there is great rejoicing and
much ceremony, each member of the visiting crew selects his
' friend ' and gives him one or more of these selected ' presents '.
' Every article so bestowed has its recognized value, and, if accepted,
the corresponding value [in sago] will be given in exchange ' (Seligman, 1910, pp. 96–120).

Trading and gift-exchange and the emergence of currency can
be seen in the *kula* system of the Massim, who spread over the
south-eastern end of New Guinea and the island groups farther to
the east. Here the trading from island to island (and the people
are keen traders and adventurous sailors) is associated with a ceremonial exchange of valuables of two kinds : *Conus* arm-rings or
bands, (here called *mwali*, which corresponds to the Motu *toia*)
made in the Trobriands and a special type of necklace (*soulava*, the
Motu *bagi*) made of a string of *Spondylus* shell disks (*sapi sapi*) with
a pendant at the end (*cf.* Pl. 13).

The arm-rings pass from hand to hand as gifts, ' gifts in solicita-
tion ', as Miss Benedict terms them, and the necklaces travel in the
same manner but in a reversed direction. These ornaments are in
no sense currency ; they are not used in barter.

But certain other articles enter into circulation in the *kula* trade,
such as the axe blades from Murua or Woodlark Islands, (*beku* or
benam), which travel as far as the Papuan Gulf ; spatulas (*potuma*)
with large concentric handles ornamented with *sapisapi* disks and
strings, and other highly prized objects. These are used in trading,
and, escaping from the *kula* circle along the southern coast of New
Guinea, increase in value and may be described as currency. We
shall meet them again in Chapter VI.

Here we may note how such trade objects can emerge from being
' presents ' or articles of exchange and barter and become ' trans-

---

[1] The use of these as currency is discussed later (pp. 172 *ff.*).

formed into reservoirs of condensed economic value ' to use Malinowski's phrase.[1]

When arm-rings are too small to be worn, but have definite equivalent values in sago ; when the overgrown axe-blades are exchanged for pigs, canoes and ornaments ; when the shell-disks, made only in certain districts, are made up into strings, and one string will buy a dozen pots ; then currency is establishing itself, and these special objects, becoming more specialized and unfit for domestic use, are acquiring the token characters that we recognize in money.

All the above examples of present-giving, whether in the Andaman Islands, New Zealand, North America, or Melanesia, show expectation of return and may be included in ' gift-exchange '.

There is another source of conventional present-giving which has its share in the early history of money, where the giving is all on one side, from a chief or headman to his followers.

In Africa and Melanesia, as in Europe, Asia and the New World the first duty of a leader is to be generous. Wealth is power, and adherents must be secured by material favours. A great man in Yap has his avenue of stone money ; in New Britain his rolls of *diwarra* ; in British Columbia his store of blankets or coppers, as insignia of rank and wealth. All are expected to act as banker and dispenser to supporters and dependants.

The Chinese chieftain must be able ' to communicate his fortune, and to distribute it from top to bottom of the scale of creatures '. Presents show respect and enhance the prestige of receiver and of giver (Granet, 1930, p. 227). A Zulu chief, like an Irish chief, depended for his popularity on the cattle that he captured and could distribute to faithful followers. When, in our own islands, gold was equated with cattle, rings were more easily, and being less prolific, probably more willingly distributed than cattle ; and court gleemen in Britain praised their *beaga bryttan* in the same fulsome strains that were used by the ' Court Praisers ' in Swaziland. Gold rings, cattle, blankets or shells, amassed as evidence of wealth, thereby acquire the prestige that equips them for developing into currency.

[1] See his account of the *kula* ring, 1922, with map, pp. 83, 90.

Chapter III

CLASSIFICATION

A place for everything and everything in its place

IT has been seen how certain objects attain accepted or conventional values when used in 'bride-price', in wergeld or as presents on ceremonial occasions. Such objects often acquire the character of tokens in trading transactions and supply the material for the study of primitive money.

Hence the difficulty in applying Temple's classification (1899, pp. 99–122) and distinguishing between barter, currency and money with any strictness. But some classification is essential in dealing with such a mass of heterogeneous objects distributed in time from hundreds, if not thousands, of years B.C. up to the present day, and in space over the habitable globe.

Various schemes have been suggested and different authors and museum curators have sorted the material into groups according to their theoretical or practical limitations.

Schurtz's classification (1898, pp. 6, 28, 75) into *Binnengeld*, *Aussengeld* and *Zeichengeld* (Internal, External and Token money) makes a valuable distinction, as it is obvious that such types as (for example) shell-strings locally made for local exchange are functionally distinct from cowries or manillas brought by traders from overseas, but the partition is not of practical application, as in most cases there is little information about the origin and actual use of the currency concerned. It is collected and labelled 'currency' or 'money' and nothing more. Neither are his divisions into *Schmuckgeld* and *Nutzgeld*, with *Kleidergeld* in between (Ornamental, Useful and Clothing money), really helpful save for superficial sorting.

Thilenius discusses the question of classification (1921, pp. 11 ff.) and, while recognizing the value of the distinction between *Nutzgeld*, *Schmuckgeld* and *Zeichengeld*, admits that the boundaries overlap and are difficult to define. Even the contrasted extremes of *Nutzgeld* and *Zeichengeld*, which correspond to our 'full-bodied' and 'token' money, cannot always be distinguished and still leave the mass of material unclassified.[1]

---

[1] Lacouperie's 'Natur- Handels- und Industriegeld', in *Int. Archiv f. Eth.*, VI, 1893, p. 57, or Montandon's 'natural money' and 'money of civilization' in *Traité d'ethnologie culturelle*, 1934, p. 615, fail for the same reasons.

Regling, in Ebert's *Reallexikon* (1926), abandoning theory, adopts a material classification into Food, Cattle, Clothing, Ornament, Tool and Metal currencies (*Nahrungsmittelgeld, Viehgeld, Kleidergeld, Schmuckgeld, Gerätgeld* and *Metalgeld*) with subdivisions. And some such practical grouping is adopted in those Museums (too few, alas!) where a separate section is allotted to currency. The Pitt Rivers collection at Oxford struck out a new path with its divisions of Raw Materials, Useful Objects and Ornamental Objects; but the grouping according to material, i.e. Textiles, Shell, Metal, &c., is the one more commonly adopted.

Such classifications may be admirably adapted for their special purposes, but they have the defect for the geographer, the ethnologist and the sociologist of grouping together things which do not belong. This is to ignore the functional interpretation of facts, and it seems better to attempt to form groups that are interrelated, so as to gain some idea of their evolution and of their interdependence, while at the same time they illustrate the culture in which they are found.

'No study so successfully combats the error of separating history into watertight compartments as the study of numismatics,' says Seltman in an earlier volume of this series (1933, p. 265), and the study of money before it becomes numismatics is even less lamenable to such separation.

In reviewing the whole world, the most obvious classification is anthropogeographical, and this is adopted here.[1]

The material forms of money are local, i.e. geographical products, as Babelon pointed out in his articles in *La Science sociale* half a century ago. The evolution of money is anthropogeographical, influenced alike by man and by his environment; and the distribution of money is by human agency; so classification by region and race gives the fullest significance to the material. Moreover, it leads to more interesting interpretations, throwing light on problems of early migrations and early intercourse, of trading and tradeless areas, and providing evidence for those who claim that trade is the basis of all civilization, as for those who claim that the love of money is the root of all evil. The abundance or scarcity of currencies is influenced by geography as well as by political and social conditions. Barter and trade develop in areas of contrasted produce, where bush and sea-coast, forest and plain, mountain and lowland offer each other novelties and encourage the exchange of

---

[1] Within the inconvenient limitations of passage wall cases in the Museum of Archaeology and Ethnology, Cambridge, the arrangement is anthropogeographical. The Knox Collection at Buffalo has the same fundamental plan, with unrivalled opportunities of display (*cf.* Mosher, 1936).

goods. Hence the chief stimulus to trading is inequality of natural endowments, animal, vegetable and mineral, but much depends also on means of transport available, the nature of the coasts, the navigability of the rivers, the canoes, boats, inland tracks, beasts of burden or human porters that can be used. It might be added that the climate and general surroundings should be favourable but not too favourable, not so satisfying that no more is required, and yet not so barren that there is no surplus for exchange. All this exchange can, however, be carried on without anything that can properly be called money.

There is also the human factor. ' The Melanesian sells ; the Samoan gives.' Geography may be at the back of this, but it is mainly due to differences in political or social organization, which have developed definite inherent characteristics, and to the ' trading instinct ' of the Melanesian may be attributed the extraordinary wealth of currency and its unique elaboration, which is described and illustrated in Chapter VI.

The African Negro shares this characteristic. He loves pro-longed bargaining, and his clinging to earlier forms of currency is partly due to this partiality. Commerce for the Congolese, says Mahieu (1924, p. 65), is ' une sorte de jeu, auquel il se livre avec passion ' and his reluctance to make use of coins of fixed values is deepened by the fact that they curtail his opportunities for argument and disputation.

There are many other factors involved. Hobhouse shows (1930) that though private property in personal things such as weapons, ornaments and tools appears to exist everywhere at the present day, yet among the lower stages of culture communal principles are strong while the concept of private ownership is comparatively weak. At the same time the proprietorship in things personally made or even personally owned is often far stronger than with us, and parting with them is like losing a part of the owner's personality.

We have unfortunately no working model of primitive com-munism in which, theoretically, money would not be needed, and it is difficult even to conceive of any social stage in which personal property is not recognized as such. A hypothetical picture of the perfect peace in which Mankind lived before the evolution of personal property destroyed its harmony is too far back to concern the modern economist, though glimpses may be seen among such moneyless cultures as those of the Andaman Islanders, the Nicobarese and the Eskimo. Generally speaking, a study of ' unrisen peoples ' suggests that desire of possession and ideas about personal ownership are as strongly developed in most communities as in our own.

Where these sentiments appear to be weak, the reason is to be sought rather in geographical, economic or political [1] conditions than in any innate human differentiation, and a cursory glance at the distribution of currencies shows that there is no generalized interpretation of the blanks, which only vaguely coincide with racial boundaries.

The Andaman Islanders, the Australians, the Eskimo, the Central Asiatics and the Maori have neither geographical environment nor race in common, but they are (or were) alike in one characteristic, a comparative self-sufficiency. In these so-called primitive societies where division of labour, save between men and women, scarcely exists, where each family group could provide for its own needs without outside help or external supplies, currency is not to be looked for ; trade can scarcely develop ; barter is rarely organized ; and though there is present-giving, it has little commercial importance. But groups so independent and so self-contained are rarely found ; even among the most aloof there are indications of extra attractions and external contacts, and women are generally the disturbing element. Abundant illustrations will be found in the following pages : a brief glance at what is happening in the Solomon Islands at the present time, showing successive stages in the evolution of the use of money, may form the prelude.

In Bougainville, the largest island of the group, there is great contrast and perpetual hostility between the bush folk of the mountainous interior and the more recent coast dwellers. Nor are the mountaineers at peace among themselves ; they live in isolated groups and are usually at feud with their nearest neighbours who may live across a valley and up the next mountain ridge. Each family, therefore, is necessarily self-contained and provides for its own needs, and if there is any exchange it is not of necessities, but of extras. Stone for tools is only found in one part, earth suitable for pottery-making in another, and there is a certain amount of barter in stone implements and in pots. But while in most of Melanesia barter is constantly going on, with markets at regular spots at regular intervals, in Buin (South Bougainville) there is nothing of the kind. Exchanges of goods take place only at present-givings, which are the essential accompaniment of gatherings and feasts on special occasions such as marriages and funerals, meetings for blood-revenge or for peace-makings. And all givers expect presents of equal value in return or another feud is started.

The most valued presents are shell-strings and *Tridacna* arm-rings, which must be obtained from the coast, and these are essential for ' bride-price ' for blood-money and for all ceremonial

---

[1] e.g. well-meaning rulers may prohibit or discourage the use of money (Sparta, Peru, Japan) while self-seeking rulers may introduce it for their own benefit (China, Bornu).

presentations. So there is exchange between the mountaineers and the coast dwellers, the former bringing taro and yams, pelts or baskets, to barter for fish, salt-water (for cooking), coconuts and, above all, shell-strings and shell-rings. For without these men cannot ' buy ' wives or pigs.[1]

Miss Blackwood (1935, pp. 439–40) describes the better-organized barter to the north of Bougainville, between the villages of Buka Passage. Here the important exchange is that of taro and fish. Few villages are so fortunate as to be self-contained as regards both these essentials of existence. The land near the coast is not very good for growing taro ; the inland people have only the small amount of fish they can take from the rivers. The fish-taro exchange is therefore a permanent feature in the life of all the villages in this area. Women's hoods, the speciality of one area, pots of another, clay pipes of another, all have their exchange values, standardized according to supply and demand and the bargaining powers of buyers and sellers. This is what is usually described as ' barter pure and simple ', although the adjectives are seldom appropriate.

The next stage is reached when an agreed rate of exchange is adopted and certain goods are given a fixed value, which remains constant. The native currency here consists in lengths of teeth, bound on strings (imun) covered with red ochre, and shell-money (beroan) imported from other islands (Pl. 10). This is not used for ordinary trading, but for marriage payments, for compensations for wrongs and for special purchases, with ceremonial significance. The ordinary currency is trade tobacco in the form of plug twist, mixed with molasses, made up into sticks about 6 inches long. Trade has also introduced coins, mainly shillings. One shilling equals three sticks of tobacco. Five will buy a fathom of shell-money. A fathom of the more valuable tooth-money is arbitrarily valued by the natives at £5. But £5 merely means ' untold gold ' or ' a lot of money '.

Thus in one island may still be seen a money-less barter, with present-giving and ceremonial exchanges developing into local forms of currency, which may be estimated in tobacco and coins.

---

[1] A wife costs 100 to 200 fathoms of shell-strings and a pig 20 to 30 ; 100 fathoms is blood-money for a murder (cf. Thurnwald, 1910, pp. 127, 138 fn.).

Chapter IV

COWRIES AND BEADS

i. COWRIES

The army marches on its stomach

IN the following chapters objects used as money will be grouped in their respective geographical provinces : Africa, Oceania, Asia, Europe and America. But there are two important currencies that cannot be confined within these limits, cowries and beads. Their distribution as ornaments and charms, if not as money, starts before the Christian era and takes us all over the Old World and into the New.

The ideal properties of money are that it shall be handy, lasting, easy to count and difficult to counterfeit (portable, durable, divisible and recognizable), so there are not many rivals to the precious metals. The most remarkable exception is the cowry, which, starting on its travels before gold and silver coinage was in general use, extended its range farther than any form of money before or since, spreading from China and India eastward to the Pacific islands ; travelling across and encircling Africa to the West Coast; and penetrating into the New World. In some of these lands gold, silver or bronze coins existed and circulated locally, but cowries formed the common currency throughout this vast expanse of the trading world. With unrestricted imports their value depreciated on the main highways, though they are still in actual use in out-of-the-way parts to-day.

The reasons for their popularity are both obvious and concealed. The surface and the shape are attractive and decorative, so that they are used as ornaments and playthings even where they are common. And when they are carried into inland regions, they acquire the added charm of novelty touched with mystery, and the enhanced value given to all exotic products. It is difficult to separate their use as decoration, as charms and amulets, and as ' givers of life ' from their use as currency, as the ornamental and magical concepts added so much to their value. But it is as currency that we are concerned with them, and we recognize at once how aptly they supply the essential requirements of money. They are easier, cleaner and pleasanter to handle than coins, which are usually regarded as ideal ; they are as easy to count in pairs, in quartettes or in fives, and practically impossible to counterfeit.

Many centuries after coins had been in daily use in China, a despairing Emperor abolished the whole monetary system riddled with forgeries and returned to an official currency in shells. And cowries surpass all other shell currencies in solidity and uniformity. They are fairly constant both in size and weight, and equal in these respects to the seeds such as crabs' eyes, beans, rice, wheat or barley-corns which provided the earliest units for weighing gold and silver.

The name cowry is derived from the Hindi and Urdu *kauri*, Sanskrit *kaparda*, but the varied names in different countries have often led to confusion. An early French name was *porcelaine*, which may contain an echo of a Roman nickname of ' little pig ' and connect it with fertility cults, and both *porcelaine* in French and cowry in English were applied to many shells that were not *Cypraea*.[1] The only cowries with claims to be called money are the large orange or tiger cowries (*Cypraea aurora*, *C. tigris*, &c.) and the familiar little *C. moneta* or *C. annulus*, which we still use as counters in domestic gambling.[2]

The large shells have been treasured in our islands for many centuries, and are not uncommonly found buried with their owners in Anglo-Saxon graves. They may have been used in presentations or exchange, as in Fiji, where they are often called ' currency ' (Pl. 5) or in barter as on the eastern coasts of Africa, where they are native, but rare.

The little cowry represents the most widely spread money of world commerce, used by the trading nations of the Old World from the South Seas to the western coasts of Africa and across to America. The original occupant of this solid, shiny, slightly asymmetrical shell with its narrow ventral opening was a gasteropod mollusc living in shallow water and preferring that water to be warm, hence its distribution in the Indian and Pacific Oceans.[3] It is usual to distinguish two varieties, the money cowry, *Cypraea moneta*, and the ring cowry, *C. annulus*, the former often called the ' large ' and the latter the ' small ' cowry, the one just over and the other just under an inch in length (Jackson, p. 156, with illustration). But size is an unsafe guide in conchology, and the *Cypraea* are notoriously variable. In Southern Nigeria the ring cowries in current use are twice the size of the money cowries, and Mahieu tabulates ' large ' and ' small ' varieties of both kinds in the Congo

---

[1] *Venus mercenaria* and other clam shells were called *porcelaine* in America, while cowries and olives are inextricably mixed in Africa.

[2] The border line between gambling counters and money is not easy to define, and it is safe to say that cowries are still used for gambling all over the world. For small stakes they are obviously superior to coins, a. they are so much easier for the winner to scoop up. When copper *atts* the value of a cowry, or $\frac{1}{64}$ of a *tical*, were used for gambling in Siam, they were bent up at the edge to avoid fumbling.

[3] Jackson, 1917, gives a map of its recorded range, p. 124.

(p. 41).   Trading interests obviously regulate size, for when cowries are bought wholesale and traded retail, it is to the merchant's interest to buy up the smaller specimens.   So, although *C. moneta* may be larger than *C. annulus* on its native Maldivian shores, it is the smaller specimens that find their way as currency to the Guinea Coast and the East Indies.

In trying to disentangle the two varieties many difficulties are encountered.   Most records are content with merely reporting ' cowry currency' with no description or further details ; some distinguish between Indian (*moneta*) and African (*annulus*) ; and some distinguish between ' large' and ' small', which it is usual to interpret as *moneta* and *annulus*, as above, but with caution.

A currency string may contain both varieties strung together and when the backs are chipped off or ground down for stringing (Fig. 1) identification is uncertain.[1]   The indiscriminate mixing of the two is to be expected in Africa, but it is surprising to find both varieties in the small change of a Panjab banker towards the end of last century.[2]

It is fortunate that civilized as well as uncivilized man is susceptible to the fascinations of the cowry.   The literature is extensive,[3] and there is no need to repeat what has been so fully and admirably dealt with. A brief summary of the travelling history of the cowry as currency will suffice here.

FIG. 1.—Cowries *Cypraea moneta*, with backs broken for stringing

Cowries (both *moneta* and *annulus*) are found in the Red Sea, and may have been used

---

[1] It is not even certain that *C. moneta* and *C. annulus* are really distinct. The animals change their colours and patterns with age and exhibit two or three different coatings of enamel at different stages, so that by some authorities these are considered as merely the extremes of one variable mollusc (Reeve, 1842, II, p. 262).

[2] Presented by Temple to the Pitt Rivers Museum at Oxford.

[3] Stearns traced the history of the cowry in his ' Ethno-Conchology', *Rep. U.S. Nat. Mus.*, 1889, pp. 297–34 ; Schurtz in his *Grundriss einer Entstehungsgeschichte des Geldes*, 1898, pp. 88–98, gave a summary and review, and Schneider in his monograph (*Muschelgeld-Studien*), edited by Carl Ribbe, in 1905 sifted, criticized and amplified the mass of information already collected (pp. 101–73).   Jackson, in *Shells as Evidence of the Migrations of Early Culture* (1917), made use of Schneider's monograph as of other writers before and after, and devotes pp. 122–94 to a study of the use of cowries as currency, amulets and charms, with a map of their distribution. Wiener, in *Africa and the Discovery of America*, (1920, Vol. II, Part III) traces their wanderings and history by means of etymological and linguistic evidence (pp. 203–23) ; Montandon, *Traité d'éthnologie culturelle*, 1934, illustrates their distribution as currency with a map (pp. 614–19).

3

as currency in Egypt in ancient as in modern times. They were highly valued as ornaments and worn as charms or talismans and buried with their owners in Pre-dynastic as in later graves (Jackson, 1917, pp. 128 ff.). They travelled up the Nile Valley and also along the coasts and may have taken part in the early trade which was carried on between the Eastern Mediterranean across the Indian Ocean and down the East African coast at the beginning of our era.[1]

The true money cowry (*Cypraea moneta*) and its career as money throughout the world starts in the Indian Ocean, with its collecting industry in the Maldives (called Divah Kavzah, or ' Cowry Islands ') and its centre of distribution in Bengal.

Sulayman, the Arab merchant in the 9th century, describes the riches of the Maldives, which consisted in cowries, and how the Queen amassed large quantities in her treasuries. (Ferrand, *Voyage du marchand arabe Sulayman* (851), 1922, p. 31). Masudi of Baghdad the Arab historian, who died about the middle of the 10th century, amplifies this account. (*Meadows of Gold*, 1861, p. 337). He records that cowries were the only money in the Maldives, and when the royal treasury was getting empty the Queen directed women to cut branches of coconut palms and throw them on the sea. The animals climbed up on to these and they were collected and spread on the seashore until only empty shells were left, which were brought in to replenish the treasury.

Pyrard de Laval, who was wrecked on the islands and spent 2 years there at the beginning of the 17th century, gives much the same description of the collecting, and adds

> They called them [cowries] *Boly* and export to all parts an infinite quantity, in such wise that in one year I have seen 30 or 40 whole ships loaded with them without other cargo. All go to Bengal for there only is there a demand for a large quantity at high prices. The people of Bengal use them for ordinary money although they have gold and silver and plenty of other metals ; and, what is more strange, kings and great lords have houses built expressly to store these shells and treat them as part of their treasure (1887, I, p. 78).

He tells how Portuguese ships brought rice from Cochin solely to exchange for cowries for the Bengal market, the shells being put up into parcels or baskets of coconut palm leaves each containing 12,000 shells ; these were negotiated like bags of silver, by weight, and between merchants taken as counted, ' though in less than no time they will take a tally of a whole parcel '. It was a profitable trade, as they were bought at 9,000 or 10,000 for a rupee and sold for 3 or 4 times as much.

When the Mohammedans overran Bengal in the 13th century

---

[1] The reference in the *Periplus* is doubtful.

cowries were already established as currency and spread thence over the trade routes of India. There is evidence of their continued commercial use down to the present day, for they may still be found in native bazaars, and were reported as in use as small change in Benares, Darjeeling and Hyderabad until a few years ago.

They never formed a currency in Ceylon, or on the Malabar coast (where they are native), but they increased in value as they travelled inland and their travels led them to Eastern Asia and to Western Europe.

Cowries were the currency of China some hundreds if not thousands of years before there is any record of the Maldive industry, the supplies being derived possibly from the Sea of Formosa, or farther to the east from Borneo and the Philippines, where later they were used for ballast. But Marco Polo clearly states that in his time the cowries in the Province of Carajan [Yunnan] were brought from India (Yule, 1903, II, p. 45). Cowries in China had a fluctuating commercial career, being highly valued,.depreciated, abolished, reinstated and abolished again, as is described below (pp. 224 ff.).

Westwards from India [1] they spread through Afghanistan into Persia, and from thence into Europe, where they encountered the stream that had trickled up in prehistoric times, probably connected with the amber trade. Occasional occurrences in graves cannot prove that the shells were used as currency here, though when 50 are found together, as at Vitebsk in Latvia, the inference is perhaps not unwarrantable.[2] The bronze cowries found in Etruscan graves may be compared with those of China, which are usually presumed to be money. The gold cowries of Cyprus (as also of Egypt) bear witness to their estimation, though there is no suggestion of commercial use.

The early history of cowries in Africa is difficult to trace. They are found in the Red Sea, and may have been carried inland from Egypt, and by sea along the coasts. Later the Arabs brought them across the Indian Ocean in their dhows as ballast and for trade with the natives, and they were dispersed all across the caravan routes of the north.[3] The ships of the Dutch and the Portuguese, the French and the English followed the Arabs, but their trade was mainly with the West Coast, as was described in the 17th century

---

[1] Only two cowries, neither of them *C. moneta* or *C. annulus*, have been recorded in the Indus Valley excavations (*cf.* p. 193).

[2] For Scandinavia and the Baltic region *cf.* Jackson, 1917, pp. 130 *ff.*

[3] Some idea of the profits of the trade in the 14th century can be reckoned from Ibn Batuta's statement that cowries could be bought in the Maldives for 400,000, sometimes even for 1,200,000 to the gold *dinar*, and he had himself seen them sold in what is now Nigeria at the rate of 1,150 to the *dinar* (1929, p. 243).

by Barbot, Agent-General of the Royal Company of Africa and the Islands of America at Paris.

> The *Boejies* or *Cauris*, which the *French* call *Bouges*, are small milk-white shells commonly as big as small olives, and are produced and gathered among the shoals and rocks of the *Maldivy* islands, . . . and thence transported as ballast to *Goa, Cochin* and other ports in the *East-Indies* by the natives of those numerous islands ; and from the above-named places are dispersed to the *Dutch* and *English* factories in *India* ; then brought over to Europe more especially by the *Dutch*, who make a great advantage of them according to the occasion the several trading nations of *Europe* have for this trash, to carry on their traffick at the coast of *Guinea* and of *Angola*, to purchase slaves or other goods of *Africa* and are only proper for that trade ; no other people in the universe putting such a value on them as the *Guineans* ; and more especially those of Fida and Ardra have long done, and still do to this day. These *Cauris* are of many different sizes, the smallest hardly larger than a common pea ; and the largest, as an ordinary walnut, longish like an olive ; but of such great ones there is no considerable quantity in proportion to the inferior sizes ; and all are intermixt great and small. They are commonly brought over from the *East-Indies* in packs or bundles, well wrapp'd, and put into small barrels in *England* or *Holland*, for the better conveniency of the Guinea trade (Churchill, *Collection of Voyages*, 1704, Vol. V, pp. 338–9).

Bosman, the Dutch factor at Elmina, describes these barrels of cowries at Fida :

> In my time the *English* sowed up their small Barrels of *Boesies* (the Money of this Country) in Sacks, thinking thereby to have secured them from the pilfring Fingers of the *Negroes* : but they were mistaken ; for as they were carrying them, on the way they cut the Sacks of the Barrels, and dug out their *Boesies* at the Chinks of the Barrel with an Iron Chissel (1705, p. 349).

Cowries thus entered Africa in two streams, and Wiener traces the Indian words derived from the Sanskrit *kaparda* (which he connects with the Chinese *ho-pei*) by the overland route from Zanzibar to West Africa ; while the Maldive name *boly*, Portuguese *buzio*, French *bouges*, travelled by sea, appearing in Benin as *abuy* and in Dahomy as *akwe* (1920, pp. 221–3).

It is interesting to note that these two streams did not flood the entire continent. The Arab trade advanced across Africa from east to west, along the northern routes to the Niger, and past the Lakes to the Upper Congo, and cowries spread down the rivers and their tributaries. Trade by sea landed cowries on the West Coast, and they spread up the rivers and their tributaries. But in between were areas where cowries never penetrated before the introduction of the usual ' trade goods ', cloth (which to a great extent, superseded cowries), beads and brass wire.

The adventures of the cowry on the East Coast were very different from those on the West. On the East there were two serious rivals : the local *C. annulus*, which anyone could pick up along the shores and the established cattle-standard inland. In a cattle area, especially one where iron is fairly abundant, other currencies are less important, and the cowry plays a small part. When, however, it first travelled into the interior, the Arab traders made sensational profits. In the days of King Semakokiro, about five generations ago, the cowry first appeared in Uganda, and two shells would purchase a woman.[1] But this high price was short-lived. In the reign of his grandson (about 1860) their value fell and 2,500 would only buy a cow, and a woman was worth 4 or 5 cows. This was at the capital and on the main trade-routes. Off the beaten track cowries were still good value. Junker, in 1886, found eggs priced at 5 cowries each and a bunch of bananas for 30. The final knell was struck by the coming of the rupee about 1921, when cowries were reckoned at 1,000 to the rupee and were of no practical value in bargaining. But strings, nominally of hundreds, can still be found, side by side with modern coinage. And some of the ancients of Wanyoro probably still talk of the good old days when 10 cowries would buy a cow and 30 a woman (J. A. Grant, 1864).

Cowries travelled along the trade routes of the North, and are recorded by Ibn Batuta in the Kingdom of Melle in the 14th century and by Cadamosto in the Songhay Kingdom in the 15th. In the same century Leo Africanus met them in Timbuktu, where 400 went to the ducat.

The Spaniards found them already established along the West Coast, and they formed the usual currency there for some centuries. Barbot includes cowries in his list of trade goods for the French trade with Senegal and Gambia about 1677; and in Dahomey in 1669, ‘ the best commodity the Europeans can carry thither to purchase slaves, cotton cloth and aggry beads is *Boejies* or *Cawries*, so much valued by the natives, being the current coin there and at Popo, Fida, Benin and other countries further east, without which it is scarcely possible to traffic there ’ (Churchill, 1704, Vol. V, p. 338).

They formed the accepted currency all along the coast from Senegal to Angola for two or three centuries, percolating slowly inland up the rivers, and had their importation been regulated, might have continued in use down to the present day.

But in the middle of last century the Hamburg merchants who had been carrying Indian cowries from the Maldives, found it extremely profitable to load up with *C. annulus* on the East Coast, at Zanzibar or Mozambique, and unload on the West Coast. At first these shells, being larger than the Indian cowries, were much appreciated, but when hundreds and thousands of tons had been brought into the continent, the new variety soon became too common, and the price of both fell so low that they ceased to be of any use

[1] J. Roscoe, 1911, p. 456.

in trade. It is difficult, as explained above, to trace the fluctuations of the two varieties. One was more popular in one district, one in another, and both kinds may occasionally be found on the same string. Along the Gold Coast importations ceased towards the end of last century, but their use continued, although 2,000 went to the ' head ' (valued between 1s. 6d. and 2s. 3d.) because they were used by the factories for paying native labour. At one time these payments were made in gold dust, but the opportunities for fraud were so easy that the natives preferred the unadulterable cowries ; and they continued to be preferred inland, though the old ratio of two farthings to the score (*tapo*) was ' a thing of the past ' half a century ago (Burton and Cameron, 1883, p. 155).

In 1896 4,000 were only worth a mark in German Togoland, but Schneider tells of a man who was unable to buy a fine horse, offered cheap for 63 marks, because he was unable to pay in [about a quarter of a million] cowries (1905, pp. 148–9). And cowries are still the common native currency in the Northern Territory of the Gold Coast, and still often preferred to coin, which is accepted with suspicion and protest.

In Nigeria cowries were in general use until lately,[1] though the ' head ' of 2,000 was only worth about 6d. They were useful because the smallest silver unit was 3d., so for minor transactions cowries were indispensable. With the issue of the *anini*, $\frac{1}{10}$ of 1d., this need for very small change was supplied, but the memory of cowry currency will long be preserved in the name for the halfpenny, *dari*, meaning a hundred (cowries).

Up-country their value increases. In the North and West currency is still almost exclusively in cowries wherever currency exists, though in the bush markets transactions are carried on without currency by means of barter (Talbot, 1926, p. 875). *C. moneta* is usually the rarer here, and when importations of *C. annulus* ceased, the former increased in value, and the price is still rising. They formerly played a large part in fines and in ' bride-price '. A chief's tribute consisted in thousands of slaves and rolls of cloth and millions of cowries ; thousands would be paid by a father on his son's marriage or presented to the wife's father after the birth of the first child.

Barth in 1851 found cowries (*C. moneta* he observes) the common currency of Kano market, 2,500 being equal to the Spanish or the Austrian dollar. With cowries so plentiful and so cheap the counting was a formidable operation, for they were not strung as they were on the coast, but had to be counted one by one, or rather five by five. The governors of towns packed them in sacks made of rushes,

---

[1] For an interesting aspect of the reappearance of cowry currency in Northern Nigeria see Nadel, S. F., 1937, p. 488.

20,000 to the sack, but no private individual would receive these
without counting them out. 'The general custom is to count them
in fives, in which operation some are very expert, and then to form
heaps of 200 or 1,000 each.' The counting of 500,000 shells
'is a really heroic work'.

Barth says that cowries were then a novelty in Bornu, where
there was no recognized currency. The ancient standard *rotl* or
pound of copper had fallen into disuse, and the usual media of
exchange were the *gabaga* or cotton strips. Cowries, here called
kungona, were introduced as a commercial speculation by the rulers,
and 8 went to the *gabaga*, and 4 *gabaga* or 32 cowries to the *rotl*.
For larger transactions shirts (*dora*), too small and unfit for wear,
were worth 6 *rotls*, and large shirts up to 50 or 60 *rotls*. But values
went up and down in response to speculation so that sometimes
45 sometimes 100 *rotls* went to the dollar. Further inland, there was
no currency at all. Agades in the Air oasis, with a population of
some 7,000, was an important trading centre for the salt caravans,
thousands of pounds' worth of salt passing through in the year, yet
'its characteristic feature is that no money of any kind is current
in the market, neither gold nor silver nor *kurdi* [cowries]' (1858, II,
pp. 310-11).

Denham and Clapperton, travelling south from Bornu, shortly
before the time of Barth, record their first meeting with cowries
as currency at Katagum, between Bornu and Kano. Farther south
they note 'the great convenience of the cowrie which no forgery
can imitate . . . as a ready medium of exchange in all transactions'
(p. 57). And another traveller exclaims, 'In what country of the
world would you find all the food that you need along the road
for a few shells?' 'A few shells' sounds like an under-estimate,
where the 'bag', the unit of value, contained 50,000 and 4,000 to
5,000 were only worth a Maria Theresa dollar. Nevertheless,
though cattle, ivory and slaves usually supplied the higher values,
large payments as well as small were effected by means of cowries,
and the cowry-counter 'a curiosity of the West Sudan trading
centres' counted daily from 250,000 to 300,000 of this small change.
(Ratzel, 1896-8, III, p. 310).

In West Africa, from Senegal to Nigeria the cowry still holds its
own, in spite of rival native currencies or Government disapproval,
and we meet it again in the Congo basin. It is curious to find that
it has vanished from the regions in between. Eastward of the Niger
delta, in what was German Cameroons and the hinterland, as all
along the Lower Guinea coast, Schneider says that cowry-currency
has disappeared without leaving a trace. (*Spurlos verschwunden*,
1905, p. 157).

The Congo area is renowned for having a more varied collection of native currency than any other part of the world: It is fortunate in having the most complete collection excellently housed and displayed at Tervueren, Brussels, in charge of Dr. J. Maes, himself an expert collector. In spite of all this wealth of native currency the cowry once introduced soon proved enormously popular, but depreciated with the unlimited importation.[1] The first cowries were probably brought inland into the Kasai-Sankuru region by the slave-raiding incursions of the Badjok (Kioto) before the coming of the Europeans. While they were still a novelty, 300 or 400 would be paid for a wife. About the beginning of this century 3,000 was the normal price. Some 6,000 or 7,000 might have to be paid to an injured husband if adultery is proved, and fines for murder or for suicide ran into higher figures. Even attempted murder or suicide was priced at 20,000 to 30,000 cowries. A slave was valued at from 30,000 to 60,000 according to the district, a female slave being more. Goats from 10,000 to 15,000, a fowl 1,200 down to a hoe iron at 300.

The Bushongo are the great traders of the Kasai and Sankuru district in which these figures were collected, and it is owing to this trade, and owing to the large numbers with which they have to deal, that they possess, what is rare in Africa, names for figures up to a million, though they admit that a million or even a hundred thousand are beyond comprehension. (Torday and Joyce, 1911, p. 229).

With the depreciation of the cowry owing to importations of thousands of tons every year from Zanzibar and Mozambique, they declined in value and only survive in use along the Kasai, as also in some of the back-waters of the Middle and Upper Congo. Cowries appear in the list of goods in payment for ivory at Nouvelle Anvers in 1885, together with a varied assortment of trade cloth, beads, brass wire (*mitako*) and an empty bottle (Mahieu, 1924, p. 65). But this is a retrogression from currency to barter.

Cowries are common in Pacific waters, but their use is decorative rather than commercial. According to Jackson's map (1917, p. 124) the recorded range of *C. moneta* and other forms is from Japan and Hawaii in the North to New Zealand and Easter Island to the South and East. And there is an important centre of distribution in the islands between Borneo and the Philippines, where for long they have served as ballast for ships. But while they constituted

[1] One of the main difficulties which besets the collector of primitive currency is to decide what is valued as money and what is valued as decoration, and in very many cases no decision is possible. The cowry belts of the Mobenge (*kamba-barakuta*) are as good an illustration of this overlap in Africa as are the shell-money belts of the Micronesians or the Solomon Islanders in Oceania ; *cf.* Maes, 1910, pp. 501–2.

currencies on the mainland of Asia, there are very few references to any such use in the islands.

Pickering visited Hawaii with the Wilkes Exploring Expedition, 1838–42, and says that an estimable and intelligent Hawaiian lady gave him particulars of former customs. ' Money was certainly known, for with a string of cowries, *Cyprea monetas*, it was possible to buy any articles wanted.' Specimens that were finer than usual were extravagantly valued, and could only be worn by the highest chiefs. (1863, p. 91). As Polynesia never developed a native currency (*cf.* p. 109) and as this is the only reference to such use of money in Hawaii, the exchanges should perhaps be regarded more as barter than as money transactions.[1] Nor is there much evidence for the use of cowries as currency in Melanesia, though Schneider records doubtful instances from the Bismarck Archipelago (1905, p. 118), and they are used as gifts in the New Hebrides (*cf.* p. 168).

There is more information from New Guinea, especially in the Mandated area, where cowries are used both strung and made up into ornaments (*cf.* pp. 175 *ff.*).

The most surprising occurrence is in Dutch New Guinea. It is surprising, because it is recorded from the interior among a Papuan people with totemistic culture, who, as a rule, have no need for and no clear conception of the use of money. The shells are called *tinale* or *tingala* and the natives in the highlands at the sources of the Mamberamo are so keen on possessing them that they cross over passes in the mountains some 10,000 feet high, to buy them from the lowlanders. They prefer them as flat as possible, and when they are almost as broad as they are long, and shiny white, they circulate as coins. Their value is high. Ten constitute a small fortune, and will buy a capable young woman or a full-sized pig. A young pig or a middle-sized one can be bought for 2 to 5 shells. Objects in daily use seldom cost more than a shell apiece (Wirz, XVI, 1924, p. 121).

With the gradual opening up of the interior of New Guinea by exploration, and the stimulus of the discovery of gold, cowries from the coast now find their way more easily into the formerly almost inaccessible mountains, and among the Mount Hagen tribes of Mandated territory it takes a fathom and a half of cowries, sewn on cord, for a bride, but there is no fixed price and five times this may be demanded (Ross, 1936).

Travellers into the interior who bring native carriers down to the coast describe their excitement at finding cowries on the beach, and how they spend all their time there, as ' on Tom Tiddler's ground picking up gold and silver '.

[1] Schneider, 1905, p. 118, quotes a record of cowries *als Geldsurrogat* in Fiji, with a query.

It is doubtful if cowries were ever used as currency in America. They have been found in mounds and in early burials which show no trace of European influence ; they were sacred emblems among the Ojibwa and the Menomini to the west of the Great Lakes, and were used in initiation ceremonies (Jackson, 1917, pp. 184 *ff.*), but there is no record of their use as money. They were imported into America, as into Africa, for trading with the natives, and stocked by the Hudson Bay Company to barter for pelts, but their function was ornamental, rather than financial.

ii. BEADS

Beads . . . the most exasperating objects [in the British Museum].

T. A. JOYCE

Cowries and beads have much in common.

Geographically they have much the same distribution, their dispersal being due to the same agency, the commercial enterprise of traders with less-civilized peoples. But while the original homes of the cowries are known, the source or sources of early trade beads are still much in dispute.

Secondly, beads, like cowries, often owe their popularity to supernatural beliefs. While the cowry may have some claim to be a symbol of fertility, it is more generally valued as an apotropaic, a talisman or a charm. Beads are also apotropaic, possibly (like the cowry) owing to their association with eyes or to their association with holed stones or rings ; and beliefs in their magic virtues were doubtless fostered, if not invented, by traders to increase their value. A third similarity is of more immediate concern. Cowries used in currency are difficult to identify and, as has been seen, impossible to classify. Just the same may be said of beads, but here the confusion is infinitely worse. For while cowries have persisted as currency in many parts, owing to the fact that they cannot be imitated, trade beads have been imitated for hundreds of years, and so skilfully imitated that it needs microscopic and chemical analysis to distinguish between a pre-dynastic bead from Egypt, a genuine ' aggry ' from the Gold Coast (if such a bead can be identified) and a Czechoslovakian product of today.

Modern trade beads are seldom of any general interest, nor are local prejudices worth noting, save by the trader, though they add variety and attractiveness to museum collections ; but old trade beads are fascinating mysteries, about which much has been written but little is certainly known.

Take first the aggry beads. Why ' aggry ' ? Read (1905) in a note on a necklace of glass beads from the Gold Coast, says frankly :

'I have never yet been able to get a satisfactory answer to the inquiry, What is an aggry bead?' The *O.E.D.* tells us that this is 'a word of unknown origin and meaning, applied to coloured and variegated glass beads of ancient manufacture, found buried in the ground in Africa; they closely resemble the *glain neidyr* or adder stone of the Britons'.

The comparison with the British 'druid stones' is due to Bowdich, who in his report of his mission to Ashanti in 1817 gives a general description of the aggry beads and their uses. The plain beads were blue, yellow or dull red, the variegated ('mosaic') ones of every colour and shade. The natives distinguished between these, which they dug out of the ground, worth their weight or twice their weight in gold, and the 'boiled beads' made locally, which were imitations, but heavier. The beads were used for ordeals, for oath-taking and, ground down and mixed with water, were rubbed on children to assist their growth. If one was accidentally broken in a scuffle the price paid was 7 slaves, but Bowdich never heard of their being used for money, for the currency was in gold (1819, p. 218). Bowdich sent a 'suite' of these beads to the British Museum, noting the similarity of the beliefs, if not of the beads, to those of the ancient Britons.

These beads were well known to the traders of the Coast. Duarte Pacheco Pereira, the Portuguese explorer who probably assisted at the founding of the Castle of Elmina (the first permanent European settlement on the Gold Coast) in 1481, speaks of the trade there and the amount of gold yearly brought to Portugal. In exchange the chief goods bartered were cloth, brass manillas, handkerchiefs, corals, 'certain red shells which they estimate as we estimate precious stones', white wine and 'certain blue beads which they call coris' (1905, p. 114).

These beads came from Benin as he tells later, describing the trading some·five leagues up the left branch of the Rio dos Forcados, in the Niger delta. There trade consisted 'principally in slaves, cotton cloths, a few leopard skins, palm oil and certain blue beads with certain red lines or stripes,[1] which they call coris'. These were bought in exchange for brass or copper manillas and sold again at Fort St. George for gold (p. 121).

Barbot towards the end of the 17th century records, among the most profitable items for trading in Dahomey, 'slaves, cotton cloths and blue stones called agry or accory, very valuable at the Gold Coast' and at Benin, besides slaves and cotton cloths 'blue coral, *alias*

[1] The description of blue beads with red lines or stripes, ridges or zigzags (*riscos*) suggests chevrons (Frontispiece, Fig. 7). Kimble, however, reads *conchas* not *contas*, and translates 'blue *shells* with red stripes' without explanation (1937, p. 128).

akory from Benin'. Barbot adds the local belief that ' blue coral grows in branchy bushes like the red coral at the bottom of the rivers and lakes in Benin, which the natives have a peculiar art to grind or work into beads like olives, and is a very profitable merchandize at the Gold Coast' (1704, Vol. V, pp. 348, 361).

The accounts of the early explorers and traders trace these ' aggry ' beads to Benin and to native industry. There they could be bought in native markets or through the agency of the factors, which suggests that they were due to overland trade, and the ' blue coral ' may have been made from the long Venetian pipes which the natives cut up and ground down on a whetstone into whatever shapes they pleased, as Barbot records of the Gold Coast (p. 274).

Philological guesses are seldom of any value, but the confusion between coral and aggries, together with the early spellings of *coris* and *accory* certainly suggest that the word ' aggry ' is no more than ' a coral ', a name used for beads in general, and that the beads were substitutes for the red coral, a royal monopoly in Benin, which no commoner could wear without the King's sanction. Mediterranean coral was exported, some centuries B.C. chiefly as amulets, but also for trading, to India in the east and Africa in the west, and reached Timbuktu and the Niger in Arab caravans. But even in Barbot's time the string of coral which in Benin was a badge of office, was made of counterfeit beads, and he tells how the officer was obliged to wear his string, and was put to death if he lost it, and how five men were killed when a string was stolen—the owner, the thief, and his accomplices—for a string of coral ' not intrinsically worth twopence ' (p. 367).

How, when and why blue beads were substituted for red coral is not clear, but it is not unreasonable to assume that the Africans then, like their descendants of the present day, showed preferences sometimes for red, sometimes for blue, and sometimes for parti-coloured beads, such as in still earlier times composed the La Tène string from the Crimea (Déchelette, II, III, 1914, Fig. 575, p. 1318) or the Merovingian string from the Rhine (Andree, 1885, Fig. 3, p. 114), either of which if dug up in West Africa would confidently be classed as ' aggries '.

There is no doubt about the high values attached to these ' aggry ' beads, which were worth their actual weight in gold, sometimes doubled or trebled, or several slaves. The natives believed that they grew out of the earth some generations ago, a belief common to many parts of Africa, fostered by finding them in the ground of old village sites, where they had been either intentionally or accidentally buried. Many natives still believe that beads when buried, not only grow, but breed, though King Suna of Uganda experimented in vain. Another native belief, that beads are the bones of a snake or petrified snakes' eggs, links them with the 'snake stones' of the Britons, and the mysteries surrounding them doubtless added much to their estimation.

Miss Kingsley, noting the African's successful resistance to civilizing influences, prophesied that travellers in the remote future will find him

> still with his tom-tom in his dug-out canoe—just as willing to sell as ' big curios ' the *debris* of our importations to his ancestors at a high price. Exactly how much he will ask for a Devos patent paraffin oil tin or a Morton's tin I cannot imagine, but it will be something stiff—like he asks nowadays for the Phoenician ' aggry ' beads (*Travels*, 1897, p. 679).

The Phoenicians are said (by Herodotus) to have sailed round Africa early in the 7th century B.C., and some beads from the Gold Coast now in the British Museum are authoritatively 'associated with the name and time of the Carthaginian Hanno' (*Man.*, 1905, 1) but the belief that the aggries were introduced by the Phoenicians still awaits proof.

FIG. 2.—West African ' aggries '.
($\frac{3}{8}$ size)

Cardinall has cleared up some confusion by showing that the name aggry was given to three different types of bead in the Gold Coast, all (he believes) of Venetian origin, and brought by the first European traders some 2,000 years later than the Phoenicians. The 3 kinds are the plain blue glass beads, or ' blue coral ' of early accounts, which are similar in shape to the red coral beads of Benin : the mosaic or eyed beads (Fig. 2 and Frontispiece, Fig. 6), described with such admiration by Bowdich, regarded by many as typical ' aggries ', which inspired the native industry of the present day : and the striped, which included the chevrons (*cf.* Frontispiece, Fig. 7).[1]

> These novelties would have come first into the hands of chiefs or great men, enhancing their worth and importance, and giving them by this association fictitious values in native estimation, although they can all find counterparts in the products of Venice or even of Birmingham (Cardinall, 1924–5, p. 298).

There is a new claimant to the name ' aggry ' which has no counter-part anywhere else (Fig. 3 and Frontispiece, Fig. 8). When

[1] Captain Wild collected some old chevron beads in Ashanti but says that they are not called ' aggries ' there.

he was in Ashanti Captain Wild noticed the large buff-coloured beads
' of ginger-beer bottle aspect ' as he describes them, worn on the
wrist as a charm (*suman*) by important chiefs (*amanhene*). They are
heirlooms, handed down like crown jewels from the chief to his
successor, and could not be bought or sold. The natives call them
' aggries ' and all believe that they grow in the ground. Beck gives
as his opinion ' not only are these beads made by natives, but they
are also of considerable age '.

The one illustrated here had been in the possession of the
Queen Mother of the village of Osai Tutu,[1] a few miles north-east
of Kumasi, but came into the market during the slump.

The problem of aggries is far from being settled, and can only
be cleared up by an expert on the spot. Meanwhile, it would
simplify the subject if the name ' aggry ', if used at all, were restricted
to special beads from the Coast, for there are early trade beads from
other parts of Africa whose history is
equally obscure and these, though all
lumped together as ' aggries ', may or
may not be derived from the same
source.

FIG. 3.—' Aggry ', Gold Coast

Their geographical distribution is
suggestive and may help to explain how
they came to Africa. They are well
known on the West Coast, as we have
seen, and used in the gold trade there.
But they do not spread into the gold-less
Congo region. Schurtz (1898, pp. 103–5)
notes their distribution also in the
South-East, where in the richest gold districts the most ancient (or
' aggry ') beads are found. These are not the ' blue coral ' of the
West Coast, but are of all colours, shapes and sizes. They were
believed to come from the Kingdom of Monomotapa (Rhodesia)
and to be dug out of the earth there. Their rarity was accounted
for by the belief that the earth had caved in and covered the place
in which they had been excavated.

Ogilby (1673, pp. 582, 605), recording the trade of his day,
described the exchange of ' Cambayan beads ' for cattle between the
Namaqua and the Portuguese of Monomotapa, and gives more details
about the trade of Sofala.

In that country [which he identifies with the Ophir of King Solomon]
the Mohammedans coming by sea in *zambuks* bring silk stuffs and ash-
coloured, yellow and red Cambayan beads, which they exchange for Gold,
as those of Sofala barter these wares again with them of Monomotapa for
Gold, which they receive without Weight.

---

[1] Osai Tutu was the founder of Ashanti, and reigned about 1700.

A little later (1700) Barbot notes ' the little glass balls . . . from Cambaia ' which were used instead of money at Malindi (1732, IV, p. 518). Merensky, Mission superintendent among the Basuto in 1860, described the ' beads or corals, especially a yellow and black sort ' only worn by chiefs and their wives. No commoner was allowed to own one. He mentions 17 different types, red, green, blue, white and variegated (1882, pp. 543–5).

Bartels describes and illustrates 15 types (1891, p. 399), many irregularly cut and asymmetrical. These are all reed beads, none of them corresponding to the West Coast ' aggries '. The most valuable here were the largish yellow beads called *talama*, a word which means ' gold ' in many African dialects. The largish angular dark-blue transparent beads familiar throughout Africa (*cf.* Frontispiece, Fig. 5) are also called *talama*. The word has been traced to the Arabic *dirham*, which means ' money ', and *dirham* is derived from *drachma*, a weight, originally a handful. Beads are still measured by the handful in East Africa.

If the association of ancient beads with ancient gold-seekers can be established, it would seem an easy matter to identify the early gold-seekers by discovering where these beads were made. But when India, China, Japan and the East Indian Islands, Egypt and the Eastern Mediterranean all have their supporters, the difficulties are complicated.

Sir Richard Temple believed that they had their origin in Egypt, recognizing types familiar in 17th- and 19th-dynasty graves ; and he assumed that the Arabs, trading under Egyptian masters, trafficked with Egyptian beads, and were followed by the Spaniards and Portuguese, using the same wares, made in Venice (1899, pp. 120–1).

Egypt is credited with the invention of glass-making, and during the Bronze Age beads spread round the Mediterranean, their occurrence in Spain, Brittany and South-West Britain indicating maritime trade. As the knowledge of glass-making also spread, factories were established and imitations were made, the Eastern Mediterranean, and especially Venice, being renowned for beads down to the present day, though Cambay was for a time, a serious rival.[1]

An extensive trade in beads spreading so widely, and over so many centuries makes identifications and dating peculiarly difficult, and it must be confessed that at present there is not sufficient evidence to prove where the ancient trade beads came from, whether from one centre or, as seems more probable, from many ; nor who were the intermediaries responsible for their distribution.

[1] Especially in the 16th century (*cf.* Wiener, 1922, II, pp. 226 *ff.*, 245).

Had Africa been the only continent concerned, the problems would be simplified, but Africa is probably the last chapter in the whole story, and West Africa the last word. Mere resemblances are misleading. The string of 'aggries' presented by Sir Richard Temple himself to Sir William Ridgeway (Frontispiece, Fig. 6) is pronounced by Beck to be comparatively modern, probably not more than a century old, and some of the beads might even be of Czechoslovakian manufacture, so superficially indistinguishable are they from those turned out at the present day.

Superficial resemblances may mislead, but comparisons are being placed on a safe foundation by microscopic and chemical analysis and the study of ancient trade beads is becoming an important aid in archaeology. Here and there a few beads are found in graves or other hoards of a definite horizon, and the evidence is gradually accumulating; and when related, if not identical, beads are found in South and East Africa, in South India, in Malaya and in the East Indies, the question is seen to be far-reaching.

These clues have been provided by Beck (1928, 1934), who has been able to identify some of the early beads found in megalithic tombs and urn-burials in South India, in early sites in the Federated Malay States, and in treasured hoards of Sarawak of the 9th and 10th centuries A.D. And the 'similarity between the majority of the beads [from Kuala Selinsing, F.M.S.] and those from the middens of South India, those from Zimbabwe and those from Zanzibar is unmistakable' (1930, **134**).[1]

The mysterious Pelew beads of Micronesia belong to the same problem and probably to the same chapter of history. Some of these are ordinary-looking cornelian or agate beads (which suggest Cambayan origin), but most are artificial, with numerous varieties, indescribable shapes and unpronounceable names.[2] Each one has its special name 'like a man'. The beads have different functions according to their class; some are used for ordinary buying and selling; some only for special purchases; one will buy a canoe, one will buy a house, another is the price of a village, and another —reverently handled—is beyond price. Some belong only to chiefs; some are lent out at interest, with different scales of interest for different classes, the system being intricately complicated and seemingly illogical.

Similar beads, equally treasured, have been found in Timor,

---

[1] Still earlier links have been recognized by the finding of a Hittite stone bead of 700 B.C. and an Italian glass bead of about the same date, together with Phoenician and early Cypriote beads, in a hoard of Roman and Indian beads in the Johore River (Gardner, 1934, p. 467).

[2] *Barak, bunau, kluk, kalebukub* and *adolobok* among the larger classes are credible, but *misnroaol, kalopthuy* and *pknalaywayu* present difficulties. *Cf.* Kubary, 1895, pp. 6 *ff.*

Flores and Savu, the beads being in some cases identical (Andree, 1885, p. 110) brought perhaps by the Hindu-Malay pearl-fishers whose language has been traced through Polynesia and as far as the Carolines and the Gilberts in the names for pearl shells and oyster (Christian, 1910, pp. 236–7).[1]

The study of ancient trade beads in Britain belongs rather to the province of archaeology than to that of currency. Nevertheless, mention must be made of the chevrons, ' druids' beads ' or ' snake stones ' [2] found in British barrows and Anglo-Saxon graves, with their counterparts on the mainland of Europe. Beads of this rather complicated pattern are conspicuous among the Gold Coast ' aggries ' (as seen above) ; one was recognized in the Pelews (Andree, 1885, p. 110) ; they have been found in pre-Columbian graves in North America (*Schoolcraft*, 1851–7, I, Pls. 24, 25) ; and a clever imitation was detected by Beck in a Sarawak hoard (p. 261).

Brent, describing the ' glass adders of the Druids ', adds ' beads exactly similar are now manufactured in England for the African slave trade ' (1872, p. 684), which accounts for their common occurrence on the West Coast (where they are of course called ' aggries ') and their dispersal inland along the trade routes.

Beads age rapidly in Africa, and burial in the ground produces an appearance of such hoary antiquity that an import of 50 or 100 years ago can easily lay claim to be a relic of Phoenician traders, a claim which only an expert can disprove.

There is evidence of intercourse and commercial interchange from the beginning of our era, (as recorded in the *Periplus*), between the Mediterranean, the coasts of Arabia and East Africa to the west of the Indian Ocean, and the Spice Islands to the east, while (according to Herodotus) traders had found their way still earlier down the coast of West Africa. Precious stones figure largely in trading lists, and even in the earliest, imitations were creeping in. Pliny records how the people of India were skilful in counterfeiting precious stones ; and in the Chinese account of Roman Syria, based on the report of the ambassador (A.D. 97), the writer describes the articles made of rare precious stones as sham curiosities and mostly not genuine (Schoff, 1912, pp. 221, 277). In succeeding centuries Phoenicians, Arabs, Indonesians and Malays carried on the trade, with gold and slaves among the most valued exports from Africa, spices, pearls and pearl-shells from the East. It seems reasonable to suppose that this early trade, using beads in barter, if not as currency, which was well established some 2,000 years ago, distributed the products of

---

[1] Other theories of the origin of the Pelew beads will be found on p. 148.

[2] *Glain nadroedd* is the Welsh form. *Cf.* Åkerman, 1851, p. 51, with illustrations.

Egypt, later of Venice and Cambay, and later still of Birmingham and of Czechoslovakia, wherever traders could foist them on the natives in exchange for goods of greater worth. But the help of archaeology or the skill of the specialist is needed to discover the stratum to which any particular bead belongs.

Chapter V
AFRICA

I speak of Africa and golden joys.
PISTOL

i. General.   ii. West Africa :   A. Congo, Gaboon to Angola ;   B. Nigeria to Senegal.   iii. North, East and South Africa

i. GENERAL

GEOGRAPHY plays a large part in influencing and determining native currencies, but the human factors are at least of equal importance, so in making a general survey the choice lies between a physical or an ethnological map for the foundation.   Fortunately the two often overlap, and they overlap sufficiently for this purpose in Africa, if we note the main outlines of geographical conditions and race distribution.

The whole of the North and North-East of the Continent, from the Red Sea to Senegal, and penetrating with the slave trade far south of this line, is the zone of Arab influence ; and Arab trade, trade-goods and trading currencies preceded, accompanied or followed the Crescent over that vast area marked ' Arab and Berber ' in *The Times* map of Races and left blank in the map of Commercial Development.   This infiltration, already visible at the beginning of our era, and stimulated with religious zeal in the 7th century, had reached Nigeria and Senegal in the 10th, blotting out evidence of former migrations in the same direction ; and with cowries, beads and finally coins, produced a uniformity irrespective of environment.

But geography overrules racial boundaries to east and west.   The West Coast, including the Congo basin, shows no marked contrasts, whether the native traders are of Sudanian or Bantu-speaking origin, though Spain and Portugal, as well as Britain, France and Belgium, left their imprints in more recent times.

Along the Mediterranean and all down the East Coast to the South, the cattle country links Africa with the early pecuniary system of Europe, however distinct the Nilotic Negroes may be from the Southern Bantu.   Abyssinia stands aloof behind its mountains ; while among the Hottentots and the Bushmen farthest south, native currencies are undeveloped.

These are the broad outlines, with the main divisions between West and East, the former with a great variety of currencies, each area, each river, and often each tributary of the river having its own special characteristic form of money.   The East (which includes the

45

North) has few primitive types, and most of it is labelled ' *Thalers de Marie-Thérèse* ' in Montandon's map.

But before proceeding to a regional survey we may note certain materials used as currency over the whole continent; shells, iron, salt, cloth and beads. Shells, here as elsewhere, ignore local boundaries, and prove their claim to be best-sellers; iron, salt and cloth are widely used, though appearing in specialized forms in different parts. These four classes can be dealt with first.

We have watched the cowries percolating along the trade-routes of Africa and noted their extraordinary popularity wherever they went. But in the Congo region and to the south of it they met a serious rival in their distant relative *oliva nana*, the little olivella

FIG. 4.—*Olivella* shells, ' simbos '

shell called by the trading Bayaka *nzimbu mbudi*,[1] corrupted into *jimbu, simbu, simbo*, &c., in trading jargon.

This is a small shell only about half an inch (12 mm.) long, much lighter and more fragile than the cowry (Fig. 4). It is found in many parts along the coast, but the great collecting centre was at Loanda.

Pigafetta, writing down in 1591 the account of Duarte Lopez, who had spent 12 years in the Kingdom of Congo, described the native industry.

An island called Loanda meaning . . . flat country and devoid of mountains, as it hardly rises out of the water, . . . is formed from the sand and mud which are deposited by the sea and the River Coanza [Kwanza], whose streams meet here. . . . This island furnishes the money used by the King of Congo and the neighbouring people ; for along its shores women dive under water, a depth of two yards and more, and filling their baskets with sand they sift out certain small shell-fish called Lumache,[2] and then separate the male from the female the latter being most prized for its colour and brightness. These Lumache are found along all the coasts of Congo, but those of Loanda are finest, being transparent and in colour somewhat like the chrysolite [topaz], with other kinds, not as greatly valued. It must be remembered that gold, silver, and other metals are not valued nor used as money in these countries ; and so it happens that with gold and silver in abundance, either in mass or in coin, yet nothing can be bought except with Lumache (Hutchinson, 1881, pp. 18–19).

Dapper a century later (1686, p. 367) describing the money used in Angola, says that *simbos* represent silver there, and that the best

---

[1] The name is given to any shells used as currency not only to olivella, hence the frequent confusion between olives and cowries, all of which, as well as beads, are lumped together, so that *jimbu, simbo*, &c., come to mean ' money ', like *wampum* in America. Wiener (1922, II, p. 221) derives *nzimbo* from the Maldivian name *boli*, meaning cowry, which became *abuy* in Africa, and, with plural prefix, *zimbuy*.

[2] Lat. *limax*, slug or snail.

come from Loanda. But importations from Brazil,[1] fished up at Rio de Janeiro, were brought back by Portuguese slavers.

Schneider (1905, pp. 94-100) quotes references and descriptions concerning these shells from the end of the 15th century, and clears up much of the obscurity which surrounded them, owing to their confusion with cowries. It is obvious that many of the earlier writers had never seen either cowries or olives.

After the introduction of the Portuguese *makuta* (1624) the inland petty trade was still carried on with *simbos*, cowries, native cloth or blocks of salt. But in the next century the fishery seems to have ceased, the *simbos* depreciated, and disappeared as currency, due partly to the foreign importations, and partly to the superior attractions of the all-conquering cowry.

But they were still used inland, especially in the Kwilu-Kwango area. The Bayaka traded them down the rivers to the Kasai, and they became the currency of the Bambala and Bahuana of the Lower Kwilu as well as of the Bateke of Stanley Pool. The Bambala have special purses for carrying the shells, among them being the baskets plaited in a ring, like miniature lifebelts, with a neck for inserting or extracting the shells (Fig. 5). One hundred *nzimbu* will buy a fowl, a slave costs 10,000, a female slave (women are always variable) may be anything from 10,000 to 30,000. The Bahuana scale in 1905 was as follows : [2]

10 *nzimbu*	=	1 *mitako* (brass rod 6 inches long)
20 *mitako*	=	1 fowl
100 *mitako*	=	1 salt (2 or 3 pounds)
2 salts	=	a he-goat
4 salts	=	a big she-goat
20 salts	=	a male slave

(Torday and Joyce, 1905, p. 398 ; 1906, p. 283 ; 1907, **52**)

The cowry has conquered the olive, but it has yet other worlds to conquer, and a snailshell currency still holds its own

[1] Loanda (founded by the Portuguese, 1576) was the headquarters of the slave trade with Brazil. John Ogilby, Royal Cosmographer and Geographick Printer to Charles II, distinguishes between ' pure simbos ' of Loanda and ' brazils ' (1676, pp. 502, 570).

[2] The value of native money cannot be stated in £ s. d. as it varies with the individual, time and place, besides being influenced by many factors inoperative in our commercial circles. Authority may fix some equivalent, but with difficulty, and the Belgian attempts to fix the *mitako* in the Congo, as described by Mahieu (1924, Chap. III) are instructive. Lugard's rough estimate that the daily wage of native labour was approximately the same as the local value of a fowl, gives some idea of equivalence, if not too rigidly applied. The pre-war (1914) rate paid by Government and by Europeans ranged from 1s. 10d. a day in the Union of South Africa, to 9d. in Nigeria, 3d. in East Africa, and 1½d. in Rhodesia ; and the price of an average fowl was about the same (1929, p. 405 fn.).

farther inland. Cowries spread along the Northern Congo: they spread along its southern tributaries, the Kasai and the Sankuru : but there is a cowry-less region between these, between the Congo above Stanley Falls (here called the Lualaba) and the Great Lakes. Here the Warega and Wazimba, the Warundi to the east of them and the Bakusu to the north (besides many others), use strings of snailshells, called *musanga, ikumi, viringi* and a variety of untranslated names (Mahieu, 1924, pp. 10, 119–22). Similar strings

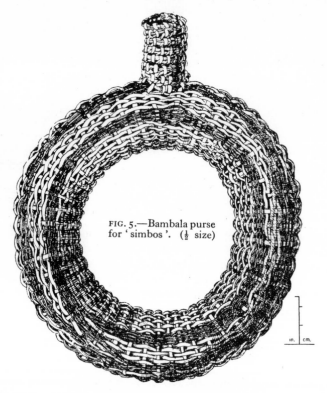

FIG. 5.—Bambala purse for 'simbos'. (½ size)

were formerly the currency of the Batetela of the Upper Lomami (Torday and Joyce, 1922, p. 52, Fig. 30). The men break up the shells and perforate them, an easy job as the shells are very thin and brittle, and then make them into necklaces and trading strings. The latter are measured from the big toe to the heel, 10 strings of this length being equal to a length of calico. These African snails are very large, some 4 to 5 inches (10–13 cm.) long, so the broken pieces are often very large too. The smaller strings are usually more evenly cut and finished, and may form necklaces, but the

coarser strings of fragments an inch or more across, with irregular
scratchy edges (Fig. 6) are unsuitable for wearing on bare skin and,
single or bunched together, have no use save as currency. The
strings are especially important in ' bride-price ' and in entrance to
secret societies, for which no other form of money is accepted. And
a currency which is almost indefinitely divisible is here essential, as
the contributions are distributed according to custom, 40 per cent
among the degree next above, and 60 per cent among members of
lower degrees. Practical demonstration of the share-out saves
dispute.

Mahieu (1924, pp. 121 *ff.*) describes the *ikumi* of the Wasongola,
on the Lualaba, of poor workmanship, and low
value, a single string a palm long being worth only
about 10 c. These are little used in trade, but
form an important part of the marriage portion,
the number of strings fluctuating with the social
position or personal attractions of the bride. The
viringi (sing. *kiringi*) of the same district are not
of local manufacture, but are obtained from near
Ponthierville in exchange for oil, fowls and other
produce. These are not worn as ornaments, but
are merely for trading, and also figure largely in
marriage settlements. The standard string is as
long as the forearm and nominally worth a franc.
The *kiringi* is a bunch of 16 strings, nominally
worth 16 francs. Before 1914 their value was
only 3 or 4 francs but later they were bought
up by traders, who often paid 25 francs a bunch.
They found that they could not buy ivory from
the natives entirely for cash—it had to be supplemented by some of the snailshell strings.

FIG. 6.—Snailshell
string, Batetela.
(⅔ size)

Snailshells also provided an important currency which Schneider has described (1905,
pp. 88–94) as stretching from Senegambia to Benguella made of
little disks of *Achatina* shells. And he distinguishes *Achatina
balteata* along the coast, and *Achatina monetaria* in the district
inland from Mossamedes in Angola. Here he quotes from Dr.
Welwitsch, who was collecting shells as well as plants and insects
in Angola in 1853–61, and indeed it needs a specialist to identify
the shell out of which these little disks are cut, especially as the
edges get polished with use, and show little evidence of their
original colour or texture. The inland industry appears to have
had its centre in the Benguella or Kwanza district, some way from
the Coast, and the disks were there called *dongo*, and were strung
in bundles of 6, about as long as the forearm, called a *quiranda* or

kirana. These strings were highly prized as ornaments as well as currency, and a *quiranda* was worth 1,000 to 4,000 *reis*, (about 5*s*.). As strings they do not attract much attention, being irregular and uneven. The Bubi currency in Fernando Po is much more effective. Here the strings are plaited into broad flat plaits, the ends of the threads being tied together where they meet, to make circular bands or belts for arm, neck or waist, and especially waist. These are called *jibbu*. A fine example nearly a yard long (90 cm.), and over 4 inches (10 cm.) deep, is illustrated in Plate 3, Fig. 5. It is believed that these shell-strings are not native to Fernando Po, but were introduced by runaway Angola slaves, who used to escape from their Portuguese owners on San Thomé, to the Spaniards on Fernando Po, (Kingsley, 1897, p. 59 ; Johnston, 1908, p. 959, Fig. 494).

Shell-strings are also used as currency among some tribes of the Upper Nile, Uganda and East Africa (see below, pp. 100–101), but their commercial and social functions are nowhere so conspicuous as in the regions to the west.

FIG. 7.—Cone shell, Manyema. (⅔ size)

One more Gastropod is occasionally represented in collections of African currency, this is the cone shell, which is so conspicuous in Melanesian ornament and currency. *Conus papilionaceus, Conus imperialis* and others are worn both in West and in East Africa as ornament, or displayed as signs of rank and wealth (Mahieu, 1924, pp. 46, 117–18). Schneider (1905, pp. 86–8) collected the early references which indicate that the shells (*papilionaceus*) were imported into West Africa from Fernando Po and San Thomé, and that the slave traders from the latter island brought them over to the mainland in the 16th century. Here they had a high value and were greatly prized, 'worth 20 shillings a shell' as Andrew Battell records (1901, p. 31).

The larger *imperialis* were imported from the Moluccas in the East Indies and may have travelled along the same trade routes as the Indian cowries. This was the kind that Livingstone met in the Balunda district (and illustrates, 1899, p. 205). Two would buy a slave and 5 were worth an ivory tusk or £10.

The basal whorl of *Conus* that Sir John Kirk collected in 1850 as currency among the Manyema, to the west of Lake Tanganyika, is illustrated (Fig. 7). These end whorls of the shells, or more often disks ground down from them, are prominent as regalia and talismans in East Africa, especially in Tanganyika Territory, Kenya and Northern Rhodesia, and though they are rarely recorded as currency they figure largely in ceremonial presentations and are used in ' bride-price ' and fines.

Next to shell-currencies the most popular and widely spread materials are iron, salt and cloth. The choice illustrates the axiom that the chief stimulus of barter and trading is inequality (either in the provisions of nature or the products of man). It also illustrates the axiom that pleasure in possession arises from its use, regarded as characteristic of Anglo-Saxon mentality, which is incapable of, or at any rate, ignores, any finer aesthetic appreciation (Schurtz, 1898, p. 112). But among the Africans, if not among the Anglo-Saxons, iron and cloth are valued for decoration, as much as for use.

It has been noted before that where nature is lavish and uniform in bounty, where wants are simple and there is enough for all, exchanges may be made but trading is not a social necessity. Commercial bartering begins with specialization. Iron, though abundant, is not found everywhere and the working of it is a specialized craft. Saline deposits are still more local, and salt-making becomes a monopoly. That cloth should become a currency is less obvious. Materials are common, cloth-making is not such a specialized craft as iron-working, but it represents a certain amount of work done, sometimes remarkably fine work, and logically or illogically, takes its place with iron and salt among the most widely spread currencies that evolved in Africa before the opening up of the continent by Europeans. Possibly neither of these owes its estimation to its intrinsic worth alone. Magic and ritual are closely associated with iron-working, less with salt-getting, but salt possesses symbolic virtues also. And both iron-working and weaving may have gained prestige, if not some supernatural character, from their introduction from the unknown, by a conquering people, which enhanced their values, at any rate in West Africa (Johnston, 1908, p. 791). And iron, cloth and salt have continued as trading currencies ever since. *Shokas* (axes) made in Birmingham are the currency of the Upper Congo, as hoes of the Upper Nile and bars of varied shapes from Nigeria to Sierra Leone. Salt is the typical currency of Abyssinia, and the common payment for carriers along the Kasai : and cloth, ' americani ', ' indigo drills ' and many other well-established lines is accepted in place of money right across Africa, extinguishing native cloth currencies on the way.

Apart from the fact that iron complies with the four primary demands of an ideal currency, that it shall be durable, recognizable, portable and divisible, it has the further essential characteristic of comparative scarceness ; and even where it occurs, it is not always worked. Smiths, as is well known, form a special class, caste or guild, sometimes highly honoured, sometimes as conspicuously despised, hence their products are not such as any man can make for himself. Further, owing to the exclusiveness of the workers, their craft is surrounded with a certain mystery, and this mystery clings to the output of the forge. The belief that there is something a little uncanny about metals appears to be almost universal, and it certainly enhances the value of iron objects used as currency.

Another point in favour of iron-currencies must be noted, though it is an advantage shared by shells—an ornamental value.

Just as shells used as currency can be used also as chaplets, necklets, armlets, bracelets, leglets, anklets,, waistbelts and other decorations, so can iron be used in the form of rings with an additional solidity and safety that shells seldom possess. There may be some feeling of enclosure and safe-keeping about the ring form, as fostered in that ' spiritual fetter ', the modern conventional wedding-ring, and here only the larger and (in Africa) rarer shells can compete with iron, but it is an obvious advantage when surplus wealth can be so conveniently stored on necks, arms and legs (own or wives').

Iron is more than potential wealth or potential ornament. It is of practical use. Hence it is impossible to insist on any strict dividing line between currency and non-currency. A man would take his iron bars, rods, *manillas* or *mitakos* to the smith to be made into axe, hoe, knife or ring : and the axe, hoe, knife or ring would have the exchange value, save for the smith's deduction, of the original metal. If the object is left unfinished, and has no practical use, it is, in Temple's definition (p. 1), reckoned as ' money ' ; but when it is shaped, polished or sharpened, although it has its exchange value all the same, it is merely a tool, or an ornament.

With ornaments the distinction between what is money and what is not is even more difficult to estimate.

In many parts of Africa iron *is* money, that is, it represents a standard of value, it is a recognized medium of exchange, and a symbol of wealth. To succeed in the last function it must be displayed ; hence it may be coiled round the arms, legs or necks of the owner or his women-folk. But it is still money.

With all these advantages, as money, acceptable in exchange, as ornament, or for practical use as tools, iron easily acquired its supremacy throughout Africa, and metal-work provides the most conspicuous objects in currency collections, although not all of the types seen there are of native metal or of native manufacture. These will be described according to their regional distribution later on.

Salt, like iron, only occurs in certain districts, and, also like iron, when once acquired, becomes indispensable. Doubtless our earliest ancestors lived happily without either iron or salt ; both are of late introduction in many parts of the world (salt usually later than iron) and carnivorous people can do without any additional salination. But as iron holds its own through its superiority over the materials it replaces, so salt, once enjoyed, spoils the taste for saltless food, especially where the food is mainly vegetable. Hence the salt trade in interior Africa often seems more like blackmail than barter.

In a country like our own, with the sea accessible all the way round us, and ample deposits of salt inland, it is difficult to realize the salt-hunger in those parts of Africa where the sea is far distant and inland deposits are sparse. Mahieu describes it vividly. Speaking of imported salt in the Congo, where it arrives in little squares like lumps of sugar, and constitutes *une veritable monnaie*, he says that the natives are so fond of the taste that successive possessors of this money can rarely resist a lick. Hence, after serving for several transactions it reaches the final consumer sticky with saliva, and thick with dirt, which happily does not affect the stomach of the negro (1924, p. 57). The importance of the salt trade in Africa, its export across the deserts, and its influence on the caravan routes and on the slave trade are well known.

Ibn Batuta in the 14th century travelling south to Timbuktu described Taghaza :

> An unattractive village with the curious feature that the houses and mosques are built of blocks of salt roofed with camel skins. There are no trees there, nothing but sand. In the sand is a salt mine. They dig for the salt and find it in thick slabs. A camel can carry 2 of these slabs. At Iwalalan [Walata] 10 nights' journey away a load of salt brings 8 to 10 mithqals,[1] in the town of Malli it sells for 20 to 30 and sometimes as much as 40. The negroes use salt as a medium of exchange just as gold and silver is used [elsewhere]. They cut it up into pieces and buy and sell with it (p. 317).

Here the salt trade was on a grand scale, with caravans of hundreds of camels all laden with salt. And it ' passed for money ' wherever it went.

In the Congo also it ' passes for money ', and is indeed preferred to money by labourers [2] and carriers in the interior. But the local salt is derived from different and humbler sources.

Torday describes and Norman Hardy illustrates (1911, p. 134, Pl. XVII) salt-making on the Sankuru. The plants are burnt, their ashes collected and water is filtered through them into troughs ingeniously made of bark. A smouldering fire is lit underneath, and the water evaporates, leaving the salt behind.

Among the Babunda of the Upper Kasai preparations for war consist in the collection by the chief of quantities of salt, neatly wrapped in banana leaves.[3] This is the currency of the district,

---

[1] The *mithqal*, an Arab weight and measure of value, was very varied, cf. Barth, 1858, Vol. V, p. 23.

[2] Roadmakers (women) round Luluaberg are paid in salt by the bucketful, and they spend it, in teaspoonfuls, in the bazaar (Norden, 1924, p. 173).

[3] M. W. Hilton-Simpson, 1911, p. 263.

and it is also used for paying the murder indemnity of a man of
another village.

On the Upper Lukenie, which runs into Lake Leopold, blocks of
salt are the only exported currency of the Bohindu (Torday and
Joyce, 1911, p. 268). At the head waters of the Lomami, farther to
the east, two or three pots of salt are the price of a slave (Mahieu,
1924, p. 38) and on the northern boundary on the banks of the
Ubangi, 'salt is a common currency' (Boyd Alexander, 1907, II,
p. 226). Imported salt was used by Moroccan traders along the
Guinea coast for several centuries, and native salt in cones
(Fig. 20) is still current in Bornu, and forms an essential item in
'bride-price' (D. F. H. MacBride).

Angola was famous for its salt trade more than three centuries
ago, as Andrew Battell records (1901, p. 37):

> In this place [the Quissame region just south of Loanda] there is such
> store of salt that most part of the country are perfect clear salt, without any
> earth or filth in it, and it is some 3 feet under the earth as if it were ice, and
> they cut it out in stones of a yard long, and it is carried up into the country
> and is the best commodity that a man can carry to buy anything whatsoever.

A commodity which inevitably depreciates in transit lacks the
'durable' aspect of money and save that it is put up in commercial
units and has a higher rate of 'acceptability' than most, it differs
little from other objects of barter. It is met with, hovering between
barter and currency, throughout East Africa. Sir Samuel Baker
described how he heard the traders in Nyoro (Uganda) calling out
'Milk to sell for salt! Salt to exchange for lance-heads! Coffee
going cheap for red beads!' &c.[1] (Alexander, 1907, II, p. 171).

Hose describes the salt trade in Tanganyika (1882, pp. 8–9):

> The most noticeable feature in Ujiji is its maiket . . . the only export
> of great extent . . . being the famous packages of salt, current all over the
> Lake shores. It is manufactured once a year on the banks of the Ruguvu
> River easc of Ujiji, where from two to three thousand people assemble for
> the sole purpose of making the salt.

It is packed up in cylindrical leaf packages weighing from 20 to
30 pounds each, and valued at Ujiji at about 2 yards of good calico
or 100 strings of the beads figured in the Frontispiece, Fig. 5.

The most familiar example of a real salt currency comes from
Abyssinia.

Francis Alvarez, the Portuguese missionary who was sent on an
embassy to the Negus, and spent 6 years in Abyssinia, 1520–6, wrote:

[1] A South American parallel could be heard last century in Corrientes
in the Argentine, where the children were wont to run along the streets
calling out 'Salt for candles! Tobacco for bread!' (Roscher, 1878, I,
p. 340).

Salt is current instead of money from the Red Sea to Congo on the West Sea. It is said to be dug out of mountains and cut into blocks a hand-an-half in length, 4 fingers broad and 3 fingers thick. When dug out 100 or 120 of these blocks were worth three-quarters of a ducket ; a day's journey distant 5 or 6 blocks less were worth the three-quarters of a ducket ; at the King's Court, 6 or 7 blocks were worth this money and as it travelled farther one block would purchase a slave and it became nearly worth its weight in gold (Purchas, 1905, Vol. VIII, p. 53. *Cf.* P. M. de Salviac, 1901, p. 159, who illustrates other forms of salt-currency).

Alexander Hamilton, the East India merchant, early in the 18th century wrote :

The current small money of Ethiopia is salt, which is dug out of the mountains as we do Stones from our Quarries, which they break into Pieces of several sizes, the largest weighing about 80 pounds, the others in 40, 20, 10, or 5 pounds, and are so expert in dividing it that they err not above 5 per cent more or less in their Calculation of Weight ; 20 Pounds is in value, 1 Shilling Sterling, and those Pieces of Salt is the current Money in their Markets for Provisions (1727, I, p. 24).

Major Powell Cotton travelling in the country in 1899 found that Menelik's smaller silver or copper coins were only accepted in the neighbourhood of the capital.

Beyond that district crystallized salt bars 10 inches long and 2 inches across at the centre were the small change. Four went to the dollar at the capital, and gradually lost value as one proceeded north, until at Adua I obtained 15 to the dollar. Changing a dollar was not the work of a moment ; each bar had to be examined and sounded, for if it were not of the right size, was chipped or cracked or it did not ring true, the first person to whom it was offered would be as indignant as a London cabby when tendered a bad shilling (*The Times*, 17.6.38).

The salt bars illustrated (Fig. 8) show the four values in use, being equivalent to $1\frac{1}{2}$, 1, $\frac{1}{2}$ and $\frac{1}{4}$ dollars, these are not only useful for barter or as small change, they are (or were until the recent reorganization) legal tender for fines and taxes (Walker, 1933, p. 195).

Cloth is of little more permanent value than salt, but it was firmly established as currency here and there in West Africa before the varieties of European cloth which now form the usual trade goods supplanted native products. And although native cloth is not durable (hence its rarity in Museum collections) it is divisible and recognizable, and has the further advantage of being particularly well fitted for transport. A large quantity can be packed into a comfortable shape for head-porterage, and, being blameless of sharp angles and projections, is always a popular load.[1]

It may owe its widespread distribution in the tsetse fly area to its

[1] Hobley describes how on his way to Uganda his porters always rushed for the bales of cloth, so these were unpacked, and 10 pounds of brass wire tucked away inside (1929, p. 78).

portability. But its acceptability in its personal appeal to the women-folk must not be overlooked. Iron in its commonest forms is potentially a tool or a weapon ; cloth is potentially a dress or at least a decoration. So in the regions where cloth is worn by women it plays a large part in pre-matrimonial as well as actual 'bride-price' negotiations.

It may be noted that cloth as currency progressed a stage further than was ever attained or attainable by salt. From *Nutzgeld* it

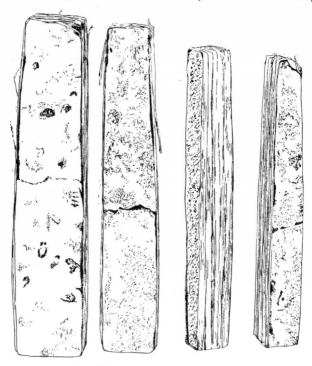

FIG. 8.—Salt currency, Abyssinia. (½ size)

becomes *Zeichengeld*, a mere token. From being a potential garment it becomes a useless strip of material (in the Sudan), a mock shirt (in Bornu) or a bundle of fibres (in the Congo).

This bunch of fibres (either Raphia palm or banana as used for weaving) called *mbadi* or *mbari*, was the unit of value in the Cataract region before the coming of the Belgians (Mahieu, 1924, pp. 15–16, ill.). These 'useless bundles of tangled hay', as Johnston calls them (1908, p. 790), were traded inland as far as the head waters of the Kasai and the Lomami, but are no longer met with, having long ago been replaced by European cloth and brass wire.

Woven cloths are more persistent. These are in different lengths, women's cloths, men's cloths, and longer pieces for wrapping up corpses for burial, each having its value according to its length. The unit of measurement was usually the fathom, measured between the outstretched fingers, and multiples of this, but a fathom might be very liberally or very stingily interpreted, and the actual length often depended on negotiation rather than on measurement. Barbot describes how in the Congo district in dealing with the king, the fathom was reckoned at 6 ft. 2 in. but, for ordinary people, at 5 ft. ; while farther along the coast it shrank to 4 ft. (1732, pp. 504, 506, 508).

In the Loango area (now in French Equatorial Africa) the Portuguese *cortade* was the unit of measurement and the same name is still used for the yard. A piece may be of 5, 10 up to 100 *cortades*, and the longer pieces are folded and counted by folds. Shorter lengths are conveniently plaited or rolled into a bundle tied at the ends, a handy shape for small purchases, but not intended for any other use. 'Mat-money' woven of native 'grass' (chiefly fine strips of Raphia palm leaves) in pieces approximately square were widely used in place of money in the Belgian Congo.[1] The *madiba* of the Upper Sankuru (some 60 by 40 cm. = about 2 by $1\frac{1}{2}$ feet) formed the tribute paid in immense quantities by the Basonge to the Arabs and used by the latter for buying goods in the markets and by Europeans for paying their men. They were the common currency along the Sankuru and the Kasai ; while from the Basonge area they were exchanged with the Baluba, who exchanged them for Katanga crosses from the south.

'Mat-money' was also current in the Lower Congo, in the Cataract and Stanley Pool region (Loir, 1935, pp. 58–9, Figs. 49, 50). Small pieces (Pl. 2, Fig. 6) were widely used and were almost the only currency at one time on the Congo border.

Dapper, describing the current money of Lovando (Angola), puts cloth (*libongos* and *panos-simbos*) first, with *simbos* next and red wood (*tukula*) third (1686, p. 367). But though inland in his list of the riches of the kingdom of Macoco, slaves come first, he notes the *simbos* and Indian cowries and 'little pieces of cloth and such bagatelles, which they esteem as much in their country as gold and silver in Europe' (p. 359).

These mats went out of use at San Salvador about 1830, but lingered on on the frontier of the Congo State until about 1900 ; 10 of the small bits were worth a small copper *macuta*, and 50 were about equal to a string of blue beads.

[1] Mahieu describes the *madiba, bongo, nlabu* and other kinds (pp. 13–17) and illustrates, opposite p. xx, a weaver making one of these mats. *Cf.* also Johnston, 1908, pp. 515, 792, 799.

The trading value was increased by sewing 30 of the small mats together in 3 rows of 10, to make the *nta*, and though the whole was worth only about a franc, this was the unit all up and down the Middle Congo among the Bateke traders. They were used for fines, compensations and marriage payments and still more generously expended at funerals. A man who had killed another had to pay the relatives 200 *nta* and a gun. A husband claims 100 *nta* from his wife's lover. This is also the average ' bride-price '. Should the girl die, her relatives must provide a substitute or refund the *nta*. Far greater quantities of *nta* are seen at the funeral of a wealthy or popular man, who is swathed in cloths provided by relatives. Mahieu tells how at Stanley Pool he saw a corpse so lavishly bundled in cloths that it was too cumbersome to be removed by the usual entrance and had to be extracted by removing the end of the hut. This bale, as he calls it, was 6 feet high, and had to be levered along by poles to roll it into the grave, in which it was planted upright. A woman never justifies this expense and the maximum number expended on her is about 20 (Mahieu, 1924, pp. 14–15).

The superior attractions of European gaily printed cottons have discouraged if not destroyed local industries, and trade goods such as ' americani ', ' indigo drills ', ' savedlist ', &c., have taken the place of grass mats and native cloth in commercial transactions.[1]

Their acceptability, however, is not universal. Torday on his expedition (1907–8) met with an unexpected obstacle in the Kasai-Sankuru region. They paid the carriers each day in salt, the local currency, to be exchanged for food in the villages where they halted. And they took with them the European cotton goods which are the common currency throughout, but in the unexplored region between the Loange and the Kasai, where missionaries had never penetrated nor white traders ventured, they found that nothing save axes would serve as currency. Salt was still useful for small change, but cloth not at all, the chief having issued an order that any one of his subjects being found wearing European cloth would be instantly put to death. This added greatly to the difficulties of exploration, as the iron bars are heavy to carry and one man's load only equals the value of one piece (about 2 yards) of cloth (Hilton-Simpson, 1911, pp. 42, 310).

Nor was cloth universally acceptable farther north, even in the early days of exploration. Barth in his journey from Bornu to Timbuktu (1853–5) had to depend mainly on native cloth and cowries for buying provisions, though his darning needles were often valued more highly. The cloth even in narrow strips was worth hundreds of cowries, so it was a far more convenient currency when transport was so great a difficulty. In some places cowries were refused and

[1] Mahieu (pp. 50–1) gives lists and values for the Belgian Congo ; and Hobley (1929, pp. 245–6) for East Africa.

only cloth was accepted, though the cloth current in one place was useless in another.

The Kano *turkedi* was the kind specially used in the salt trade, 6 cloths for 9 slabs of salt, but on the way from Say to Timbuktu he had difficulty in disposing of his *turkedi* (worth 3,000 cowries) as the local currency was in *faravel* or narrow cotton strips worth only 300 shells. Many other kinds of cloth are mentioned in his travels as forming the currency, including, in Bornu, the shirts, which were also the currency of Kanem, in French Sahara. These had ascending values, like coins, from the *dóra*, too small, coarse and unfit for wear, to magnificent *tobes* fit for presentations (II, pp. 311, 471; IV, pp. 290-2, &c.).

Native cloth is still essential in marriage payments in parts of Nigeria (*cf.* pp. 85-6), and native mats are used as currency, as they were more than three centuries ago up the Gambia.

Jobson (1620-21) says

Now through the whole Countrey there is no use of any Coyne or Money neither have they any, but every man to choppe and barter one thing for another, and the onely nominated thing is matts, as in asking the price of this or that I desire, the word is How many matts shall I give you? (1933, p. 168).

Likewise Ogilby (1676, p. 357): ' in case they want Money [at the Petty Market] they exchange all other things for Matts ', while Barbot (1732, p. 78) calls mats ' properly the coin of the country '.

Neither native cloth nor native mats provided currency in East Africa, though imported calico is often the favourite substitute for money in modern times.

Calico here [Northern Rhodesia] is the staff of life. For most purposes it takes the place of hard cash. Men draw their rations in calico, they are buried in calico, marriage dowries are often paid in calico. The headman who brings you presents is recompensed with a yard or two and returns wreathed in smiles. Calico is to the plateau what . . . shells are to the South Sea Islanders (Gouldsbury and Sheane, 1911, p. 10).

Beads in general have been already discussed (Chap. IV, ii). In Africa there is little evidence of currency beads of native manufacture. Exceptions are found, as might be expected, along the Upper and Middle Congo, where copper is so popular both for ornament and for exchange. Strings of copper beads are currency both above and below Stanley Falls; Mahieu records their former use farther north (1924, p. 27); and brass beads strung on leather are popular ornaments, sometimes described as currency, in South-East Africa. Balfour collected the string of brass beads or pendants of peculiar shape, used by the Munshi in Nigeria (Fig. 9) and also the large stone bead (Fig. 10) used for buying slaves.

It has been stated that some of the more roughly made blue

annular beads of the Congo are of native manufacture. Sir Harry
Johnston believed that they were the work of the Katanga people
(influenced by metal-workers from the north some 600 years ago)
and made out of the vitreous substances in the slag of their copper-
smelting furnaces (1908, p. 790 *fn.*) ; and there is a little Bakwese
(Upper Kwango) bunch of these beads (fastened to a charm in the
shape of a pair of bellows) in the British Museum labelled ' native-
made Katanga ' (Torday and Joyce, 1907, p. 147). But Dr. Maes
says definitely ' *toujours de fabrication étrangère* ' and further discussion is waste of time.

The early ' aggry ' beads of the Benin and the Gold Coast were
used in exchange, though scarcely as currency, and imitations have
been made in both regions for generations. Bowdich (in 1817) had
heard in Ashanti of the local industry of ' boiled beads ' but dismissed

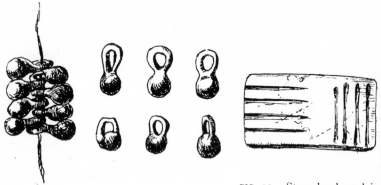

FIG. 9.—Brass beads, Nigeria

FIG. 10.—Stone bead used in
the slave trade. (⅔ size)

it as mere conjecture, as he could not verify it ' by observation or
discovery ' (p. 219). And the technique which has been described
and illustrated by Wild is still kept secret, the replies of the natives
to questions being more than usually evasive ' apprehensive that their
patent might be infringed and a rival firm set up ' (*Man.*, 1937, **115**).

These coarse and clumsy beads are used in trade both in Nigeria
(Pl. 3, Fig. 2) and in the Gold Coast, and as in the latter region
they are intended to represent the precious ' aggries ', the makers
charge six or seven times more for them than for the European
trade beads.

There is a close relationship between beads and holed stones
(which may be their ancestral type) and the holed stones of the Gold
Coast and Togo (Pl. 3, Fig. 3) have found their way into many
currency collections.[1] These are pierced quartz disks, some 2 to

[1] The quartz balls, another Stone Age problem in Africa, are sometimes
used as currency in the Northern Territory of the Gold Coast (R. F. Wild).

$2\frac{1}{2}$ inches (5 to 6·5 cm.) in diameter, and about 1 inch thick. Suggestions for their use are : spindle whorls, digging-stick weights, loom weights, net sinkers, necklaces, arrow and implement sharpeners, fire-making apparatus, and sacred insignia. But as they have been found in considerable numbers, one hoard under an old tree (Worobong, Kwahu district) containing hundreds if not thousands, they may be an early form of currency.

There is less uncertainty about their modern use, which is as charms or amulets. The natives believe that they have fallen from the sky, some regarding them as the female counterpart of the miniature stone implements or ' god axes ' of the same region (Wild, 1927, pp. 182–4 ; *Man*, 1943, **18**). The holed stones collected by Rattray in Togoland (now in the Pitt Rivers Museum) were placed in water and the water thus impregnated was used for washing and drinking, and stones were occasionally ground and the powder administered for medicinal purposes, just like that of ' aggry ' beads.

ii. WEST AFRICA

A. CONGO ; GABOON TO ANGOLA [1]

Portuguese money was carried to West Africa by explorers and traders, so coins have been familiar along the coast for centuries, and penetrated, though very slowly, inland. Yet even at the present time barter is the sole method of trading in many of the inland districts and European coins are altogether useless. On the Coast itself coins are not always accepted and commodities are preferred, as Miss Kingsley's sprightly description illustrates in the scene between the ship's captain and ' King Coffee ', the head of the Kruboys engaged to work the ship.

The Captain took Miss Kingsley for a temperance missionary and ostentatiously proposed to pay the boys off in money and not in gin and gunpowder,

which are unpopular in missionary circles. King Coffee's face was a study. If Captain X, whom he knew of old, had stood on his head and turned bright blue all over with yellow spots before his eyes, it would not have been anything like such a shock. ' What for good him ting, Cappy ? ' he asked. ' What for good him ting for we country ? I suppose you gib gin, tobacco, gun, he be fit for trade, but money——' Here his Majesty's feelings flew ahead of the royal command of language, great as that was, and he expectorated with profound feeling and expression (*Travels*, 1897, p. 647).

This reluctance to accept modern coins has preserved Africa, and especially West Africa, as a happy hunting-ground for collectors

[1] Except where other references are given, place and tribal names are spelt as in Maes and Boone, 1935.

of primitive money, and it is fortunate for them that the reluctance is not likely to be easily overcome ; for it is not primarily due to suspicion or distrust, though these certainly exist. Mahieu, from whose admirable survey much of the following is drawn, explains why a fixed currency such as is provided by Government is so unpopular.

Commerce provides for the Congo native, as for the blacks in general, a sort of game into which he flings himself with enthusiasm. He finds in it the opportunity to indulge his excessive love of talking and gesticulation. It is in the local markets that one must see him exert himself and puff his goods with a volubility which none of our salesmen could achieve, though our ears and noses suffer cruelly if forced to endure these gatherings for any length of time. The native excites himself to such an extent that he loses sight of his own interests ; it is not rare to meet men who, after having in the course of a day in the market, bought and resold, exchanged and re-exchanged goods twenty times, return home with diminished capital. The custom of exchange by which the seller is forced to over-estimate, because the buyer depreciates, is naturally more favourable for interminable discussions which the black loves, than purchase by fixed value, which permits of rapid sale. Therefore he is reluctant to accept nickel or silver coinage, and limit his entertainment (p. 65).

Neither silver, copper, nor even nickel coinage really supplied his needs. A coin represents far too high a value to be of daily use. When the ' head ' of 2,000 cowries was worth about 1s., a handful of the shells could be profitably spent in the market, so neither the copper centime nor the nickel anini, the tenth-of-a-penny, was sufficiently minute.

At the other end of the scale coins are unserviceable for more important transactions, not merely because potential danger lurks in uncanny metals, but because (not unreasonably) the natives feel that European money lacks the magico-religious virtue possessed by their own. So in a life permeated by religion and fearful of offence, it is safer to follow in ancestral footsteps, and for large purchases, especially those attended with ceremony, it is risky to use alien money with no blessing in it.

In a survey of the materials of West African currency the first impression is of the predominance of iron among the earlier objects, with local patches of copper and a later popularity in brass. But it must not be forgotten that the more perishable salt and cloth were equally popular and more generally distributed. Many of the iron currencies have a very restricted range, and some of the most spectacular, which figure so conspicuously in museums, are local symbols of wealth rather than of active currency. They may have an exchange value, but do not pass from hand to hand in commercial transactions.

The less-spectacular iron currencies are seldom found in museums at all. These are the ingots in lump, bar, or other shapes, that are commonly used in barter and as currency throughout so much of Africa. As ' money ' they have been recorded in the Kasai area where a bar weighing a kilo will buy a couple of fowls or 10 small cloths (madiba).[1] Large ingots (gamba bete) worth 80 mitako are currency on the Lomami to the east, and large lumps (dundu), 3 or 4 inches across weighing 2 to 3 kilo, are worth a he-goat, or from 2½ to 5 francs among the Azande and other people of the Aruwimi-Welle region to the north (Mahieu, 1924, p. 117). Very little has been recorded about the use of ingots as money, although it is of special interest, for it provides a living illustration of the stage which European currency passed through many centuries ago, as the Argive ' spits ' and our own ' currency bars ' bear witness.

From the 15th century onwards imported iron was a popular trading medium all round the coasts, and was used by the Africans to make their weapons, tools and ornaments, and took the place of the native metal. Barbot says that all of the iron for Guinea was of the same size and weight, ' called in London by the name of Voyage-Iron, and is the only sort used all over the coasts of North and South Guinea and in Ethiopia '. Slaves, and all other goods were reckoned in iron bars usually 8 to 12 for a man, and less for a woman (Churchill, 1704, Vol. V, pp. 44, 273).

The largest and most conspicuous exhibits in collections or African currency are the decorative axes, kasuyu, popularly called ' zappozaps ', of the Lulua, and the gigantic spearheads, liganda or ngbele, of the Lomami.

It is doubtful if the ' zappozaps ' have any right of entry at all. They take their name from that of a notorious brigand chief and slave raider of the Lulua, whose followers, collected from various neighbouring tribes, settled at Luluaberg and are renowned for their skill in iron working.[2]

The axes were insignia of rank worn for parade and ceremonial display ; they could not be owned by a commoner, and though they may represent wealth, they are not used as currency. The earlier ' zappozaps ' (and many are far earlier than the name)

[1] Torday and Joyce, 1905, pp. 407–8 ; illustrated by Schmeltz and de Jong, 1904, Pl. 68, Figs. 6–8. But the Bashilele iron-bar currency in the same area appears to be derived not from an ingot, but from the throwing-knife (Torday and Joyce, 1911, p. 94).

[2] The life-size group of smiths at work in the Tervueren Museum, Brussels, are Zappozaps. Cf. Johnston, 1908, II, pp. 441–2, 516 ; 1913, p. 394 ; Torday and Joyce, 1922, II, p. 2 ; Maes and Boone, 1935, pp. 209, 356.

are veritable works of art, with radiating spokes indulging in complicated loops that would test the skill of any craftsman, and characteristic rows of human faces Janus-like on the bars (Pl. 1, Fig. 13).
They travelled far afield, and an early specimen was found buried
in the Khami ruins, and was recognized as belonging to the Zimbabwe culture.[1]   In later years these axes were turned out in large
numbers for European trade ; florid specimens in polished copper
flooded the market and were used, together with imported goods, for
native trading.   This may give them a claim to mention here, as
being used in place of money, but though included in currency
by Schmeltz and de Jong (1904, Pl. 64, Fig. 72), and Mahieu
(1924, pp. 18–20), they are definitely excluded from the Tervueren
Collection.

The *liganda* or *ngbele* made by the Turumba (or Barumbu)
below Stanley Falls, illustrated in the centre of Pl. 1, is the currency
between the Congo and the Lomami.   This is an enormous spearhead, over 5 feet 6 inches long (1·677 m.) and weighing 4½ pounds.
Cumbrous though these are, they are still in use among the neighbouring tribes, though mainly for ' bride-price ' and for the purchase
of canoes.[2]   They have a definite value according to their size, being
worth from 10 to 25 *shoka*, 100 to 250 *mitako*, 2½ to 5 francs, or
between 2s. 6d. and 5s. in English money.   A fine specimen may
fetch twice as much and the price is rising with their scarcity.   They
are no longer made now that the country is more open to European
goods, but they still play an important part in marriage palaver and
are not unknown in native markets.[3]   Thirty will buy a male slave.

The Topoke (or Tofoke) of the Lomami also use this huge spearhead (*ndoa*) currency.   Thirty will buy a male slave and 40 to 50
might buy a female, though a purchaser may have to go up to 100.
Smaller spearheads, axes and hoes are used for less important goods
(Torday and Joyce, 1922, II, p. 202).

This Stanley Falls region is the centre of spearhead currencies
and there are many different types and values recorded among the
neighbouring tribes.

The Mobenge to the north need 20 to 30 *makongo* for a male
slave and 50 to 100 for a female, according to estimation.   The
Wanande to the east, near Lake Albert Edward, have a less valuable
spearhead, *ituma*, only worth a fowl or about 6d.   The Mangbetu
in the North-East, show in their *mapuka* that evolution (or degenera-

---

[1] Neville Jones, *Occasional Papers of the Rhodesian Museum*, No. 40.
[2] Ten will buy a canoe 35–40 feet long (Bentley, 1900, II, p. 295).
[3] In the photograph taken by the Rev. K. Smith, reproduced in Pl. 3,
Fig. 4, the little Lokele boy is holding a *shoka* in one hand and supporting
a *ngbele* nearly twice his height with the other.   The value of the latter was
quoted as 10s. 6d. (Smith, H. S., p. 18).

tion) from weapon to currency that marks so many African examples, for the spear-blade has become blunted at its edges, and tip and tang are twisted into decorative spirals (Mahieu, 1924, p. 24, ill.).

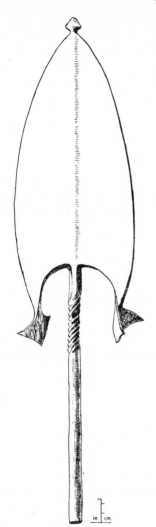

Nor could the 'Bangala iron money' between the Ubangi and the Congo (Fig. 11) serve any practical purpose with its characteristic twists at tip and flukes (Schmeltz and de Jong, 1904, Pl. 68, Fig. 5).

There are spearhead currencies farther south too between the Upper Lomami and the Upper Sankuru. Here an *ikonga*

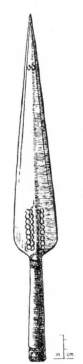

FIG. 11.—Bangala iron money, Congo   FIG. 12.—Congo spearhead

(Fig. 12) is worth a fowl, 2 or 3 a dog, and 5 or 6 a male slave; Torday and Joyce (1922) give other examples with illustrations and values, but to obtain some idea of the variety in this region a visit must be paid to the Tervueren Collection at Brussels.

Spears made wholly of iron, twisted, split, barbed, and blunted, decorative rather than useful, are used in barter in the Congo region. The 'currency spears' of the Bapopoie of the Aruwimi to the north-east of the Congo are worth 1 or 2 'pieces' of cloth, according to the metal ornamentation of the handle (Mahieu, 1924, p. 24). But most of these decorated spears should be classed, like the 'zappozaps' above, with objects of parade and insignia of rank, rather than with currency.

All of the preceding may be classified as spears or spear-blades, even if their original purpose is blunted or contorted, but there is a large class of objects used as money to which it is difficult to give a generally descriptive name, as they have so little resemblance to their ancestral weapons or implements. They are neither spears nor axes, hoes, spades nor trowels, but are likened by collectors sometimes to one, sometimes to another, of these prototypes.

Of such the *shoka* (which means axe in Swahili) of the Stanley Falls region, and the *kundja* (or *iwenga*) of the Kasai-Sankuru, are well-known examples. The common *shoka* (Pl. 1, Fig. 7) has the outline of a broad spear-blade broken off short, and though accepted widely as conventional currency it varies considerably in size and weight. The larger ones are some 11 inches (28 cm.) long weighing about 8 ounces, with smaller ones 9 inches (23 cm.) long weighing about 4 ounces. There are still smaller ones. The Bakusu *shoka* is the chief standard of value between the Congo and the Lomami, south of Stanley Falls. This is only just over 6 inches long (16 cm.) and was worth from 25 to 90 centimes before the Great War and 1 franc 50 centimes after (Mahieu, 1924, p. 22; Johnston, 1908, Fig. 452, p. 749). Mahieu estimates the large *shoka* at 10 *mitako*, 50 centimes or 6*d*., but as its value varies with time and place, rising and falling to two or three times above or below its average, estimates are of little use.

When European imitations of the *shoka* were introduced, they were at first eagerly accepted, until the natives found that the iron was inferior and would not make good tools. The accumulation of unwanted stores, together with the variations in native-made *shoka*, led to an inquiry, and finally an acceptable model was sent to Birmingham to fix the standard, and that provided the ordinary currency up to the coming of the franc.

Grenfell, writing in 1903, says,

All the smiths in the Stanley Falls district depend on these [*shoka*] in making axes, knives, spears, arrowheads, &c., and households depend on them as a market currency. All our Yakusu food for workpeople and children is paid for with *shokas*—three bundles of plantain = one *shoka* —and without these we are in difficulties at once.

He adds that the imported *shoka*, cut from a rolled plate of iron,

not worked at all, was a popular substitute, but one with a thickening
in the middle in imitation of the native pattern 'has not caught on
at all . . . I think the fault is not with the pattern, but with the
quality of the iron, the natives requiring an article that will not
run to slag into the charcoal pits as it is being worked up'. (Johnston, 1908, p. 797. His illustrations, Fig. 452, p. 794, show *shoka*
of different shapes.)

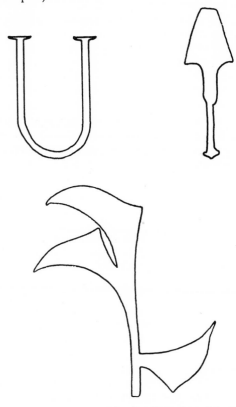

FIG. 13.—Outlines of *boloko*, *kundja* and *woshele*, Congo

The *kundja*, the unit of value among the Basongo Meno on the
Sankuru above its junction with the Kasai (and also of the Bohindu
of the Lukenie, to the north of them), is equally enigmatic. It
varies in size, though not to such an extent as the *shoka*, and is
vaguely trowel-like in outline. The Basongo Meno are not iron-
smelters and they do not make the *kundja*, but obtain them by
bartering salt, their local currency, with the Bankutu farther inland.
They obtain from them also iron throwing-knives (here called

4*

woshele) and U-shaped copper bars (*boloko*), but the iron *kundja* is the standard of value (Fig. 13).

2 small *kundja*	= 1 big *kundja*
10 big *kundja*	= a *boloko*
1 *boloko*	= a he-goat (or more)
2 *boloko*	= a male slave
3 *boloko*	= a female slave
10 *boloko*	= a wife

(Torday and Joyce, 1911, p. 268)

Congo knives have a character and a ferocity all their own, and it seems inappropriate that some of the most fearsome should have come into common commercial use. The knife currency with the most extensive history and the most extended use is the *trombash* [1] or throwing-knife of the Sudan and the Upper Nile, which, travelling across Africa as the *pinga* of the Azande, the *bo* of the Ubangi and the *woshele* (*oshele*) of the Sankuru, gave its name *shongo* to the Bushongo and Bakongo on both banks of the Kasai.[2] Its prototype seems to be the wooden F-shaped *trombash* originating in Libya, which developed into a weapon characteristic of the Shari-Chad region ; it achieved great effectiveness in the hands of the warlike Azande, who, with a well-directed hurl of a well-balanced knife, could cut off an enemy's leg at 20 yards. Dr. Maes, experimenting at Tervueren, cut through a $\frac{1}{2}$-inch deal plank at 15 metres.

The history of the throwing-knife illustrates the transition from weapon to currency, with reflections of geographical and racial influences.

In the Sudan, whirled along the open plains, the Zande *pinga* is a useful and barbarous weapon. But even in this area it has a definite currency value. Nachtigal (1887, p. 362) tells of his difficulties in buying grain at Baghirmi, as the traders would take nothing but throwing-knives in exchange. He needed two a day, and the supply was inadequate.

Among the peoples of the savanna it is still a weapon of war, it is also a tool, and is used for cutting trees, clearing bush, and in agriculture. And another type is developing side by side, not for use, but for show, as is the case with so many of the Congo knives.

Coming westward or southward into the forests of the Congo,

[1] *Trombash* is one of its names in the Sudan, and has been adopted for the iron throwing-knife though it belongs properly to the wooden throwing-club.

[2] Bushongo means they of the throwing-knife. Bakuba (= Bushongo) means they of the lightning, and is probably from the same source. Both names were given by the Baluba, who had never met throwing-knives before (Torday and Joyce, 1911, p. 2).

throwing-weapons are of little use. They retain their characteristic shape, but, without finish or polish or cutting-edges, become currency iron, capable of being made into tool or weapon if required. Among the Bangala and their neighbours in between the Congo and the northern curve of the Ubangi, they are the recognized currency, 2 to 4 being paid for a goat, 6 to 8 for a male slave and up to 30 for a woman.

The throwing-knife occurs again as currency in the region of the Kasai and Sankuru under various names, the most widely known of which is the *shongo* or *woshele*. The *shongo* is neither tool nor weapon, it is merely the conventional unit of iron, made by the Bankutu and spread with the extensive trade characteristic of the region by its intermediaries the Bakuba, more properly called Bushongo, whose name is reminiscent of their fame with the knife like lightning. This was once the typical weapon of the Bushongo, but its use was officially prohibited on humane grounds, ' lest it should kill the innocent' by one of the most remarkable of their chiefs, Shamba Bolongongo, the great Bushongo hero, who is computed to have reigned about 1600.[1] Shamba was an adventurous traveller opening up friendly relations with neighbouring peoples which developed into the extensive trading for which the Bushongo were and still are, famous. Among the Basongo Meno, to the north of the Kasai and Sankuru, there is no evidence or tradition to suggest that the *shongo* were ever of any practical use, they are merely iron currency, and the same name is given to the iron bars of European manufacture which ousted the work of native smiths (Torday and Joyce, 1911, pp. 26, 94). The *shongo* were so eagerly and easily converted into tools, weapons or ornaments that they were rarely preserved in their original form, save possibly in the secret treasury of a chief. This rarity gives surviving specimens a fictitious value. ' The throwing-knife on the Sankuru is a veritable bank-note', says Torday; ' its actual value in metal is a hundred times inferior to its estimated value, which is that of several slaves' (*Causeries congolaises*, pp. 178–9).

The throwing-knife on Pl. 1, Fig. 20, shows the Bangala type from the Ubangi region (collected by Dr. J. B. Hurry) and should not properly be classed with ' money', though it was collected as such, for it has been sharpened and polished and made into a weapon —transformed from *Zeichengeld* to *Nutzgeld*, from a monetary token to a potentially murderous weapon of war.

The Bubu of the northern curve of the Ubangi, have a throwing-knife currency which could not possibly be used as a weapon of war or a tool of any sort. It is not even called a knife or a tool, but *ngindza*, which means ' money'. Here the blades have dissipated

[1] His image, carved in wood, is in the British Museum.

into bloated plates of very thin metal (Fig. 14), which, save as money, have no practical use.[1]

It has been suggested that the throwing-knife has other derivatives used as money, and that the weapons used by the warlike Fan, from the Welle district, have degenerated into the Fan 'axes' of the Gaboon (Fig. 16). A parallel can be seen from the Ubangi area, where a bundle of Bubu so-called 'arrowheads' are tied together

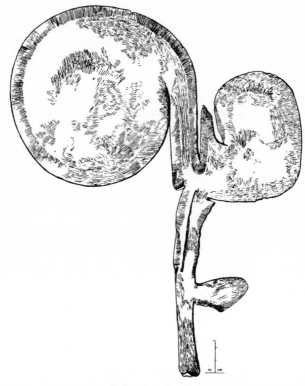

FIG. 14.—Bubu throwing-knife, Congo

rather like the Fan 'axes', and serve as a unit of exchange. (Thilenius, 1921, p. 15, Pl. I, Fig. 8, illustrates a specimen in the Hamburg Museum). The Bangala 'execution knives' (Pl. 1, Fig. 19), in some of which the influence of the throwing-knife can be detected, are on the border land where so many 'ceremonial' objects are balanced between wealth and currency. Some (but usually those without handles) are known to have been used in ordinary trading trans-

[1] Thomas, E. S., 1925, ill., Pls. 2 and 3 ; Thilenius, 1921, p. 19, Pl. 1, Fig. 1. Cf. Schmeltz and de Jong, 1904, Pl. 110, Fig. 5 and Pl. 117, Fig. 1.

actions ; others have no such guarantee ; but as all have a certain exchange value they find their way into currency collections (Johnston, 1908, II, p. 694 ; Thomas, 1925, p. 139, Fig. *n*, XI, p. 137). The knife or chopper of sinuous outline on Pl. 1, Fig. 17, is attributed to the Bayanzi [1] lower down the river.

Johnston (1908, p. 775) regards the choppers as coming from the North, together with the throwing-knives ; and one in the British Museum, collected by G. Burrows, is from the Welle District. The chopper and ' flounder ' money illustrated by Johnston (1908, Fig. 433, p. 774) belong to the same group, and the Cambridge specimen has special interest as both it and a ' currency spear ' are labelled ' brought home by one of Stanley's men '. The knife, with deep ' blood-groove ', and ornamental punch-marks, illustrated on Pl. 1, Fig. 15, and in more detail in Fig. 15, is a fine specimen of the so-called ' currency knives '. It was collected on the Kwilu (Angola) but its shape and workmanship are more characteristic of the Ubangi farther north. This ' mean term between sword and dagger ', as Ratzel describes it, suggests Arab influence (*cf.* Schmeltz and de Jong, Pls. 87–90).

The Fan ' axes ' (Fig. 16) are among the most familiar examples of token-money derived from weapons or tools.[2] The Fan (Fang, Pahuin, Mpongwe, Pangwe or many other names, either synonymous, or those of related tribes) formed one of the most dreaded races between the Niger and the Cunene, owing to their superior vigour, their reputation for ferocity, and their terrifying throwing-knives—now replaced by muskets. They came from the East, probably from the Congo–Nile divide, and are found as ivory and rubber collectors and traders in the Gaboon, especially along the Ogowe and its tributaries.

Miss Kingsley described their mode of life as she saw them at the end of last century, collecting ivory and rubber

to exchange with the rich men of the village for a very peculiar and interesting form of coinage—*bikĕi*—little iron imitation axe-heads which are tied up in bundles called *ntet*, 10 going to one bundle, for with *bikĕi* must the price of a wife be paid.[3] You cannot do so with rubber or ivory or goods. These *bikĕi* pass, however, as common currency among the Fans for other articles of trade as well, but I do not think they will pass *bikĕi* out of the

---

[1] The name Bayanzi, it may be noted, covers a number of tribes and especially those engaged in trade along the course of the Congo, from the Lower Ubangi to the Lower Kasai. Kiyanzi was the trade language in this section of the Congo.

[2] *Cf.* Ridgeway, 1892, p. 40, ill., Fig. 11 ; Temple, 1899, p. 118 ; the British Museum Guide calls them ' razors ' and spells them *beki* (p. 243). Tessmann (1913, II, p. 212) spells them *awumbekie*.

[3] Miss Kingsley's bundle of ' axes ' is in the Pitt Rivers Collection.

tribe. . . . Thousands of these *bikĕi* done up into *ntets* go to the price of a wife. You do not find *bikĕi* close down to Libreville, among the Fans who are there in a semi-civilized state, or more properly speaking in a state of disintegrating culture. You must go for bush (1897, pp. 320–1).

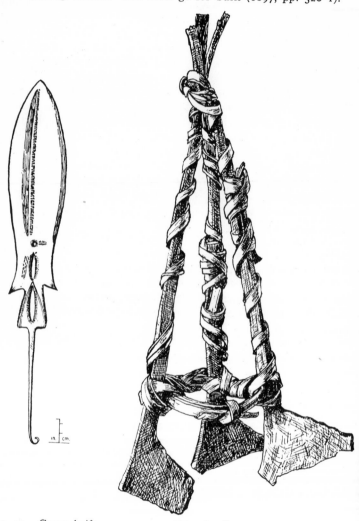

FIG. 15.—Congo knife   FIG. 16.—Fan axe money

The little 'axes' can no longer be found as currency, even though you go for bush, as they are superseded nowadays by spear-blades of various shapes. Tessmann (1913, II, p. 212, Fig. 66) illustrates 5 of these and also a chief counting out his money arranged in piles of spear-blades (Fig. 65).

The Fan ' axes ' are not the only currency of this type in French Africa. Thin little pieces of iron, ranging from 3 or 4 inches up

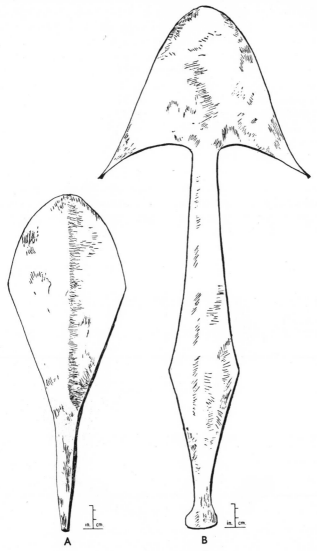

FIG. 17.—Hoe-money, Congo

to 8 inches (8 to 25 cm.) usually flattening out at one end have been collected as ' conventional arrowheads ' (if small) or ' conventional spearheads ' (if larger) (*cf.* Mosher, 1936, Fig. 10, p. 28).

They are of small value, some 50 of the little ones go to the centime, but the more familiar ' sombies ' of the Ivory Coast are quoted at a penny each.[1]

In an area of hoe-culture such as West Africa, hoes themselves, iron for making into hoes, and inchoate forms in between may all be used instead of money, varying in name, shape and value from district to district, playing an important part in marriage palaver, but presenting no specially interesting features.

The *shoka* (commonly included in the hoe group) of the Stanley Falls region, have already been described (p. 66). Mahieu illustrates (p. 25) the Bayaka hoes *ntsengo* of the Kwango, the Lower and Middle Congo, worth 300 *simbo* shells, and the fluked *lukasu*, in copper, from the Katanga and Kasai region, worth 50 copper rings (*nsambu*), one or two lengths of cloth or 4 fowls. An ordinary slave was worth 40 *tukasu*. The *jembe* of the Lomami is a larger implement, long, thick and solid in construction (Fig. 17*a*). There is a still larger type, described as a hybrid weapon-hoe-knife form, which has been found more widely distributed. The one illustrated in Fig. 17*b* comes from the Lomami ; Thilenius illustrates one in the Hamburg Collection from the Cameroons (1921, Pl. 1, Fig. 12) ; one in the Berlin Collection is from the Ogowe, A.E.F. ; and Schmeltz and de Jong illustrate one from Tanganyika, Pl. 63, Fig. 14. They also illustrate the typical Bangala ' axes ' or hoes made of soft iron, for currency, some much like *shoka* in outline, others fluked with queer twists at the tips (see p. 65, Fig. 11). The making of these was an important industry at Bopoto on the northern bend of the Middle Congo. It was here that in 1884 Grenfell exchanged his beads, wire and cloth for these ' axes ' which were the usual currency farther east. One ' axe ' was here valued at two brass *mitako*, but farther up the river one would sometimes buy a goat (Johnston, 1908, p. 122).

In this Middle Congo region, and in the Welle-Ubangi region to the North, iron gongs or bells [2] are doubtfully included in currency (Fig. 18). These are made of lengths of iron, beaten out and hammered together down the edges ; they have no tongues, but are beaten with rubber-headed sticks. They are found singly or in pairs rigidly connected by a curved handle, and they range from about 6 inches (15 cm.) in height, to a couple of feet (50 to 60 cm.).

---

[1] The little bits of iron, like large pins, about an inch long (3 cm.), with curved ends like hockey-sticks, or ' with a small semicircle at the end like a half-moon ' as described and illustrated by Barbot, may belong to this class of currency. They were used at Accra, Barbot says, as current money instead of the little bits of gold (*krakra*) (Churchill, 1732, Vol. V, pp. 251, 264, Pl. 22, Fig. 4).

[2] Their name, *gunga*, may be onomatopoeic, like the Chinese *ch'ing* or Burmese *gong*.

Five of the smaller ones would buy a pot of palm oil, 100 would buy a slave. Those of the Mobenge between the Welle and the Middle Congo, huge upstanding fellows, were worth a wife, or 2 male slaves (Mahieu, 1924, p. 26). These native-made gongs or bells spread over a wide area, from Togo to East Africa, and often have ritual significance ; several have been found in the diggings at Zimbabwe and other contemporary ruins in Southern Rhodesia, and they occur in Northern Rhodesia also. One old and dilapidated specimen in the Livingstone Museum is preserved as the *lukano* or insignia of the Lunda chiefs, and wars have been waged for the possession of a *lukano*. (Brelsford, 1937, pp. 82–3).

Since metal is used almost universally for barter throughout Africa, most objects made of metal hover on the edge of currency,

FIG. 18.—Iron bells, Congo. (¼ size)

and bells, spears, knives or hoes can be readily turned into ' money ', while on the other hand ' money ' can be turned into spears, knives, hoes or bells. This is even more clearly seen in metal ornaments of various kinds, such as necklets, armlets, leglets and anklets [1] among which the dividing-line between ornament and currency cannot be distinguished.

As ornament copper is preferred to iron, and as it is found in abundance in many parts of Africa, and is so easily worked, besides possessing superior decorative value, it is not surprising to find it forming both ornaments and currency.

There are three chief copper areas, to the north, the west and the south-east of the Congo basin. The northern area includes the Ubangi, and the upper bend of the Middle Congo, where copper is worked in most of the villages on both banks. Bopoto was a

[1] The suffix -let has here no diminutive sense.

distributing centre and the Bapoto specialized in copper ornaments that were traded up and down the rivers. Mahieu (p. 33) illustrates a Mupoto woman wearing a neck-ring, and H. H. Johnston (1908, Fig. 305, p. 588) illustrates the same type from the same district. These are both of brass which superseded copper on the main trading-routes, having the same estimation as gold among the Congo natives. But the earlier examples are of copper, and some are of incredible weight: a Bongo necklet from the Ubangi may weigh over 20 pounds or 10 kilo. This would be worth 1,000 *mitako*, with 30 *mitako* to the franc.

The Gombe (Ngombe) anklet on Pl. 1, Fig. 2, measures some 6 inches (15 cm.) across and weighs nearly 5 pounds. Torday illustrates (*Causeries congolaises*, opp. p. 38) a woman wearing a brass collar of this type and adds that these may weigh 12 to 15 kilo (25 to over 30 pounds) so cleverly forged on to the neck that a woman captured by enemies risks having her head cut off, owing to the difficulty of disengaging the collar. Weeks (1909, p. 99) assumes that this is the only method, but a less drastic procedure was described to Grenfell (Johnston, 1908, p. 586).

The machicolated collar (Pl. 1, Fig. 5) is a specialized product of the Bateke near Leopoldville, with a doubtful claim to be classed with currency (*cf.* Mahieu, p. 33; Johnston, 1908, II, pp. 589, 590; Figs. 306, 307; Schmeltz and de Jong, 1904, Pl. 31, Fig. 4).

The second of the copper regions mentioned above is in the West, in the Crystal Mountains of the Cataract Province, below Stanley Pool, with its trade centre at Manyanga. Here the currency was in copper ingots, 4 inches (10 cm.) long, and less than 1 inch (2 cm.) thick (surprisingly like our own ' currency bars ' from Money Hill, illustrated on p. 290). These were traded up and down the river by the Bateke and Bayanzi and by the Bangala farther north. But they soon gave way before the *mitako*, which became not only the currency but also the official money of the Congo Free State.

Originally the *mitako* were merely short lengths of copper (*cf.* Pl. 1, Fig. 4), but rings were handier for transport and became the popular form, varying in thickness, in weight, and in size, sometimes single, sometimes interlinked, sometimes in bunches, sometimes elaborately laced in bundles with cane, all formerly of copper, but later of imported brass (Pl. 2, Fig. 1).

The ordinary brass wire sent out to Africa in coils was cut up into lengths to suit local prejudices, and traded in rods, loops or rings as required. The Bangala standard *mitako* was a length of 20 inches (50 cm.) in 1890 with a value of 15 centimes, but the brass workers cut an inch or half an inch off each rod, so its length and consequently its value lessened and lessened as it passed from hand to hand. Still everything was reckoned in *mitako*, from a basket of manioc worth 10 or 12 to an ivory tusk, worth several thousand. The price being fixed in *mitako*, payments would be made in beads, cloth or any approved goods (Overbergh and de Jonghe, 1907, 1 ; Weeks, 1909, p. 107 ; Mahieu, 1924, pp. 29–30, 52–3, 60).

'Brass rods' under various native names became the ordinary currency of the whole of the Upper Congo, and everything was priced in them. One egg, 1 brass rod, 1 fowl, 10 brass rods, 2 yards of cloth, 20 brass rods, up to a slave 600 and a female slave possibly over 2,000 brass rods. But the length was always variable, owing to the process of 'sweating'. The Lower Congo rods, which were 27 inches long (70 cm.) in 1884, shrank to 10 inches in 1894, and barely 4½ inches (11 cm.) in 1909 (Bentley, 1900, II, p. 398 ; Weeks, 1909, p. 107). The introduction of coins did not interfere much with the traffic in brass rods, which maintained their usefulness in barter, and were at the same time, material for making native ornaments.

Neither the Bapoto nor the Cataract copper areas can rival the riches of the Katanga region, one of the most famous in the world. This is the boundary of the Congo basin to the south-east, and is marked by the projection of the Belgian tongue into Northern Rhodesia, with its modern commercial centre in Elizabethville or Kambove, or perhaps, by the time that this book sees the light, at some other place not yet marked on any map.

Here were made the well-known 'Katanga crosses' also called St. Andrew's crosses, saltires, croisettes, &c., with still more variable and less-expressive native names,[1] which may be found from the Cape to Cairo and from Mombasa to Boma.

The one illustrated on Pl. 1, Fig. 3, weighs rather more than a kilo, (2 pounds 3½ ounces) and measures 9 inches (23 cm.) across. This is the average size for currency crosses, though they are very variable and in the old days many were several times this size and weight, while there were little ones with knobby arms, dwindling down to only a couple of inches across, compared by Mahieu to knife rests (p. 27). The larger ones usually show the characteristic rib across the centre, and being cast in sandy moulds have a rough surface flattened on the under side.

Arnot, who was in the Garenganze district just north of Katanga from 1886 to 1888, describes the native copper-working, a business handed down from father to son for generations. He noted how at one place the copper was cast in the form of a capital H 'and the angles of this figure are perfect'.[2] At other mines it was cast 'in

---

[1] Often the native names mean merely copper or ring.

[2] A soap-stone mould from Zimbabwe, with a cast of an ingot of this type, is in the British Museum (*cf.* Mahieu, p. 27, upper figure).

the form of a Maltese cross,[1] the mould being made in the sand by
the workers with their fingers ; and out of twenty casts from such
moulds scarcely a fourth or an eighth of an inch difference is
discernible ' (1889, p. 238).

Cameron, crossing over Lake Tanganyika to its western shores
into the country of the Warua in 1874, found that his trade-beads
which had served him well up to the borders of the lake (*singo-mazzi*,
of opal glass, as large as pigeons' eggs) were of no further value,
and he had to use the Urua crosses, here called *handa*. These were
larger than the average type, 15 to 16 inches (38–40 cm.) across
diagonally, and weighed from 2½ to 3 pounds. Many of these—
he illustrates one of them—have a raised rib along the centre of
each arm, as if the man, in preparing the mould, had traced its
skeleton in the sand [2] (Cameron, 1877, I, p. 319). But the *handa*
were not acceptable everywhere, and at Nyangwe on the Lualaba,
a trading station of the Zanzibari, with a large market every fourth
day, no purchases could be made save for slaves, goats and cowries ;
Cameron, having neither, was utterly stranded (1877, II, p. 7),
and his difficulties have been described above (p. 6).

The value of a cross of about 600 grammes (nearly 1½ pounds)
is quoted as being, at Katanga, worth 10 kilo of native flour ; 5 would
buy a fathom of cloth or 4 fowls, and 10 a gun. In the Kasai region
in 1910 the value was fairly steady. One cross would fetch 5 to 6
fowls, 2 lengths of good cloth, 3 or 4 kilo of rubber or 6 axes ;
4 to 6 would purchase a she-goat (Mahieu, 1924, p. 28). But
elsewhere the value appears to be very variable. The Babengele
of the Lualaba make one cross into a *manilla* or bracelet, and this
is worth a she-goat ; 5 or 6 would be the average payment for a
wife. Their northern neighbours the Bakusu, along the Middle
Lualaba need 2 crosses for a she-goat, and 2 *manillas*, made from
crosses will buy 4 goats or a slave (Mahieu, 1924, p. 124). Mahieu
quotes a typical ' bride-price ' paid for a Basonge bride in the
copper district. It consisted of 14 large crosses, 1 large she-goat,
1 piece of indigo drill, 1 flint-lock gun, and 1 female slave. The
total was estimated at 100 crosses of a local value of 350 to 400
francs.[3] Two slaves or 6 goats would be paid by a simple mortal,
says Mahieu, but for one of the great ones of the land 200 goats,
100 slaves and 300 crosses were claimed, as well as powder and
shot (p. 35).

[1] More Greek than Maltese, with equal arms at right angles, but without
indented ends (Fig. 38), these *nyambu* are still current in Katanga and
Northern Rhodesia.

[2] Monteiro illustrates a cross with a still more prominent ridge, suggesting
the junction of two bars ; this was brought down to Benguella by caravan
(1875, p. 190, Pl. XIV, Fig. 1).

[3] The market price was calculated as between 3 and 4 francs.

Montpellier d'Annevoie, who was pioneering in Katanga with the Benedictine Mission between 1910 and 1912, places the centre of the copper-cross industry at Kabinda on the Lomami, to the east of Luluaberg, but they were no longer being made in his time (1921, p. 155). They were a convenient and easily recognizable trading medium, but were valued by the natives mainly for the sake of the copper which they made into weapons, tools and ornaments, though some were stored for emergencies ; and they are still valued and still used for making wire bracelets and anklets, and are also made into bullets for native muskets (W. Ff. Fisher). As currency, their main use is in ' bride-price '. A local magistrate finding on his table ' a pair of suspenders, some pieces of *madiba* (raphia cloth) and a pile of copper crosses recognizes the signs at once, " Hullo, a dowry returned. Another divorce." ' Crosses are the one form of currency that is never refused. Cattle may die, cloth will rot, but neither misfortune can happen to copper, so many of the natives still insist that marriage payments should be made in Katanga crosses (Norden, 1924, p. 177).

Besides the crosses, copper was used in two other forms, both very popular, and widely distributed. One, as is expected, was the ring form, and these were also ornaments ; the other was the croquet-hoop or U-form, and this was equivalent to rod or ingot currency.

The Katanga rings, such as the *nsambu* in the Lukafu district, north of Elizabethville, may be in the shape of actual rings, worn usually on the ankles, or they may be coiled copper wire or bangles. (Mahieu, 1924, pp. 29–35).

Along the Sankuru and Kasai copper rods are bent into croquet-hoop form with blunted ends. These, called *boloko* by the Bushongo, and *konga* or *kunga* by the Basonge, together with *shokas* and *woshele* (incipient throwing-knives) form the ordinary trading currency as has been described already (p. 65).

The value of these rods is very variable. In some districts, one will buy a fowl or a dog ; in others it takes 6 or 8 ; a male slave may be anything between 3 and 10, while among the Batetela a female slave ' of guaranteed fecundity ' can be bought for 2. They are important also in marriage payments. The Olemba (Batetela) youth approaches the girl of his choice and says, ' I love you.' If she is willing she replies, ' All right, bring the money.' The first payment is usually a dog, followed by 8 copper rods (*kunga*), more dogs, and also fowls (Torday and Joyce, 1922, pp. 52, 67, 167, 186).

Copper was abundant down the West Coast, but was ornament rather than currency. Andrew Battell, at the beginning of the 17th century, was impressed by the wealth of copper. ' The women wear a ring of copper about their necks which weigheth 15 pounds at the least, on their legs rings of copper that reach to the calves of their legs ' (1901, p. 18). But in his time he expressly states that ' they take no more than they wear for a bravery '. His trade was by barter. He carried

all commodities fit for that country as long glass beads, and round blue beads and seed beads and looking-glasses, blue and red cloth and Irish rugs which were very rich commodities

and he exchanged these for ivory palm fibre, cloth and elephants' tails. These were to be traded again, the elephants' tails in particular fetching a high price, 50 hairs being valued at 1,000 *reis* and one tail being equal to 2 or 3 slaves.[1] So the trade was very profitable as Battell proved : ' I bought 20,000, which I sold to the Portugals for 30 slaves and all my charges borne ' (p. 58).

The last class of Congo ornaments to be mentioned represents veritable currency and provides another comparison with Bronze Age (and later) ornaments in Europe. These are the coiled arm- or leg-rings called *minkata*, by the Wangata between Nouvelle Anvers and Coquilhatville. Those worn by chiefs are of iron, and the one with a dozen spirals in the Tervueren Currency Collection is enormously heavy (ill., Mahieu, p. 33).[2] When Chief M'Kuba was asked if such a weight on his leg did not make it awkward for walking, he replied that it suited the dignity of a chief to have a slower and heavier walk than that of ordinary mortals (Montpellier d'Annevoie, 1921, p. 155).

This long catalogue may end with the cakes of red powder which represent money in the Congo belge.

Dapper, in his *Description de l'Afrique* (1686, p. 367), speaks of red wood in pieces about a foot long taking the place of money in the West. This refers to the cakes of *tukula* (*nkulu, ngula*) which, besides being in daily use, are popular in present-giving (especially at funeral ceremonies), in barter and as money, and are traded along the Sankuru-Kasai in the south, and from the Upper Congo to its mouth.

Various redwood trees (especially *Baphia nitida* or camwood) grow abundantly in the Congo forests, but are not found everywhere. The wood, of a beautiful deep-red colour, is hard and heavy, which

---

[1] Elephant hairs and bracelets made of them are common as charms and amulets from the West Coast to the East, and as they were popular in barter they are sometimes found in currency collections as at Vienna (Loehr, 1936, p. 20) and Buffalo (Mosher, 1936, p. 30, Pl. VIII).

[2] *Cf.* Schmeltz and de Jong, 1904–16, Pl. 35, Fig. 18. Weeks (1909, p. 107) describes how these leg spirals are made by the Bangala across the river. The same type of ornament being made of commercial brass wire has an exchange value in East Africa also.

discourages transportation, but when it is rotten it is easily ground
down with a stone and water, and the powder made into cakes.
The flat cakes stamped with patterns suggest comparisons with brick
tea, though the uses are different. The powder is mixed with oil
and smeared over the body, it is used for stiffening the coiffure, for
dyeing cloth, both native and European, and for colouring woodwork
and pots. The red colour appears here as elsewhere to have special

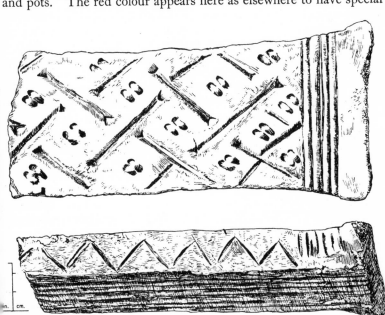

FIG. 19.—*Tukula* paste block, Congo

virtues and it is *tukula* that provides much of that general reddish
tinge so characteristic of West African material culture. The *tukula*
cake from the Bushongo between the Sankuru and the Kasai, illustrated (Fig. 19), is fresh and red, but after much handling, the
cakes become black and shiny, and scarcely recognizable (Torday
and Joyce, 1911, Fig. 111, pp. 129, 165 ; Maes, 1920 ; Mahieu,
1924, pp. 39–40).

B. NIGERIA TO SENEGAL

Travelling westward from the bewildering jungle of currencies
in the Congo, those of Nigeria appear scanty, and there are scarcely
a dozen different types in the Cambridge collection. Modern coins
are supplanting earlier forms here as elsewhere, though there are still
many districts off the trade-routes, especially in the eastern provinces,

where cowries, salt and iron bars, gin (illicit) and tobacco are preferred.

The natural reluctance to accept European coins was actively fostered by the Royal Niger Company (1886–1900) because it was believed that barter was more profitable, so any money that found its way up the rivers had to be returned to the Coast before it could purchase goods. Under the Protectorate the policy was reversed; native currencies were discouraged, if not suppressed, as a hindrance to trade, since it was recognized that no stable rate of exchange could be maintained with such fluctuating values.

Cowries had been in circulation for centuries, and were almost universally current, but had depreciated so much owing to unlimited entry that they were useful only for very small payments. Salt was also long established, and formed the usual medium of exchange from the Sahara to the Coast, but it was bulky and inconvenient, and prices shot up and down with the fortunes and misfortunes of the camel caravans. Iron bars, though always serviceable, were heavy and awkward, and transport was a difficulty, so their price increased unsteadily from the Coast to the interior.

After 1900, therefore, English silver coins were introduced, which achieved such unexpected popularity that they were speedily withdrawn. The natives accepted them eagerly but made them into personal ornaments, and headdresses of shillings became the latest fashion. Coins in substituted alloy possess less ornamental appeal, and are everywhere in official use at the present day. They are not always accepted in outlying districts, and this is especially the case with coins that are worn, or those dating from earlier reigns. Money is supposed to die with the sovereign, and after the Queen's death, Victorian coins were refused as ' dead money '.[1]

The important part played by cowries, and their depreciation owing to importations from East Africa, have been described above (p. 32). In 1860 a bag of 20,000 cowries cost from £1 to £2 at the Coast. Inland an average of 40 went to the string, and 50 strings to the ' head ' and 10 ' heads ' to the ' bag ' (Talbot, 1926, p. 875).

To the West of the Niger *C. annulus* was the kind preferred. To the East of the Niger in Iboland the Indian ones were worth twice as much as the East Africans (Basden, 1921, p. 195). The Ibo counted them in groups of 6, called *ekpete*, they collected these into groups of 10, to form the *ukwa*, or ' string '; 20 of these strings or 1,200 cowries made the *akpa* or ' bag ', which was a man's load. This was worth about a shilling. The native was extraordinarily

---

[1] The same belief is recorded by Mahieu on the Lomami (1924, p. 66) although it does not affect the popularity of the Maria Theresa dollar, which is acceptable over a third of the continent.

adept in calculations, but it was not easy for a European to make a quick estimate as to whether a fowl was worth 16 multiples of 90 cowries (when 90 equalled a penny) and the introduction of coins was a boon.   Cowries gradually faded away from the main trading routes, and by 1923 had entirely vanished from such centres as Kano and Zaria.

But in spite of Government exhortations and prohibitions the cowry dies hard.   It even seems to be reviving farther south.   When the importations ceased in 1900 the depreciation also ceased, and from an exchange of 20 to 25 *ukwu* to the shilling, they soared to 16, 15, even 12 to the shilling, in market quotation.   And as they are still preferred in native trading—many natives refuse to sell except for cowries—a buyer can often get better value for cowries than for coins.

Even though a single money-cowry is only worth $\frac{1}{90}$ of a penny and a ring-cowry $\frac{1}{180}$, not a shell is ever wasted.   Basden noted how, should one fall on the road, the next woman passing that way would deftly pick it up with her toes and store it in her bag (1921, p. 200). The trading in the markets is all done by the women and the surprising fact is that there is no barter.   Goods are sold for cowries not exchanged for other goods.   *A* buys *B's* yams for cowries and *B* buys *A's* oil for cowries.   There is no attempt at direct exchange. But when it comes to accumulation of wealth, then the advantages of metal over shells encourages the new introduction.   Treasure houses of cowries are like barns of newly threshed corn but natives are slowly learning to appreciate the smaller bulk for banking purposes.

Cowries undoubtedly owe much of their popularity to their symbolic and ornamental value and they will still be worn as decoration and used in games and gambling (as with us) long after their monetary use has vanished.   The little red black-spotted peas or ' crabs' eyes ', *Abrus precatorius*, are even more decorative than the shells and had at one time almost the same value as cowries, being current in Southern Nigeria and the Cameroons at the rate of 100 to the penny.

The general use of salt as a form of currency throughout Africa has been discussed already (pp. 52 *ff*.).   It has special importance in this region.   The great salt trade-routes—which also formed parts of the great slave-routes—both led to Northern Nigeria ;   the Great Road of the West to Timbuktu ;   the route from Tunis through the salt regions of Bilma and Lake Chad to Kano ;   and these were the great distributing centres of a commodity more important than gold.

Jobson, exploring up the Gambia (1620–1), tells of the eagerness of the *Tawny Fulbies* to exchange their milk and butter, ' as good as we have at home ', for salt.   The trading started with small

beads and poor knives ' but after they once saw and tasted of salt
. . . there was no other thing could so well please them, although
it were never so little ' (1933, p. 50).

There was a regular exchange of salt from the Coast for slaves
up-country but that salt was ' of a course and durty kinde . . . which
doth rather looke like durte or Sea-Coale ashes than resemble the
Salt we have in use ' and ' after they saw our salte no other thing
was esteemed amongst them ' (p. 119).

The inland salt was dug out in large slabs, some 3 feet in length
weighing 50 to 60 pounds, or an average man's load. The price
naturally varied and a journey over difficult or dangerous country
would double its value.   In Barth's time a middle-sized slab was

worth 3,000 cowries (about a dollar) in
Timbuktu, but the price always rose in
the spring, when the salt caravans became
scarce on account of the number of blood-
flies which infested the town and the
river.   And prices naturally went up
when, owing to tribal feuds, the routes
were particularly unsafe for travel.   From
Barth's account the tribes appear to have
been continually at feud during his travels
but the price did not ever exceed 6,000
cowries a slab.   Binger (1887–8) quotes
far higher estimates.   The price was
always calculated in cowries, but as
cowries were rare, salt was bartered for
goods, and a load of salt (about 25 kilo)
bought for 8,000 cowries at Salaga
(Northern Territory, Gold Coast) would
be sold at Kintampo (Ashanti) after

FIG. 20.—Salt currency, Nigeria

crossing the Volta for 16,000, or about 10 francs (II, p. 142).

Salt is still currency in Bornu, and is a customary, if not an
essential part of the ' bride-price ' in the hills.   It is boiled down
in conical pots, evaporated, the pots are broken and the cones form
the currency.   Fig. 20 illustrates the Hausa and Fulani *mangul* of
the Bornu-Yola caravan-route from Lake Chad.

The local price varies in direct proportion to the distance from
its place of origin, and also reflects fluctuations in money values.
The price of a cake at Madagali in recent years was 6d.; at Mubi,
50 miles farther south, 1s., and at Yola, 100 miles south of Mubi, 2s.

Of the cakes sold in the markets in the pagan area of the Northern
Cameroons only a small proportion is immediately broken up and
used as salt.   Most of the cakes are bought as a means of locking
up capital, and are freely used as currency in local transactions

These are an almost invariable item in any ' marriage negotiations ',
and are collected for this purpose, the father or guardian of the girl
reserving the cakes paid for her, to provide for the marriage of a
son or nephew (D. F. H. MacBride).

In the interior of Nigeria among the people of Bornu and
Adamawa cloth currencies still thrive. Brass bracelets or bangles
are used also, one is illustrated Fig. 21, but cotton thread, a strip of
cloth or a gown all have their trading values. Ten rolls of thread
equal a strip of cloth (*kuntu*) ; 10 strips of cloth equal a gown (*bul*)
and a gown is worth 5 brass bracelets (Meek, 1931, p. 144).

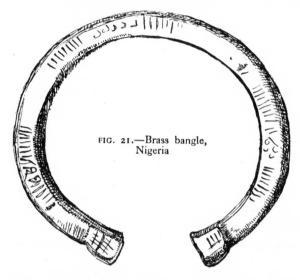

FIG. 21.—Brass bangle,
Nigeria

The roll of cloth illustrated in Fig. 22*a* (with detail) is a long
narrow strip of very loosely woven cotton, rolled up like a tape-
measure, to form the unit. This is chiefly used in marriage transactions. The larger roll (Fig. 22*b*) is the *langtang*, woven in Sensi-
dong, used as currency by the Mumuye in the extreme south of
Adamawa Province. In 1929 a strip was worth about 4*s.* or a
medium-sized goat or 16 currency bars (*taji*). Neither bars nor
cloth were used as much as salt, but cloth was necessary for ' bride-
price '. Not that it was used, as the men wear goatskins and the
women green leaves. In Benin the ' pawn ' [1] originally a cloth worth
about 2*s.*, was taken as the standard of value and figures largely in
local trade (Talbot, 1926, III, p. 875).

[1] Usually assumed to = Fr. *pagne* or loincloth. But there is some doubt
about the derivation of the word and it may not be as simple as it looks.
Possibly it represents the ' head ', i.e. *paume*, of tobacco (*cf.* Ling Roth,
903, p. 139).

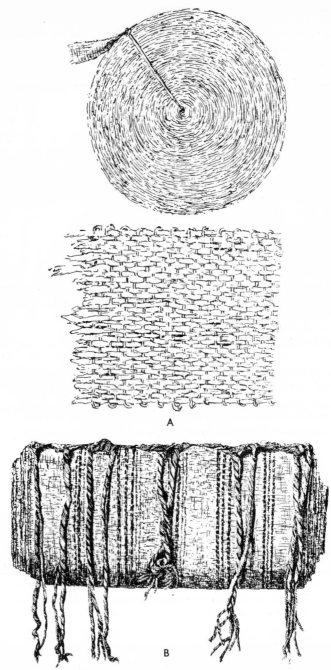

FIG. 22.—Cloth currency, Nigeria

Currency bars of iron are found in different forms in different districts. Some are merely rough bars of a foot or less in length, with no distinguishing features; some have a slight twist here or there; some are splayed out in the middle; some at the ends.

The bars called by the Eastern Fulani name *losol*, or the Western Fulani *tajere* (more commonly in the plural, *taji*) of the Batta of the Benue Valley and the Mumuye to the south of them, are more distinctive in shape. These bars are carefully finished, and have usually a flat expansion in the middle and slight twists at both ends. The one illustrated (Fig. 23, and Pl. 1, Fig. 6) comes from the Mandated Area, Adamawa Emirate, and the local price in 1934 was a penny or a little less. Their ultimate use is for making hoes and other implements, but they are much used for currency both among the non-Moslem tribes and in the Moslem markets where the pagan tribes come to trade. (MacBride).

A special development of iron bars or rods across West Africa is the Y-form. Typologically they may be attenuated spearheads, cutlasses, throwing-knives or any other weapons, or they may be merely local fashions in currency bars.

These bars are definitely Y-shaped on the Ubangi (Schmeltz and de Jong, 1904, Pl. 63, Fig. 12) and in Southern Nigeria (Pl. 1, Fig. 10) where they are popularly called 'Ogoja pennies', although their value ranges from a penny to less than a halfpenny each. Their native names here are *iyayaw* or *akaju* and others. Westerly extensions of more irregular shapes may be recognized in the 'sombies' of the Ivory Coast, some 8 to 10 inches (20–25 cm.) long with one projecting end, worth a penny, or the well-known 'Kissi pennies' of Liberia and Sierra Leone (Pl. 1, Fig. 11), but these are usually described as degenerate or conventional hoes (*cf.* p. 92).

Brass wire cut into lengths of about a yard and usually traded in croquet hoop form (Pl. 2, Fig. 2) provided the common currency from the Coast inland, one length being worth about 3*d*. Importations were stopped after 1904 and the brass rods' or 'Calabar bars' that played so large a part in early

FIG. 23.—Iron bar currency, Nigeria

trade ceased to be legitimate currency after 1907. *Cheetems* [1] are
bunches of finer wire, usually 9 or 10 to the bunch (Pl. 2, Fig. 3),
which take their name from their inventor, Captain Cheetem, who
introduced them as small change,
at 18 to the ' bar '.

Southern Nigeria has a queer
little iron currency of its own, called
by various names in Nigerian dialects as well as in English. In currency collections it may be labelled
' arrowhead ', ' axe ' or ' needle-
money ', its native names being *aiyu*
(*ieyu*), *ozala, umumu*, and others.

The Bank of West Africa, which
presented the specimens to the

FIG. 24.—' Needle money ', Nigeria

FIG. 25.—Munshi axehead

British Museum, gives the value as 3s. a pound, and calls then
arrowheads, but N. W. Thomas, recording their former use (a
Awka, to the south-east of Onitsha) says that the local name mean
' needle '. They are barely ½ inch (12 mm.) long, as is seen in th
illustration (Fig. 24) and 50 of them weigh less than a halfpenny
so it would take about 5,000 to make a pound weight. The exchang

[1] The word is sometimes given an African form and spelt *chittim*.

value was reckoned roughly at 45 to the penny, or twice as much as
a cowry, though cowries were not accepted in exchange (Basden,
1921, p. 201).   Basden describes this Awka currency as ' resembling
squashed tin-tacks ' and says it was used for buying slaves, though
how many hundreds of thousands would have to be counted for
such a transaction is not mentioned.

Pl. 1, Fig. 8 and Fig. 25 illustrate a ' Munshi axe-head ', from
Northern Nigeria, said to have been used as currency.

The Slave Coast is, as one would expect, the home of the *manilla*
currency which, as its name implies, is closely connected with the
Portuguese or Spanish slave-trade.   Originally of copper or brass,
later of iron or a mixture of metals, this became the dominating
currency from the Gold
Coast to the Lower Niger,
and though no longer legal
tender, *manillas* are still met
with up-country, with a
trading value of about 3*d.*
(Cowan, 1935 and 1936).

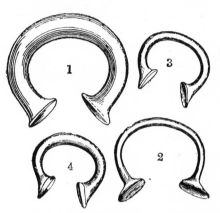

FIG. 26.—Manillas

1, 2, Bronze Age, Ireland.   3, 4, West Africa

Pacheco Pereira, whose
Esmeralda is a guide to the
commerce round the coasts
of West Africa at the end of
the 15th century, says that
at Sierra Leone, the Gold
Coast and Benin [1] the exchange is in *manillas* either
of brass or of copper, with
fluctuating values, 8 or 10 for
a slave being regarded as a
air price (Kimble, 1937, pp. 105, 107, 132, &c.).   Barbot at New
Calabar in 1699 bought up 500 slaves at two copper rings apiece
1723, p. 460), but most of his trading was done with iron bars.

Rings and bangles worn as ornaments, or used as currency—and
we cannot always discriminate—are found in all metal-using countries
but the West Coast *manillas* are especially interesting, as they are
believed to perpetuate an ancient type, and their resemblance to
prehistoric penannular rings, perhaps themselves a form of currency,
is remarkable.   Tons of *manillas* used to be exported annually from
England, and the mischance of a wreck of these on the Irish coast
in 1836 led to the comparison of the product of a Birmingham foundry
with the Bronze Age bangles in the Dublin Museum (Fig. 26).

[1] Coffey drew attention to the 16th-century bronze castings from Benin,
showing Europeans and natives holding large *manillas* in their hands (1913,
p. VI, p. 70 ; *cf.* also Ling Roth, 1903, Fig. 147, p. 142).

An attempt was made to cheapen the product and improve the profits of the trade by turning out *manillas* in cast iron. But it was a failure. They would not ring when struck, as all good *manillas* should. The natives would not accept them and the loads were returned as worthless. The best-ringing quality was obtained by a due proportion of copper, tin and spelter. The rough edges, both inside and out, were a flaw from the manufacturer's point of view but, if filed down, rendered the *manillas* useless for trade (*cf.* W. Hawkes, *Arch. Journ.*, XII, 1855, pp. 179–80).

The *manilla*, like the *mitako*, is merely one form in which a length of metal can conveniently be shaped for trading purposes, and all curves, sizes and patterns are found, from the impressive ' King manillas ' over a foot long, to tiny ones weighing only a few ounces. The varying shapes represent waves of fashion in different districts and at different times. The commonest type is worth about 5 or 6

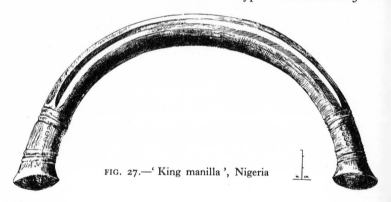

FIG. 27.—' King manilla ', Nigeria

to the shilling in Southern Nigeria, but with a change of fashion they are immediately worthless. ' King manillas ' (Pl. 1, Fig. 14 and Fig. 27) are thick curved bars with slightly splayed-out ends and represent high values, being worth 100 of the smaller ones. They are made of iron, copper or a mixture of metals and were commonly the price of a slave. One of these in the Wilberforce House Collection at Hull, which was used in this traffic, is said to have been worth £12 to £14 in the old slave-trading days. But values of ' King manillas ' and of slaves were very fluctuating, and traders of the Coast will tell you that a ' King ' would purchase a hundred slaves (R. P. Wild).

There are ' Queen ' and ' Prince ' *manillas* also, worth 75 and 5 smaller ones respectively, but there is very little information about them. The large ones were undoubtedly highly valued along the Coast and inland, and were used in funeral offerings. A large number were found in the Andoni country in Southern Nigeria in a fetish hut which was destroyed by order of the Government in 1905, in consequence of the human sacrifices offered there. The hoard of skulls and ivory and ' King ' manillas are in the British Museum.

If the common *manillas* are derived from Bronze Age bangles, ' King ' *manillas* may be compared with Bronze Age torques (*cf.* Johnston, 1908, p. 794, Fig. 452). But perhaps, as old Coasters will tell you, they are nothing more than the bolts of early wooden ships, broken up on the shore.

The Slave Coast lies next to the Gold Coast, a juxtaposition not without significance in West African history, which lends itself to metaphorical application and moral exposition. A proverb of the Gold Coast, ' There is no market wherein the dove with the pouting breast is not traded,' preserves the memory of the cowry as currency and cowries are still in ordinary use in the Northern Territories. But the chief medium of exchange here was gold dust, used either in grains or by weight. The dust permitted of almost infinitesimal division, and Burton and Cameron describe how even a farthing's worth could be paid by balancing a grain or two on a knife tip (1883, II, p. 144, 154).[1]

Barbot describes the weighing of the gold by means of seeds ; *taccoes* with ' little pease, black on one side and red on the other ' ; and *dambas* with ' little red berries with black spots ' weighing 2 *taccoes* (or 2 dwt. at Almina) : 12 *taccoes* made the *akye* (*ackie*) and 16 *akyes* the ounce Troy. (Churchill, 1732, Vol. V, p. 234).[2] But weights as well as measures were adjustable by bargaining with chiefs or kings. The ' small money ' was also in gold, but in gold adulterated ' with several ingredients and of little value, cut into small bits called *krakras*' (which Barbot illustrates on Pl. 22).

Bosman describes these little bits (spelt *kakeraas*) cast into *Fetiches*, about the worth of 1, 2, or 3 farthings.

'Tis a common Proverb *That you cannot buy much Gold for a Farthing*, yet even with that value in Gold you may here go to Market and buy Bread or Fruit for your Necessities. The *Negroe* Women know the exact value of these bits so well at sight that they never are mistaken ; and accordingly they tell them to each other without weighing as we do coined Money (1705, p. 82).

Bowdich described the revenue and currency of Ashanti in 1817. The gold, a royal perquisite, was valued by weight, with two sets of weights, heavier ones for the King and lighter for current use. The *ackie*, $\frac{1}{18}$ ounces av. was then worth 5*s*., and the *periguin* (2 ounces)

[1] They also refer to the earlier money consisting of holed quartz stones described above (p. 60).
[2] *Damba* is a common name for *Abrus precatorius* on the Coast but both names and seeds are often confused.

5

was worth £10. Tribute, fines, compensations and 'bride-price' were all reckoned in *periguins* and *ackies*. The King's son was redeemable at the price of 20 *periguins*, a commoner at a few *ackies*; murder cost 20 ounces of gold dust and a slave, but accidental killing only 5 ounces and the funeral expenses; a 'captain' would pay a *periguin* or £10 for a wife; a poor man, 2 *ackies* or 10*s*.; damages for adultery in the former rank was 10 *periguins*, in the latter 1½ *ackie*, and a pot of palm wine (1873, pp. 209–10, 243).

All along this much-harried coast from the Slave Coast itself to Senegal, trading through many centuries spread the use of cowries, trade-beads, iron, brass or copper rods or rings, cotton, cloth and, of late, coins, so any traces of native currencies are rare. But one distinctive form of native money is still current on the borders of Sierra Leone and Liberia, in the shape of the well-known 'Kissi pennies', (Pl. 1, Fig. 11) so-called because the Kisi (also spelt Kissi and Ghisi) use them, though the local name is *kilindi*. The length is variable, with an average of some 16 to 18 inches (40 to 46 cm.). The stem is usually twisted, and the ends are hammered out into the 'ear' *nileng*, and 'foot' *kodo*. These are still the common currency used, not only by the natives, but by all polite travellers in the hinterland, as it is considered a compliment to the local chieftain to use his local money. Now that coins are beginning to penetrate into the interior there has to be a money-changer in the market, who sits on a mat with a pile of the irons in front of him, and exchanges them, at some 46 or 48 to the West African shilling—though a shilling is seldom seen, as it represents a mine of wealth. Two irons will buy a score of oranges, a large bunch of bananas, or several kola nuts. They may be seen as offerings made on the death of a chief, first broken, then stuck in the grave; and they provide an essential part if not the whole of the 'bride-price'. This may consist of only a few bundles, or, in the case of a favoured maiden, may make a large pile. Among the Gbande of Liberia the man places an iron on the woman's head, saying 'This is my wife' as he hands over the first instalment of his payments to her father. (Earthy, 1934, **180**; 1936, **271**).

iii. NORTH, EAST AND SOUTH AFRICA

North, East and South Africa have been for so long the home of cattle-keeping peoples that cattle, whether in the form of camels, sheep, goats or cows, but chiefly cows,[1] are the standard of value.

[1] The connexion between 'cattle' and 'chattels' and 'capital' or chief property has often been quoted to emphasize the fact that wealth in Europe in early days consisted in cattle. When dealing with examples of such

The larger animals are rarely and reluctantly sold, but everything is calculated on a cattle basis. They constitute real wealth, and are parted with only in important transactions such as ' bride-price ', or under compulsion, as for fines and compensations (*cf.* Ankermann, 1929, pp. 114 *ff.*).

Still, though cattle provide the dominant occupation and sub-sistence they can rarely support the whole group ; they cannot flourish in fly-infested areas, and in fly-free areas they are often the privilege of the rich or of the overlords alone. So grain and vegetables support the non-pastoral and semi-pastoral groups and a subsidiary standard of value is set up in the essential African implement, the hoe. In Bechuanaland a man could have as many wives as he liked, or rather as he could purchase ; for the price of a wife was 10 head of cattle among the wealthier cattle-keeping tribes and large hoes or spades among the poorer (*cf.* Gordon Cumming, 1850, p. 232). Native hoes in East Africa may be regarded as the local form of iron ingot, for they were exchanged for goods by the tribes in the districts where iron was plentiful, and worked up else-where into other implements, weapons and ornaments by the local smiths.

As the country was opened up, cowries, beads and cloth advanced along the trading routes, but throughout the greater part of this eastern side of the continent, native currencies are scarce compared with the west, and often entirely lacking, all trading being by barter.

To begin with Egypt. Egypt, in spite of its skill in the working of metals for thousands of years, does not appear to have developed a coinage before the 4th century B.C., when coins with Egyptian devices were struck in imitation of the Greek gold staters. Before this time gold and copper, and silver which was more highly valued, circulated as currency here as elsewhere, with values determined by weight. Rings (Fig. 28) are usually accepted as currency, and Plato speaks of ' engraved stones of which a Spartan could make no use ' which may refer to scarabs (*Eryx*, 400*c*).

The wealth of Rameses III, the Croesus of ancient Egypt, was in grain, cattle, silver and gold, the gold depicted in reliefs being in the form of rings, bags of gold dust and solid ingots. From the XVIIIth dynasty onwards articles were valued in terms of weight, the *dbn* or *deben* (1,400 grains) and the ring or $\frac{1}{12}$ of the *deben*. But the hieroglyph of the standard weight (*deben*) is ⟁ or ⟁ which represents a bent metal strip or rod, and this may have been the native currency, the far-away precursor of the *larins* of the

wealth and its use in actual exchanges or payments, it is unfortunate that the English language has no singular neuter form for animals of such con-rasted sex, and the collective word ' cows ' in Africa, must like ' pigs ' in Melanesia, be stretched to include the male of the species.

Persian Gulf and the forerunner of the ' brass-rods ' or *mitako* of the Congo, though material evidence is lacking.

Maspero describes how the dull and sleepy towns of ancient Egypt woke up completely only three or four times a year for the religious festivals. These attracted crowds from far and near, some travelling great distances in caravans and in boats ' for religious sentiments did not exclude commercial interests '. The religious exercises ended, the market began. Peasant folk with their cattle, market gardeners with their vegetables, fishermen and hunters with their spoil, potters and small tradesmen all offered their wares.

Business was mostly carried on by barter. The purchasers brought with them some product of their toil, a new tool, a pair of shoes, a reed mat, pots of unguents or cordials ; often, too, rows of cowries and a small box full of rings, each weighing a *tabnû*,[1] made of copper, silver or even gold, all destined to be bartered for such things as they needed.

FIG. 28.—Gold rings
(1) Egyptian. (2) Abyssinian

Lists of the goods exchanged (in the XXth dynasty) can be seen, in which beds, sticks, honey, oil, pickaxes and clothes make up the price of a bull or a she-ass, and Maspero, taking his illustrations from the Saqqara tombs and contemporary market scenes, gives a lively description of Egyptian trading, but no money enters into the picture (1910, pp. 223–4).

The gold rings from Abyssinia (Fig. 28) form a link with those of Egypt, and rings or bracelets or bangles of various metals from Nubia, the Sudan and Uganda trace their spread up the Nile Valley.[2] Tin rings were the only currency at El Fasher, in Darfur (there called *tarneih*) ; for higher values cloth, *toukkiyeh*, was used and 30 pieces of cloth were the price of a good slave, i.e. one measuring six spans from his ankle to the lower part of his ear and 20 cows with a male and female slave were the usual price of a wife (Ridgeway, 1892, p. 44). Brass rings strung on a leather thong were the currency farther south (Pl. 3, Fig. 1), and copper rings or beads were recognized as currency at Mapungubwe (Fouché 1937, p. 109, Pls. XXXVIII, Fig. 4, XXXIX, Fig. 1).

[1] i.e. *deben*.

[2] Barth noted that most of the gold brought into Timbuktu was in the form of rings (1858, V., p. 22).

Among warriors and among agriculturists iron is more desirable than other metals, and over most of Africa provides, as has been seen, the nearest approach to currency, sometimes in the form of ingots, large or small, sometimes in rings, sometimes in weapons, more often in East Africa in actual or potential hoes.[1]

The *hashshash* (Fig. 29) from Kordofan and Darfur is tentatively included with the hoes. It has been likened in shape to the cross of St. Anthony, to the cross-section of a mushroom, to the semicircular knife used by leather-cutters, which is believed by some to be the tool from which it is derived, or an arrowhead, believed by others to be its prototype. But it is more likely that it belongs to the large class of hoe-currency. The extinct Darfur hoe was of this shape (Arkell, 1937, p. 146, Pl. XX, A2). The typical Kordofan hoe illustrated by Ratzel (1896, I, p. 91) was also, he says, currency. The hoe-money of the Western Sudan in the British Museum, the

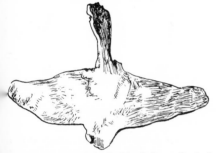
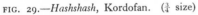

FIG. 29.—*Hashshash*, Kordofan. (¾ size)   FIG. 30.—*Sakania*, Lake Chad

hachâchah of Wadai (Ridgeway, 1892, p. 45), and the *sakania* (Fig. 30) in the Pitt Rivers Museum form intermediate links. This derivation is also supported by a note contributed by Dr. Hubert Loewe, whose grandfather, a pioneer in Egyptology, collected the specimen here illustrated.

Hash-shash in the dictionaries of Lane and Belot is given only in the conventional Arabic sense of ' a man who cuts grass (Hăshásh) '. But Dozy's *Supplément*, p. 289, adds ' Morceau de fer en forme de faucille et taillé en pointe aux deux bouts, avec un manche au milieu, qui remplace dans le Kordofan tous les instruments aratoires ; bêche ou pelle, qui a la forme d'un petit croissant dont la partie concave offre un trou dans lequel pénètre le manche en bois de l'instrument. Le mot espagnol " aciche " qui en dérive, signifie hachette de carreleur.'

This second definition favours the leather-cutters' knife derivation.

[1] De Salviac, 1901, illustrates p. 159, Fig. 5, the iron currency of the Galla of Abyssinia ; Ratzel, 1898, III, p. 37, that of the Jur, Azande and others.

Fifteen of these pieces were equal to the piastre, or about 6d., and 60 pieces went to the *feogar* or piece of cloth, some 9 inches wide (23 cm.) and 18 to 20 feet long. This compares with the values given by Powell Cotton for his 'kokey', a similar blade from the Sara district near Lake Chad (now in the British Museum) 15 of which were worth 1 franc.

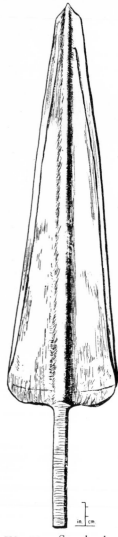

The Bongo spades provide an interesting evolutionary series. The Bongo live on the higher land to the south of the Bahr el Ghazal, in a country rich in ironstone, which is entirely unknown in the swamp region. So the raw iron is an important article of trade with the tribes to the north. It is exported in three shapes:—*mahee* or spearheads, 1 or 2 feet long[1]; *loggoh-kullutty*, 'ill-formed spades' with the characteristic antennae at the top (*cf.* Temple, 1899, Pl. XX, Fig. 16; Thilenius, 1921, Pl. I, Fig. 10); and *loggoh*, called *melote* in the market, which are actual spades (Fig. 32). 'The *loggoh-kullutty* is the only equivalent which Central Africa possesses for money of any description', said Schweinfurth (1873, p. 279), but there are even simpler forms, such as the Tula spade in the Pitt Rivers Museum (Fig. 32), and, simpler still, the flat iron pancakes of the Madi.

Among the Madi (Moru) of the Upper Nile, wrote Felkin (1884, pp. 350-1)

cattle form the chief wealth; a rich man may have as many as 200, a very poor one only 3 or 4. . . . The nearest approach to money is seen in the flat round pieces of iron which are of different sizes, from ½ to 2 feet in diameter and ⅔ of an inch thick. They are much employed in exchange. This is the form in which they are kept and used as money, but they are intended to be divided in two, heated and made into hoes. . . . Compensation for killing a woman or any serious crime must be paid for in cattle. . . . Payment for a wife must be made in cows of a year old or in bulls of 2 or 3 years.

FIG. 31.—Spearhead, East Africa

The payment for a wife is still the feature which distinguishes licit from illicit marriage in the Anglo-Egyptian Sudan, though cash often supplements or is substituted for the cattle and

[1] Resembling the spearhead illustrated, Fig. 31.

iron bars formerly demanded (Nalder, 1937, p. 47). The iron bars are destined, as Felkin noted, to be made into hoes, and there are many other references to 'currency hoes' in East Africa, though the exchange is seldom distinguishable from barter.

Temple figures hoes from the Dinka and Shilluk (Pl. XX, Figs. 11, 12); Schmeltz and de Jong illustrate one from Tanganyika (Pl. 63, Figs. 4, 5). It was in Tanganyika that a chief tried to buy Grant's umbrella for a hoe, and only gave up bargaining when Grant declared that he would not sell it for 20 cows, a currency the chief really understood (1864, p. 87). Grant was told that travel through the unexplored land to the east of the Wanyoro would be quite easy

FIG. 32.—*Melote*, Central Africa   FIG. 33.—Tula spade money

if he were provided with a horn filled with charms, and carried 600 iron hoes for presentation, two by two, to each chief whose district he wished to traverse (p. 279).

The Wabena of Tanganyika Territory, south of Iringa, at the upper streams of the Rufiji, trade among themselves mostly by barter, but have a clear idea of what is currency and what is not. Cattle, goats, cloth and hoes are currency and are accepted as legal tender for any claim, while salt and fowls, rice and grain are not ; and though these may be commonly used in exchange, no man is bound to accept them in payment of a debt. So in disputes over marriage payments (which are paid in instalments) the man will state : ' I gave her father 15s., 3 hoes, 2 she-goats and 4 *kaniki* [lengths of black cloth] ', but will make no mention of the salt, rice or *simsim* oil which were included in the contributions.   Three hoes was the recognized ' bride-price ' in the old days, each hoe being a separate payment and fulfilling a special function.   Some of these were made specially for the purpose and were never used on the land, but were stored away in the rafters as special treasures.   They might be used if a son wanted a wife, but were often kept in the family as treasured heirlooms, called *jembe la maboka*, ' hoes of the spirits ', and handed down from generation to generation.

Now that native-made hoes are supplanted by imported ones at 1*s*. apiece, the hoe standard is going out of fashion, and payments are mainly in cash, the average marriage payment being between 20*s*. and 60*s*., for public opinion, the influence of the chiefs and that of the missions all unite in opposing extravagant demands (Culwick, 1935, Chaps. XII–XV).

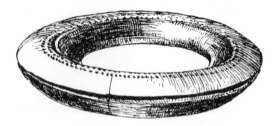

FIG. 34.—Brass bracelet, Uganda

Among the Kavirondo, hoes are exchanged for cattle, a sheep being worth 3 hoes and a cow 30 (Hobley, 1928, p. 248).   Captain Stigand mentions axes and hoes as ' sometimes used as money ' in the Angoni area, Nyasaland, North-East Rhodesia and Portuguese East Africa.   Large hoes (*khasu*) are equal to 4 yards of calico or 1*s*. ;   small hoes 2 yards or 6*d*., and axes the same (1909, p. 43).   Special ' marriage hoes ', too large to be of practical use, were made solely for payments to the father of the girl.   One of these, from Northern Uganda, is seen in Pl. I, Fig. 1.   The value of this one was about 10*s*.

The region of the Great Lakes and Uganda was reached by influences from the Upper Nile and Egypt, but communication can never have been easy and, save on the slave-routes, it was scarcely explored by the Arabs before it was opened up by Europeans in the latter half of last century.   So its primitive currencies are the more easily traced, and Roscoe (1911, pp. 450 *ff*.) collected information about the earliest stages.   The cow naturally formed the standard of value, and ivory and slaves had their equivalent in cows, smaller values being expressed in goats or fowls.   Brass bracelets were also used as currency (Fig. 34) and, earlier still, beads and cowries.

It was probably in the time of Semakokiro, grandfather of Suna (who died about 1857), that cowries were first introduced into Buganda. He had many elephant hunters, and traded with ivory in exchange for cotton goods (reserved for royal use) and cowries brought from the coast at Mombasa. At this time two cowries would buy a woman. Earlier still small roughly made blue beads, *mpeke* and *nsinda* (Frontispiece, Figs. 3 and 4), were highly valued, and, still earlier, disks of shell or ivory and strings of wild banana seeds. As trade with the Arabs increased and cowries came more freely into the country a disk or a blue bead was valued at 100 cowries. In Suna's time a cow or a male slave was worth 2,500 cowries, a goat 500, and a fowl 25. The larger blue beads were used for fines on special occasions, particularly for any breach of the marriage regulations. The defendant might be fined one bead, which was equivalent to 1,500 or 2,000 cowries. One suspects another royal monopoly here, to maintain the high price of beads, for the common people were officially forbidden to traffic in them, cowries being their 'current coin'. Farther to the west,

FIG. 35.—Cowries, Uganda

among the Banyoro, cloth and beads had not yet arrived when Grant was travelling through; cattle and barkcloth were their currency with cowries which had only lately become abundant. A middle-aged man could remember the time when 10 cowries could buy a cow, and 30 a woman (1864, pp. 229, 271). During the reign of Mutesa, son of Suna (1857–84), beads dropped in value, and after the introduction of the rupee cowries were exchanged at 1,000 to the rupee.[1] But when the rupee was firmly established, mainly owing to the building of the railway, and trade goods were current throughout the country, 'bride-price', fines and compensations for injuries had still to be paid in livestock. And even today, although tribal

[1] The memory of the cowry-currency is picturesquely preserved in the first postage stamps printed by the mission press in Uganda, with denominations of 5 and 10 cowries (Hobley, 1929, p. 247).

5*

payments are in cash, they are referred to in terms of cattle. The 'bride-price' will be quoted as 4 cows, even if it is paid in rupees or florins, at the recognized market-price for a cow (Hobley, 1929, p. 248).

The use of strings of shell and other disks as money is interesting in comparing the similar development in Oceania. Here in East Africa there were strings of ivory, ostrich egg shell and snailshell as well as seeds (Figs. 36, 37) which were valued as ornament, and are all included by Roscoe in 'currency', even single disks having high values (1911, pp. 412–13). Ivory came first in Buganda, and as

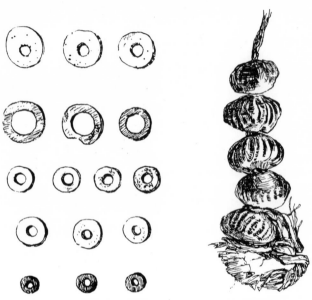

FIG. 36.—Discs of ivory and shells, Uganda

FIG. 37.—Banana seeds, Uganda

most of the ivory belonged to the King, and most of the skilled ivory workers were in the royal service, there was a certain restriction on its output, though it was not a royal monopoly.[1]

Ostrich egg shell disks, which are found again among the Bushmen of South Africa, are characteristic of many tribes on the eastern borders of the Victoria Nyanza, though their use as money is not established. They are not accepted for 'bride-price', which has to be paid in cattle (Northcote, 1907, pp. 59 *ff.*).

[1] It is doubtful if worked ivory, apart from tusks, was ever used as money, for the strings of disks had special significance, and could only be worn by unmarried girls (J. H. Driberg).

Strings of snailshell disks are found as ornaments among many of the Upper Nile peoples such as the Shuli, Makaraka, Bari-speaking people and the Madi, and are occasionally used as money. Grant noticed the large white spiral shells bleaching on the housetops in the Bari and Madi country. The natives cut them into circles the size of shirt-buttons and strung hundreds of them to be worn as ornamental white girdles round the waist. They formed the ordinary coinage, and if beer or fowls were required, they were used in the purchase (1864, p. 356). But all of these East African strings are primarily ornament, and rarely developed into 'shell-money' for general commercial use, as they did to the west of the Great Lakes.

Kenya and Tanganyika Territory have little to show in the way of primitive money. Cattle provide the standard of wealth and medium of exchange, with salt and iron in worked or unworked shapes for ordinary barter. Iron could be used in purchase of slaves or negotiation for wives, for paying taxes and fines, and had an accepted, if not a fixed, price. The Kavirondo hoe was worth 15 strings of pink beads, and 3 hoes equalled 1 sheep. The hut tax could be paid in hoes, sheep or rupees, but the tax collector had to take what he could, and near Victoria Nyanza he collected it in crocodile eggs (Hobley, 1929, p. 247). Towards the end of last century imported iron was one of the main articles of exchange, used by the agricultural tribes for making hoes, for the Masai for their enormous spearheads, and by all for ornament (Stuhlmann, 1910, p. 73).

In the Tabora district of what is now Tanganyika, Speke and Grant found that our coinage of gold, silver and copper was there represented by brass or copper wire for sovereigns, calico for silver and beads for coppers. But not *all* beads. *Goolabee* (*golabio*), rose-coloured beads, were very popular, but when they ran out, everything doubled in price ; sea-green beads, *magee bahr* (*maji bahari*), and pure whites, *kanyera*, were refused point blank, and Indian reds, *kuhunduguru*, were rejected as only fit for uncivilized peoples to the north. Everything was, however, valued in cattle. Cows were always at hand to be paid over for services rendered, for repairing a gun, for curing a chief of blindness, mending a split ear or extracting a bullet (Grant, 1864, pp. 86, 96).

Indian cowries were brought by the Arabs to Lamu, their trading emporium, and shipped to Mombasa, the string of 100 being called *simbi*. A hoard of these gave its name to the House of the Cowries at Gedi dating from the 15th century; copper bangles, a common currency, were also found (Kirkman, 1954).

Trade-beads were among early importations. In the 16th century 'small red glass beads made in the Kingdom of Cambay' were used as money in the Kingdom of Monemugi,[1] ' gold not being valued ' (Pigafetta, ed. 1881, p. 124) and beads are still in common use. The blue and white beads in the frontispiece came from Ujiji at the end of the notorious slave-route to Zanzibar. Fifty years ago a string of 20 of these was the unit, and it took 100 strings to buy a length of white calico. The string is the *kete*, which is Swahili for cowry, 2 strings are a *timba*, a bunch of 10 is a *fundo* (a knot).

Maes described the trade-bead currency of the Wania- (or Bania-) bunga south of Lake Kivu, far in the interior. There the usual trading medium consisted of strings of red and blue beads. The red string was worth about a penny. Blue beads were estimated by weight, and were worth 6 times as much as red ones. But everything was valued in red strings. A cow was worth 500 bunches (of 10 strings) ; a large goat or sheep 8 or 10 bunches, 2 lengths of indigo drill, or 1 small goat and 2 lengths of ' americani '. Two strings would buy 5 eggs ; 3 strings, a fowl ; 4, a stem of bananas. One string would buy a small pot of *pombe* beer, and a bunch a large pot (Maes, 1911, p. 64).

In the Tabora market Captain Stairs noticed that the food was set out in small quantities equivalent to a string of beads. Thus for 1 string you could buy 7 small pieces of dried manioc or 10 fresh, an ounce of *bhang* (hemp), 3 large sweet potatoes, a small cup of ground nuts or beans, or 2 spoonfuls of native salt. The highest unit was the *shuka*, 30 strings of beads or a length of cloth. This would buy a native hoe or a dozen eggs. The beads were exchanged for cloth as soon as a seller had collected enough, just as we exchange our coppers for silver, and the cloth was used for purchases of higher values. Two pieces are the *doti*, 8 pieces the *jora* and 20 the *korja* (*cf.* Mahieu, 1924, pp. 124–5).

In the Rhodesias and Nyasaland currency can scarcely be said to have existed before the coming of the whites. Cattle, sheep, goats and hoes were the recognized values for ' bride-price ' and fines. All trading was done by exchange, and still is, except where there are towns, or natives returned from the mines or otherwise influenced from outside. Arab and Portuguese traders introduced cowries and trade-beads, blue and white representing different values, measured in teaspoonfuls or dessertspoonfuls for small amounts, and handfuls for large. Beads were the popular trading-goods of the Swahili and Chikunda slaving and ivory parties up to the end of last century in Northern Rhodesia, and large translucent barrel-beads about $1 \times \frac{3}{4}$ inch (28 × 17 mm.) were used in exchange. A girdle sufficient to encircle the slave offered for sale was the price of a male

[1] Monemugi, in Pigafetta's map, is mountainous country due west from Zanzibar, perhaps Unyamwesi.

or female, and a long necklace was usually added to the cloth paid for a tusk. The beads were used by the natives for fines, especially as damages in action for adultery, and could be paid by a chief to ransom a slave (Brelsford, 1937, pp. 74–7).

Together with cattle, slaves and ivory, the handsome *impande* ornaments of *Conus* whorls were regarded as wealth. These, as well as pieces cut from the sides, were worn as charms and as insignia of office or rank. Long cylindrical beads, 2½ inches (6–7 cm.) long or large round beads nearly 1 inch each way have been handed down for many generations and are used in presentations and exchanges over a wide area.

According to tradition it was Bulongo, the arch-demigod in the Ba-Ila pantheon, who first brought these shells and beads into Northern Rhodesia. ' In the old days you took a string of beads, long enough to go round your neck and down to the navel, and bought an awfully nice girl with it ' (Smith and Dale, 1920, II, p. 195, *cf.* illustration, I, p. 100). The Ba-Ila have no idea of the value of gold, silver or copper, and men return from Kimberley with the belief that the white people are digging there for *impande* shells. Cattle are used for wergeld, 20 for homicide, and misdeeds other than witchcraft, are atoned for by lesser fines. *Impande* shells figure largely in *chico* or marriage payments, together with cattle, salt, tobacco,

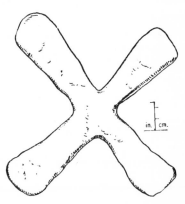

FIG. 38.—Katanga cross, N. Rhodesia

beads and, nowadays, shillings (*ibid.*, II, p. 50). Salt may be called a form of currency. It is obtained, as in the Congo, by evaporating saline earth, and is collected in long, cylindrical baskets, 5 of which are the price for a male calf, 3 for a suckling calf, and 20 for a heifer (*ibid.*, I, p. 148).

Copper crosses of Katanga type (*cf.* pp. 77 *ff.*) are not uncommon in the Rhodesias ; they are found in ruins associated with Zimbabwe culture in Southern Rhodesia and are still current in trading in the North. The usual form here weighs about 1¼ pounds and lacks the typical central ridge (Figs. 38, 118 (*c*) and Fig. 3 on Pl. 1).

Ingots in lumps and bars are also of local origin. Copper was formerly extensively worked in the rich districts of Northern Rhodesia, and the conquering Kasemba (Lunda) extorted tribute from subjugated chiefs in the form of copper bars. These were given as presents and used in exchange for salt, flour and other provisions (Burton, 1873, pp. 110, 125, &c.).

One of the roughly smelted bars now in the Livingstone Memorial Museum measures 3 feet 10 inches (1 m. 17 cm.) long by 4 inches (10 cm.) thick, it weighs 70 pounds and consists of 98 per cent pure copper. A slightly smaller example in the Hamburg Museum currency case is just over 1 m. long, shaped like an exaggerated capital ' I ', spreading out over 15 inches (39·5 cm.) at top and bottom.[1]

Cowries and beads lingered on in parts of Portuguese East Africa, though cattle, especially goats, provided the standard of value and the chief items in *lobolo* or ' bride-price '. Other goods, such as barkcloth, hoes, beads or rings, used in exchange for goats thereby acquired a definite *lobolo* value.

Junod gives the sequence of the objects used for *lobolo* among the Thonga.

First it consisted in *mats* and *baskets,* in those remote times when White people had not yet made their appearance. The *large iron rings* were produced by barter from sailors who anchored off the shore, and were employed for the purpose. Later on white traders settled in the country. *Beads* were bought from them (*nkarara*) especially large ones (*mubatlwana*). A chief used to *lobola* with 10 handfuls of them, a subject with only 5. Large *brass rings* [some weigh more than 2 pounds] were also used in old times. . . . They were called *litlatla,* and were very much sought after. One was enough to buy a wife (1912, pp. 258-9).

Cattle here, as among the Zulu, were the regular means of getting a wife, but when, early in the 19th century, the Thonga were raided by the Angoni, all their cattle were taken, and they had to fall back on hoes and beads. Ten oxen were the usual *lobolo*, and 10 hoes, unless oxen were available. This was from 1840 to 1870. But when the natives began to work in the mines and coinage was introduced (about 1870) 10 hoes were equivalent to £1, and the chiefs fixed the *lobolo* money at £8. Later it went as far as £20 for an ordinary girl, and £30 for a chief's daughter.

Oxen and hoes enter into fines and wergeld. It was explained to Junod :

Should you have killed a man by accident in a hunting trip, for instance, you will try to arrange matters directly with his relatives if you were good friends ; your relatives will give them a girl. . . . They will accompany her with 10 hoes and an ox, saying ' This is fat to smear our daughter.'

The girl is not regarded as ' a life for a life ' but as a means of supplying the deficiency caused by the accident. As soon as she has borne a child, she is free (1912, p. 415).

[1] The Horniman Museum exhibits a piece of copper in the form of an elongated axe-head neatly finished and polished as Northern Rhodesian currency.

In Gazaland white beads (*tshifula*) were probably introduced by the Arabs or by early Portuguese settlers, and these are worn in initiation ceremonies and were exchanged for goats for *lobolo*. Bright blue beads of Dutch origin came later and these are still of intrinsic if not of currency value, and are worn by medicine men. Metal rings (*tibbetu* or *titlata*) of solid brass (Fig. 39) are probably of Zulu origin, as they are used in Ngoni ritual dances. The mother of the bridegroom held aloft one of these rings bemoaning the loss of cattle which her son had paid for *lobolo*. The bridegroom would present the ring, with nowadays a coin in the middle of it, at the feet of the bride. These rings, together with all the other gifts or payments, would have to be returned if the marriage negotiations were broken off or the marriage dissolved. They are kept tied up in a bundle, and the father of the bride would use them to *lobola* another wife for himself or for one of his sons (Earthy, 1933, p. 137).

FIG. 39.—Brass *lobolo* ring, Portuguese East Africa

FIG. 40.—Gold bar, Mozambique

Gold ingots are rare in currency collections, so attention may be called to the *barrinha* (or little bar) of Maria II from Mozambique (Fig. 40). These were issued in 1835, weighing about 222 gr., and worth $2\frac{1}{2}$ *maticaes*. The star, which shows that it is genuine, was added over the M. for Mozambique, after 1851. The gold comes from the Sena district up the Zambezi, and the pieces were still legal tender, with the value of 6,600 *reis*, in 1892 (*Numismatic Chronicle*, 1892, p. 330).

Before leaving North and East Africa, a word should be said about the most popular money, the *talari*,[1] or Maria Theresa dollar of 1780, even though it is not primitive currency. Quite why this particular coin should have such a widespread popularity is not clear. It went out of use in Austria in 1854, but the issue was continued for export, and over 2,000,000 were minted between 1891 and 1896. The demand still exceeded the supply, and in 1936 the Royal Mint was authorized to strike these coins to assist British trade, and issued 150,000. In *The Times* (30.5.38) we read

Perhaps the most picturesque coin issued [from the Royal Mint] in 1937 was the Maria Theresa thaler or dollar. This coin which bears the

---

[1] *talari* : Arabic form of thaler.

effigy of the Empress Maria Theresa and which is dated 1780, circulates freely in the Anglo-Egyptian Sudan, the Colony of Aden, and the Arab territories along the Red Sea. During the past year or two the Royal Mint, for some reason, has been called upon to strike large quantities of this historic coin. The Italian Government has also struck large quantities of this same coin for use in Abyssinia.

As a rule coins of dead sovereigns are not acceptable, as the coins too, are considered ' dead '. Maria Theresa certainly died in 1780, so it is curious that it is the coin of that date which has continued in circulation so generally for more than a century and a half. At Kanda Kanda, on the Upper Sankuru in 1920, the Albert I francs were worth 100 little blue beads, *mitunda*; but the francs of Leopold II, he being dead, were worth only 80. The Sower, being an immortal symbol, might be expected to maintain a steadier value than a coin of Maria Theresa, but the natives, being accustomed to busts, called it *makulu*, ' the legs ', looked on it with disfavour, and estimated it at only 60 little blue beads (Mahieu, pp. 66, 71, 130–1).

Maria Theresa,[1] however, supplies the trading-currency all across Africa, and is met with even in the markets of Nigeria and the Gold Coast. But values are very variable, ranging from 2s. to 6s., and the coins are used by the traders rather than the natives, who, even in Abyssinia, often reject them altogether.

Major Powell Cotton started from Addis Ababa in 1899 with 1,500 Maria Theresa dollars,

but the natives were most particular about the look of these coins and the farther one got from the capital the more difficult they were to please. Every piece offered was carefully scrutinized, generally in consultation with one or two friends. A new one or one that was much worn, or on which the ornaments of the neck, especially the points of the star, were not clear was at once rejected. I had as many as thirty of these coins refused out of fifty, but fortunately no two men agreed, so that when I reached Asmara only twenty-five out of the fifteen hundred remained unacceptable (*The Times*, 17.6.38).[2]

Officially the Maria Theresa dollar is doomed in Abyssinia, as the patented rust-proof Acmonital steel coins, issued on October 28, 1938 (17th anniversary of the Fascist March on Rome), were intended to replace all earlier issues. But a people who still use salt and

---

[1] Barth gives the value of the dollar as worth 2,500 cowries in Kano, 3,200 in Bornu, though they were not accepted in the market there (1858, II, p. 311) ; Binger in 1887 found it worth 5,000 cowries (or the equivalent in gold) at Salaga in the Gold Coast (1892, II, p. 104).

[2] The same suspicions and, it may be noted, the same preferences for a portly female on the coins, may be seen in many other parts of the world, and Queen Victoria shares the popularity of Maria Theresa. Le May tells how a whole consignment of King George V rupees had to be returned by road and rail to Bangkok, as the coolies refused to take them.

cartridges [1] as their currency may not be quick to recognize the superiority of patented rust-proof Acmonital steel over the handsome Maria Theresa dollars, with a silver content of over 83 per cent.

Some of the Congo currencies trickled over into South Africa, and copper crosses and iron gongs have been found in early gold workings or settlements, while cowries, beads, and iron bars were common in coastal trading here, as in the rest of Africa.

There is one form of native currency which has, so far, been found nowhere save in the Palaborwa district of the North-East Transvaal. This is the *lirali*, which may be described as a copper ingot arrested in making a rod or bar.

A common method of making copper rods was to choose a reed, cover it with clay, with a clay funnel at the end for the molten metal to pour in. When the metal was cooled the clay and reed were broken away. The *lirali* consists of the long copper rod, still attached to the ' runner ' or mass of copper in the funnel, from which there still project (in most examples) a varied number of short rods or ' root-like bars '. The first specimen to attract attention in Europe was the one exhibited and described by Bartels (1893, p. 320, ill.) which was obtained from the Makwapa (Thonga) nick-named Knobnoses. The projecting rods were taken to represent air vents in the original funnel, but this interpretation is not alto-gether satisfactory, and the origin and significance of these pro-jections is so far unexplained.

Haddon procured two specimens of *marali* in 1905, one of which is illustrated on Pl. 1, Fig. 9. These rods were used in former times in ' bride-price ' for wives of chiefs, and were worth 10 cows, but reduced later to 2 cows and 3 she-goats. Copper ore is abundant in the North-Eastern Transvaal, but the low-lying area is infested with tsetse fly and unsuitable for cattle, so it is suggested that the *marali* (probably the work of the Balemba) were used instead (*cf.* Haddon, *Man*, 1908, **65**; Hemsworth, *ibid.*, 1908, **66**; Lindblom, *ibid.*, 1926, **90**).

Among the Hottentots and the Bushmen no native money is met with, though rings had exchange values among the Hottentots, as among the Zulu. The only claimants for admission to a collection of currency are the strings of Bushman beads. These are made of ostrich shell which is chipped into disks like the shell-money of Oceania. And, like the shell-money of the Gilberts and Malekula, these white disks are interspersed with black, the contrast being provided here by disks of skin instead of coconut. These strings were traded, as well as pelts, for tobacco and iron, a string 12 feet long, taking 3 months to make, fetching a handful of raw tobacco, worth 2s. or 3s. (Goodwin, 1937, p. 189).

[1] The cartridges must be new, with paper band intact, when they equal $\frac{1}{10}$ of the dollar.

Chapter VI

OCEANIA

i. Australia. ii. Polynesia. iii. Micronesia and Melanesia in general. iv. Micronesia. v. Melanesia : A. Bismarck Archipelago ; B. Solomon Islands to New Caledonia ; C. New Guinea ; D. Rossel Island

i. AUSTRALIA

His best riches, ignorance of wealth.

GOLDSMITH

OCEANIA provides illustrations of all the stages in the evolution of money, for it includes Australia and Polynesia, in which no native currencies developed : and Micronesia and Melanesia, in which we can recognize all the human gradations from present-givers and barterers to communities of commercially minded traders, with monetary systems more complicated than our own.

Australia is one of the largest areas occupied by man with no native currency. This blank may be attributed to several causes, among which geographical isolation and uniformity, together with a lack of acquisitiveness among the inhabitants, are recognized as the most conspicuous. This ' lack of trading instinct ' is primarily due to their mode of life, for to a wandering folk property has little appeal. When an Arunta man decides to move camp he picks up his spears, his wife snatches up the household goods, grinding-stones, babies, puppies, and digging-stick, and in three minutes they are ready for the journey. The woman, being the carrier, does not encourage her husband to acquire extra property. This may to some extent account for the absence of all inquisitiveness and eagerness to trade noted by many early travellers, especially when comparing the Australians with their Melanesian neighbours. The Australians were not even interested in beads and gew-gaws, though iron and glass, substituting stone for their implements, were greedily welcomed.

There is, however, organized trading in the North of Australia, where the natives may in this as in other ways owe something to influence from Melanesia. And the dependence of trade on inequality of natural products is clearly seen in Queensland.

The principal trade articles are shells, only procurable on the Coast ; ochre for personal decoration ; stone for implement-making from the Selwyn Ranges, and, most important of all, *pituri* or wild tobacco leaves,[1] which are chewed as a narcotic. ' Man

[1] Not *Duboisia hopwoodii*, as commonly stated ; *cf.* Johnstone and Cleland, 1933-4, pp. 280-2.

must sometimes seek relief from his memory ', and this means of producing a pleasantly voluptuous dreamy sensation was widely appreciated and traded in quids which could be stuck behind the ear.   Shells found their way down to Merion Downs and beyond ; *pituri* returned to the Coast.   In between, ochre and stones travelled north, south and west, and various articles were made specially for exchange ; here a special type of boomerang or spear ; there fishing-nets or throwing-sticks, but none of these developed into what can be called money.[1]   This may be described as trading and attributed to the natural working of the laws of supply and demand, but it probably owes its inception to the system of present-giving or gift-exchange, which is prominent in the Northern Territory where it has been specially studied by Stanners (1934, pp. 156 *ff.*).   The system of ' delayed economic exchanges ' here called *merbok*, may be compared to the *kula* cycle of the eastern end of New Guinea, in which certain articles—in Australia red and yellow ochre, white clay, hair belts, boomerangs, spears, beeswax and pearl-shell ornaments—travel along definite routes in friendly exchange.   These are supplemented nowadays by imported trade-goods, of which trade tobacco is the nearest approach to currency.

McCarthy has mapped the surprisingly extensive ' trade ' routes in Australia and notes the special significance of red ochre and of *pituri*, which are not uncommonly found in collections of primitive money, but he insists that ' no [native] medium of exchange or measure of value was or is employed anywhere in the continent ' (1939, p. 178).

ii. POLYNESIA

At first sight it appears surprising that the Polynesians, the most advanced people of the South Seas, never developed a currency, while most intricate systems were evolved by their less advanced neighbours in Melanesia.   Money is a curious companion to pottery and the bow and arrow, which appear to have been lost on the way to their ultimate island homes.   But geographical conditions and the social systems supply the explanation.

' If man does not work, neither shall he eat ' is unintelligible in Polynesia.   Bountiful nature encourages careless giving, rather than niggardly hoarding or commercial keenness, and although ' presents ' here, as elsewhere, expect a return, native currencies are unknown. When all that a man wants can be had for the asking, or taken without explanation, there is no need for money, and in the social system of Polynesia, with strong kinship obligations, money plays no part.

[1] See Ling Roth's map, 1908, opp. p. 2.

There was no money or any articles which could be used as a standard of exchangeable value in Samoa. . . . The communistic customs according to which every member of the family could beg without fear of refusal any articles belonging to a member of the same family practically prevented any great extension of trade. Each household supplied itself with almost everything that was necessary for common use, or for the purchase of imported articles (Brown, G., 1910, pp. 304-5).

Firth has made a special study of a people without money, and with no need for money, in Tikopia (*cf.* p. 7), and describes how their economic activities are admirably managed not only with no medium of exchange, but without markets or organized barter.

Fiji stands midway between Polynesia and Melanesia and shares the characteristics of both, but no development of commercial activity can be expected, first, because of its natural endowment, next, on account of Fijian social customs.

The Fijians have no spur to the acquisition of money except the desi.e for some particular luxury. The earth need only be tickled to laugh back in harvest. Most of the necessities of life are produced equally in every village. When a native takes produce to the market it is for no abstract desire for the possession of money ; he has in mind a definite object upon which the proceeds should be spent ; a new *sulu* [cloth], a lamp, or a contribution to the missionary meeting. If he has no such object, he will let the surplus produce of his garden or his net decay rather than undergo the trouble of taking it to the market (Thomson, 1908, p. 83).

Neither does Fijian society provide a stimulus to money-making. Present-giving is exalted into prominence [1] but the prevalent communism discourages individual enterprise. ' The commoner reckons his wealth, not by the amount of his property, but by the number of friends from whom he can beg ' (p. 79).

Present-giving attained such prominence that the borderline between presents and currency is very faint. Certain objects used in presentations acquired a conventional value and were used also in exchanges, and hoarded as wealth ; Fijian *tambua* are found in almost all collections of primitive currency, and orange cowries, *tapa* and feathers are equally admissible—or inadmissible. *Tambua* (Pls. 4, 5) are traditionally derived from wooden banana-like objects which were later made in cachalot whale ivory. They were bartered for sandalwood by early traders, but their chief function was, and still is, to serve in ceremonial present-giving. A youth when courting a maiden will take a tooth in his hand, and its acceptance implies a sacred obligation on her part similar to that of an engagement ring, and no important official reception is complete without presentation of *tambua*. The larger and ' redder ' the tooth the higher the value, so sections were joined together to make abnormally sized

---

[1] The Fijian *solevu* is described above, pp. 15-16.

tambua a foot and more in length, and a deep orange colour was artificially produced by turmeric dye.

The orange cowries, *Cypraea aurora* (Pl. 5), were ornaments of high value, usually worn on the chest. A Fijian chief told Baron A. von Hügel that one of these was worth many whale's teeth, and whales' teeth are carved to represent the shells ; but neither shells nor teeth were used as money.

Plaited mats are often called currency in Samoa, and may be seen in company with African mat-money in museum collections.[1]

Mats were evidence of wealth and position ; they were security for house or canoe building ; they were part of the bridal dowry, especially for daughters of chiefs ; they secured adherents in battle and rewarded services rendered. They played their part in political alliances and in peace-makings, and were presented or exchanged on all important occasions. The fineness of the plaiting, the age and history of the mats all contributed to their estimation, and the older ones, darkened with age, with red feathers or fringes of red along the edges would be up to a hundred dollars in value. Their function in mercantile, social and political life gives them a claim to be considered as the nearest approach to currency in Polynesia (G. Brown, 1910, p. 304).

Pieces of Samoan tapa have been described as ' paper money ' as they are used not only for presentations but also for interchange of property. These were small bits worth 1s. or 2s., with larger sheets for mosquito screens, valued at four or five dollars. Pieces of tapa served the same purposes of present-giving and exchange in Fiji, and there the value was enhanced by a stamp, the purple circle associated with chiefs.

The early traders fostered the use of whales' teeth, shells and mats in barter with the natives and this justifies their inclusion in collections of primitive money as illustrating a transition stage in its development.[2]

iii. MICRONESIA AND MELANESIA IN GENERAL

In a world map showing the distribution of currency many thousands of square miles covering Australia and the Polynesian Islands including New Zealand must be left blank.

In direct contrast Micronesia and Melanesia show the most abundant, most varied and most complicated forms of money, the delight of the collector and the despair of the cataloguer. In some parts, notably New Britain and the Banks' Islands, money and

[1] There is a fine collection in the Hamburg Mus. f. Völkerkunde, and Mosher illustrates one at Buffalo (1936, p. 42).
[2] The string of flying-fox teeth collected as currency in Fiji is noted below (p. 128 *n*., Fig. 48).

money-making are more all-important and absorbing than in civilized communities, and the complexities of the monetary system of Rossel Island, though (or for some readers because) described by economists by means of mathematical formulae, are not easy to grasp.

In any chance collection of currency (ignoring those of special areas) the commonest labels (if any) are 'spear', 'axe', or 'hoe' money from Africa; or 'shell-money from the South Seas'. And it is perhaps significant that these two areas are the eastward and westward limits of the Negro or Negroid race. Also that while iron is one of the most valued products of Africa, there is none available in Oceania, and shell takes the place of metal for use, and far more successfully for ornament.

Cowries and olives may serve as 'money' here, as in Africa, though their appreciation is less commercial than artistic. The ordinary cowries are not counted in thousands, but are back-broken for threading and stitched into decorative strips: olives are not valued by the basketful, but in necklaces.

Further comparisons between African and Oceanic currencies may be made. Iron is not evenly distributed over Africa, and the smiths form a special class, if not a special caste, the mystery of their craft enhancing the value of their products. Similarly, although shells are abundant in Oceania, they are not always easy to collect in shark-infested waters and the making of 'shell-money' is a special craft, requiring skill and training as well as magic, and usually shrouded in such secrecy that even those who habitually used it for trading knew nothing of its origin.

Lastly, in Oceania, as in Africa, the development of currency is attributed to a clash of race and culture. The modification of a negroid stock by a higher infiltration produced the Bantu in the West and the Melanesian in the East; and some of the objects used as money gained their prestige from their association with intrusive culture.

A lively trade, elaborate currencies, keen traders and grasping money-makers seem out of place in Oceania. The islands are commonly pictured as being naturally supplied with all the necessaries of life; roots, fruits and vegetables &c. on the land; molluscs, fish, turtle &c. in the sea. But while this may serve for a description of much of Polynesia, or even of Micronesia, closer investigation shows that it is rarely true of Melanesia or New Guinea. Islands, in spite of their 'double larder' advantages, cannot escape the comparative poverty imposed by isolation, and it is the smaller outlying coral islands that supply most of the currency. Foodstuffs here are not superabundant, sometimes there is no soil or space for gardens or even for pigs; all provision comes from the sea, and food is actually scarce. There is no superfluity to be used in exchange ; nothing will keep for long to provide for hungry times. So some form of storeable wealth is desirable and ' shell-money ' or its equivalent provides the obvious ' durable, portable, divisible and easily recognizable ' form. Its social and religious uses increase its significance. For when not only life in this world, by rising in social grades, but happiness in the next, depends on accumulated wealth, money attains an exaggerated importance, and the love of it is the despair of missionary effort.

Rivers when discussing Communism and Money ascribes the change from communism to individualism to the effect of immigrants from Polynesia into Melanesia.

A thoroughly communistic people can have no use for money among themselves. If they possess anything which can be regarded as currency it can only be used in transactions with other peoples (1914, p. 385).

There is evidence of various streams of migration into Melanesia, especially of a kava-using people with secret society cults and special burial rites, and a betel-using people with different forms of burial. The intimate connexion between shell-money and secret societies shows that they belong to the same culture, and suggests an explanation of the use of money in an area which formerly had no need of it. This need was primarily the purchase of wives.

It was suggested in an earlier chapter that a main factor in the evolution of money was the custom or necessity of making presents or payments on marriage. In Melanesia the immigrants arriving in canoes would bring few if any women with them and the necessity was urgent. Sister-exchange being impossible some substitute had to be found and some bribe offered.

The custom of paying for a wife [says Rivers] would result as the need of the immigrant men for women among whom they had settled. . . . The origin of payment for a wife and the beginning of the use of money in Melanesia may thus form two aspects of one and the same problem (1914, pp. 384-9).

Admission into, and steps up in, the secret societies were accompanied by money payments which emphasized its importance. Money was also essential for burial rites. So it is easy to see how its acquisition could develop into an obsession.

' Shell-money ' is the popular name for the strings of disks which form the principal ornaments and currency in Oceania, and ' Shell-money, South Sea Islands ' used to be considered an amply descriptive label for all the varieties of the Western Pacific. Further classification is beset with difficulties.

The identification of the shell itself is complicated by the loss of its characteristics in the process of shaping into disks, especially when these are very small and artificially coloured. The source is difficult to discover in objects passing so readily from hand to hand and from island to island, and specially made for distribution. For shell-strings are rarely currency, though they may be prized as ornaments, in the places where they are made. To enhance their value, as has happened with beads and cowries, the secrets of their source and their manufacture were carefully guarded, information is still difficult to obtain, and where obtained from the natives has often been intentionally misleading. This is the more tantalizing since shell-money has special significance in theories of distribution and borrowings. Those who are impressed by the similarities, assume the spread of an invention from a single centre throughout the Western Pacific. Others, more struck by the contrasts, and especially by the variations in the methods of manufacture, cannot recognize this unity, and claim that this diversity and the occurrence of similar types in Africa and also in America, point to separate origins and independent invention.[1]

Fortunately both shells and shell-money have attracted considerable attention, and the labours of Schneider, edited and amplified by Ribbe (1905), of Lewis (1929) and of Petri (1936), to name but a few, have cleared the way for the cataloguer. Schneider, with 13 plates and a few text figures, illustrates over 70 different types; Lewis has 25 plates and about 70 types also. But the casual observer finds it difficult to recognize overlaps, and the confusion of names, the contradictory statements of competent observers, besides the absence of colour in the illustrations, all make classification the work of a specialist. Strings that to the unpractised eye look exactly alike may be made of entirely different shells, and belong to different island groups, if not to different cultures, so that any attempt at identification by means of book-illustrations is unwise.

Labels on museum specimens add to the confusion. Shell-money strings were used by the early traders and spread by them from island to island. ' Black-birding ' mixed the products and upset the culture of Melanesia, as the slave trade did in Africa, only on a smaller scale. Red strings were bought for 1s. in the Solomons at the end of last century and traded for 25s. worth of gold dust in New Guinea. Travelling in the contrary direction a string of New Guinea *sapi-sapi* in the Cambridge collection is marked ' Ulawa, Solomon Islands ' on one label and ' Santa Cruz ' on another. The name of one kind was transferred to another kind and became the pidgin-English for shell-money, or even, like wampum in America, for money in general. Hence such names as *sapi-sapi* in New Guinea, *tapsoka* in New Hanover, *diwarra* or *tambu* in New Britain, *pele* in Duke of York, *arangit* or *kokonon* in

[1] *Cf.* Schurtz, 1898, p. 164; Heine-Geldern, 1932, map; Petri, 1936, pp. 551–4.

New Ireland, *som* in the Banks' Islands, &c. &c., are very loosely used and have often lost their original significance.

It will simplify descriptions and avoid repetitions if shell-money strings are roughly classified, not according to the shell, which is often unidentifiable, but according to the technique, which is obvious to all. For convenience the four main types may be called :

1. South-Sea or *sapi-sapi* type. Disks strung parallel like ordinary beads in a necklace (Frontispiece, Figs. 1, 2).
2. Edge-to-edge or ' pig-money ' type, Pl. 15 (detail in Fig. 71).
3. *Diwarra* type, when the backs of *Nassa* shells are broken and the mouths strung parallel (like beads) typically on stiff cane (Pl. 10, Fig. 1 and Fig. 55).
4. *Tautau* type, when the mouths are strung so that they lie flat or overlap (Figs. 69, 70).

The ' South-Sea ' or *sapi-sapi* type is found generally throughout the Western Pacific including Micronesia, the coasts (but only the coasts) of New Guinea, and all of Melanesia, attenuating towards New Caledonia. Inside this wide circle the *diwarra* type has its well-known centre in the Gazelle Peninsula in the Bismarck Archipelago. The *tautau* type is a method of attaching *Nassa* shells in New Guinea, but is often used for cowries also, and is more common for ornament than for currency. The edge-to-edge stringing, characteristic of New Ireland, where hundreds of fathoms are made up into *birok* or ' pig-money ' is found in ornamental dangles at the ends of currency strings in the Solomons (Pl. 16, Fig. 1), and attached to currency objects in New Guinea (Pls. 13, 14 and Fig. 71) (*cf.* Foy, 1913, pp. 134–47).[1]

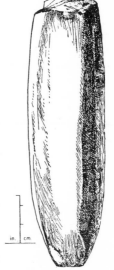

FIG. 41.—Shell hammer, Reef Islands, Santa Cruz

The methods of making shell disks are naturally influenced by the size and shape of the shell, but the methods also differ widely from island to island, if not from generation to generation. The central hole may be bored laboriously by means of a pointed stick or stone, sand and water ; but the pump drill (Pl. 13, Fig. 14) is used in Micronesia, the Bismarcks, the Solomons and New Guinea and as far south as the New Hebrides and New Caledonia. Men or boys usually collect the shells, but the disk-making is woman's work.

[1] It is seen again in currency strings in Borneo (Pl. 24) and in decorations of Pomo jewel feather baskets in the New World (p. 297 *n.*).

The usual plan is to break up the pieces of shell into suitably small fragments roughly circular,[1] which are then pierced for stringing. When threaded, the whole string can be ground down between two stones, to make it even. This is suitable for the finer pieces of shell, but thicker pieces need to be ground down before stringing. This may be done by fixing the fragment in the end of a stick or piece of wood, which is rubbed on a stone and the shell ground down to the right smoothness, first on one side, then on the other. Each disk may be ground separately, as in the Bismarcks and the Banks' Islands, or several may be stuck on to a large piece of wood,

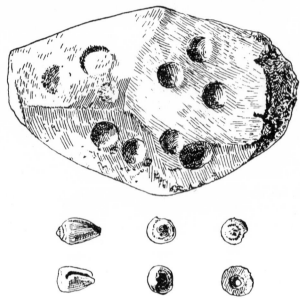

FIG. 42.—Rubbing stone and shells, Reef Islands, Santa Cruz

as in the Admiralties, New Guinea or the Solomons, or into depressions in a block of soft stone, as in the Reef Islands, Santa Cruz (Fig. 42).

Small pointed shells such as *conus* do not require drilling, and Codrington's account of *som*-making in the Banks' Islands [2] describes another process.

The body of the shell is broken, and the tip rubbed on a stone by means of a pointed stick inserted in the broken end till the hollow of the shell

---

[1] Steps in the process can be seen in Pl. 6.

[2] Codrington collected his information in the Banks' Islands between 1863 and 1887. When Rivers was there in 1908 the method of making *som* was slightly different, and is described below (p. 165).

is reached ; into the hole thus appearing at the tip of the shell the stick is then inserted, and the broken base ground smooth on the stone. There is thus a shell used for each disk, and no drill is needed, as indeed none is known (1891, pp. 325–6).

Shell-strings are vanishing from most of Melanesia, their place being taken commercially by trade-tobacco and coins, and as ornament by European beads, so that the manufacture is almost a lost art. It is still lively in the Bismarcks, but in the Solomons persisted lately only in a few outlying islands. Fifty years ago Elton noted how tobacco and axes were used by the traders in the Solomons, for paying the natives who had no idea of the value of coins. One man, being paid a sovereign, paid it away to another trader for a box of matches (1888, pp. 90 ff.). Shillings were accepted in most parts, but tobacco was necessary for small change. The standard Melanesian stick is 7 inches long (18 cm.), ½ inch wide and ¼ inch thick, and this is the official payment for carriers in the Bismarcks : 2 sticks per man per day in New Ireland. One stick = a copra string (of 10 nuts) in the Solomons. Three sticks = a shilling in the New Hebrides.[1] Nevertheless, for all-important transactions, for buying pigs, and above all, wives, native money is essential. In the Admiralties, where dogs' teeth are the money most highly valued, many a young fellow returning from the plantations rolling in riches is unable to marry owing to his lack of dogs' teeth (Bühler, 1934, p. 4).

Shell-money is practically indestructible. Coloured disks may lose colour, and strings often break, but value does not lessen with age. The Southern Solomon Islanders, however, think differently. In Malaita all important payments must be in new money and it may be that this necessity has preserved a flourishing industry here. Auki is a small island off the South-West Coast of Malaita and the centre of the shell-making industry for the eastern islands. The island is an artificial one, and is almost covered by the village, with no space for gardens, so that the people are forced to obtain their food from the mainland. Although constantly at war, there are regular market days two or three times a week when a truce is declared and the people meet in some neutral spot on the mainland shore. The women advance towards each other, offering a fish or a yam, as the case may be, while behind each stands her husband, with poised spear (Woodford, 1897, p. 32 ; 1908, **43**).

The women (and the baby) in Pl. 6 are engaged in money-making at Auki.[2] First the shells (*Spondylus*) are broken up into bits of convenient size, by pounding with a stone hammer on a stone anvil.

[1] Miss Cheeseman found tobacco sticks indispensable on Malekula as no one could otherwise be induced to work (1935, p. 45).

[2] The photograph was taken by Mr. Templeton Crocker, by whom some handsome strings, together with the manufacturing outfit, were collected and presented to the Cambridge Collection.

The bits are next put in indentations on the flat face of a wooden block, which has been covered with paste to keep them in place, and rubbed down with sandstone. The bits are then drilled, threaded and ground down evenly between two boards, making a noise (as Woodford describes it) like a wood-sawyer's yard.

It is difficult to decide how far ornaments made of shell-money strings still retain their exchange value. The strings are looped round the neck, but are also ordinary currency, a length being detached or added as necessity arises. When the strings are made up into necklets, it may enhance the money value (as in the case of the *samakupa*) or it may relegate them to the class of mere ornament.

A good illustration is provided by the necklaces or girdles, fore-head or arm-bands made of parallel strings of shell-money with spacers, treasured from Micronesia to Santa Cruz, that may be re-garded as either the most valuable of ornaments or the most decor-ative form of money. Finsch illustrates 2 made of *gau* and *tekaroro* from Ruk (1888–93, Pl. VIII, Figs. 23, 24), Lewis figures 4 from New Ireland (1929, Pl. XI, Figs. 3, 4, and XII, Figs. 2, 3), McCarthy figures 1 from the Solomons in his currency collection (1935, Fig. 8). Speiser illustrates a similar one (also currency) from Santa Cruz, where it was not worn. as a girdle, but kept wound on a wooden winder (1916, Fig. 40). Two larger ' girdles ' of this type collected by Woodford as Santa Cruz currency, still wound on their wooden frames, are in the British Museum.[1]

There are certain areas in the Western Pacific where native money is especially developed or especially abundant, and it will simplify our review if these areas are taken separately. At least five centres may be recognized :

1. Yap in the Western Carolines, linked commercially with the Pelews, 400 miles to the west, and less closely linked with Eastern Micronesia.
2. The Bismarck Archipelago, with its *diwarra* centre in the North of New Britain, and abundant currencies throughout.
3. The Solomon Islands (a prolific centre of strings of shell-disks) with their southward neighbours Santa Cruz and Banks' Islands.

---

[1] Beasley (1936, pp. 382–3) draws attention to the similarity between the terminations of shell-money ' girdles ' and the ends of the feather-money, and finds in the similarity support for his belief that the feather-money is merely an elaborated belt. Shell-money made up into belts, which are used as money units, have been noted in the Belgian Congo in the cowry belts (*kamba-barakuta*) of the Mobenge, 10 of which were the price of a wife, and the Bubi belts (made of *Achatina*) of Fernando Po (*cf.* Pl. 3, Fig. 5).

4. New Guinea, with its easterly extension to the Trobriands, D'Entrecasteaux and Louisiades.

5. Rossel Island, 200 miles south-east of New Guinea, which has developed a shell-currency of such special character that it has to be treated separately.

These will be dealt with in turn, but some of the objects used as currency generally or sporadically throughout the Western Pacific may be considered first. These are rings, teeth, mats and feather-money.

Rings are money or something like it, from Micronesia to the New Hebrides, but they vary so much in material and in shape that although certain generalizations can be attempted, detailed descriptions must be relegated to the special areas in which they belong.

Teeth pass for money throughout Melanesia; boars' tusks, especially the artificially deformed ones, in New Guinea and South-East Melanesia, with teeth of dogs, porpoise, cuscus (' opossum '), bat (*Pteropus* or ' flying-fox '), fish and cachalot whale scattered here and there.

Woven strips or mats are currency in San Matthias and Santa Cruz; plaited mats in the New Hebrides; strings or cord in Matty Island, New Guinea, Santa Cruz, New Caledonia and the Loyalties.

Feather-money has its special home in the Banks' Islands and Santa Cruz.

This warning should, however, be noted. The frequent statements that shells, rings, teeth, mats and feathers were used as money in Oceania, and their inclusion in currency collections, are explained by the fact that after the coming of the whites, traders and natives adapted the articles used in gift-exchange, in payment for services rendered, in marriage-payments and in fines, for secular and commercial transactions; these articles cannot properly be called ' primitive money ', though their use illustrates a stage in the history of its development.

The close relationship between rings and money has already been noted (p. 52) and it links together Europe, Asia and Oceania, for rings have presentation and exchange, if not actual currency value throughout. In Europe and Asia stone preceded metal; in Oceania stone is usually replaced by shell, which is still in use. The Stone Age rings of China or Annam, and the shell-rings from the ruins of Ponape and Kusaie in the Eastern Carolines may have been merely ornaments, but they were evidently ornaments of special, if not ceremonial value, and it is legitimate to presume that their use in presentations is not a modern development.

The earliest reference to rings in Micronesia is in the picturesque description of the ' Order of the Bone ' by Captain Wilson of the *Antelope*, who was one of the first Europeans to make a protracted (though involuntary) landing on the Pelews in 1783.   The ring or *klilt* was of bone, the atlas vertebrae of the Halicore dugong, but there were rings of stone and shell as well, used as currency (Pl. 7).[1] (Keate, 1789 ; Ratzel, 1896–8, I, p. 247 ; Petri, 1936, p. 298, Fig. 7).

A century later Kubary dispelled much of the picturesque mystery surrounding the *klilt*.   The dugong was rare in the Pelews, and a chiefly perquisite, but the ' bone ' was not in his time the insignia of rank, or even a special mark of honour.   It was only a valued ornament, which could be worn by anyone who could afford the high price (1895, pp. 175 *ff.*).

In New Guinea, along the coasts as in the little-explored interior, in the Bismarck Archipelago, the Western Solomon Islands, and sporadically farther south, rings are often the recognized currency, though fashions vary from group to group, from island to island, and even from village to village.

The best-known types are :—

1. The *Conus* arm-rings or arm-bands of South-Eastern New Guinea.
2. The *Tridacna* arm-rings of the islands to the east of New Ireland especially Nissan and Tanga.
3. The currency rings, also of *Tridacna*, from the New Georgia or Rubiana (Roviana) group in the Western Solomons.

It will simplify a confused subject if these main types are singled out here and local variations described later in the localities in which they occur.

The typical New Guinea arm-rings which play such an important part in the *kula* trade cycle (p. 18) are made of the larger shells (either *Conus millepunctatus* or less often *Conus maculatus*) by simple and laborious processes ; and while shell-money is usually women's work, arm-rings are the work of the men.

Malinowski explains why the industry is restricted to a few centres.   The shells are scattered all over the lagoon and fishing or diving for them is not especially difficult.   The main reason for the exclusive monopoly is the inertia of custom and usage, which traditionally assigns the manufacture to the natives of certain areas, who alone are in possession of the necessary magic (1922, p. 502).

The natives knock out the circular base of the shell with a heavy stone, and also knock out a circle at some distance from the base and parallel with it, by which means the broad band of shell is cut off.   The outside is polished by rubbing on a flat stone, and the

---

[1] Wilson's *klilt* is in the British Museum.   Similar dugong rings are exhibited in Berlin and Dresden.

inside on a long cylindrical stone
or a branch of coral fixed in a
cleft stick (Fig. 43). The largest
and most valuable are large
enough to be worn on the upper
part of a man's arm, but few
attain this size, and value depends
as much on added decorations as
on dimensions.

The main centre of production is in the Trobriands, and
the finished rings travel along the
coasts of New Guinea into the
Papuan area, being used in trading for sago, as well as for wives
and canoes. Finsch describes
the making of them also at Port
Moresby, where the shells are
not abundant, and have to be
imported from the East. A good
ring would buy 300 or more
pounds of sago, and was worth
25s. to 30s. (1888–93, p. 314: cf.
Schneider, 1905, p. 68; Seligman, 1910, p. 513). Local variations in *Conus* arm-shell-rings
used in exchanges in the Fly
River and Torres Straits are
described below (pp. 172 ff).

To the east of New Ireland
lie the islands of Tanga, Aneri
and Nissan, in a row. Both
Nissan and Tanga (and probably
Aneri also) are notable for their
shell arm-rings used for trading
with the mainland, and although
the material is the same on all
the islands, the processes of
manufacture and the products
are very different.

The giant clam, *Tridacna
gigas*, provides ample material,
one shell often being several feet
across, and several hundred-
weight in bulk. On Nissan the

FIG. 43.—Rubbing
stone for shell arm-
ring, New Guinea

technique suggests that of stone rather than of shell.   A thick piece
is chosen, broken roughly into shape, and the centre is pecked,
hammered or pounded out with hard stone or shell, or it may be
bored with a piece of pumice fixed at the end of a stick.   The result
is a solid heavy ring, more like a holed stone than an arm-ring,
and of no possible use as an ornament.   Pounders and rings in
various stages of manufacture are on view in the Field Museum
at Chicago. (Lewis, 1929, p. 10, Pl. ; II *cf.* Parkinson, 1907,
pp. 495–6, Pl. XXXV).

At Tanga another method is used.   Here was the most important
centre for rings of high value.   The shell, after the preliminary
breaking up and pounding into shape, was bored by twisting on the
end of a stone shaped like a blunt-headed axe-head, fixed at the end of
a bamboo stake planted in the ground.   When a hole had thus been

FIG. 44.—Tanga arm-ring. (⅝ size)

made a special stone tool fixed in a piece of bamboo was used to
grind it out to the required size, and a large round stone ground
down the edges.   The Tanga ring was not yet finished.   The outer
edge is not flat or convex, as in the Nissan or the New Georgian
arm-rings, but has a deep groove made by rubbing on a stone shaped
for the purpose.[1]   This external groove is useful in the case of
smaller rings worn in the distended earlobe, but has no functional
value in arm-rings.   It is found again in the arm-rings of the
South-Eastern Solomons, (possibly influenced by the Tangan
type).

The multi-grooved or fluted Tangan arm-rings (Fig. 44) are of
a different shape, and of even higher value.   These are wide or
narrow bands, 1 to 2, sometimes more inches (25–50 mm.) deep,
but ground very thin, only about ¼ inch (5 mm.) thick.   They are
distinguished by a number of conspicuous parallel grooves on the

[1] Lewis, 1929, p. 10, Pl. II, Figs. 4–8, illustrates the set of implements
used.

outer surface.   McCarthy figures one (1935, p. 388, Fig. 8) [1] which would buy 500 pounds of sago in New Britain (*cf.* Parkinson, 1907, p. 303, and Petri, 1936, p. 537).

Rings are synonymous with wealth in the Solomons, as in Beowulf, and the more golden the shell the more valuable the ring. Here, also, the material is provided by the giant clam *Tridacna gigas.* Rings made of the yellower fossil shell are more highly valued, and the yellowest parts near the hinge most highly of all.

The general name for these shell-rings is *poata* [2] which also means money in the Western Solomons, and the most important centre of their distribution is in the New Georgia or Rubiana (Roviana) group of islands.   The older and more valuable are called *bakia* (Pl. 7), and narrower cheaper ones, either *hokata* or just *mbokolo*, the name for arm-rings in general.   Smaller rings of the type worn pendant on the chest are also *bakia*, if they are a rich yellow.   When these are mounted, bound round with red plaited grass, [3] these are ornaments, rather than currency, though Coote calls them ' legitimate coins ' (1883, p. 146), and a fine one, collected by Ribbe in Choiseul is in the Münzkabinett in Berlin.

The plain arm-rings are used for buying food and articles of ordinary daily use, but the older ones have exaggerated values.   A single one would purchase a wife or 1,000 coconuts, and on Florida Coote assessed a *bakia* as worth a head, a very good pig or a middling youth.

The method of making these rings is slow and laborious.   A piece of shell is roughly sawn into a circle by means of a strip of fibre (sometimes stretched on a bow ; *cf.* Schneider, 1905, p. 82, Fig. 27, from Ribbe's sketch) assisted by sand and water.   Nowadays wire is often used instead of fibre.   A hole is pecked or hammered out [4] nearer the centre, first on one side then on the other, and when made, the cord or wire is passed through and the inner circle sawn out. The ring is then placed on a horizontal bar and ground down with sand and water or shark skin inside and out (Schneider, p. 84, Fig. 29).

Rivers brought back examples of arm-rings finished and

[1] McCarthy also figures on the same plate an extraordinary Solomon Island currency arm-ring (Fig. 2), with an outline like a large cotton-reel, 5 inches high and 5½ inches in diameter.   There are five of them in the Australian Museum, probably from Ulawa.

[2] The names of these *Tridacna* shell-rings are often confused.   Compare the accounts of Coote (1883), Schneider and Ribbe (1905), Rivers (1914) and Hocart (1922).

[3] Schneider's illustration (p. 89, Fig. 32) is upside down.

[4] Schneider figures (p. 83, Fig. 28) a stone hammer fastened by rattan vithes to a flexible wooden handle, used for making the rings ' a typical Stone Age implement ', as he terms it.   A number of these were collected by Rivers, but they are all labelled ' nut-crackers '.   The stone hammers used for arm-ring making are heavier and are held in the hand.

6

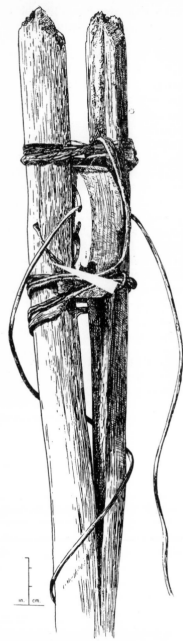

half-finished from Eddystone Island (Narovo) in the New Georgian (Rubiana) group. Fig. 45 shows a small ring fixed in a cleft stick for the sawing process, and the strip of fibre in place. (If neatly sawn out, the centre makes a convenient ear-plug.) For currency, the inner edges are left squared, but when the rings are to be worn on the arm the angles are ground down on a cylindrical stone similar to that used for grinding the *Conus* rings (Fig. 46.)

The rings are very varied in size, symmetry, thickness and values, and though they are not associated with secret societies, they enter largely into the economic and ceremonial

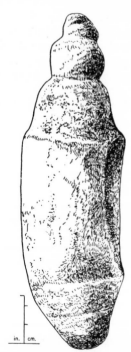

FIG. 45.—Shell arm-ring construction, Solomon Islands

FIG. 46.—Rubbing stone for arm-ring, Solomon Islands

life of the natives, as gifts, payments for services rendered, presentations to the living and more particularly to the dead, besides being amassed as wealth. Their abundant variety can be seen in Hocart's illustrations of offerings at skull houses on Eddystone (1922, pp. 71–112).

Farther south, rings lose any currency use with the exception of the Erromanga *navela* in the New Hebrides (Pl. 7).

Farther south again, in New Caledonia, *Conus* arm-rings of the New Guinea type were formerly worn, and decorated with strings of the flying-fox fur associated with money ; but, although Sarazin calls them ' *Geld-Surrogate* ' there is no evidence of their ever having been regarded as anything more than valued ornaments, and their use even as ornaments has by now almost entirely disappeared (1929, pp. 171, 183).

Throughout almost the whole of Melanesia the pig, and especially the male pig,[1] is the most highly valued and treasured beast. All the thoughts, cares and aspirations of the native centre round it, for by its means he can satisfy all his desires. He can therewith clear an enemy out of the way, he can buy many wives, he can rise to the highest social grades, and he can, with enough pigs, secure Paradise. No wonder that it is thought an honour for little girls to be called pig-nose, pig-tail or pig's-trotter.

The place of pigs in Melanesia compares naturally with that of cattle in Africa. They are a symbol of wealth, possession gives prestige, they play a large part in atoning for offences and in payments for wives. ' Pigs so often form part of the price paid for any valuable object,' says Seligman (1910, p. 517), ' that they may almost be regarded as currency.'

In Africa cows' tails are proudly worn and horns have magical virtues. In the Pacific pigs' tails are less decorative, but they are added to adornments as well as to shell-money strings. These are the ordinary tails of undistinguished pigs. Boars with tusks are on a far higher plane and tusks are artificially deformed to increase the distinction. The upper canines are knocked out and the tusks, having nothing to stop them, keep on growing and curving spirally. In time they may pierce the animal's jaw forming one complete spiral and start off on another. The more spirals, the higher the value. A double- or triple-circle tusker is renowned far and wide, and people make long journeys and pay entrance fees to see the sight. These animals are destined for sacrifice in connexion with the men's societies, and although a circle-tusker is usually beyond price, the lesser grades have relative values depending on the growth of the tusks and the prospect of the animal's longevity, ranging from about £4 up to £15 or £20. The lesser tuskers are essential in

[1] See fn., pp. 92–3.

'bride-price', in fines and compensations and in death ceremonies; they are paid to skilled workers, especially rainmakers and sorcerers, who can increase the crops; they are also used as currency in exchange for special products of neighbouring islands (Layard, 1940, Chap. X).

In the New Hebrides only the live animal can be considered as money, and though, after its death, the tusks are preserved and may be worn as ornaments they have no commercial value. Farther north, in the Torres Islands, the jaws with tusks *in situ* are an accepted form of currency. The tusks are not only ornaments, they have a trading value in New Guinea. They are carried along the Gulf in the pottery trade and they form part of the price of a canoe in the Massim district (Seligman, 1910, pp. 534–6). An unusual ornament of split, though not artificially deformed, tusks was a medium of exchange on the Sepik in Mandated Territory.[1]

Other teeth used as money are those of porpoise, dog, cuscus (so-called 'opossum' or 'kangaroo'), *Pteropus* or fruit-eating bat, commonly called flying-fox, cachalot (or sperm) whale and fish. These are used freely for ornament, and usually have a barter or currency value throughout Melanesia, New Guinea and Torres Straits. Here and there they are used like shells or shell-money for ordinary daily purchases.

Each of these animals can be treated separately, beginning with the porpoise.

Porpoise teeth have been collected 'as currency' in the Gilberts, and, together with dogs' and cuscus' teeth, in New Britain, and they are used as small change in the Southern Solomons. The 'string' here is usually 100, which forms the unit, and has the same name (*ha'a*) as the shell-money string. Four-in-a-bunch is a convenient 'coin' for small purchases, and a single tooth would buy 10 coconuts. Hopkins (1928, p. 240) calculated their value in English money as 10 to the shilling.

Porpoise, cuscus, bat and fish teeth are often bound on to cord, projecting at intervals, and such bands may be ornaments or currency. In Buka, Northern Solomons, strings of the valuable *imun* are made of porpoise and of bats' teeth (Pl. 10, Figs. 2, 5). The porpoise is peculiar in having a large number of even teeth, some 80 to 100, so they are not difficult to collect and to match in bunches or strings.

Dogs' teeth are more valuable, as only the canines or those immediately behind the canines are used. Finsch describes dogs' teeth in New Guinea as equal to 'large silver coins' (1888–93, p. 303). Coote goes further and calls them 'the gold of the coinage' in the Solomons, and gives the following scale:

[1] Petri (1936, p. 544) denies any currency value to boars' tusks.

10 coconuts = a string of ' white ' money or a flat stick of tobacco
10 strings of ' white ' money = 1 string of ' red ' or one dog's tooth
10 strings of ' red ' money = 40 porpoise teeth

(1883, p. 147)

The ratio was very variable, depending on the whiteness and condition of the teeth and their rarity in different islands.   Ivens says that the teeth are extracted after death.   Hopkins describes how the unfortunate animal was buried up to its neck in the sand, while the teeth were hauled out.   He also reports the slump in value after a rabies scare in Sydney, when all stray dogs were rounded up and killed, and the teeth exported to the Solomons (1928, p. 249).   As only 4 teeth are provided by the dog, the unit is naturally 4, and this probably influenced the four-to-the-bunch unit of porpoise and flying fox.   In Northern New Guinea the numeral system is based on the dogs' teeth, as 4 = a dog ; 8 = two dogs, &c.[1]   Dogs' teeth

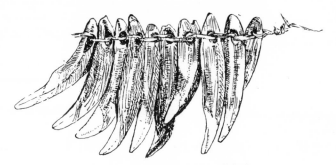

FIG. 47.—Dogs' teeth, New Britain

were used for barter and trading in Torres Straits, taking part with boars' tusks in the canoe trade (p. 17) and they were also prominent in the *kula* trade of South-East New Guinea (p. 18).   They are used along the North Coast of New Guinea in trading for sago, pots and pigs.[2]   Dogs are rare in the Bismarcks and their teeth are of high value ; a string of 30 called *rongei na gauni* (a portion of which is drawn in Fig. 47) comes from Sag-sag on the extreme West.   Their essential part in the ' bride-price ' in the Admiralties has been referred to (p. 117) above.

Cuscus teeth are used singly or in bunches, like those of porpoises, but more often they are made up into strings, firmly bound on to a cord, and worn as ornaments.   Necklaces of these occur in the South of New Ireland, and across Duke of York to New Britain, and in the Blanche Bay district under the name of *angut* they are used

[1] Hans Nevermann, 1933, *cf.* review in *Anthropos*, 1936, p. 289.
[2] P. J. Schmidt, *Anthropos*, 1923-4, p. 723.

together with *diwarra* in trading.   The teeth are also found inserted singly at intervals to divide lengths of shell-money (Parkinson, 1907, p. 494).

McCarthy (1935, Fig. 3) illustrates a string in the Australian Museum collected at Bougainville.

The fruit-eating bats, called from their foxy faces and colour flying-foxes, have only 2 teeth more than Man, but they are all much the same in shape and size and are used as ornament, while teeth as well as hair figure largely in currency.[1]   The teeth are easily recognized by the flattened-out crown and marked longitudinal grooves.   In New Ireland strings of projecting bats' teeth bound on a cord called *agut* or *angut*, are used for buying nets and weapons, and Petri illustrates a string from Nissan (1936, p. 543).   In the

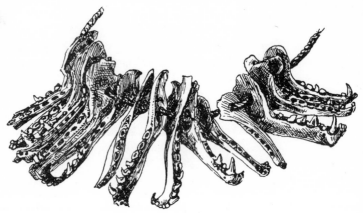

FIG. 48.—Flying fox jaws, Fiji

Solomons the teeth are pierced like those of dogs and porpoises, and bunched in fours for small change.   They are also strung with porpoise teeth or with fish vertebrae.   A string of the latter has not only currency value, but is used in ritual, being worn on the arm as a sign of peace at a peace-making ceremony on San Cristoval (H. Drew).

Fish teeth, being very small, are usually bound on to a cord, like porpoise, cuscus and bats' teeth, either in short strings of necklace length, or in long strings like shell-money.   They are of low value, 4,000 being quoted, together with pigs and shell-money as the price of a white man's head in the Solomon Islands some years ago (Hopkins, 1928, p. 241).   They are useful for distribution, as coppers with us ; the boys of the bridegroom's village have a custom

[1] A string of the jaws, with some of the teeth in place, was collected as currency in Fiji, and is now in the Pitt Rivers Collection (Fig. 48).

of shooting arrows at the wedding party from the bride's village, just to frighten and annoy them, until bought off by payment of a fish's tooth (Codrington, 1891, p. 238 *fn.*). The more valuable *imun*,[1] the native money of Buka and Northern Bougainville, is made of fish teeth as well as of small porpoise teeth, bound on to a length of cord, and covered with red ochre.

The sperm whale or cachalot has a number of large teeth, maybe 50, in its lower jaw, and these were among the most valued ornaments and presents in Eastern Micronesia. Bored as pendants, they are found among the ruins of Ponape and Kusaie, belonging to the same early culture stage as the shell-disks, and tongue-shaped pieces ; and they are so frequently attached to fathoms of the valuable red shell-money that they have become associated with money transactions. Owing to this association and to their use throughout Melanesia in present-giving and exchange they have been collected as ' money ' in the Gilberts and the Solomons, as well as in Fiji (Pls. 4, 5) where *tambua* play so important a part in native ceremony and social life.

The white man's toast ' Women, wine and song ' is rendered by the hill men of Fiji as ' *Tambua, yangona* [*kava*] and pigs '.

Brewster describes the place that *tambua* take in Fijian eyes.

With constant oiling and polishing they assume a very handsome appearance and in the eyes of the Fijians, unacquainted with gold and precious stones, they seemed the most beautiful things in the world. When Great Britain assumed the reins of government the native officials were paid regular salaries in sterling coin of the realm. One of these [officials] requested that his recompense might be made in *tambua* as in his estimation they were much more chief-like than mere money. He added that in the days of his unregenerate youth he had assisted in the capture of a trading brig which had a certain amount of gold coin on board. Not understanding its value then, he and his companions utilized the coins in matches at ' ducks and drakes ', which the Fijians play in the same way as we do, thus dissipating their fortune according to our own homely proverb (1922, p. 17).

The shell-money commonly called *diwarra*, which dominates native life and thought in New Britain, is there called *tambu*, the Melanesian form of the familiar *tabu* of Polynesia (which we have adopted, limiting its scope, in our word taboo) ; and *tambua* is the Fijian equivalent, meaning something holy or sacred. These teeth are surrounded with ' a subtle aura . . . breathing of mystery and religion'; they are treasured, kept in special baskets, only taken out occasionally to be oiled and polished and admired.

Hardly any act of ceremony is possible without the exchange of

---

[1] Portions of the strings collected by Miss Blackwood are reproduced with her permission in Pl. 10 from *Both Sides of Buka Passage*, 1935, Pl. 67. McCarthy illustrates a similar string from the Australian Collection, 1935 (Fig. 1).

tambua. When a youth seeks a wife, the request must be accompanied by the presentation of a whale's tooth, and its acceptance constitutes a binding contract of marriage. Should it be desirable to get an obnoxious person put quietly out of the way, *tambua* are employed to effect the purpose. Their acceptance implies consent to the request and then the bargain must be carried out with the strictest honour. They are associated with primitive cults and offered at the *tambutambu* or Holy of Holies in the ancient stone-enclosed *nang-a* dedicated to ancient rites. Nowadays they are presented to distinguished visitors. But, as explained above (pp. 110-11), they are not properly included in primitive money.

The use of cloth as currency in Oceania shows no likeness to its use in Africa, save that it is sporadic in both areas.

In Africa native cloth was a common object of barter, and here and there developed into token-money before the coming of trade-goods. The loom was an early introduction, and there was no obstacle to its spread throughout the continent.

In Oceania its progress was very different, and weaving only gained a precarious foothold in a few islands. Its conjectural route from the mainland to Micronesia and Melanesia is by way of the Pelews and the Carolines and then southward through the Mort-locks to San Matthias and Squally Island to the north of the Bismarck Archipelago. The native loom vanished from the Pelews and most of the Caroline Islands, though fine woven strips are worn as girdles in Kusaie in the east and the mats of Yap (p. 147) may mark a stage in the migration.[1] It did not establish itself on the main islands of the Bismarcks [2] or the Solomons but proceeded by marginal islands to the east of the chain to Santa Cruz and the Banks' Islands, and trickled on to the most northerly of the New Hebrides, where traces of its former existence can be detected (Rivers, 1914, II, p. 444, and Pl. VIII).

In spite of their novelty or rarity in Oceania woven mats or strips can seldom be included in a list of primitive currency. The beautifully made girdles of Kusaie, the finest to be seen in Oceania, were made for presentation and exchange rather than for use, for the idea of money had scarcely been born in these scattered Eastern Micronesian islands (Sarfert, 1919, p. 197). The idea was already familiar on San Matthias (also called Musau Island), north of the Bismarck Archipelago. San Matthias is best known by currency collectors for its effective strung beetle-leg money made of the brilliant peacock-blue joints of a member of the *Buprestidae* family

---

[1] *Cf.* Finsch, 1888–93, pp. 343–7 ; Ling Roth, 1917, pp. 356 *ff.*, with map.

[2] There is a loom in the British Museum, which is said to have come from New Britain.

strung either on stiff fibre (colour plate facing page 184) or on softer two-ply twine.   One fathom equals a mark or a chicken.

But San Matthias also has a form of currency in woven girdles (Pl. 8, Fig. 3), similar to those of Kusaie, though with less elaborate patterns, very finely woven with thread-like *Pandanus* fibres dyed red and orange.   Parkinson describes and illustrates these girdles (1907, p. 320, Figs. 3–5, Pl. 55), but does not suggest that they were ever used as currency.

The loom established itself firmly in the Santa Cruz group and the plain currency mats, which are never opened, and the simple apparatus for making them, together with the narrow variegated strips like book-markers, of no practical use, are commonly found in museums.

Trading in these islands is mainly by barter, notably the exchange of Nitendi sago for Reef Island girls to be trained as village prostitutes, yet there is a variety of currency, more varied than in many of the larger groups.

The ' feather-money ' (Pl. 9) is the best known, and the most effective ; the woven mats and strips are unique ; but shell-money strings are also used, besides tooth-money, turtle shell-rings, and rolls of sinnet.   The mats are made of banana stem, beaten out like barkcloth, scraped, the fibres dried in the sun, and combed out.   They are about a yard square, but they are never unfolded or used.   Neatly folded up and tied, with the fringes tucked inside, they form units of currency (*cf.* Speiser, 1916, p. 192, Fig. 38). The narrow strips for smaller change have characteristic patterns in overlaid wefts of blackened banana fibre.   These are very varied with fringed ends, and one of average size and pattern is illustrated (Fig. 49).

The loom may have reached as far south as the New Hebrides, but it has long ago disappeared.   In the north-eastern islands where there is no feather-money and little or no shell-money, plaited mats

FIG. 49.—Mat-money, Santa Cruz

are the recognized currency. These are long and narrow, made of finely split Pandanus leaves, plaited in various designs, mostly in diagonal stripes and chevrons, dyed with red, and on Maewo (Aurora) and Oba (Aoba) they have fine openwork patterns at the ends resembling Indonesian technique. As the women are the mat-makers and mats represent wealth the number of a man's wives adds to his prestige, though in some islands mat-makers may be hired to add to the store. It is not always easy to distinguish between mats made for use and mats made for exchange, but in many of the islands money-mats are entirely distinct. They are made solely for money and used in trading, for buying pigs, for buying wives, and, with pigs, for buying steps in the secret societies ; they are essential in ceremonial presentation besides being used in funeral rites.

The mats, their estimation and their uses differed in different islands. In Raga (North Pentecost) finely made mats (*bwana*) were worth about 5*s*. and 100 would be equal in value to a boar with circular tusks. In Oba (Leper's Island) size mattered more than elegance and the actual condition of the mats was of no importance,

the ancient and rotten ones which have long hung in the house are very choice, though the value still goes by the number of folds. A rich man will keep 50 mats and more in his house, hung up and decaying, a proof of ancient wealth. Mat money is also lent at interest, and so becomes a source of wealth ; there is no fixed rate of increase, the lender gets what he is able to insist upon up to a double return (Codrington, 1891, p. 324).

Some of these mats may be 100 fathoms long and worth some £12.

In Maewo (Aurora), where the mats with openwork ends are made, there are special huts in which these are kept and allowed to rot. Coote describes them (1883, p. 65) :

From the roof of the hut were suspended 8 or 10 mats, their sizes as they hung down from the beam being about 2 feet by 15 inches. They reached within a foot of the ground and under them a small wood fire is kept ever burning. In course of time the mats become coated with shining black incrustation, which gradually accumulates in such a quantity that it hangs down in stalactic forms called by the natives ' breasts '. The fire, it will be seen, requires very constant looking after for if it becomes at all large, the mats would be set alight, and if it went out, the process of coating them would be arrested. A man has therefore always to be watching these curious moneys and it is the time thus spent on them that makes them of value. This kind of money is, as far as we could learn, only current in the matter of club advancement. A fairly old mat is worth as much as a large boar with finely curved tusks. Of all the forms of money which I have seen this is certainly the most curious, for it cannot be carried about, and is never moved, even when it passes from one owner to another.

A form of mat-money made in the same way and smoked over fires (called *mangau* on Vao, *ni-mbwen* on Atchin) is used also in the Small Islands off the North-East Coast of Malekula and on the adjacent mainland. These mats are also used for wrapping up dead bodies for burial. Speiser records that when (after some months) the flesh has decayed the mats are dug up, rolled up and used as money (1923, p. 274, Pl. 75, Fig. 6). These special mats are quite plain and very narrow, only 6–8 inches wide, with fringes 2 or 3 feet long, like those that the women wear on their heads when mourning for their dead husbands. For currency they are tied up with coconut string with the fringes hanging down on either side (Pl. 8, Fig. 2). In the Small Islands off Malekula these mats are inferior in value to pigs and are used in the lesser types of ritual exchange and as small change in cases where payment in pigs would be too high. They are never undone and pass from hand to hand until the fringes have worn away and the mats are considered valueless (J. W. Layard).

Matwork or plaitwork provides currencies of somewhat similar type in the Marshalls and in the Solomons.

In the Marshalls it is in the form of a long tube, *ihrik*, of fine cylindrical plaitwork in black and white palm leaf strips in checker-work patterns alternating with bands, over a foundation of twisted coconut fibre cord (Fig. 50). This is measured by the fathom and many fathoms may be worn coiled round the waist as a girdle. Short lengths can be cut off and used in exchanges of small value.

The same technique of cylindrical plaitwork in short, stiffer lengths and in gaudier colours is used in the Solomons for nose-sticks or small

FIG. 50.—*Ihrik*, plaited belt, Marshall Islands

change. These are illustrated by Dupuy (1927, p. 753) and McCarthy (1935, Fig. 10).

The most familiar example of plaitwork currency is the shield used as the equivalent of a wife or £5 on Guadalcanar (Pl. 8, Fig. 1) (*cf.* Ling Roth, 1908, Fig. 5).

A girdle in the form of a hank of soft black cord is used as currency in Matty Island to the south-west of the Admiralties (Fig. 51). Chinnery who gave this to the Cambridge Collection says that it is very rare and expensive, being worth about £5 in

FIG. 51.—Matty Island belt

English money. The soft two-ply foundation is bound spirally with very fine blackened coconut fibre wound so tightly that it makes a cord of only a millimetre thick, and the spirals are so nearly parallel that the effect is almost that of a string of tiny black beads.[1]

A coil of red cord, *dorei*, made in the same way is currency in Dutch New Guinea. The foundation of soft fibre is the same but the spiral strip is slightly wider, made of a leaf, red on one side, and the effect is that of bright shiny red string.

In Santa Cruz rolls of sinnet are units of currency.[2] The coconut fibre is plaited in a three-ply plait, and wound diagonally as balls of string are usually wound in European fashion, making a solid block some 7 inches (18 cm.) across and 4 inches (10 cm.) deep.

In New Caledonia and the Loyalties string made of the fur of the fruit-eating bat or 'flying-fox' may be regarded as currency, as it is not only used by itself in short lengths, but is invariably attached or added to 'heads of money', shell-money strings, strings of beads and purses (Pl. 17). It is made by twisting the fur from under bats' ears in between the strands of a fine two-ply cord, the whole making a fluffy or woolly looking string (*cf.* Codrington, 1891, pp. 324–5).

Barkcloth represented wealth in Fiji, whether piled up in the owner's hut, or wound round and round his person. Pieces were also used for presentation or exchange there as in Samoa. Pieces were also used for presentation among the Baining in New Britain. These are long narrow girdles decorated with bold patterns in black, yellow and red worn by

[1] A similar string in the Horniman Museum is labelled Aua Island.
[2] They are used in 'payment for the woman' in Tikopia (Firth, 1936, pp. 6, 551–2).

candidates at the end of the initiation ceremonies, and also worn at dances.

The predominance of mat-money in the Northern New Hebrides is attributed to Polynesian influence and the feather-money of the Banks' Islands and Santa Cruz is probably due to the same culture contact.

Feathers are so generally used in the decoration of uncivilized man that they are common objects of organized barter in many parts of Oceania, though they scarcely cross the borderline into currency save in two or three areas. Cassowary feathers and bird of Paradise plumes are 'presents' in the Torres Straits canoe trade ; they are traded widely in New Guinea, and are added to the shell ornaments in the 'bride-price' (*cf.* Seligman, 1910, pp. 94, 535).

Feathers are still more highly valued in Polynesia and are conspicuous in present-giving from Hawaii to New Zealand. This explains why 'feather-money' is found only on the islands nearest to Polynesia, the Banks' and Santa Cruz, possibly spreading to the nearest islands of the New Hebrides.

Codrington described the *wetapup* of the Southern Banks' Islands.

In Santa Maria and Meralava, where the *som* shells are not found, feather-money of a special kind is in use. The little feathers near the eye of fowls are bound on strings and generally dyed a fine crimson.[1] These are used as necklaces or anklets, by way of ornament and distinction, but also pass very much in the way of money (1891, p. 324).

The red-feather-money coils *tan*, *ta* or *tavan* (Pl. 9) of Santa Cruz are among the more sensational of the 'curiosities of currency' in the South Seas, and much has been written about them. The last word has been said by Beasley who minutely describes the coils, the eleven grades of value, the process of making, and the accompanying objects, summarizing (and criticizing) earlier authorities (1936, pp. 379–92).

In structure each unit of feather-money is composed of a long belt formed of fibre rolled over two strong cords and two weaker middle cords as a base. This belt throughout its whole length is composed of tile-shaped overlapping scales of dove feathers, and these scales have again attached to their upper surfaces delicate red feathers. . . . The ends are bound with pieces of palm leaf and braided cord work running to a point which terminates in bunches of fibre, and two cords which are themselves fastened to the spirals of bark on which the coil is wound. Attached to the coil are pigs' teeth and certain stones which have a religious signification, and are said to be worth more than the money itself (pp. 380–1).

An average coil made of about 1,800 overlapping scales (*lendu*) is about 30 feet (10 m.) long, wound in double spirals of 6 turns each

[1] Nowadays longer and coarser feathers are used.

on to circular drums of bark. The little honey-bird *manga* (*Myzomela cardinalis*) which supplies the red feathers is the size of a sparrow and mostly black, with red only on head and breast, and 400 to 600 birds are needed to make a good coil.[1] This takes at least a year to make and the value is not less than £12. In 1932 there were only 10 natives on Santa Cruz who could make the coils, and as it is a skilled art, descending from father to son, and sons can now make money more easily by other means, the art will probably disappear. Speiser, writing in 1916, believed that no new coils were being made even then.

Although this feather-money is prominent throughout the group of islands and beyond, and the whole life of the natives is centred in it, it is used more for prestige and for ostentation than for trading.

The feathers themselves are articles of trade, and the small pieces (*lendu*) can be used as small change. But coils are too valuable to be expended save in transactions of high importance such as the purchase of large ocean-going canoes (in earlier days), marriage payments,[2] and fines for fornication. On Vanikoro a good wife was worth as much as a small canoe, that is 10 coils, possibly not all of first-rate quality, but among outlying islands the price would drop to perhaps half this. There are no settled prices and a tremendous amount of haggling goes on, the least sign of wear being hotly discussed, and exaggerated by the prospective purchaser. When worn, the coils are of little value, small worn coils being worth no more than 6*d.*

Accompanying the coils are objects which Beasley, for want of a better word, calls 'stretchers'[3] whose presence he says 'has not so far been accounted for' (p. 390). These objects found with the coils appear to have no functional purpose, and their shapes are very varied, sometimes merely a pronged stick in Y shape, sometimes broad flat slats of wood. The ones in the British Museum (illustrated in Pl. 9) are described as 'unique in that they consist of a pair of flat boards decorated with tassels of [*coix*] seeds[4] for use as charms, and have typical Santa Cruz painted motifs in black, white and red'. There is a similar pair of these with the coil in the Cambridge collection.

---

[1] The birds are attracted by call on to a gummed twig, but they are not necessarily killed; they may be plucked and released.

[2] Nowadays 'bride-price' is no longer paid in feather-money, but in tobacco, the amount rising to as much as two chests, worth £14 (Speiser, 1916, p. 202).

[3] The name 'stretcher' should, however, be reserved for the tenter-hooks or gauges made of bats' bone, notched at the ends used to keep the parallel cords evenly apart.

[4] *Coix* seeds were also used as currency. *Cf.* those collected by Codrington in the Pitt Rivers Museum.

iv. MICRONESIA

The Micronesian Islands speckle a stretch of more than 45 degrees across the Pacific, from the Pelews and Carolines in the west, to the Marshalls, Gilberts and Ellice in the east. Their early history is vague and relics of former glories are largely unexplored and unexplained, but there is evidence that navigation and trade were highly developed, and shell-currencies are found throughout. There is naturally great diversity over the immense and scantily habitable area, and there is notable contrast between the eastern and western island groups. While the eastern islands have shell-money strings and little or nothing else ; in the west currency includes the famous large stones (fae, fé), mysterious beads of legendary origin, mother-of-pearl shell, turtle shell, and perhaps mats. The Carolines, in particular, appear to have been on the highway of cultural streams, and to have formed stepping-stones for many adventurers into the Pacific.[1]

When Kubary was exploring the islands towards the end of last century he found that although everywhere trade goods were displacing the natural island barter of the South Seas, Micronesia, being more isolated and less profitable, suffered less than Polynesia from the influence of European civilization. The usual native trading was still going on with turmeric powder, ornaments of coconut shell, and strings of shell-money, the latter regarded more as ornament than as currency. Truk (Ruk) was the centre of trade in the Central Carolines, as Yap of the western group. Generally speaking the islanders needed no money ; they were self-supporting and self-sufficient. There was little specialization in industry and no development of luxury objects. Nevertheless, on Yap money played a large part. As far as the necessities of life are concerned, food, shelter and clothing are abundantly provided by nature and man has enough for his needs. But if he wants to get a wife, to found a family, and to become a member of the community, he must have money or the local equivalent of it. Marriage can only be achieved by payments and interchange of objects of recognized value ; these are essential in social life from birth to death ; and the existence of the community depends on the wealth of the heads of families which compose it. On Yap, therefore, which lies in so favourable a position in the Western Carolines, currency developed in many forms with a highly complicated monetary system.

Broadly speaking, the shell-money in Micronesia, as elsewhere, may be classed as ' red ' (which generally means orange-pink, and fades sadly with age and exposure), and ' white ' (which includes yellows and greys), the ' red ' being the more highly valued. This

[1] *Cf.* map Heine-Geldern, 1932.

estimation may be due to the greater difficulty in collecting red shells and their conseq ient rarity (*Spondylus* and *Chama pacifica* are both deep-water shells); it may be due to the universal human preference for coloured over non-coloured, and to red in particular; or it may be related to the world-wide appreciation of the colour symbolic of blood.

It is difficult, and certainly unwise, for a non-expert to attempt to distinguish between *Spondylus* and *Chama pacifica*, or any other sources of the ' red ' strings (*cf.* Schneider, 1905, p. 7), save by noting that *Chama pacifica* appears superficially to be a little brighter and a little rarer than *Spondylus*. The latter has three special centres in Oceania : Micronesia (especially Truk) where it dominates ornaments almost everywhere ; South-East New Guinea, spreading north and south along the coasts ; and Northern New Ireland, including New Hanover : but, owing to its popularity and its common use in trading, it is found many hundreds of miles from its island homes.

Usually the pieces of shell are chipped and rounded in the normal ' South-Sea ' or *sapi-sapi* pattern (p. 115), and *gau* and *sapi-sapi* are easily confused. But Micronesia shows a characteristic preference for spade- or tongue-shaped pieces which are very common in ornamental strings, and may be used for currency (*cf.* Schneider, 1905, p. 6, Fig. 1 and Pl. 2*b*).

Red shell-strings in varying forms and under varying names, of which *gau* [1] is perhaps the least unfamiliar, spread throughout Micronesia, though they are now scarcely to be found. They were already in existence at some unknown period on Ponape in the Eastern Carolines, where the disks and the spade-shaped pieces are abundant among the ruins.

It may be possible to trace them farther back, and this leads us to the mainland of Asia.

In the caves of Minh-can in the Province of Quang-binh in Annam rich Neolithic deposits have been found, including skeletons, remains of pottery, stone axe-heads and abundant ornaments of shell. The stone axes (*Schulterbeilkultur*) are of the Austroasiatic shouldered type in the lower layers, and later, quadrangular (*Vierkantbeilkultur*) or Austronesian. The abundance of the worked shells is striking. Close to a child's skull were over 400 disks, 166 pierced *Nassa* shells, 86 more with their backs broken off, and 10 pierced cowries. These were all still lying so close together that it was easy to reconstruct the strings, and they are so closely allied to the Melanesian and Micronesian strings that their relationship can

---

[1] In Ponape the shells and the strings are called *pake* ; in Yap *gau, kau, thau,* &c. ; in Truk *assang, asson, faubar* ; in the Marshalls, *aacht* ; in Uliai (Wolea) *chamotsch,* &c. &c. *Cf.* Finsch, 1888–93, Pl. VIII, Figs. 7–11 in colour ; Schneider, 1905, pp. 4–6, Pl. 1, Figs. *a, c* ; Pl. 2 ; Petri, 1936, p. 197, 2–4, and for Ponape *pake,* 1*a.*

scarcely be doubted. The *Nassa* shells with their backs broken off were prepared as for the making of *diwarra* ; the pierced disks would make the ordinary strings of shell-money.

These are not the only links with the mainland of Asia.

Heine-Geldern points out (1932, p. 553) how stone-rings are met within almost all deposits of quadrangular axe culture and the mixed culture of Further India, and can be recognized in Yang-Chao and Sha-Kuo-Tun. So it is possible that the rings of China and Further India, which were not mere ornaments but had some cult significance, and were used in presentations and as money, may be linked with the stone, bone and shell-rings in Micronesia and Melanesia, and the abnormally developed stone-money of Yap.

Thus the earliest and most widely spread forms of currency in Oceania can be traced back by those in search of cultural origin to the work of neolithic peoples of South-East Asia, and associated with the elements of the Austroasiatic-Austronesian mixed culture, which spread into the South Seas. Although little is known about the early history of the Micronesian Islands they were within the range of cultural influence from the mainland, and stone- and shell-money, the earliest types in Oceania, may have travelled by the same route followed later by the loom (Petri, 1936, pp. 553–4).

The red strings were not used as money in its ordinary sense. That would be sacrilege. They were treasured and hoarded by the chiefs of the larger districts, and were essential to their fortunes and prestige. They were only brought out in time of war or other states of emergency, and were decisive factors in negotiations for peace. On Yap the strings were amassed and used as loans, interest being paid in labour. A man, for services rendered, was privileged to borrow and wear a string for a certain number of days.

Furness, who was there early in the century, was unable to buy a good string as no one would part with one at any price.[1] But he bought an inferior one for ' the staggering sum of seven and a half dollars '. To clinch the bargain the owner told him ' Here you have the price of a murder. Offer it to a man and tell him whom you want killed, and it's done ' (1910, p. 91).

The exaggerated value of the red strings was doubtless partly due to the scarcity or absence of red shells, so that there was little chance of local manufacture. This lack has been filled of late by Japanese importations, and necklaces of *gau* strings are being turned out abundantly by the Chamorro, who have settled in Yap (Petri, 1936, p. 196).

The red strings so highly prized in the Carolines and Marshalls are seldom seen on the Gilberts, although—or perhaps because—

[1] Schneider quotes a demand of the equivalent of 1,770 marks for a string of *gau* on Yap (p. 6).

the 'red' shells, especially *Chama pacifica*, are fairly abundant there. But the Gilbert Islanders have a partiality for *tekaroro*, the effective black and white strings made of alternate disks of *Conus* and coconut (Pl. X, Fig. 6 and Fig. 52). The industry has its centre in the southern Gilberts and the strings are the usual currency of the northern Gilberts and the Marshalls (Schneider, 1905, pp. 9, 11). They are widely distributed, sometimes as currency but more often merely as ornament, and the pleasing effect of black and white strings on black skin goes far to explain their general popularity.

They were traded not only through Micronesia, but to far distant islands as well. Or there may have been various centres of manufacture.[1]

Finsch (1888–93, p. 356) describes and illustrates (Pl. VII, Figs. 1–4) four varieties. One was the regular currency on Tasman Island (also called Le Maire or Nukumaru), north of the Solomons, where, according to Parkinson, it was made (Lewis, 1929, p. 32, Pl. X, Fig. 3). Krause illustrates a string from Nissan (1906, p. 154); similar strings, doubtless brought by traders, are found on the mainland of New Britain, and a string (in the Cambridge collection) indistinguishable by the unpractised eye from *tekaroro* was collected in Fiji.

The coconut disks that provide the black for these black-and-white *tekaroro* strings have also a currency value of their own. Strings are made on Truk in the Central Carolines of a special coconut which has no kernel, called *losil* (Petri, 1936, p. 203), and the strings are called *sek* or *sak*. These appear to owe their estimation to their attractive appearance, and as they are tedious and irksome to make they are not very common, and are highly valued and traded from island to island. They find their way to Yap and take part in the inter-insular trade with the Pelews. Normally the strings are of small disks, no larger than those of shell, but there are also particularly well-made double strings of larger disks, nearly an inch across, from the same area.

FIG. 52.—*Tekaroro*, shell-money, Gilbert Islands

To-uba is the name of a very rare and attractive type of *Conus* string from the Gilberts, formerly used as currency.[2]

---

[1] Schneider, 1905, Pl. 3, illustrates eight varieties, but mostly without *Vaterlandsangabe*; cf. also Petri, 1936, p. 199.

[2] Illustrated by Finsch, 1888–93, p. 350, Pl. VII, Figs. 15, 16; Edge-Partington, I, p. 174; Schneider, 1905, p. 11, Pl. 1, *b*, *g*; Petri, 1936, p. 200, Fig. 6. Similar strings are worn as ornaments in South-East New Guinea.

The strings are made of *Conus eburneus* apices of various sizes from ½ inch to over 1 inch in diameter, and may be of girdle, necklace (Fig. 53) or only arm-band length. The disks are not strung like ordinary *Conus* tips through the central hole, but are drilled at the projecting edge of the spiral, and bound on to a cord so close together that the circles overlap.

These strings are usually classed as ornaments, which they undoubtedly are, but the trader from whom Schneider obtained his specimens said that they were in use as currency in the middle of last century, though no longer procurable. Finsch (before 1888) was able to collect only a few, as shells of suitable size were then rare.[1]

Shell-money strings, whether black-and-white *tekaroro*, or red *gau*, were used in exchanges in both Eastern and Western Micronesia,

FIG. 53.—*To-uba*, shell-money, Gilbert Islands

but in the West there are (or were) many other forms, consisting mainly of pearl shell and of turtle shell ; there are also the equivalent of ' cloth currencies ' in mats and girdles, besides the perplexing Pelew beads and the best known of all strange fashions in primitive currency, the ' stone money ' of Yap.

Pearl-shell currency played an important part in the social life of the Carolines, for position depended on its possession and distribution. All services, such as the building of a house, or of a canoe, or the laying out of a field were paid for in money, and pay-days were the occasion for feasts and for further distributions. There was even a more or less developed credit system. And while other currencies of the Carolines belonged mainly to the past, these pearl-shell forms, owing to their social function, were until lately a still living factor in native life.

Fae (*fai* or *fé*) is the name for pearl shell in Kusaie, and *fae in*

[1] Two single disks of *to-uba* are set up *obverse* and *reverse* in the Dresden *Münzkabinett*.

Kosa or ' pearl shell of Kusaie ' is the name for the ordinary piece used as currency. This is a spade- or tongued-shaped piece cut out of the central part of the shell (*Meleagrina margaritifera*). It is pierced at the end and hung on a thick cord for suspension.

The larger the piece, the higher the value, and as there is a limit to the size of the shell it was imitated in stone (the same aragonite which makes the stone-money of Yap) the ridge of the shell being reproduced in the stone. The ' coin ' in shell and its imitation in stone from the Hamburg Museum are seen in Pl. 11, Fig. 2.[1]

As these are the same shape as the taro spades of *Tridacna* shell they may be related to ' tool currencies ' ; but, as has been seen, small tongue- or spade-shaped pieces of shell, usually pierced at one end, are found together with shell disks, among remains of the early culture in the ruins of Ponape and Kusaie, and if the Yap stones are gigantic developments of the latter, these pendants may be abnormal enlargements of the former.

Pearl shell supplies a smaller currency in actual or vestigial fish-hooks. These were the most valued treasures of the Ellice Islanders, used in presentations to chiefs and dedications to the gods, and often buried with their owners. They acquired, ' as conveying a

FIG. 54.—Fish-hook, Marshall Islands

[1] Sarfert, 1919, Fig. 115 ; Petri, 1936, p. 198, Fig. 8*a*.

maximum of wealth in a minimum of space, an artificial value approximating to the coins of more advanced civilizations ' (Hedley, 1896–1900, p. 226).

In the Marshalls (as in the Solomons) fish-hook money consists in serviceable-looking hooks (Fig. 54), but in the Eastern Carolines the series passes from the backs of fish-hooks (without hooks) to breast-ornaments (*fae metmet*) with no obvious break. These are made of the hinges of the shell and belong to the same early culture as the red shell disks and the *Conus* arm-bands, but they were still in circulation in the Eastern Carolines, and especially in Kusaie, in recent years.

These ' fish-hooks ' illustrate once more the difficulty of separating currency—in the sense of useful articles used as media of exchange—and money, with merely token value. The Marshall Islands' fish-hooks have been cited as the only form of Oceanic shell-money coming under the head of *Nutzgeld* (Schneider, 1905, p. 10, Fig. 2). The Caroline *ka muäk*, which means ' fish-hook money ', have no hooks, and can scarcely be separated from the pendant *fae metmet*, which are merely ornaments.[1]

Pearl shell is less abundant in the Western Carolines than in the Eastern, so these currencies increased in value in Yap and the Pelews, and in Yap they are still in circulation. In Kusaie pearl shell is called *fae*, but in Yap it is *yar* or *gar* while the stones are *fae* (*fai* or *fé*).[2]

The shell is ground at the edge into something of a spade shape, a hole is bored near the hinge and the shell is bound on to a strong cord. These are often traded in pairs, the cord serving for the handle, or a number are attached to a cord at regular intervals Pl. 11, Fig. 1. *Yar nu ao* is a small local and lowly valued shell ; 5 or 6 are bound on to a length of cord some 5 inches (13 cm.) apart, and the whole forms the unit, called the *botha a yar*. Show strings may have as many as 200 or even 500 shells, and files of natives march along with them when presentations are to be made. This kind is used for local purchases and is commonly regarded as women's money while stone-money is that of men. Kubary recorded the payment for a pig made up of a small piece of stone-money and about 20 *yar*, and the complicated barter was often concluded by the additional make-weight of turmeric powder (1895, p. 6). A string of 6 shells is now worth about 100 coconuts, 10 packets of cheap cigarettes or 50 matches.

Yar y en a vo-tsai means ' pearl shell-money from elsewhere ', and describes the gold-lip shells (Finsch calls them *Avicula*

---

[1] Sarfert, 1919, pp. 213–16, Figs. 115–19 ; Petri, 1936, p. 198, Fig. 8*b*. *Cf.* also the series in the museums of Berlin and Hamburg.

[2] Christian derives the Kusaie *fae* (*fai*) from the Hindustani *pais*, money, introduced by Hindu-Malay pearl fishers (1910, pp. 236–7).

margaritifera, Schneider, p. 8) no longer found in the islands but imported by white traders.

Yar nu valeu or 'pearl shell-money from the Pelews', consists of shells with black rims, much more valuable, being worth 5 or 6 gold lips and 200 up to 500 of the Yap ones. These are valued according to their size, measured from the finger-tips up the arm. One of a hand's length is worth a row of *botha a yar*. Every finger width beyond this almost doubles its value (Müller-Wismar, 1917, pp. 127–8, Pl. 36, Fig. 3).

All these shells are used for the purchase of land, for payments from victims to victors after a war, and in 'bride-price'. The *mespil*, or village prostitutes, are always paid in *yar*, and it also figures largely in funeral ceremonies.

Turtleshell, owing to its pleasing appearance and to its uneven distribution, is prized by most of the Pacific Islanders, and it has been called 'money' among the Chamorro, the inhabitants of the Mariannes (Ladrones) before the coming of the Spaniards. Small disks were strung like shell-money and called *alas*. Arm-rings are often classed as currency as well as the spoons and small trays or saucers made in presses, which were valued possessions, given as bridal dower, and used by the women in trading (*cf.* Meinicke, 1875, p. 409; Petri, 1936, p. 204).

The stone-money of Yap (Pl. 12) is the best known of all the 'curiosities of currency' though the largest specimens are necessarily absent from museums. The circular wheels or mill-stones, called *fae* (variously spelt) or *palan* (the name in the Pelews), are made of a kind of limestone (aragonite) and vary in size from a few inches to 10 or 12 feet across (50 mm. to 4 m.). The rock is found on Babelthuap and other islands in the Pelews some 400 miles away, and the quarried stones are ferried across on rafts to form the Yap currency. Each stone has a hole in its centre so that it can be carried on a pole.

Why these stones should have become not merely visible signs of wealth but actual money is not clear. It has been suggested that they represent an exaggerated and overgrown form (*Wucherform*) of shell-money; that shell disks were first imitated in stone—the Kusaie stone imitations of pearl shell pendants are a parallel development—and that these grew and grew, acquiring merit and prestige, into their present size. Or they may be a local development of ring-money. Stone club-heads in disk form are still used as money in the South-West of New Britain (Thilenius, 1921, p. 16, Fig. 16, *a, b*) and with the central hole enlarged, the smaller Yap stones would be similar to the older shell-rings of the Solomons.[1] The connection

---

[1] In the Pelews the old disk beads as well as the Yap stones are called *palan* (Kubary, 1895, p. 7).

with rings is supported by Heine-Geldern's recognition of stone-rings as characteristic of the neolithic culture of South-Eastern Asia, whence the Micronesian may be derived (1932, pp. 591 *ff.*) and the two lines of evolution may be harmonized by regarding rings and disks as developing from the same original source (Petri, 1936, p. 207).

When Kubary was in Yap in 1870 the large stones were rare and represented high values. At that time there was only one German trading firm in the Carolines, whose agents on Yap did not take advantage of their favourable monopoly, and were merely amused at the ' stone-money '. Some years later came a more sharp-witted trader who, without capital and without much outlay, made a fortune where well-established firms were working at a loss. He was his own agent and he was a practical man. This was the notorious Captain O'Keefe, notorious in no better and no worse sense than the rest of the traders who exploited the Carolines for their own profit. He saw that it was cheaper to help the islanders to get their stone-money and to be well paid for it, than to leave this to others and exchange trade goods for native produce. So he bought a Chinese coasting boat, had a keel fitted, and took the native Yappers across to the Pelews. When Kubary returned to Yap in 1882 he found the German firms powerless, and their agents in deadly enmity with O'Keefe. They could do nothing while O'Keefe fetched over thousands of stones until the whole island was in his debt.

Kubary himself crossed the 400 or so miles to the Pelews (with 62 native passengers on the 60-ton schooner) and found hundreds of men at work in Koryor, one of the most important quarries. The deflation of stone-money led to appreciation of the larger stones and eagerness for ever-larger and larger examples. Stones two fathoms across were not uncommon, and the son of a Yap chieftain worked hard at a three-fathom stone, but, unluckily for him, it cracked before it was finished.

About this time a stone three hand span broad would buy a good-sized pig or 1,000 coconuts. Ten years earlier a stone scarcely twice as large was given Kubary's own name and travelled in great honour from district to district. Later, overshadowed by its gigantic rivals, it sank into obscurity (1895, pp. 4 *ff.*).

It is not only size that counts. Much depends on whiteness and on shape, and certain old stones are more highly prized than new. And values were very different on different islands. On Guam, in the Mariannes (Ladrones), a stone only 1 foot in diameter (30 cm.) was lately worth goods up to about £15. In the Pelews an ordinary waist-high specimen would be worth about 4,000 coconuts or £4. A man-high one would be worth a village or a plantation and a two-man-high one is beyond price. These would never be owned by individuals, but would be communal.

Small and portable *fae* are used for buying fish and pigs, and in the Carolines one the size of a plate would keep a family in food for a month. A lady of rank, going to market, is followed by a number of slaves, each of whom carries a large stone, some 2 to 3 feet across, supported by a bamboo pole across his shoulder. All payments for services rendered, material and spiritual, are paid in *fae*, which is also important in ' bride-price ' negotiations and in funeral ceremonies. The larger stones are stacked outside the house and theft is said to be rare. Not all of those exhibited belong to the house. Some may belong to others, but being difficult to move the owner is content with his ownership, and the stones remain where they are.

In earlier days the method of obtaining the stones was for the chief of a Yap village to give permission to a number of youths to go over to the Pelews and bring back a hundred or more stones, some large ones among them. These were exchanged on their return, so many baskets of taro per stone, until they were exhausted, the chief taking all the larger stones and a proportion of the smaller ones. The larger stones would very rarely be parted with, their chief value being the prestige acquired by the possessor. In this way all the larger villages of Yap were provided with stones, and kept the smaller ones dependent on them. Having acquired the stones they began to gamble with them. Alliances could be made, neutrals won over, wars begun and ended by means of stone-money.

There do not appear to be any traditions about the origin of the stones or of how and why and how long ago they first came over to the Carolines. Until lately they were still being quarried, but although they are still in use, it was reported in 1936 that no more were being made. The only tradition regarding them tells of the stone of enormous size that is lying at the bottom of the sea. This was being towed across to Yap some generations ago when a storm arose, and raft and stone sank to the bottom. Public opinion, however, concedes that its purchasing power is not thereby impaired, and the family is credited with the wealth just as surely as if it were gold stored in the bank. Many large stones are always stored outside the bachelors' house (*failu*) to indicate the wealth and add to the prestige of the village. When the German administrators had difficulty in enforcing labour for road-making they hit upon the ingenious plan of marking the stones with crosses to indicate that they were confiscated until the work was done. This was equivalent to utter bankruptcy for the owners ; the roads were soon made, the crosses were eradicated, and all were happy again (Furness, 1910, pp. 97–100).

The stones are not the only ' curiosities of currency ' on Yap. There are also the pestles and mortars *ma* which have no parallel as far as is known. These are often of enormous size, the mortars over 1 foot (30 cm.) high and wide, made of soft wood and thus useless as a mortar. The pestles are of *Tridacna* shell,[1] 1 foot to 2 feet (25–50 cm.) long and very heavy, the thick end just fitting into the mortar to which it is firmly bound (Pl. 11, Fig. 1). Thilenius and Müller recognize this as an exaggerated development of an original areca nut stamper, belonging to the earlier culture, for that also had a pestle made of *Tridacna* shell, though only a few inches long. Müller ranks them as wealth (*Geldwert*) though not as circulating media. They were held in high estimation and were used in distributions at funeral feasts. They probably have some symbolic meaning, as they, as well as the stones, are carved on house boards and house posts of club houses, as can be seen in the Museum für Völkerkunde, Berlin. (Thilenius, 1921, p. 16, Fig. 15 ; Müller-Wismar, 1917, p. 126. *Cf.* Petri, 1936, p. 211).

It is curious to find in Micronesia this love of the abnormally large, shown in the coconut disks, the pearl-shell currency, the pestles and mortars, and the stone-money. These exaggerations are not unknown in currency as may be seen in the stone axe-blades of New Guinea or the spearheads of Africa, but it is nowhere so remarkable as in the tiniest of all the scattered island groups of the Pacific.

Mats and woven strips are used in Micronesia as gifts, in presentations, as payments in tribute or fines, and in ' bride-price ' (Sarfert, 1919, p. 213 ; Petri, 1936, pp. 214–15). In Yap special mats called *mbul*, *ambul*, &c., are described as currency, but, says Christian (1899, p. 237), they are seldom bartered. He describes them as coarse, shaggy and white, resembling a goat or dog skin, made from the beaten-out bark of the *kal* or lemon hibiscus tree. They are not used, but are kept always rolled up in a safe corner, usually in the club-houses. Furness, however, says that they are ' woven ' of extremely fine soft threads of banana fibre, with loose ends sticking out all over them, almost like fur (1910, p. 104). Both say that the mats themselves were not visible as they were kept rolled up and enclosed in matting and were never exposed to view.[2] When used in exchange their value was estimated by diameter measured by span between thumb and forefinger, and they ranked with large sized pearl shells or good white stones. The large bundles were worth from £7 to £10.

Mat-making has been called a lost art on Yap, but it seems doubtful if mats were ever made there. The high value attached to these rolled-up treasures indicates an importation of unknown date,

---

[1] The shells are not found on Yap, but are fetched like the stones from the Pelews.

[2] One is illustrated, Pls. 36, Fig. 2, and 47, Fig. 3, Müller-Wismar, 1917, *cf.* pp. 99, 132.

though if they have never been properly seen and the technique identified it is useless to attempt to link these cryptic examples with the mat currencies of the New Hebrides or Samoa.

On Kusaie both plaited mats and woven strips are made for presentation rather than for use, and these can be used in exchanges. The Russian captain Lütke, who spent three weeks on the island in 1827–8, before the coming of the American whalers upset native economy, said that the inhabitants had as a rule no notion of trading nor even of barter, and he and his companions found it impossible to negotiate exchanges. The natives gave generously, but without apparently expecting a return present. This present-giving was the normal way of testifying friendship and welcoming visitors, and, as in the Nicobars and in Polynesia, was entirely dissociated from trade. Nevertheless, trading in pearl shell and in mats was not unknown (Sarfert, 1919, p. 213).

The *Pandanus* mats for ordinary use, which every native carries about tucked under one arm or hung on behind, are the stitched not plaited variety, and these are too humble for presentation or exchange. But plaited mats are less common and the better made ones (*saki*) are often designed more for gifts than for daily use. These are the customary presents at feasts, and, folded up, serve as pockets for other gifts, including pearl-shell money. They are often decorated along the edge with *Hibiscus* stitching in patterns which appear not to have altered in the course of a century. It was these *saki* mats which Finsch records as tribute. They were paid to the King at full moon, and might not be used by commoners (1892, p. 469). Woven girdles, of the same type, but even better craftsmanship than those of San Matthias, were also made for presentation only (Sarfert, 1919, p. 197).

The bead-money, *andauth*, of the Pelews is another mystery of the Pacific. The collection made by O'Keefe and Kubary is in the Museum für Völkerkunde, Berlin, and Kubary described 15 types and illustrated 54 beads in colour (1895, pp. 6 *ff.*). These are distinguished by material (stone, baked clay, glass) sizes, shapes and patterns, but the varieties are too many to make a general description possible.[1]

Captain Wilson of the *Antelope*, who was wrecked on the Pelews in 1783, and was the first European to reside on, if not to visit the islands, mentions the beads. Some he calls cornelian ; some he says were made by the islanders of baked earth ; some they made by grinding down pieces of glass from broken bottles off the wreck. They were used for ceremonial presentations, and he himself was

[1] Andree recognized a chevron among these beads as identical with one from the Gold Coast, and, noting the juxtaposition of beads and cowries in both areas, suggested that both were distributed by the same agency (1885, p. 110).

given two strings, one (which he illustrates) a handsome girdle of graduated red beads 'a coarse sort of cornelian'.

The different types of beads are used for different purposes. Some are for ordinary buying and selling in everyday life ; some are never in the possession of commoners, but are only owned by the richest families, carefully guarded and never exhibited. Specimens of these are said to be worth as much as 1,500 marks, but it is useless to speculate on their value, as they are 'above price'. The Pelew Islanders regard their bead-money as something sacred and derive it from supernatural sources.

Non-native theories of its derivation are various and are summarized by Petri (1936, pp. 210–11). Kubary traced the beads to an earlier culture formerly existing both in the Pelews and in Yap, derived from an Asiatic source possibly due to Malay adventurers some 300 or 400 years ago. Andree connected them with the worldwide distribution of the mysterious old trade beads found in Africa, North America and also in Merovingian graves. He traced these to Egypt and attributed the distribution to the Phoenicians. He regarded the similarity between the Pelew *baraks* (yellow) and *bunans* (red) and the old Japanese Usi-isi beads (which he calls a variety of aggry) as an indication of Japan as an intermediate link or secondary starting-point. Schmeltz rejected Japanese intervention, and attributed them to early Buddhist pilgrims from Asia. Niewenhuis recognized the identity of these beads with the old beads treasured by the Bahau and Kenyah in Borneo (*cf.* p. 261). The same types are found (he says) in Flores, and in the string of islands to the south, Sumba, Timor, Allor and Timor Laut. Roffeaer derives all these beads from the Indian factory of Cambay, north of Bombay, which was exporting beads to Greece and South Africa four centuries B.C., and maintains that the same were carried into Indonesia by Malay traders. Petri accepts this last possibility, but with caution.[1]

v. MELANESIA

A. BISMARCK ARCHIPELAGO

The second of our commercial centres in Oceania defined above (p. 118) is New Britain, in the Bismarck Archipelago, and much has been written about *diwarra* (or *tambu*),[2] which here enters so largely into the religious, social, and economic life of the people.

---

[1] If philological evidence is any guide it gives support to an Indian origin. The Indonesian name for beads is *muti*, Malay *mutija* and Sanskrit *mutja*.

[2] *Diwarra* is not its name in New Britain, where it is called *tambu* or *palatambu* ; it is called *diwarra* in the Duke of York group of islands and the name has spread with the currency. For literature see, among others,

Unfortunately the name has been used to include other, and indeed any, shell-money of Melanesia, and the label occurs on many museum specimens.

True *diwarra* (Pl. 10, Fig. 1 and Fig. 55) is made from *Nassa camelus*, a small shell, about ⅜ inch long (8–10 mm.), with a cowry-like hump on its back, which makes it nearly as high as long.

These little molluscs thrive in the mangrove swamps that surround the islands, and are especially abundant along the coast of the Nakanai district, at the north-west end of the Gazelle Peninsula. In the spring, after the north-west monsoon has subsided, men go out to collect the shells in palm leaves or sections of bamboos, and in spite of the stink (this is summarized from Schneider's account, pp. 15 *ff.*) they keep the decaying wealth in their huts. When the south-west monsoon has set in and the sea is calm to the north and north-west of New Britain, a flotilla of canoes comes from along the coast between Cape Stephen and Cape Lambert and the neighbouring islands to fetch the *palatambu*. They get out their largest

FIG. 55.—*Diwarra*, New Britain

outrigger boats, for the journey lasts a month or so, and they stack one end with trade goods, axes, knives, spades, cloth, and above all, special kinds of shell-money *pele* or *tapsoka*.

They travel day and night, hugging the shore, for it is unsafe to land save on an uninhabited island, and the trading is done in an atmosphere of suspicion and mistrust. Sometimes the exchange is made from boat to boat, out at sea, and the Nakanai people always try to pass off too large or too small shells among the right-sized ones. When the bargaining is over the laden canoes return home. Sometimes the shells are buried for a year, to destroy the occupants and improve the colour, for colour is important. To prepare the strings the shell is stuck in the cavity of a coconut shell to keep it firm, the back is then broken off with a knife (formerly with a hard shell) thus making a hole for threading and the skilled worker can prepare 20 to the minute. The shell, if it has not been buried, is still grey or brown, so it has to be bleached or scoured, until it is white. Then comes the hard task of making the finished *diwarra*. Each shell has to be forced on to the stiff strip of rattan with much patience and with fingers as hard as iron. The strips are from 1 foot to 20 inches

Romilly, 1886; Parkinson, 1907; Danks, 1888; Stearns, 1889; Schneider, 1905; Stephan, 1907; Brown, 1910; Foy, 1913; Lewis, 1929; Petri, 1936. For theories of its origin and distribution *cf.* Heine-Geldern, 1932, pp. 553 *ff.*

(30 to 50 cm.) long, and joins are made by slipping a shell over a sliced junction, and so the fathom lengths are made with 300 or 400 shells to the fathom.[1]

The shells must not touch, but must be evenly spaced a little apart. This is important, as it enables the shells to be easily counted, it enables short lengths to be broken off, and it also distinguishes true *diwarra* from mere ornament.

Short lengths obtained by work [2] or by trading or by less equitable methods were stored in decorated coconut shell bowls, with a preference of late for glass bottles, through which they could be more easily seen and more constantly gloated over. But the great ambition of every man was to collect enough to make a ring or *loloi*.[3]

For this tens or hundreds of fathoms were all joined into one long string coiled round and round and bound with leaves and rattan, looking like a stout life-belt. The *loloi* might contain 40 to 50 fathoms up to 100 or 200. A chief might have rings as large as a cart-wheel, and so heavy that they had to be slung on a bamboo pole, with two men to carry them like the stone-money of Yap. Schneider noted how handy the shape was for transport, the ring could be put over the head, and a woman fleeing from hostile attack, would fling away her children rather than her *loloi*.

Diwarra can be called a true currency, as everything purchasable could be bought with it, from wives and canoes, for 100 to 150 fathoms, to pigs, from 7 to 10, fowls, half a fathom, or vegetables for smaller fractions, market prices naturally varying from place to place and time to time. It never formed the currency on Nakanai itself, though it was used there for barter, and for ornament. Its use as money spread over the Gazelle Peninsula, and the Duke of York group, and over parts of New Ireland.

> *Tambu* or *diwarra* was the national currency just as much as the coinage of any civilized country. A man wanting betelnut would twist off a few shells and tender them as recognized payment. Fish, yams, taro, lime, bananas, puddings, birds, pigs, canoes, slaves, turtle-shell and wives all had their recognized value, and were paid for by twisting off the required number of shells or measuring off the number of fathoms agreed to as the price of the purchase (Brown, 1910, pp. 196–7).

This recognized value was, moreover, affected by the law of supply and demand as in more civilized communities, and in the

---

[1] The size of the shells and the spacing varied in different parts, hence the varied numbers of shells to the fathom counted by different collectors.

[2] A man might earn 50 fathoms during his fishing season and make 10 or 12 from his plantation (Danks, 1888, p. 315).

[3] Properly *a loloi*. Finsch says the ring is called *tambu a loloi*, the latter word meaning chief (1888–93, p. 94).

recognition of this law New Britain shows a marked contrast to Samoa. When the price of cotton rose during the American Civil War traders gave a high price for cotton. After the War, when the price fell, the Samoans let their cotton rot on the trees rather than accept a lower price. But the New Britain natives always noted the state of the market, and regulated their prices accordingly. With the coming of the whites *diwarra* did not immediately suffer eclipse like so many native currencies. The German Government wisely forbade its use by European traders, seeing that modern fishing methods would flood the market with the shells, destroy the industry and depreciate the currency ; and although it was officially prohibited in 1900, it was too firmly established in native estimation to be easily discarded. For the native conception of money differs in many ways from ours. Its main use was not as a circulating medium to facilitate exchanges ; it was not for spending, but for keeping.

All this greed for *diwarra*, which fills the *kanaka's* whole life, is all for one end, not for possession, not for comfort and luxury in this world, or to enrich his family—but for distribution at his death, so that men should bewail, praise and honour him with feasts (Schneider, 1905, pp. 36–7).

As much as 2,000 fathoms might be distributed at the death of a wealthy man. Finsch saw 20 *loloi* at a funeral. ' There are million-aires among the savages of Blanche Bay,' he says, ' and each one essays to become one, for wealth is power here, as with us.' Wars are caused and settled by *diwarra*. Theft of it, the greatest of all crimes, is punished by death ; though, in practice, life can be pur-chased by sufficient payment. With *diwarra* a man pays his fines, condones adultery (3 to 5 fathoms), and atones for murder (50 or more fathoms). A specially constructed *loloi* of colossal size was brought as compensation for the four Fijian teachers who were murdered on the island (Finsch, 1888–93, p. 94).

The position of women is influenced by the dominance of *diwarra*. It naturally provides a scale for ' bride-price ' which has a wide range, from a mere 10 to 20 fathoms (the price of a fair-sized pig) to 100 or 150 (the price of a good canoe), while a chief might pay over 200 fathoms besides much other wealth for a choice specimen. As the women make *diwarra*, they are a steady source of income. The wife may amass wealth, too, as long as it is by her own exertions ; her husband is not responsible for her delinquencies and her fines are paid, not by her husband, but by her own family. At the same time the husband can often drain his wife's savings by trumping up accusations of adultery (Burger, 1913, p. 26).

Lastly, but this is the most important of all its functions, *diwarra* is essential in all the activities of the ' secret societies '. A candidate has to collect several fathoms, perhaps 50 or 60, from his relatives

before admission. Often small boys are admitted, as the relatives
are afraid of their being fined for breaking some taboo, or for some
inadvertent disrespect to the members, which would cost more than
initiation fees. Each successive step is usually accompanied by
successive and increased payments. All ceremonies, dances and
feasts are the occasion of further contributions by the members,
and often of extortions from non-members. The activities of the
dukduk of New Britain savoured so much of blackmail that to
outsiders its main purpose appeared to be the acquisition of *diwarra*.
These societies were the chief power in their communities, and
everything that was wrong in their eyes gave them an opportunity
to extort shell-money. They represented public opinion, and were
a terror to evildoers, but in their lust for gain might was often
mistaken for right, and the weak, especially the women (who could
not be members) were the victims.

In petty cases the *Tubuan* (female *Dukduk*) simply goes to the home and
drives ' her ' spear into the ground, and squats beside it, perhaps to hide
' her ' legs, which might be recognized by some mark on them, till some
shell-money is offered to ' her ', which, if not sufficient ' she ' rejects. . . .
A great deal of the society's income is from fines for various reasons, e.g.
speaking disrespectfully of the ' bird ' [masked figure] . . . by calling its
dress ' leaves ' instead of ' feathers ', for speaking about it in the presence
of women, &c. . . . Any excuse is availed of to fine non-members, e.g. a
lad was fined 3 fathoms of shell-money for accidentally breaking a member's
pipe, which might have been bought for a finger's length (Brown, 1910,
pp. 60, 69–71, 81).

Even the fairies in New Britain are concerned with the amassing
of *diwarra*, and instruct lucky mortals in ways of making and increasing it by charms and spells.

Parkinson (1907, pp. 83–4) describes how astute natives take
advantage of the superstitions with which *diwarra* is regarded, and
incidentally how women sometimes pay the men back in their own
coin. He cites the case of a woman who claimed to be able, with
the help of the spirits, to double or even treble any sums of *diwarra*
entrusted to her. Many natives eagerly invested in this attractive
and easy scheme. But the spirits were not always amenable and
often had to be placated with further offerings. When an influential
investor became too impatient he would be repaid, while others were
kept waiting. When the place became too hot to hold her the
woman started business in another part.[1]

[1] It is curious to note a parallel superstition in an unexpected locality.
A few years ago a respectable shopkeeper in Cambridge sued a gypsy for
sums which had been entrusted to her to place under a stone in order to
bring money into his business. The first £5 did not have the desired effect,
and more and more was extorted, until the total added up to £60, the man's
patience was exhausted, and the case was brought into court.

In no other part of the world had money so powerful an influence on savage life and customs as in New Britain. All the energy of the natives was spent in collecting it. No service, however slight, was given without demanding payment, no present without return. The commercial spirit was everywhere uppermost. Danks, who was a missionary for nearly eight years in New Britain, deplored the influence of *diwarra*. He regarded it as responsible for the

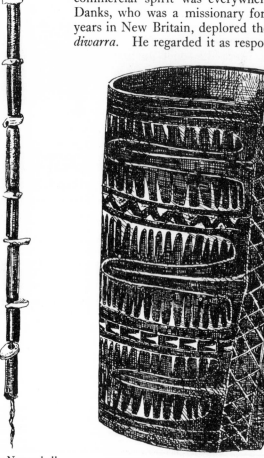

FIG. 56.—*Nassa* shell and cassowary quill string, New Britain

FIG. 57.—*Navoi*, arm-band, New Britain. (⅞ size)

intense and glaring ingratitude met with everywhere. ' Gratitude means expense, and is too expensive to indulge in ',[1] (1888, p. 315)

[1] To show gratitude is often bad form in Melanesia.   It implies that you regard the donor as a poor man whose gift involves a sacrifice. *Cf.* Coombe 1911, p. 182, also Codrington, 1891, p. 354.

Lack of foresight and general thriftlessness are commonly attributed to 'savages' in general and South Sea Islanders in particular ; the Polynesians accused the missionaries of teaching them to be greedy. But in New Britain greed was already strongly developed, and in missionary opinion the love of money was the root of all evil.

Diwarra itself has a limited range, including only the north-eastern end of New Britain, the southern end of New Ireland and the islands in between. Strings or strips of *Nassa*, often called ' false *diwarra* ' (the native name is *eddi*) with the shells close together instead of separated, are found along the southern coast of New Britain, at Hansa Bay and Möwehafen (Schneider, 1905, p. 14, Pl. 4, Fig. *f*). *Nassa* shells, broken and threaded singly, eked out with bits of cassowary quills, ½ inch (15 cm.) long (Fig. 56), are also currency along this coast (Finsch, 1888, Pl. III, Fig. 2 ; Lewis, 1929, Pl. VII, Fig. 1).

Ordinary shell-money of strung disks is either made locally, or introduced in exchange from other islands. Thus *pele* strings from the Duke of York group came in exchange for *diwarra* ; and from New Ireland *tapsoka* spread south, together with the common white money from the Admiralties (Lewis, 1929, Pl. VII, Fig. 3).

At the western end of the island the general name for shell-money is *na ma yu yu*, made of black (*pa taw*), white (*bori boria*) and brown or grey (*ra vali*) disks, sometimes strung separately but often mixed together, and decorated with cuscus or other teeth at intervals. Dogs' teeth were formerly used as currency here, as in New Guinea and the Solomons, and fetched high prices, as dogs were scarce.

From Sagsag at the westernmost end of New Britain comes a form of currency not met with elsewhere. This is an arm-band made of turtle shell called *navoi*, with patterns scratched on it, filled in with white chalk (Fig. 57). This is an importation from New Guinea and is used as the local currency and forms one of the principal items in the ' bride-price ' (H. Sherwin).

Another local form of special interest and higher value consists in the stone club heads of the south coast, and specially of Möwe-hafen. These are flattish disks, some 4 inches to 6 inches (10 to 16 cm.) across, made of fine-grained stone, and highly polished.[1] These have been recognized as a link between the ' stone-money ' of Yap and the shell-money disks (p. 144), but they are little more than valued objects of barter or exchange, like the flint strike-a-lights from the same area in the currency collection in Vienna, or the stone axe-heads, sometimes included in currency, from the Solomons.

[1] *Cf*. Thilenius, 1920, Fig. 16, *a*, *b*.

The Duke of York group, lying between New Britain and New Ireland, is the centre for manufacture and distribution of the *pele* strings which are the general money of the area (Pl. 13, Figs. 6–13) and are especially used for buying *Nassa* shells for *diwarra* (see p. 150).

Pele is made of many different kinds of shells strung in short lengths. It is not measured by the fathom, like most shell-money; each string is only about 7 inches (20 to 25 cm.) long, with a long end of string left, so that several strings can be tied together in a bunch. The shells are broken up with a pounder of stone or shell, often a stone axe-head is used, and they are chipped into a more or less circular shape. The disks are bored with a sharp stone or a shark's tooth bound on to a handle, or with the pump-drill; then threaded and ground down with pumice to make an even and well-polished string.

As the shells are thin, the disks are usually only ground at the edges, though inequalities may be rubbed down with sand and water, and in recent years the strings are often left rough and un-polished. Schneider describes and illustrates 12 kinds of *pele* (pp. 52–4, Pl. 6); Lewis, 10 kinds (p. 14, Pl. IX); and Petri sketches details of 4 (p. 521, Fig. 11). The orange-red *munbun* or *biga* of *Chrysostoma paradoxum* is the finest and most highly prized, worth 25 pfennig a string on Mioko (south of Duke of York Island) where it is made, and double that in New Britain.

The commonest dark brown strings are *mbiu*, of *Modiola plume-scens* : *mui* is 'white', made of *Strombus luhuanum*. *Pirr*, made of *Cypraea*, is white on the concave and purplish on the convex inner surface, and is probably the best known, as its common use by European traders gave it additional value. This is the favourite in the *diwarra* trade, and the usual currency of the Nakanai district. A light purplish-grey (lighter than *pirr*) is *bingam*, made of *Conus geographicus*, a creamy-white string, *lillie*, is made of *Nautilus pompilius*, dark brown strings *kalakalang murmuru minne* of *Perna vitrea* and *kalakalang kambang* of *Perna ephippium*. All these strings, the shells from which they are made, the broken bits and disks (Figs. 6–12), the stone pounder (Fig. 15) and the stone-tipped pump drill (Fig. 14) are illustrated in Pl. 13.

Crossing over to New Ireland we plunge into the most perplexing and complicated of all the shell-money complexes. There are at least a score of different kinds in use here, and there is little illustra-tive material in English museums. Owing to the mountainous character of the country, the unsociable nature of its inhabitants, and the lack of communication between them, the currencies are local and very varied. Both here and in the Solomon Islands it is difficult for a general surveyor to avoid losing the way in a jungle of unintelligible names, for a string may have a dozen different names (recorded in different spellings by different observers) in as many districts.

Tapsoka is the best known here, as, although it is made on New Hanover and smaller islands to the north, it travels widely in New Ireland, and also into New Britain. This is made of *Chama pacifica imbricata*, and as the whole shell which is 'red' on the outside and 'white' inside is used, the strings can easily be recognized by the alternate and irregular patches of bright pinky red and creamy white. Boys dive for the shells, which are broken up, and ground down by the women, making small thin disks about ⅛ in. (3–4 mm.) in diameter, but the strings vary in fineness. The men bore the holes by means of sticks with stone points—iron nails are now preferred—and the disks may be baked on stones to improve the colour. A length of 2 to 3 feet (60–90 cm.) was worth from 3 to 6 marks or more, but much depends on colour. Five strings of the best kind was the average price of a woman and 6 to 7 that of a pig of the best kind (Schneider, 1905, p. 55, *fn.*; Parkinson, 1907, pp. 301–2; Lewis, 1929, pp. 19–20, Pl. XII, Figs. 4–6).

'False *tapsoka*' is made of *Spondylus*, and shows a different shade of red with more orange in it. These strings in Schneider's illustration (Pl. 7, Figs. *d*, *e*) are as fine as the finer strings of *tapsoka*, but were only valued at 25 pfennig a foot. Chinnery (p. 29) says that *Spondylus* strings (*levene dasilok*) are the most highly prized kind in the north where he equates them with *sapi sapi*, imported from New Guinea. And as similar strings are found also in the Solomon Islands, he attributes the spread to the 'blackbirding' of earlier days.

Kokonon seems to be a general name for shell-money in the north of New Ireland, and in Finsch's collection at Vienna various kinds can be seen, all (including *tapsoka*) labelled *kokonon* (*cf.* Finch, 1888–93, p. 128, Pl. III, Fig. 3). The commonest sort, *kokonon luluai*, is made of the tiniest of white *Conus* tips strung alternately with equally tiny coconut shell disks (Finch, *ibid.*, Schneider, 1905, p. 59, Pl. 8, Fig. *k*; Lewis, 1929, pp. 23–4, Pl. XIII, Figs. 8, 9). This is of low value, but in constant use. It is so necessary for small purchases and for fines that some is usually worn in the hair in case of sudden need or accident. *Arangit* is a 'red' string,[1] though finer and darker than *tapsoka* and more brown than red. It is found mainly in the central region where it is worth about 50 to 75 cents a fathom, though far more highly valued farther south (Schneider, p. 56, Pl. 7, Fig. *f*; Lewis, p. 20, Pl. XII, Fig. 10).

Other 'red' strings are *mait*, which is finer than *arangit*, and

---

[1] In the Finsch Collection in Vienna 'white' as well as 'red' strings are labelled *arangit*.

tingerib (the name is used for other kinds of shell-money also) which is finer still (Schneider, pp. 56–7, Pl. 5, Figs. *g–i*).

The difficulties of identifying shell-money in New Ireland are increased by the custom of stringing several different kinds together, and mixed strings are a special characteristic, the meaning of which is unexplained. There are many fine strings of white, whitish, greyish, brownish, and reddish disks, the prevailing tinge being grey; *bau* is the name for the whiter kind and *tikutkut* and *titpele* for the greyer shades, while the red-brown shades would be classed as *arangit* (Schneider, Pl. 8, Figs. *a–e*; Lewis, p. 18, Pl. XI, Figs. 7–8). *Miu tikutkut* or ' black *tikutkut* ' is the darkest of all the strings, made of disks less than 3 mm. in diameter. This is strung in short lengths, measured across the breasts, and one length was worth 8 pfennig (Schneider, p. 57, Pl. 5, Fig. *k*).

Tapsoka, arangit, bau, tikutkut, titpele and *kokonon luluai* are the only kinds in the Cambridge Collection at present (*cf.* Pl. 13, Figs. 1–5), so whether *mangin, lolat, (lollot) lideran, kemetas, pukheo, kabon, kawas* and others are variations in shell-strings or merely in nomenclature must be left for others to decide.

The really interesting money of New Ireland is the *birok* or ' pig-money ' (also called *nulpap*) especially characteristic of the south, and entirely distinct from any other kind. This consists in a composite string made according to a general plan which is described by Lewis (1929, pp. 24–5) and illustrated, by kind permission of the Field Museum, Chicago, in one of his strings (Pl. 15).

First comes a fathom (or more) of shell disks, usually mixed sorts, up to a rattan square a couple of inches across, usually red, black and yellow, through which the string passes diagonally. After this it bifurcates into ' pig-money ' proper, consisting of a fathom or so of edge-to-edge disks (*cf.* p. 115) in two parallel strings. Dogs' teeth and more shell-money separate this section from another stretch of ' pig-money ' in more numerous parallel strings, terminating usually in pigs' tails. The whole string may be 15 yards long, containing 20,000 separate disks. The rattan squares are believed to be charms and to contain some special magical objects such as hair, &c. But they are too valuable to destroy in confirmation of this belief. One was opened by Lewis and contained nothing but the folded strip of *Pandanus* leaf which was the foundation for the plaited rattan.

The meaning of the pig-money and of the pigs' tails at the end of it lead into a maze of contradictory statements by competent authorities.[1] The popular idea is, so many tails, so many pigs, and that a string with 10 tails is worth 10 pigs. Lewis (1929, pp. 26–7) argues that this is improbable, as a string in the Field Museum Collection in Chicago with 17 tails is not much longer than one with

[1] *Cf.* Petri's summing up of reports and opinions (1936, p. 524).

only 5. But this seems an unnecessary appeal to reason, for the value of shell-money is fixed by custom rather than by common sense. A more obvious explanation is that the number of tails represents the number of pigs which it has been used in buying, but this lacks proof. Some travellers state that the strings were used in purchase of wives as well as of pigs, and also at funeral ceremonies. Some say they were never used for wife-purchase. Some doubt if they were ever used for buying pigs. Some doubt if they were 'money' at all, or anything more than symbols of wealth imbued with magic. And now that the generation that used these strings is passing away, a clear solution of the uses and abuses of pig-money cannot be expected.

The place of *diwarra* in native life as described by contemporary writers nearly 50 years ago has already been noted (*cf.* pp. 151 *ff.*). A general survey of the function of money throughout the archipelago is given by Bühler (1934). He claims that shell-money here really deserves the name of money as it fulfils all the functions of a recognized currency. It is convenient to handle, to measure or to divide, and the values if not fixed are fairly steady within local groups ; the supply is limited, either because of the scarcity of the material, the tedious labour of manufacture, the small number of people qualified to make it, or by intentionally restricted output. It is used in exchange, as a standard of value and for payment for services. Yet it differs from our money in certain important ways. Not only does the value vary from place to place, and district to district, and also from time to time, more erratically than that of civilized currencies, but it differs from the latter in its restricted uses, whereby one kind alone is used for one purpose or purchase and another for another, notably pigs or wives. Thirdly, it is far more commonly used as mere ornament, and enters into necklaces, armbands and girdles, and in the Admiralty Islands the shells are used to make whole dance aprons.

The transition from the old shell-money economy to the new shilling and tobacco standard was difficult. White traders were forbidden to use the native money, as abuses could too easily result. Though the shell-strings can scarcely be imitated successfully and profitably, imitation shell-rings and imitation dogs' teeth were imported by Chinese and Japanese traders, and the teeth were very popular as decorations in New Ireland, where the real teeth have gone out of circulation as money.

The first trade with the natives was necessarily by barter, but with the development of plantations, the payment of wages, and the enforcement of a head tax by the Germans, silver marks came into native use, and the Australian shilling, still called a 'mark' by the natives, is current throughout the archipelago.

In most parts of the world, in defiance of Gresham's Law, 'good' (i.e. civilized) money has driven out 'bad' (i.e. uncivilized), and native currencies have disappeared. In Melanesia the essential association of money with important native institutions has necessarily preserved it, wherever the social structure and beliefs are still maintained. Meanwhile, owing to economic changes, the value has increased rather than diminished. The making of shell-money is almost a lost art, as wages can now be earned by quicker and less laborious methods, and the strings are more and more difficult to obtain. The prices asked for *diwarra* in curio shops today would astonish traders of 50 years ago. Then a fathom roughly equalled 2 to 3 shillings or marks. A fowl was worth a quarter or half a fathom according to size, one fathom would buy a piece (2 yards) of calico, and 1 to 3 fathoms an axe or spade.

Workers were paid a fathom a month, with food. Pigs, wives and canoes fetched fancy prices according to size and attractions. Wages are nowadays paid in money or in tobacco, and the value of coins is appreciated. But for all ceremonial payments, especially for pigs to be sacrificed at feasts, for payments on marriages, or for carvers of masks, or of dancers on various occasions, native money alone suffices, and is indeed essential, no substitute being acceptable, as it lacks the necessary religious content.

B. SOLOMON ISLANDS TO NEW CALEDONIA

In the Solomon Islands, as in the Bismarcks, strings of shell-money are met with everywhere, although their significance appears to be more ornamental than economic. There are three main interests in life, women, pigs and money, but money comes last, not first. The making of the strings is usually, as far as can be discovered, the industry of the smaller less productive islands, where the women are not able to support the family with garden produce, so they use the strings for buying supplies from the mainland, strings supplementing or supplanting fish in the ordinary inter-insular fish-taro or fish-yam exchange.

The chief centres are in the smaller islands of the Shortlands, south of Bougainville in the north ; and in the small islands south of Malaita in the south. But here as in the Bismarcks, strings pass from island to island, acquiring new names in each district ; and again, a list of the illustrated types and references to the literature form the only non-controversial introduction.

It is usual to distinguish between 'red', 'white' and 'black' strings, although strings of either or all three colours often have the same name. The red disks are mostly of *Spondylus* or *Chama pacifica*, and, being more valuable, are seldom used in trading, though short lengths are threaded in with white or black to enhance the value of the commoner strings.   The white are mainly *Conus*, and the black may be very dark brown shells of various kinds ; they may be coconut, or more often seeds.

To begin with the commoner ' white ' strings.   Schneider describes and illustrates (pp. 70-2, Pl. XII, Figs. *f–h* and *k*) some strings of *Conus, perasali* and *salesale*, made on Alu, circulating through the Shortlands to Bougainville in the north, Choiseul and Ysabel to the east and Rubiana and the New Georgia group to the south, by way of trade.   *Moremore* or *mimisi* of *Spondylus* or *Chama pacifica* are among the many names for the ' red ' strings, and series of these reds are interspersed with whites and characteristically separated by single ' black ' disks or seeds.[1]

Bougainville, the most northerly and formerly the least explored of the larger Solomon Islands, shares shell-money strings with other island groups, but has two distinct types of its own.

Biruan or *beroan* is best known in the North.   These are white *Conus* strings often enlivened with black disks that occur irregularly

FIG. 58.—*Mauwai*, shell-money, Solomon Islands

here and there.   These can scarcely be distinguished from the *Conus* strings such as *perasali* from the Shortlands to the South, but Parkinson says (1907, p. 494) that they are made on the little Carteret islands to the north of Buka, and the Buka natives believe that they come from New Britain or even from the Admiralties (Schneider, Pl. XII, Figs. *f* and *k* ; Lewis, 1929, p. 32, Pl. XXIII, Figs. 1-3). ' Purple ' *biruan* takes the place of ' red ' money on Buka (Pl. 10). To the south *abuta* (*aputa*) or *mauwai* can easily be distinguished from anything in Oceania or elsewhere (Fig. 58).   It is made of the speckled tops of small *Conus* shells (either *C. sponsalis* or *C. hebraus*) $\frac{1}{4}$ inch to $\frac{1}{2}$ inch (5–13 cm.) across.   These are broken up into bits almost as long as broad, but not ground down into disks, so that the string of only 5 bits to the inch (25 mm.) looks ' like weather-beaten flotsam ' as Schneider describes it (p. 69, Pl. XII, Fig. *e*).

A better-made, ground and polished type of *abuta* is used for pig purchase (ill., Petri, 1936, p. 521, Fig. 15).   *Abuta* is measured by the fathom and a fathom is worth about a shilling.   A length of

[1] On Ysabel *mimisi* is the name for whitish strings, or for strings in general.

10 fathoms with a snailshell at each end is looped 6 times and firmly bound for a few inches, leaving the ends dangling (*cf.* Thurnwald, 1934–5, Pl. II). Ten of these strings, making 100 fathoms in all, are packed in a netted bag and placed in the sleeping hut as a pillow for the ancestral ghosts (*ibid.*, Pl. III).

Thurnwald drew up a fairly definite scale of values (1912, pp. 39–42). A quarter-fathom would buy a small carrying net, a basket or a pot. One fathom was equal to a good arm-ring, which could also be used as currency, and would buy a large pot, a large basket of taro, a large forehead shell, a club or spear. Ten to twelve fathoms would buy a large pig. For the same price a man can hire a murderer or purchase a widow. It needs 100 or more to atone for murder and more still may have to be paid for a girl wife.

In a Buin song the lovesick girl appeals to her lover :

> Buy me with arm-rings,
> There are many arm-rings
> Down there at the mouth of the river
> Where the men work on the land.

And in another song the outraged lover upbraids a fickle maiden—

> If you did not want me,
> Why did you tell me to give you a string of red shell-money ?
> Your father demanded two hundred fathoms of *abuta* ;
> That was your price.

and he ungallantly adds—

> You unwashed scarecrow
> You are as old as an opossum.
>
> (Thurnwald, 1910, p. 120).

The other money peculiar to Bougainville is *kuriri*, a whitish string that a conchologist (but only a conchologist) would recognize as unique in this oceanic world in being made of land-snails (Schneider, p. 71, Pl. XII, Fig. *i*).

Guadalcanar is renowned for its plaited shield used in ' bride-price ' (Pl. 8, Fig. 1 ; it also has strings of shell-money not found elsewhere (Pl. 10, Fig. 7). These are made of thick heavy dark brown coarse irregular disks nearly ½ inch (10–12 mm.) across, which Woodford collected in the island, though they were already obsolete in his time and little was known about them (1908, **43**, Pl. F, Fig. 3).

In the Southern Solomons *rongo* is the general name for shell-money ; *rongo pura* for white strings, and *rongo sisi* for red, though mixed strings are the commonest ; red strings with patches of white in the middle are called *sapi*. The white disks are made from *Arca* shell and the red from *Chama pacifica*. There is a very special kind of brightest red, made from the very reddest part of the shell ;

sometimes a whole shell provides only one disk, and a short string measured from the elbow joint to the end of the middle finger may take two years to make (Woodford, 1908, **43**).

Codrington describes a very fine kind made at Haununu on San Cristoval of disks only $\frac{1}{16}$ inch (little over 1 mm.) in diameter with about 50 disks to the inch (1891, p. 325, *fn.* *Cf.* Petri, 1936, p. 526).

Black disks may be made from black *Pinna* shells ; more often from seeds. These are not strung by themselves but are mixed in with white and red either for effect or to mark divisions for measurement. The alternate black and white in the middle of otherwise white or red strings is a special characteristic of the Solomons (Fig. 59 ; *cf.* Lewis, Pl. XXIII, Figs. 3, 5–7). The red shell-money is scarcely in circulation, though it is used for 'bride-price', 60 strings being a fair average. It is mostly owned by chiefs, who store it in secret, and only distribute it on great occasions such as feasts, and as rewards for war service, distribution on the owner's death being a frequent cause for quarrelling.

FIG. 59.—Shell-money, Solomon Islands

From the farthest south of the Solomons, off the south-east end of San Cristoval, the natives of the atolls of Santa Ana (or Itapa) and Santa Catalina (or Aquari) make fine strings to exchange for mainland goods. These are long strings, made for currency, not for ornament, of the usual Solomon Island type, with red and white separated by alternate black and white disks (Pl. 16, Fig. 2), but some of them show in their termination a curious likeness to the 'pig-money' strings of New Ireland (Pl. 16, Fig. 1). The unusual technique of dividing two or more strings and joining them together again is the same ; bits of shell are used at the junctions in place of the dogs' teeth, and there are the same halved seeds. More striking still are the dangles of edged disks, the chief characteristic of 'pig money', while the terminating strips of cloth suggest an imitation of former pigs' tails. These strings travel far, as one was collected lately on Guadalcanar.

Ivens (1927, p. 391) sums up the part played by shell-money in the social life of the smaller islands Sa'a and Ulawa, and the larger Malaita near by.

7*

Strings are used for

the furnishing of the bride-price and the blood-money, the buying of canoes [100 shell-moneys for a decorated canoe, 10 for a bonito canoe and 3 or 4 for an ordinary one], the payment of fees and fines including redemptive offerings to ghosts : the buying of pigs and of food ; single strings of varying lengths are in common use for making purchases. The one term *ha'a* is used for a unit of shell-money of 4 or 6 strings, for the unit of porpoise teeth, 100, or the unit of dogs' teeth, 40. . . . In the bride-price or the blood-money each unit of 10 may include so many units of porpoise teeth and of dogs' teeth. In the buying of pigs or canoes the shell-money is usually generally the only one employed.

The Santa Cruz group to the South-East of the Solomons is famous for its woven mats and strips (p. 131) and its feather-money (p. 135) ; strings of teeth or seeds and turtleshell rings (Fig. 60) are also used as currency, but shell-money appears to have gone out of

fashion. It was in general use in former days, made of white or greyish white strings like those in the Solomons, and, as in those islands, strung with black coconut disks, black seeds, fish vertebrae and European beads as variations or decorations.[1]

In between the Santa Cruz group and the Banks' Islands are the Torres Islands formerly famous for the ' very pretty little arrows ' which were ' used in the way of money ' (Codrington, 1891, p. 327 ; Rivers, 1914, II, p. 386 ; *cf.* specimen in Pitt Rivers Museum).

FIG. 60.—Turtleshell nose ring, Santa Cruz

Codrington noted the absence of shells and of shell-money, but belts (*te titi*) made of snail-shells bound on to cane (Fig. 61) are a form of currency (W. J. Durrad). Boars' tusks, and jaws with the tusks still *in situ*, are valuable in exchanges here, together with strings of shiny black bead-like *evodia* seeds.[2]

Continuing southward we reach the Banks' Islands where once more shell-money reigns supreme. It is rough, white or dirty-white, unpolished and unattractive (which may account for its rarity in museum collections) but for the Banks' Islanders it is the prime necessity of life in this world and the next.

Most of it comes from Rowa near Vanua Lavu ; the largest island of the group.

[1] *Cf.* Speiser, 1916, p. 191, Fig. 39. *Cf.* also Rivers, 1914, II, p. 397. The girdle of shell-money used in exchanges in Tapua, the central island of the Santa Cruz Group, is referred to above (p. 118).

[2] The occurrence of this tree prevents the round shiny black beads, otherwise so popular in trading, from being ' acceptable '. The natives have no use for them, as they explain ' all same trees '.

Rowa consists of 5 tiny islets on the bight of an irregular reef some 5 miles long. One of the islets is the jagged point of a volcanic rock, and this is the only one inhabited. It was believed that if any food was grown on this island there would be a famine on Vanua Lavu, its nearest neighbour, also that if a sow were taken thither it would devour the people, so they were obliged to support themselves by exchanging fish and shell-money (Pl. 10, Fig. 8) with the larger islands. It supplied the common money called *som*, made of tips of shells (as described above, pp. 116–17), and also finer sorts used only for ornament. In Codrington's time *som ta Rowa* was so fine that 60 disks went to the inch (Codrington, 1891, pp. 17, 298, 325–6).

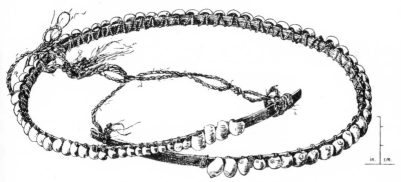

FIG. 61.—*Tetiti*, shell belt, Torres Islands

Rivers watched the *som* disks being made by a simple process on Rowa, and collected the apparatus which is illustrated in Fig. 62. The shells are broken up with a hammer of giant clam shell and the pointed ends collected, sun-dried and washed. They are chipped down till they form small pieces pointed on one side corresponding to the outer surface of the shell and hollow on the other side, corresponding to its interior. To rub down the fragment, the woman takes a stem of *Hibiscus* about as thick as her finger, sliced diagonally across, and fixes the little shell-tip with its hollow surface inwards in the end of the stick. The tip can then be rubbed on a stone sprinkled with water and volcanic sand, until it is worn down and a hole appears in the centre. The disks thus made are collected in a coconut cup, and strung on *Hibiscus* bark string. ' Nothing could have been simpler and more expeditious than the conversion of the fragments of shell into disks ', a woman working from sunrise to sunset could make a fathom of money (Rivers, 1914, pp. 167–8). This coarse kind of shell-money quickly and roughly made with the corrugations still left, and not ground down after stringing, is of paramount importance in native life, taking the same place here that *diwarra* does in New Britain. It is used daily for ordinary transactions; a length of about 4 feet would buy enough yams to keep a family of five for a week and it is essential in all important payments.

Social advance is secured by possession of shell-money because the steps in the Suqe Club cannot be taken without it; social eminence is maintained by it, because the moneyed man has his debtors under his thumb, and by the power he has of imposing a loan, he can make rising men his debtors and keep them back.

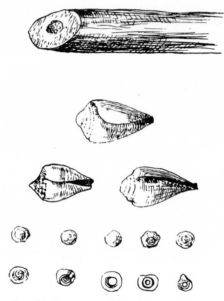

FIG. 62.—Shell-money making, Rowa, Banks Islands

A debt is not only contracted by borrowing. A rich man may impose a loan which his friend may not for his own credit refuse, though he has to make a double return.

The pressure put upon a debtor who does not pay when payment is demanded is admirably effective. All the men of the creditor's place come and sit, bringing their wives with them, in the debtor's premises; the debtor lights his fire and cooks food for them; if the payment is not forthcoming they stay overnight, go home next morning and after a while repeat the visit. The debtor's neighbours and friends pity him and help him with food and money until he scrapes enough together to pay the debt (Codrington, 1891, pp. 326–7).

From Micronesia down to the Solomons Schneider's monograph has led the way through the mazes, but south of the Solomons he himself goes astray. Not having seen the Banks' Islands shell-money, *som*, he was puzzled by Codrington's description [1] and assumed that it was the same as the shiny white shell-money which is found, though sparingly, in the New Hebrides (Schneider, Pl. 7, Fig. *l*, *cf*. pp. 82–3). These latter strings ground and polished, are worn as ornaments in the more northerly islands, the string (part of which is illustrated in Fig. 63) was collected as currency in Aoba, and in Espiritu Santo a woman wears her 'bride-price' round her neck (Speiser, 1923, p. 182).

The white disks are often interspersed with black coconut, as in the fine string (part of which is seen in Fig. 64) given to Miss Cheeseman by King Ringapat of the Big Nambas in the interior of Malekula, but European beads are replacing shell-strings, which are now no longer made (Speiser, 1923, p. 270).

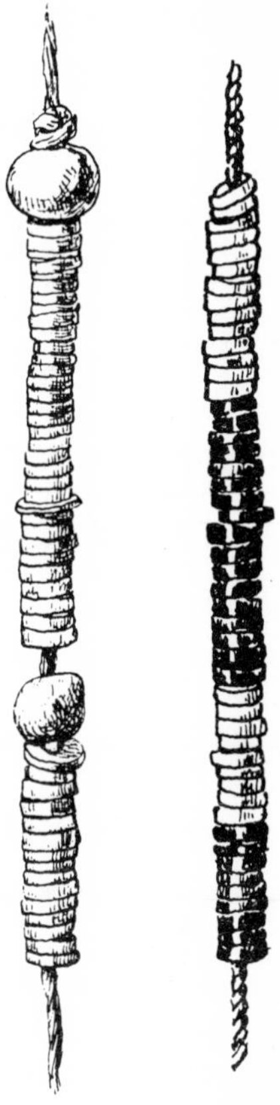

Pigs are the real currency of the New Hebrides, and though shell-money is used in the purchase of pigs or of wives in parts of Santo, mats are the ordinary substitute for money in the East (Maewo, Aoba (Oba) and Pentecost); teeth are more important in Malekula and Ambrym; Erromanga is noted (in museums) for its stone-rings, which are not used as money; and Tanna has no currency at all.

The mats and teeth—mainly boars' tusks —have been described above (pp. 126, 131); the use of rings as currency in Melanesia has also been discussed, and the *navela* or *navila* of Erromanga is often included as the last link in the chain of ring-money and of stone-money stretching from Micronesia through the Bismarcks and the Solomons. Robertson describes these rings (1902, p. 389):

FIG. 63   FIG. 64
Shell-money, New Hebrides

These *navilahs* they believe were not made by human hands; they were given to them as heirlooms by their forefathers, who, in turn, received them from the spirits. When a man was dying, he generally sent for his son or nearest male relative, and told him where the family *navilah* were buried,

---

[1] Schneider found Codrington's description of *som* 'etwas schwer verständlich' (p. 49). Petri (1936, p. 527) follows Schneider.

for the ground was the bank of deposit where these precious relics were usually stored. Sometimes he died before he could tell this, or perhaps, out of anger, he preferred to be silent, and thus deprive his successor of his heritage. Thus these stones might be buried for years and then suddenly be found. There was no risk of a stone not being recognized by the family to whom it belonged, for each *navilah* has its own name and history. Some bear a man's name, others a woman's. . . .

The *navilah* is in the form of a ring or of the crescent moon, though sometimes almost straight. They are of all sizes and when they are ring-shaped, a man can easily crawl through the largest, which weigh from 40 to 50 pounds and are about 5 feet in circumference. They were also given as purchase money for wives and often at their feasts a chief will present another with a *navilah*, there being always an exchange of the compliment at the return feast.[1]

Humphreys (1926, p. 164), who collected the *navela* illustrated (Pl. 7), says that these rings can scarcely be classed as ordinary currency. They are chiefly used in present-giving, though never without expectation of a return gift in kind, and are used as presents in the purchase of a wife in the same category with boars' tusks and *numpuri* [cowry] shells.

A unique medium of exchange is found on Santo in the form of bits of black coral (a Gordonid, probably *Plexaura antipathes*, Esper).[2] This is a very finely branching species and the shiny black twigs are treasured as charms, though rarely owned except by chiefs. They are used in exchanges, a fragment of a colony, say a branch 7 inches to 8 inches (18–20 cm.) long with its associated branchlets, having the exchange value of half a dozen pigs—the staple wealth of the island—or a wife (Richie, 1913).

Throughout New Caledonia and the Loyalties trading is almost all by barter, and money rarely changes hands save in the more costly purchases such as canoes and valuable ornaments. Nevertheless, money is all-important in native life, though its significance is far more ceremonial, religious or magical than economic. It enters into all functions from birth and marriage to death, and the accompanying rites and ceremonies ; it takes part in all feasts, all alliances and peace-makings ; it is used for the accomplishment and atonement of crimes, and is essential in all ceremonial presentations.

It consists solely in shell-money and is distinguishable from that of any other part of the world by its fineness, its accompanying ornaments, and the addition of string entwined with the hair of the fruit-eating bat (*Pteropus*) commonly called ' flying-fox '.

This fur string is highly valued in New Caledonia and the Loyalties being used not only for personal ornament, but for decorating weapons and other articles of value, such as the becket, which

[1] *Cf.* also Meinicke, 1875, p. 204 ; Speiser, 1923, p. 273 ; Petri, 1936, p. 547.
[2] Specimen in the Royal Scottish Museum, Edinburgh.

serves as a spear-thrower as well as currency (Fig. 65), necklaces and purses. The bats are caught in nets or knocked down with sticks or sling-stones, and the hair pulled out. This spread out evenly

FIG. 65.—Becket, with flying-fox fur string, New Caledonia. ($\frac{3}{4}$ size)

and fixed between fine banana fibres is twisted to make a furry cord, which should not be thicker than a quill. It is dyed in a concoction made from a root to give it the reddish-brown colour (Sarazin, 1929, p. 102). A string or tuft or plaited tail of this appears to be an essential accompaniment of money in New Caledonia, even if it no longer possesses money-value in itself.

Miu is here the general name for money, and 'black money', *miu bwarre*, is the most valued and extremely fine. It was originally made of tiny bits of the tarsal bones of lizards, but is imitated in very fine *Conus* shell-tips of incredible minuteness, less than a millimeter each way. It is greyish-white and the darker the colour the higher the value. This was used more for presents for great chiefs on special occasions, and for fines, than for trading, and many natives had never even seen a string of it. A short piece with its accompanying tail of plaited flying-fox fur is illustrated in Fig. 66.

'White money', *miu me*, is lighter, but not white, and is also very fine and also has a tail of flying-fox fur string, and different kinds have different values, though all are remarkably high. A

FIG. 66.—'Black money', New Caledonia

few inches of the finest sort were worth 30 to 40 francs, an ell would buy a wife, and half a fathom a canoe. But there is also a cheaper kind of white money, where the little shell beads are separated from each other by knots in the string. (This method of stringing is peculiar to New Caledonia and found nowhere else.) This was the kind used by the whites in trading with the natives, and their price was 1 franc a meter; 5 francs' worth was measured by a man standing with the string in his outstretched arms, the ends falling to the ground from either hand (Sarazin, 1929, pp. 177-8, Pl. 51, 1).

No one knows how the strings are made, and the natives, if they know, will not tell. They are no longer current, as trade is now transacted with paper-money of the Indo-Chinese bank at Noumea (Nevermann, 1933, p. 212).

The white strings are illustrated in Fig. 67; a fine string with its fur tail to the right, the cheaper kind with knotted string next, also with a fur tail, and coarser white strings, which have lost their tails, to the left. The fine white string was said to be worth from £1 to £1 15s.[1] No less characteristic of New Caledonia are the ornaments attached to the strings, which consist in shells, and in the little pendants of pearl-shell with serrated edges, seen in the same illustration. These pendants have been variously interpreted (Sarazin, 1929, p. 179). They often have bifurcated ends, and a pisciform or even anthropomorphic appearance, but the natives explain that though these are customary, they are not essential, any more than the heads on our coins. They are merely added for ornament.

The more valuable money, which is said to be used only by chiefs, is kept in the characteristic wrapper or purse. This may be a piece of barkcloth or other material, but it is always bound round with flying-fox fur string (Pl. 17). More characteristic still is the 'head of money' go miu, of varying shapes. This may be a solid roll wound round with flying-fox fur string and/or plaitwork, with dangles of shell-money and ornaments below. Or it may be in the better known form of a canoe-shaped piece of wood, bound with the string, carved with a human face with large prominent nose (Fig. 68). This type is probably connected with ancestor cults but it has a practical use, as it constitutes a safe, being tabu to all but the owner, guarding him against thieves.

Another form of purse, or 'head of money' (for so Sarazin identifies it, 1929, pp. 181-2, Pl. 51, Figs. 10-11), is composed of a pair of frigate bird bones about 1 foot (30 cm.) long, fastened together at one end to form a sort of handle of almost the same length, and again at the other end, both fastenings being of flying-fox fur string. These have been taken for ornaments, possibly for combs, but Sarazin recognized them as Münzkopfe on which to hang strings of shell-money.[2]

---

[1] Lewis (1929) illustrates two fine strings, Pl. XXIV, and the cheaper kind Pl. XXV.

[2] Cf. specimen in the Horniman Museum Collection.

FIG. 67.—' White money ', New   FIG. 68.—' Head of money ', New
            Caledonia   Caledonia

Characteristic of New Caledonia, and often included in collections of currency, are the handsome strings of beads (*mejir*) labelled
jade or nephrite, but mineralogically speaking gabbroid amphibolite
(Sarazin, 1929, p. 169). These are large green beads of irregular

sizes, irregularly drilled, and of unknown origin, to which long strings or bunches of the flying-fox fur are attached, an association which gives them a claim to be classed as currency (Pl. 17). These are worn as necklaces both in New Caledonia and the Loyalties, with the fur strings over the shoulders.

C. NEW GUINEA AND TORRES STRAITS

Round the fringe of the Eastern part of the large island of New Guinea ·the natives are keen traders and reference has been made already (pp. 17–18) to the *kula* cycle of the South-East, and the pottery trading voyages, *hiri*, from Port Moresby. The routine of the former has almost raised such valued objects as the red *Spondylus* strings, in the form of *bagi* and *samakupa* necklaces, and the *Conus* arm-rings (*toia, mwali*) into the ranks of currency ; with stone axe-blades (*benam*), lime spatulas (*potuma*) and nose-sticks (*wanepa*) following in their wake.

White shell-money is made on Tami Island, in the Huon Gulf on the Northern Coast, but serves more for ornament than for currency, though the strings are traded to New Britain. The industry was, until lately, flourishing here, and the apparatus is described and illustrated by Schneider, 1905, pp. 66–7, Fig. 13 ; and by Lewis, 1929, p. 14, Pl. VII, Fig. 5, Pl. V, Figs. 1–2.

Nassa callospira shells are used as currency round both the Northern and the Southern Coasts. The backs are broken off, not as for *diwarra* to be fixed on to stiff cane, but to be threaded, like buttons, through two holes, and bound on to a cord ; Fig. 69 shows the *tautau* (its Motu name) of the central district of the South Coast and Fig. 70 *maij* of the Sepik district in the North.[1]

The ordinary shell-money of British New Guinea is the red *sapi sapi* which the Massim people of the islands of the south-east, and especially the Trobrianders make from the shells of *Spondylus* or *Chama pacifica* (see Frontispiece, Figs. 1, 2). This currency is in full use along the Coast, and is made at a few villages near Port Moresby, where its Motu name is' *ageva*.[2] One string is worth about £1 and the two strings essential for a *bagi* or a *samakupa* £2 (Lewis, 1929, p. 11, Pl. VII, Figs. 6–7 ; Petri, 1936, p. 531, Fig. 16).

Seligman, whose photograph of a *bagi* is reproduced in Pl. 13, says that

A really fine specimen is worth from £5 to £7, this being the price which

---

[1] *Ssanem* and *darram* are other names on the North, and *movio* or *mowi* on the South. *Cf.* Schneider, pp. 64–6, Pl. 12, *b, c.*

[2] It was imitated by white traders, who found it a profitable industry but their strings can be recognized by being threaded on European twine in place of the native *Pandanus.*

natives earning from 10s. to 15s. a month are prepared to pay in cash to any traders possessing a really good one (1910, pp. 514–15).

The central point of the *samakupa* is marked by a series of white disks and a row of black banana seeds, with dangles of finer disks like those of the *bagi*. These dangles are of the edge-to-edge technique (Fig. 71) characteristic of New Ireland ' pig-money ', and the same type of decoration is added to the shell arm-rings, to the lime spatulas and to the stone axe-blades used in exchanges.

While these shell-strings are worn as ornaments purists will not accept them as ' money ', but their uses afford an excellent illustration of the evolution of money as suggested in Chapter I. They are used in presentation for ' bride-price ' ; for wergeld, and in peace-making ; and they accompany a dead man on his last journey (though removed by his heirs before burial). (Seligman, 1910, pp. 545, 556, 570, 610, 613, &c.).

When a formal peace-making is due, the blood accounts between two communities being tolerably even, exchange of valuables forms the opening ceremony. Seligman describes how the Wagawaga and the Maivara neighbouring villages on the south side of Milne Bay concluded peace a few years ago.

About 20 Maivara canoes, carrying spears and shields so as to be prepared for

FIG. 69.—*Tautau. Nassa* shell - money, New Guinea

FIG. 70.—*Nassa* shell-money, New Guinea

hostilities, came to Wagawaga to propose peace. They lined up silently some 200 yards from the shore. Some of the older Wagawaga men went off to discuss whether it should be peace or war, and, deciding for peace, some stayed in the Maiwara canoes, while the rest paddled back to shore and hastily collected the essential presents in the form of shell ornaments, axe-blades and pigs. A man from each hamlet called up a Maivara canoe which paddled in, and

was tied up to a stake close to the shore ; then the man waded out, bringing his ' presents ' and sat in the canoe for a short time. On this occasion the presents included 15 pairs of *Conus* shell arm-rings, 9 red shell-strings (*bagi* or *samakupa*), 10 stone axe-blades, 4 nose-sticks, 2 boars' tusks, 1 decorated lime spatula and 3 pigs (Seligman, 1910, p. 545).

The same ' presents ' are used in compensations for wounds or death. Injuries caused by trouble over a woman or a pig or by accidents were all compoundable by necklaces, *Conus* arm-rings or other valuables. At Wagawaga the blood-price for a man killed in a brawl was quoted as a pair of really good shell arm-rings, one shell nose-stick and one *samakupa* necklace of *sapi-sapi*. A broken arm would be atoned for by a *samakupa* necklace and 3 arm-rings ; an eye was worth far less than an arm (Seligman, 1910, pp. 570-1).

FIG. 71.—Detail of *samakupa* string

Arm-rings in New Guinea as in the Solomons have a confusing variety of names in the different dialects, and there are also various names for different sizes and qualities, while each really valuable one, like each Pelew bead, has its own individual name, given it by its maker or owner.

The arm-rings which form the currency of the Mandated area of New Guinea are altogether different from those of the Trobriands, being made of *Tridacna*, like those of the Bismarck Archipelago and the Solomons. Lewis describes the method of manufacture on the small islands of Seloe and Angel in Berlin Harbour. The centre of the piece of shell is bored out with a hollow bamboo, sand and water, leaving a smooth round hole of the required size. The rings are here used for buying sago from the mainland, one ring buying 500 to 1,000 pounds of the meal, which is the chief foodstuff. One man there refused to sell Lewis a partly-finished ring at any price, saying he needed it to buy food for his family for the coming rainy season. (Lewis, 1929, p. 11).

The smaller rings measure 3 to 6 inches (8 to 15 cm.) across, and the larger and much rarer ones 8 to 10 inches (20 to 25 cm.).

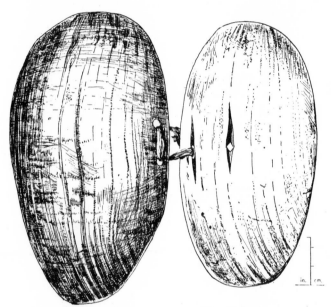

FIG. 72.—Breast ornament, New Guinea

These are the standard valuables in which to express important exchanges or ceremonial payments, though many other objects may be used interchangeably with them. The list includes shells of various kinds, *Turbo, Melo, Conus*, ' gold lip ' (*Meleagrina*) *Nassa* and cowries ; besides dogs' teeth, cuscus teeth, and boars' tusks ; and there are coarse strings of shell-money, and arm-rings of *Trochus* as well as *Tridacna*. (Mead, 1938, p. 193).

The *Melo* shells shown in Fig. 72 are rare and difficult to obtain and this adds to their value, whether regarded as breast ornaments or as a form of currency. Necklaces of the apices of *Conus* or other gastropods are made in different ways. They are strung through their pierced tips, and ground smooth, like shell-money, but firmly

knotted with cord, as seen in Fig. 73. Or the apices are fixed on
to a plaited band as shown in Fig. 74 and secured by a toggle of a
piece of shell. Both of these are primarily necklaces. Cowries
threaded in bunches (Fig. 75A) or knotted on parallel cords, *tsimua*
(Fig. 75B), are a more usual medium of exchange (G. Bateson).

FIG. 73.—*Conus* string, New
Guinea

FIG. 74.—Shell necklace, New
Guinea

Mead's careful analysis of the part played by exchanges, buying
and sellings among the Mountain Arapesh and their neighbours in
the Sepik district illustrates the use of these various objects and their
claim to be looked upon as substitutes for money. Here 'bride
price' is not an important factor. In this extraordinarily diversified

area payment for wives is the custom on the plains inland ; sister exchange on the Coast, and the Arapesh came in between the two.

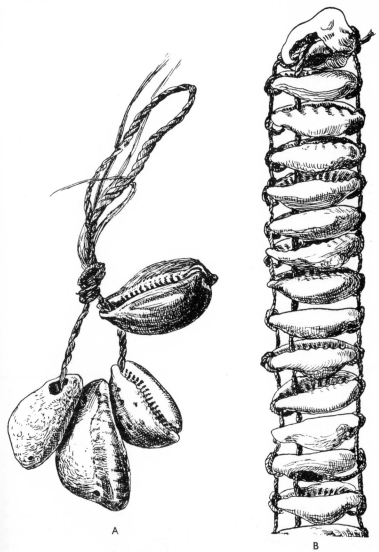

FIG. 75.—Cowries, New Guinea

We pay a little for our wives, but we also like to exchange sisters when that is possible,' as one explained (1938, p. 177). Few of these little groups are self-supporting, for most of them depend on markets for exchange of sago for fish ; and even when they are self-supporting as regards food, like the Arapesh, they depend on lines of hereditary trade friends for the supply of weapons and tools.   Trade crosses every boundary, linguistic, social and geographical, and accounts for the diffusion of magical beliefs and social customs as well as of material objects, ornaments and currency.   But the evolution of actual currency or money from this exchange of goods for rings and shells is hampered by the sentimental and personal value given to each possession by its maker or owner.   Like the more valuable arm-rings to the South, so those of the Mandated Territory often have individual names, and no one will admit that two similar valuables are genuinely interchangeable.   Work produced by hand with inefficient tools, the construction of which takes a long time, is felt to reflect and partake of the personality of the producer. Such objects are often considered so much a part of the maker that they are inalienable, and until they come to be regarded objectively instead of subjectively, they cannot form a currency (Viljoen, 1936, p. 213).

The trading activities of New Guinea are largely confined to the coasts and to the villages near the Coast.   The interior is still difficult of access, thinly occupied by unsociable and isolated communities, and, as has been seen above (p. 35), cowries only trickled in very sparsely.

In the Mt. Hagen area cowries are less rare ; gold-lip (*Meleagrina*) shells are more prized by the women (for ornaments) and the large bailer shells by the men.

Present-giving is here a firmly established custom, always reciprocal.   The man receiving a present is bound in public opinion to return something of equal value to the giver, or fall in social estimation.   Shells and axes are the usual presents, especially on the occasion of feasts.   A father seeking a wife for his son will take with him presents of shells and pigs, and more shells have to be paid before the negotiations are complete.   When all is fixed, the bride decorated with ropes of cowries, and gold-lip shells, perhaps bailers also, brings these as dowry, back to her husband.

Cowries are the commonest currency, either loose in the hand, or sewn vertically on to cord with value calculated by length, 2 feet being the unit.   The largest ropes of about 9 feet buy gold-lip shells, pigs or wives.   A gold-lip will buy a small pig, a bailer shell a large one, but prices fluctuate, and the coming of the white man has upset native currency values.   (Ross, 1936).

Among the most remarkable and by far the most impressive articles of high value, on the borderline between presents and currency, are the large stone axe-blades *benam*, which form a link not only between barter and money but between the ages of Stone and Steel. These all come from Murua or Woodlark Island in the South-East of the Trobriands, where the special stone (ash or lava) with specially valued banding is found. The blades are much too large and thin to be of practical use as tools and their exchange value is much the same as that of the arm-rings.

They are used according to value to buy pigs, food, canoes and land ; to procure sorcery, to pay for those slain in battle, to appease an enemy, to buy dances . . . as an exchange for other wealth. Placed under the head of the dying or on the breast of the dead, they placate Topileta, the keeper of the ways in the underground world of spirits : they are brought out at harvest feasts or rejoicings so that the spirits of the departed may see them and be glad. They are used as gifts to the relations of her whom the man would marry. Sometimes they are buried with the dead (Seligman, 1910, p. 518, quoting Gilmour ; cf. ill., Pl. LXII).

Stone blades were traded along the Southern Coasts of New Guinea to the Gulf, and they passed in exchange from village to village. The Motu of Port Moresby got theirs from the Koiari of the hinterland, who said that theirs came from farther inland, and these from somewhere else, and the Motu have a story to account for their origin. Only a certain people, they say, and only certain men of the tribe can procure these stone blades. They wade in the streams with a hand-net, and stone adzes, ready-made, swim like fish, and are caught in the nets. They believe that it is easy to know one of these stone-blade fishers (who is especially *tabu*) because of the scars on his legs caused by the stone blades trying to avoid his net (Seligman, 1910, p. 115).

The lime spatulas (*potuma*) used as presents or as minor currency can also swell into *Wücherformen*. They are made of bone (whale or dugong) or of wood, often elaborately carved, and decorated with strings of *sapi-sapi* or crabs' eyes (*Abrus precatorius*), but show no signs of ever having been used.

The largest and most decorated (*gabaiera*) come from the Lousiades, where they form part of the ' bride-price '. (Seligman, 1910, pp. 515–16, 528, Figs. 39, 40).

There are two more ornaments which must be included in this large group of valued objects used in present-giving and exchanges, in ' bride-price ' or in ordinary trading ; these are the pearl-shell crescents (Fig. 76) and the turtleshell chest pendants (colour plate, facing p. 184).

Pearl shells (*Meleagrina margaritifera*) are fairly abundant and are valued for making into ornaments throughout the region, so they are traded round the coasts and inland. The crescents (*mairi*) made by the Hula South of Port Moresby are something more than mere ornaments as they commonly accompany the arm-rings in the *hiri* trading voyages, and are used in ' bride-price ' as well as in ordinary exchanges for sago.

The fretted turtleshell chest pendants (*koio* or *koiyu*) are made by the Roro people in Hall Sound, to the north of Port Moresby, who, having learnt from the Motu people to make pottery and to build canoes, have trading voyages on a smaller scale, and these ornaments are among their valued articles of trade. They have a certain ceremonial and social importance too, and a young Roro, after his first kĭll, has one tied to his headdress at the end of the purification ceremony (Seligman, 1910, p. 298).

Money cannot properly be said to exist in the islands of Torres Straits, so the stages anticipating its evolution can the better be distinguished.

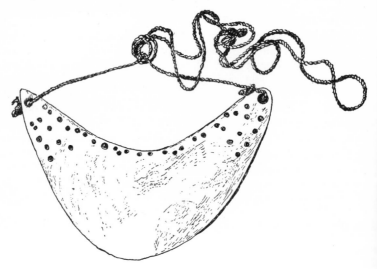

FIG. 76.—*Mairi*, breast ornament, Torres Straits

Various articles in daily use or which were occasionally worn, had a recognized exchange value, depending on the fineness of the specimen or its rarity. There were certain objects which were the units of highest value, and approximately equal in exchange, the standard being, as usual, a wife, and their main use was in presents made to the bride's relatives (Haddon, 1912, p. 236).

The most valued possessions of these island peoples were naturally their canoes and their dugong harpoons, which were handed down from generation to generation. The more easily exchangeable objects are the *Conus* shell (*wauri*) (Fig. 77), olive shell necklets (*uraz*) (Fig. 78), strings of dogs' teeth (*umai dangal*) and the *dibidib* pendants made of *Conus* top whorls (Fig. 79).

These have already been recorded as participating in the

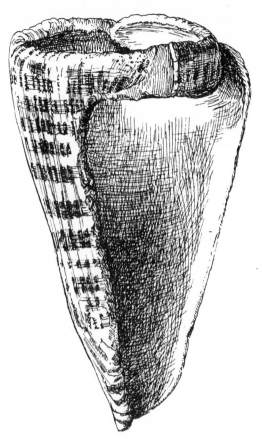

FIG. 77.—*Wauri, Conus* shell, Torres Straits

presents' in the canoe trade with the Fly River (p. 17) in which
barter, the shell arm-rings and strings of dogs' teeth are essential as
final payments (Landtman, 1927, p. 214). But the cone shell (*wauri*)
(Fig. 77) is no longer an ornament; it is a token of value, and so
can almost be regarded as money. It can be recognized as a *Conus*

FIG. 78.—Olive shell necklace, Torres Straits

shell, from the side of which an *o* pendant (Fig. 80) [1] has been cut, and a *dibidibi* [2] from the top. The chief interest lies in the fact that the value is merely conventional and the *wauri* represents the first step towards actual money, and the farthest step reached by the Torres Straits' Islanders uninfluenced by Europeans (Haddon, 1912, p. 236). A further step was marked by the 'needles' or pieces of iron 6 inches to 8 inches long (15–20 cm.) obtained from wrecks paid by the Muralug people for canoes, 6 to 24

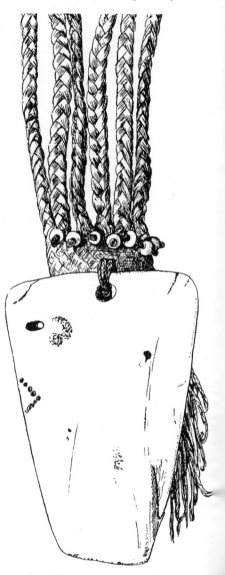

FIG. 79.—*Dibidibi*

according to the size of the canoe required (Haddon, 1904, pp. 196–7). Nowadays the final stage has

[1] The *o* pendants were frequently used in exchange and in marriage presents (Haddon, 1912, pp. 47, 169, Fig. 64).

[2] The *dibidibi* are especially interesting from their parallel use as both ornament and currency in Central Africa (p. 50). In Torres Straits 10 or 12 of these of a fair size would equal a canoe, a dugong harpoon or a wife (Haddon, 1912, pp. 43–4, Fig. 61).

FIG. 80.—*O* made from *wauri*, Torres Straits

been reached, when European trade goods, tobacco and coins have established a new standard of value, in which local products, even if they still survive, have no place. Local products with ceremonial and sentimental value are still in demand in 'bride price' as has been seen above, though with decreasing frequency.

Courtship in Torres Straits in earlier days consisted mainly in presents to the bride's relations. There was no fixed price, but a canoe, a dugong harpoon, a shell armlet, with perhaps necklaces of olives or dogs' teeth or *dibidibis* thrown in, were considered the equivalent of a wife. Fifty years ago, when European importations were still rare, a knife and a glass bottle might be sufficient. Nowadays payments are almost all in trade goods, and the occasion of much haggling. More is naturally expected from a chief than a commoner. Maino, chief of Tutu, recorded his payment consisting of a sandalwood chest containing seven pieces of calico, a dozen shirts, a dozen singlets, a dozen pairs of trousers, a dozen handkerchiefs, two dozen axes, a fish spear, fish lines and hooks, besides a pound of tobacco and two pearl shells, ending the list with ' by golly he too dear ' (Haddon, 1904, pp. 223-4, 231).

D. ROSSEL ISLAND

The currency of Rossel Island, some 200 miles south-east of New Guinea, is of peculiar interest.

It is a small island, about 100 square miles in extent, with a population of about 1,000, who differ in many respects from their Melanesian neighbours, particularly in their unique currency system, by the aid of which they carry on their mutual trafficking in pigs and concubines, in canoes and wives.

The outstanding features of the Rossel Island money are that, of each grade of the tokens in use, there is a virtually unchanging stock that has come down to the present generation from time immemorial, and that into the grading of the tokens—their value-relationships to one another—there enters the novel element of a time-element or interest-element, in place of the more familiar principle of simple proportionality (Armstrong, 1924, p. 423).

Armstrong, himself an economist, shows how large a part this monetary system plays in the life of the islanders. Payments of money are the most important constituents of marriage rites, mortuary rites and many other ceremonial activities. He says, ' I use the term " money " advisedly, for the objects are used primarily as media of exchange and standards of value ; they are systematically interrelated as regards value ; and any commodity or service may be more or less directly priced in terms of them ' (1928, p. 59). But while most of our ' primitive money ' claims the title mainly because it represents wealth, here there is no such claim ; as although chiefs alone appear to own the higher valued pieces, this is not for ostentation or display, for it is bad form to make any parade of possession.

There are two kinds of money, *ndap* and *nkö* (Pl. 18). The *ndap* money consists of single pieces of *Spondylus* shell, ground down and polished, varying in size from about 2 to 20 sq. cm. These pieces are generally roughly triangular in shape, with rounded edges, and are perforated near one of the corners.[1] The colour varies from white to orange, yellow and red, and the value appears to be indicated primarily by colour. All the *ndap* money is believed to have been made by the gods before man appeared on Rossel, and all the shell was then used up, at any rate shells for the higher values. Some of the lower values may still be made, but this is doubtful. There are special *ndap* canoes used either for collecting the shells, or for transporting the *ndap* from place to place, and the possession of these canoes is the most important attribute of chieftainship, suggesting that the making of the money is a chiefly perquisite. Moreover, only chiefs possess *ndap* of the higher values.

These shell ' coins ' form a series of 22 values each with a separate name, and there are subdivisions of these, making about 40 distinctions of value altogether. Individual coins of the higher values have individual names ' not etymologically descriptive ', and are recognized by their colour or their irregular shape, no two being exactly alike. The number of coins in each denomination is known, only 7 of some and 10 of others of high values, existing on the island ; but there are more of the lower ones, perhaps 1,000 altogether. A *pwomondap* (or No. 4 coin) is illustrated in the colour plate opposite ; this is perhaps the commonest coin on the island and there may be some 200 of them altogether.

The monetary system is so complicated that it is safest to quote extensively from Armstrong's account (1928, pp. 63–4). Value does not depend on scarcity, but on custom, and the economic law of supply and demand has very little effect. Moreover, owing to the peculiar nature of the system, some values are more in demand than others either above or below. Some coins have to ' work ' much harder than others, (No. 18 is in constant request for wives), but this does not affect the value relationships.

The 22 values are related in a peculiar way, which makes the Rossel system one of exceptional interest. The values are not regarded as simple multiples of some unit of value—the usual principle in most monetary systems. The relationship of any value to any other in this series may be expressed by the formula

$$\text{Value of No. } n = \text{value of No. } m \, (1 + k)^{n-m}$$

---

[1] *Cf.* the similar pendants of *Spondylus* from Ponape illustrated by Finsch, 1888–93, Pl. VIII, Fig. 17.

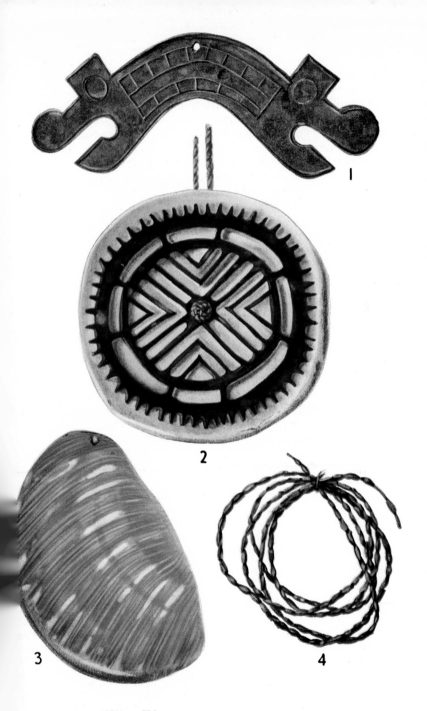

1. *Ch'ing*, China, p. 233
2. Turtleshell chest pendant, New Guinea, p. 179
3. *Pwomondap*, Rossel Island, p. 184
4. Beetle leg string, San Matthias, p. 131

where m and n are the two integers representing the number of the value in the series and k is a constant. One way in which the No. m value is related to the No. n value is by the length of time a No. m coin would have to be let out on loan in order that a No. n be repayable. Now this time interval is dependent on the value interval $(n - m)$ to which it is roughly proportional.

If a coin is borrowed for a few weeks, the next above has to be repaid. If the loan is for a longer time, it requires for repayment a coin two stages higher. The price of any commodity or service can thus be reckoned in terms of time, i.e. the time required for the loan to increase through the value series. E.g. a basket of taro could be said to cost a week, a wife to cost a year, and so on. This appears to represent the native point of view, rather than the supposition of a more or less definitely evaluated rate of interest.

The higher coins (Nos. 18 to 20) have also a magic or sacred content. *Työmundi* (No. 18) in particular, when passing from person to person, is handled with apparent reverence and a crouching attitude is maintained.[1] The higher values are proportionately more sacred and are almost always kept enclosed and are not supposed to see the light of day. It seems to be rare nowadays for there to be any transactions involving payments greater than No. 18. No. 20 was, however, used some years ago as compensation for ritual murder. The death of a chief used to involve the eating of one or more victims drawn usually from a neighbouring friendly village, and the compensation to relatives involved elaborate payments with ramifications extending over many years (1924, p. 428).

The *nkö* money is made of roughly and irregularly shaped disks, probably of the shell of a giant clam, perforated and strung in tens. The manufacture of this, and apparently that of *ndap* also, is a lost art, and the natives believe every piece to be of great antiquity.

Ten disks form the monetary unit, and several strings of tens may be strung together to make a long rope containing some thousand or more disks, the larger the disks the higher the value. There is a fiction that *nkö* is women's property while *ndap* is man's ; there are only 16 values compared with *ndap*'s 22, but otherwise, save for a few minor differences, both kinds are used in the same way. It is very difficult to collect any of the *nkö* money. Armstrong tells of the trepidation of the native who sold him quite a low value of *nkö* for over £1), imploring him not to reveal the sale as he feared the anger of the older men.

Birth, marriage and death rites all demand payments in *ndap* and *nkö*. No feast is complete without them, and they are necessary for fines and compensations. The prospective bridegroom brings a high value *ndap* (No. 18) for the father of the girl, while the

[1] *Cf.* Pelew beads, p. 149.

negotiations are not complete until various claimants have all been paid in *ndap* coins.   A rope of *nkö* is presented to the bride's mother a few months after the wedding.   Children play games with small stones to represent *ndap* and *nkö*, with sometimes cats' eyes (opercula) for higher *ndap* values.

Owing to the complications of the monetary system a profession has arisen in Rossel, very similar to that of a London bill-broker working with different material.   The members of this profession on Rossel render an important service by transferring the possession of a coin from one who does not want it and lending to another who does.   Their profit is made by increasing the time unit for their debtors and decreasing it for their creditors, and by keeping their capital on loan as far as possible ; in other words, borrowing at a lower rate of interest and discounting at a higher.   In practice, a form of magic is employed, by means of which these brokers claim to act on the minds of their debtors making them repay within the customary time, while the minds of their creditors are affected in the reverse way.   As wealth is power in Melanesia such a person may become a chief.

Chapter VII

ASIA

The first Invention . . . of that coy Lady *Pecunia*.
RICE VAUGHAN

i. General. ii. India. iii. Further India : A. Andamans and Nicobars ; B. Assam and Burma ; C. Siam and Indo-China. iv. China. v. Japan. vi. Malay Peninsula. vii. Borneo. viii. The Philippines. ix. Dutch East Indies

i. GENERAL

THERE are over one hundred different examples of primitive money from Africa in the Cambridge Collection. There are rather more from Oceania. From the far larger area of Asia, far more densely populated, containing some of the oldest civilizations in the world, yet with large areas scarcely civilized at all, some 30 types have been collected from the mainland (Assam, Burma, Siam, China and Indo-China) and about the same number from the Malay region, Borneo, the Philippines, Sumatra, Java and successive islands. Japan is doubtful ; and India is almost unrepresented.

There are several reasons for this lack of material, and one of the most obvious may be mentioned here.

Throughout the greater part of the immense region which includes Europe to the West and stretches to Further India in the East, cattle were the chief form of wealth, and, as is seen in Africa, where cattle form the standard of value, varieties of primitive money are undeveloped.

Ridgeway compares the system of currency in Annam with that formerly in use in Greece, India and Persia. He argues (1892, p. 26) that there were definitely fixed relations in value between the cows, horses, gold, rice and cloth of the Vedic people.

But absolute proof is at hand, for their close kinsmen, the ancient Persians, have left us in the Zend Avesta ample means of observing their monetary system. Thus we read in the ordinances which fix the payment of the physician that ' he shall heal the priest for the holy blessing ; he shall heal the master of an house for the value of an ox of low value ; he shall heal the lord of the borough for the value of an ox of average value ; he shall heal the lord of a town for the value of an ox of high value '.

Women were appropriately doctored for payments estimated in values of cows, mares and she-camels according to the position of their husbands.

Ridgeway traces this cattle-currency-complex through ' Aryan,

Semitic and Hamitic races ', all alike possessed of flocks and herds, from India in the East to the Gauls and Britons in the West, and to Egypt and the Sudan to the South, and he points out that

> There was no insuperable barrier between Indian and Persian, Persian and Mede, Mede and the dweller in Mesopotamia, or again between Persian and Armenian, Armenian and the Scythian . . . of what is now South Russia ; the Scythian was in contact with the tribes of the Balkan peninsula who in turn were in contact with the Greeks and the dwellers along the valley of the Danube, who in their turn joined hands with the peoples of Italy, Helvetia and Gaul. Hence the value of cattle would be more or less constant from one end of this entire region to another . . . though the purchasing power of the cow might be greater in some parts than in others (pp. 50–2).

Cattle, however satisfactory as wealth, as a standard of value, or even as a medium of exchange in the larger affairs of life, cannot properly be called money ; and need must often have been felt for some more easily transportable and divisible form.

> A simple invention it was in the old-world Grazier [wrote Carlyle]— sick of lugging his slow Ox about the country till he got it bartered for corn or oil—to take a piece of leather and thereon scratch or stamp the mere figure of an Ox (or *Pecus*) ; put it in his pocket and call it *Pecunia*, Money. Yet thereby did Barter grow Sale, the Leather Money is now Golden and Paper, and all miracles have been out-miracled ; for there are Rothschilds and English National Debts ; and whoso has sixpence is sovereign (to the length of sixpence) over all men ; commands cooks to feed him, philosophers to teach him, kings to mount guard over him—to the length of sixpence

Whether token money in skins or leather [1] can be regarded as a natural development from cattle-currency is doubtful. Pelts were certainly used instead of money throughout the northern regions of Europe and Asia, like the beavers of North America, but the dividing line between bartered goods and currency is here impossible to define.

In Russia, according to Herberstein, the ' simple invention ' of token money was made, not by the Grazier, but by the Hunter.

> In early times before they had money they made use of snouts and ears of squirrels and other animals, whose skins are brought to us in lieu of coin and bought the necessities of life with them as with money (1851, p. 111).

When Herberstein was ambassador in Moscow (1517–20) the ordinary currency was in silver, but the use of skins as money was artificially fostered, with the hope of keeping coin from leaving the country ; so pelts of sable, marten, ermine, fox and squirrel were made up in regularly graded bundles of ten, and sold for 1 or *deng* (p. 114). These bundles of 10 skins were too heavy to carry about, so the ' tokens ' of snouts or ears were cut off, and acted as

---

[1] Leather has often been used for emergency money, and *cf.* p. 248.

tallies. The purchaser fitted in the bits when he claimed his goods.

A currency in squirrel skins still continues in Mongolia.

Squirrels are hunted by Solons, Numinchen and Reindeer Tungus in North-West Manchuria, and are the principal means of paying the Chinese for the wares bought (almost always on credit) from the latter. As these tribesmen are chronically in debt to the Chinese firms, cash is practically unknown ; and any payment for sums less than the value of a horse (or more rarely cattle, sheep or goats) is likely to be made in squirrel skins.

The Reindeer Tungus pay debts to each other as well as to traders (Russians in their case) in squirrel skins ; but when they remove the skin from the animal, they roll it up into a ball, into which shape it stiffens, thus differentiating the skins obtained by these Tungus from those obtained by Russians or by other tribes.

The skin illustrated in Pl. 27 was payment for drink.

During a shaman performance to celebrate the shaman's cure of an official's son after an illness the official ran short of spirits, and asked whether our party could supply him with a little more. In view of his reputation for slashing at his neighbours when drunk, less than half a pint of alcohol was given him, for which he paid with this skin (E. J. Lindgren).

ii. INDIA

Cattle and barter sufficed for the more primitive peoples of Asia, pelts were traded all across the northern regions and Chinese silk provided a currency along the trade-routes down to medieval times. When we turn to the southern civilizations, so much earlier than our own, examples of primitive money are remarkably lacking. One cause is evident from a glance at the types exhibited, for a large proportion consists of coins, or coins in embryo, and when coins are in circulation the currency can no longer be called primitive. Rectangular and rounded coins were in use in India several centuries before the Christian era, anticipated here as in Ceylon, and in Further India by lumps and bars of metal (Pl. 19).

Another cause is the absence of information about prehistoric or even early historic times, and archaeology is only slowly filling up the blank. Tavernier, who was specially interested in the subject, wrote in 1684 : ' This is all I could collect of most certainty concerning the Money and Coins of the East. Nor do I believe that any person has undertaken before me to write upon the same subject ' II, p. 13). The serious study of Asiatic numismatics is little more than a century old and the Numismatic Society of India only came of age in 1937.

For India, history scarcely begins to be trustworthy before Alexander, who quickened the dispersal of Greek culture and Greek coinage to the Orient. By this time metallurgy was already well advanced, gold and silver were abundant, coins were already in existence and forms of primitive money are not to be expected.

As early as the 3rd millenium B.C. the high level of the gold-smith's art and the use of gold, silver and copper ·in beads, rings, bangles and other objects are illustrated in the civilization of Mohenjo-daro and Harappa, although nothing belonging to the early culture was recognized by the excavators as money. It was, however, suggested that the ring-stones found in large numbers at both sites might be a form of currency, comparable to the stone-money of Yap, and forming a link in the world-wide distribution of holed stones or rings with currency or ceremonial value, from West Africa to Eastern Asia and the Pacific. These ring-stones of the Indus Valley vary from ½ inch to 4 feet across (1 cm. to nearly 1 m. 50 cm.); the larger ones are of stone, the smaller include shell, imitation carnelian and faience.

Marshall makes the significant comment: ' The wheel-money of Uap (Yap) undoubtedly presents a striking parallel to the larger class of ring-stones in the Indus Valley ' (1931, I, p. 61). But he argues that even though stone was rare there it was not so rare as to warrant its being used as money, nor were people of such high culture as the inhabitants of these wealthy cities, with commercial relations with Persia and Mesopotamia, likely to use so cumbrous a form of currency. He regards it as more likely that these ring-stones were treasured on account of the magical properties that all holed stones are believed to possess, a belief that persists down to our own day in our own villages ; and that their special preservation was due to the awe in which such stones are held, either as fetishes or as actually imbued with divine power.

For commercial purposes far more suitable material was at hand.

It has indeed been claimed (Acharya and Gyani, 1937, p. 11) that round and rectangular pieces of copper or of silver, fore-runners of the punch-marked coins, were the currency of the Indus Valley in the 4th or 3rd millenium B.C. The similarity, if not identity of signs on the Mohenjo-daro seals (which may have passed as currency or I.O.U.'s) and those on punch-marked coins is remarkable (Fábri, 1934, pp. 307, 316 ; Prasād, 1934, pp. 9, 36 Pls. XXVII, XXIX), but as Allan says (1936, p. lxxiii) 3,000 years is a long period to bridge. Thick slightly bent bars of silver stamped with various designs appear early in the North-West adjusted to the Persian weight standard, and are assumed to date from the 4th or 5th century B.C. when that part of India was still under Persian domination. The earliest authentic and official coins of India, the punch-marked coins, found north, south, east and west over the whole peninsula, which, from their ubiquity and uniformity indicate a central organized and imperial authority, can scarcely be place

earlier than the Mauryan Empire (*post* 322 B.C.). The Mauryan
coinage is, however, by no means primitive in type, and ancestral
stages will doubtless be recognized as archaeological research fills
up the gap between the civilization of Mohenjo-daro and that of
Chandragupta (*cf.* Whitehead, 1938, p. 337).

Although this is an intrusion into the domain of numismatics,
Cunningham's description of the making of these silver *karshapanas*
or *panas*,[1] (which were already called *puranas*, meaning ' ancient '
in the Buddhist Sutras), must be quoted here, as it illuminates the
obscurity of the transition stage between primitive money and coins.

Pana probably means a handful, and the handful equalled 80
cowry shells ; 4 *panàs* equalled a *tanka*, whose weight was fixed by
the *māsha* (mace) or bean (*Phaseolus*). There was also a copper
pana, weighing 80 *rati* seeds (*gunja, Abrus precatorius* the black-
spotted pea) or twice that number of barley grains, and valued at
80 cowries. The interdependence of cowries, seeds and coins and
their contemporary use can scarcely find better illustration.

The metal was adjusted to the equivalent of the shells or seeds
as follows :

> The mode of fabrication is evident at once from an inspection of the
> coins. A piece of silver was first beaten out into a flat plate of about the
> thickness of a shilling. . . . Narrow strips of about ½ inch or more in
> width were then cut off. Each strip was then cut into separate pieces of the
> same weight of about 56 grains,[2] and a final adjustment of the weight was
> made by cutting small bits off one or more corners of the heavier blanks.
> The marks of the chisel still remain on the edges of the thicker pieces which
> were broken off when the cut did not go clean through the strip of metal.
> The earliest specimens are generally thin and broad, and of irregular shape
> (Cunningham, 1891, p. 43).

If we turn on to historic or modern times we do not find in India
those incentives to the multiplication of forms of currency such as
have been evolved either in Africa or in Oceania. It is still not a
need of the social system.

The basis of society is cultivation of the soil. Even today three-
quarters of the whole population is classed as agricultural. And the
main crops are grain and pulses, which are not only sufficiently
' portable, divisible, durable and recognizable ' to serve as money,
but are sufficiently uniform to serve also as weights and measures,
with which, here as elsewhere, the metal currency was closely linked.

The village community, the social nucleus of which appears to
have persisted for centuries, is essentially self-contained and is still
singularly independent of coined money. The peasants till their

---

[1] The Sanskrit *karsha*, through Portuguese *caixa*, has become *cash*
Cunningham, 1891, p. 47 ; Chalmers, 1893, p. 372 *fn.*).

[2] Prasād (1934, p. 10 ; 1937, pp. 76–7) distinguishes the early pieces
weighing 24 *rati* (= 42 gr.) from the later, weighing 32 (= 56 gr.).

plots, the artisans, smiths, carpenters, weavers and potters ply their trades, and their payments are in grain, not in coin. Barter is still the normal exercise of trade, and though there is probably a money-lender in every village, money plays a minor part in local transactions.

Nevertheless, when early records come to be explored a few picturesque currencies, such as salt and almonds, come to light; mulberries are 'currency' in Turkestan (Temple, 1899, p. 105); cowries start on their conquering career; coconuts form the currency of the Nicobars, and the *larins* (so-called 'fish-hook money') spread throughout the territory of the Moguls.

Salt, here as everywhere, is an important object of barter, and large deposits in rock salt or in salt marshes are centres for export. Marco Polo describes how in Tibet ' they use salt instead of money ' and the stamped cakes, like brick tea, were the ordinary currency for traders (1903, Book II, Chap. 47). Salt still has a currency value, and is often preferred to coins by carriers in the hills.

Ogilby, writing about the Empire of the Great Mogul (1673, p. 163), described the *Fanos* (fanams) of ordinary gold, like the scales of a fish, worth 5½d.; the silver *Ropias* (rupees) worth 2s. 2d.; and the copper *Peysa* (pice) like farthings, 43 or 44 to the rupee. He adds

Moreover Almonds in the Shells pass for Money, 36 of them making a Copper *Peysa*, as also a sort of Cockles with a black Spot, in the Country Language call'd *Cauries*, which are found along the sea Coast, 8 whereof make a *Peysa*.

This was a hearsay account. Tavernier not only travelled in the country but collected the almonds and cowries, as well as coins, and illustrates his collection.

For small Money they make no use of these Shells [in the Province of Gujerat] but of little Almonds which are brought from about Ormuz and grow in the Desarts of the Kingdom of Larr. If you break one of the shells it is impossible to eat the Almond for there is no *coloquintida* [colocynth] so bitter; so that there is no fear lest the children should eat their small Money. Some years the Trees do not bear and then the price of this sort of Money is very much raised in the Country and the Bankers know how to make their benefit (II, p. 2). They call these Almonds *Baden*.[1] They give for a *pecha* sometimes 35 sometimes 40 (I, p. 22).

Nicolo de' Conti, the Venetian merchant and explorer in India early in the 15th century, gives the following scanty information.

In some regions they have no money but use insteade of money a certayne small stone which they name Cattes eye, and in some other places they do use peeces of Iron like needles, somewhat bigger. In other place they do use the Kings name written on paper insteade of money (1937 p. 143).

---

[1] Bādām, *Amygdalus communis* L., *var. amara.*

The travels of the cowry have already been traced (Chap. IV) and archaeological evidence shows that they had reached Asia in prehistoric times. Only two, and those neither *C. moneta* nor *C. annulus*, have been found in the Indus Valley, but *C. annulus* occurs among the ruins of Nineveh. Bengal was, as we have seen, the great distributing centre of the money cowries, and they spread over the whole of India right up to the hills. Their use as small change is illustrated in a treatise on Hindu mathematics, formerly attributed to the 7th century, but more recently, to the 12th.[1]

'Twice ten cowries are a *ćaćini*; four of these are a *pana*, sixteen of which must be considered as a *dramma*, &c.' When dealing with reduction of fractions, a moral is introduced and the avaricious man held up to scorn.

The quarter of a sixteenth of the fifth of three-quarters of two-thirds of a moiety of a *dramma* was given to a beggar by a person from whom he asked alms. Tell me how many cowry shells the miser gave if thou be conversant in arithmetic with the reduction termed subdivision of fractions.

Except along the West Coast cowries were the small change throughout India, and they persisted on the borders of the Empire until recent years.

Tavernier describes and illustrates (1684, I, p. 22) the 'small Money' consisting of 'little Shells which they call Cori the sides whereof turn circularly inwards' and reports that they were traded

into all the Territories of the Great Mogul . . . and into the islands of America and serve instead of Money. Near the Sea they give 80 for a Pecha (pice). But the further you go from the Sea the less you have. So that at Agra they will not give you above 50 or 55 for a Pecha.

Cowries were still the usual currency in many parts of the Indian Empire at the beginning of last century and they are still officially recognized in revenue assessments in Bengal. The estates register records the amount due from shares in an estate, in annas, pice and cowries (J. H. Hutton).

In the 18th century the yearly revenue of Silhet, Bengal Province, amounting to a quarter of a million rupees, was paid entirely in cowries, at the rate of 5,000 to 6,000 to the rupee. Large warehouses were needed to store them and when the annual collection was complete a large fleet of boats transported them in 50-ton loads to Dacca (Hamilton, 1820, I, p. 195).

In 1740 2,400 cowries went to the rupee; in 1756, 2,560; in 1845, 6,000 and more. Even when 4,000 or 5,000 went to the rupee, large payments were nevertheless made entirely in shells.

Reeve, after stating that cowries 'still pass current for money amongst the lower classes in some parts of Hindostan', quotes the

[1] *Lilavati of Bhaskara Acharya*, p. 301; *cf.* Ridgeway, 1892, p. 177.

case of 'the gentleman at Cuttack' who was said to have paid for the erection of his bungalow entirely in cowries.

The building cost him 4,000 rupees sicca (= £400 sterling), and as 64 of the shells are equal in value to 1 'pice' and 64 pice to 1 rupee sicca, he paid for it with over 16 million of these shells (1842, p. 262 *fn.*).

Next to cowries, and far higher in value, come the *larins* (Fig. 81), short lengths of silver wire doubled in two, which take their name from Lar in Laristan, formerly an important point on the caravan route from the Persian Gulf. They were traded inland and along

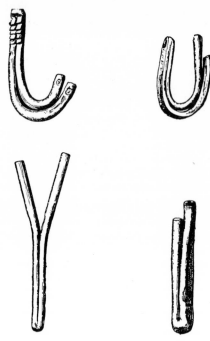

FIG. 81.—*Larins*, Persian Gulf

the coasts, and there are many references to their use from the 16th century onwards through the Indian Empire, including the Maldives and Ceylon, and as far as the East Indies. They were imitated locally, and the different types are difficult to distinguish. They were usually struck on both sides with a die, containing Persian or Arabic legends, only a few letters of which appear vaguely on the coin. These, when imitated, are still less legible and no help in identifications. They were especially popular in Ceylon, where they were bent up in the familiar 'fish hooks' and the locally made 'hook silver' (*koku ridi*) was current for some time after the British occupation in 1815. A cut or nick at the bend is often found, apparently to test the purity of the metal (*cf.* Allan, 1912).

All the *larins* are often lumped together as fish hooks, and it was believed that they were derived from actual hooks, the most important of all objects of barter for the fisherfolk of the Gulf, coasts and islands, and that the evolution into current money and from hooked into straightened forms was similar to that of the Chinese or African ' tool currencies ', illustrating successive stages of barter with useful objects, currency and token money.[1] But the comparison should be rather with the rod, bar or wire currency of Africa, which there was bent into hoop, ring, or *mitako* form to suit the demands or whims of local traders, and here was doubled and bent for the same reason. So the occurrence of straight *larins*, (which, if the genealogy of the *toweelah* (p. 196) be admitted, stretched back for more than 1,000 years), represents the earlier, not the degraded form.

William Barret, the English merchant, writing of the money and measures of Basra at the mouth of the Tigris in 1584 describes the *larin* as

a strange piece of money not being round like all other current money in Christianitie, but is a small rod of silver of the greatness of the pen of a goose feather wherewith we use to write and in length about one-eighth part thereof, which is so wrested that the two ends meet at the juste halfe part, and in the head thereof there is a stamp Turkesco and these be the best current money in all the Indies and six of the larines make a ducat (1904, p. 12).

There were thicker coins at Lar itself. Sir Thomas Herbert, writing in 1665, says

near this Buzzar [of Lar] the Larrees are coyned : a famous sort of money, being pure silver, but shaped like a Date-stone,[2] the King's name and some sentences out of the Alcoran being stamped upon it ; in our money it values tenpence (1665, p. 128).

The doubled bits of finer wire current along the coasts are often opened slightly at the end into a Y-form, which has given them the

[1] Unmistakable fish hooks are not unknown in currency collections. There are plain and serviceable ones used in barter with the Indians of Alaska (Mosher, 1936, Pl. XVIII) ; silver hooks from the Laos States (Loehr, 1935, p. 18) ; besides the pearl-shell blanks and hooks of Micronesia (Fig. 54), and the decorative and decorated hooks of the Solomon Islanders (Mosher, 1936, Pl. XII).

[2] This ' date stone ' shape is met again in the Java *tang*, the local name for *larin*. The Dutch found *larins* in use on their arrival, and they issued pewter *tangs* about 1660 to supply the deficiency of small change on the island. (Bucknill, 1931, pp. 55–6, illustrated the only known survivor.) A bronze *tang* of the 18th century is in the Vienna coin collection (Loehr, 1935, p. 20).

8 *

name of ' nose-clips ' from a belief that they were used by the divers
of the Persian Gulf.

Ogilby, writing in 1673, describes the popularity of the *larins*
throughout India :

> The *Laryns* or *Lari* are two Pieces of Silver of a certain weight bow'd
> together in two parts and stamped at the end with the Governor of Lar's
> Arms, and hath its name from the Princes of Lar when they were absolute
> and not subject to the Kings of Persia.   And because the value of the Coyn
> consists only in the weight and goodness of the Silver it passes currantly
> through all the Eastern Countreys. . . .   The Turks, Persians, Moguls
> and others coyn the same with their proper names (1673, p. 63).

Larins were the ordinary coinage of the Maldives and Ceylon.
Pyrard de Laval, who was wrecked on the Maldives in 1602, wrote

> This kind of money is current throughout all the Indies and is made
> at many places, but the best is coined at Ormuz.

And in his description of Ceylon he says :

> The coin of the realm is silver only and of one sort.   These are pieces
> of silver of the value of about eight sous of our money as long as the finger
> and doubled down.   The King has them struck on his island and stamped
> with his name in Arabic characters.   Though foreign coine are current, they
> are only taken at their just weight and value, and must be silver or gold, all
> others are rejected.   The King coins *larins* only and no pieces of less value.
> In place of copper they use *boly* or cowrie shells of which 12,000 are worth
> a *larin* (1887, I, p. 232).

Knox, who was a prisoner on the island in the 17th century, says:

of money they have but three sorts that passeth for coin in the King's
dominions.   The one was coined by the Portugals, with the King's Arms
on one side and the Image of a Friar on the other called *tangom massa*.
The value of one is ninepence English.   There is another sort which all
people by the King's Permission may and do make.   The shape is like
a fish hook, they stamp what mark or impression on it they please.   The
Silver is purely fine beyond Pieces of Eight.   For if any suspect the good-
ness of the Plate it is the Custom to burn the Money in a fire red hot, and
so put it in water ; and if it be not then purely white it is not Currant
Money.   The third sort of Money is the King's proper Coin.   For none
upon pain of death may Coin it.   It is called a *Ponnam (fanam)*.   It is as
small as a spangle ; 78 make a Piece of Eight, or a Spanish Dollar.   But
all sorts of Money is here very scarce.   And they frequently buy and sell
by exchanging Commodities (1679, pp. 156-7).

Along the western coast of the Persian Gulf a currency of *larin*
type is a relic of the former glory of El Hasa.   Here compressed
Y-shaped coins were issued in gold, silver and copper (mixed with a
little silver), and though the gold and silver have been melted down
long ago, the copper coins are still in use.   They are usually longer
than the *larins*, which has earned them their local name of *toweelat*
or ' long-bit ' from *tawil*, long (Fig. 82).   Along one or both of the

flattened sides run a few cubic characters, mostly illegible, but said to read Mohammed-al-Sasod. The coins have neither date nor legend, but are attributed to one of the Carmathian princes about the year A.D. 920. This Moslem sect owed its origin to Carmath, a fanatic enthusiast born at Cufa, who first had a following about the year 277 of the Hejira. The centre of their power remained at Hasa for some years, and here the coins were struck. And while the Carmathian doctrines are held in abhorrence these little bars of copper still buy rice, dates and such daily necessities in the market. Palgrave (1865, II, p. 179) calls them ' copper nails ' and gives their value as about three-farthings each. He says that they were current at Hasa alone, which gave rise to the local proverb *Zey toweelat-il-Hasa* ' like a Hasa long-bit ', meaning a man who could only make himself useful at home.

Nevertheless, they were current throughout Arabia, and the examples illustrated in Fig. 82 from the Royal Scottish Museum in Edinburgh are from Nejd.

FIG. 82.—*Toweelah*, Persian Gulf

The *larin* represents an unexpected return to a form of ingot currency long after coins were in ordinary trading use, and Codrington suggests that its special shape was due to its convenience for carrying, stuck into the folds of turban or waistcloth (1904, p. 118). It may be that the varieties and complexities of the coins of the 17th and 18th centuries, their varying values at different ports, and the impositions of the money-changers led to a preference for this full-bodied currency of pure silver [1] by traders of the Persian Gulf. But from Tavernier's account we can discover a more potent reason for its use. He illustrates the *larins* and half-*larins* (I, p. 2), 5 of which were equal to a French crown (= 3s. 10d.).

only the Five *Larins* want in weight eight sous of our Crown. This is that which the Emirs or Princes of Arabia take for the Coining of their Money ; and the profit which they make by the Merchants that travel through the Desert, either into Persia or into India. The Emirs change their Crowns, Reals or Ducats of Gold for their *Larins*. For they must of necessity pass that way. And they must use very smooth words to boot. For there is nothing to be got by rough Languages (1684, I, p. 1).

f the merchants would not submit to this extortion, the Emirs would not take their toll or give them a safe conduct, but would go off on a hunting trip of some weeks, leaving the wretched caravan waiting and waiting, eating up all the provisions for the journey. Tavernier

[1] Tavernier carefully enumerates 13 different ' goodnesses ' of silver 1684, I, p. 26).

spoke from his own experience.   Should the merchants start without
paying toll they would either be cut to pieces, their camels seized or
the caravan robbed with impunity, which often happened even if
toll was paid.

Coming from Babylon to Aleppo, Tavernier and his company
were met by an Arabian Prince :

> He would not let us go a step further unless we would exchange
> 200 piastres in specie for *larins*, the Money of the Country ; and he forc'd
> us to take them, what ever we could urge to make it appear how much we
> should lose by them.   And indeed we said as much as we could, for the
> dispute lasted two and twenty days to no purpose ; might overcoming
> right (1684, p. 59).

iii. FURTHER INDIA

A. ANDAMANS AND NICOBARS

The *Periplus* of the first century A.D. is a traders' guide as far
as the Ganges, but no farther.   ' The regions beyond these places
are either difficult of access because of their excessive winters and
great cold, or else cannot be sought out because of some divine
influence of the gods.'   So, though occasional voyages were made,
and Chinese records tell of adventurous merchants from the Roman
Empire in Siam, Annam and Tongking, Further India remained
little affected by Greek and Roman influence, except for such
indirect infiltrations as might percolate along the interior trade-
routes in return for Chinese silk.   And, save for the coasts, and
the establishment of a few trading-posts on river banks, these regions
were little affected by Western influence down to the 19th century.

This part of the world—especially if we include the Andaman and
the Nicobar Islands—makes an ideal field for economic investigation,
showing all stages in the money-concept : firstly, the moneyless
islanders, with their ceremonial presentations and exchanges and,
in the Nicobars, their coconuts as a medium of exchange : next the
isolated hill folk of the mainland, with no conception of money
before the coming of the rupee, yet with certain articles emerging
into a sort of currency : then the more advanced people with metals
in lumps or ingots, at first estimated by weight, and finally officially
cut up, stamped and issued as coins.

This part of the world is especially favourable for this investigation for another and more practical reason.

Such pioneers as Radcliffe-Brown, Hutton, Skeat and le May
not only collected valuable information, but supplemented it by
presenting the actual currency, or potential currency, to the Cambridge Museum, providing a lively background for the specimens
in the cases, and a complete picture of native economic phases.

The absence of money among the Andaman Islanders has already been noted, and also their universal custom of present-giving or gift-exchange as a sign of goodwill with no idea of barter (p. 13). Every present anticipates a return of at least equal value, save in the case of wedding presents, which alone are one-sided. (Radcliffe-Brown, 1922, p. 238).

Certain articles such as a special white clay (*tol*) could only be found in local deposits, and red paint [1] (oxide of iron mixed with turtle fat) and *dentalium* shells could only be obtained from the coast dwellers, and as these were essential for ceremonial costume, they were especially prominent in present-giving. Certain particularly ornamental shells (*Hemicardium* sp.), which were also rare, came very near to being a medium of exchange (J. H. Hutton).

The coconuts which are the medium of exchange in the Nicobars must be considered at greater length, as they are so often referred to in arguments about the origin of money.

The Nicobarese live on small islands, well protected from enemies, they have no lack of food or need of clothing. They are self-supporting, and independent of all external trade. Coconut palms supply them with food, drink, houses and furniture, as well as with a surplus for barter and medium of exchange. ' Because it acts as a sufficient currency they have no use for money as Europeans understand it. The coconuts are their money,' wrote Temple (Whitehead, G., 1924, p. 9). The islands produce millions of nuts annually ; they constitute wealth ; they provide a standard of value ; they are the recognized medium of exchange. For the latter purpose they are counted in pairs to reach a score, and then in scores of scores.

Pigs are used as presents on important occasions, in ' bride-price ', as fines, and in promoting general friendliness. The Nicobarese, therefore, may be included in the widely spread cattle-currency complex, with pigs to represent cattle, and coconuts to represent grain. Within such a culture, as has been seen, money is not essential and it is doubtful if a ' coconut currency ' would have developed, but for the visits of traders.

The Nicobars lie in the path of an ancient trade-route, so the islanders have been subject to the same alluring temptations in the shape of trade goods, as the rest of the world, but they have remained singularly indifferent. Buying and selling and even barter, are practically unknown among themselves, and the only exchanges are in the way of present-giving.

[1] Red ochre or red paint has been recognized as the nearest approach to currency among widely separated groups. It was used in exchanges by the Australians (*cf.* p. 108) and ' as currency ' by the Mohave and Apache in Arizona (Pitt Rivers Collection). Such lumps were trade, if not exchange objects in Europe in Aurignacian times, and possibly represent the most primitive money-substitute of all.

If a man has been very successful in his fishing—he would then make presents to his friends. Similarly if he has much ripe fruit on his hands, or an abundance of pork, he gives away some to his friends : but a very well-marked mental note would be made of such ' friends ' as do not make a return of gifts some time in the future. ' I your friend, you my friend ', says Offandi . . . when he brings me a piece of pork, and receives at the same (or some other) time a quantity of Burmese cheroots or Chinese tobacco (Whitehead, G., 1924, pp. 69–70).

But to offer a man some tobacco or anything else he may want for some fruit or a chicken would seem to him unnatural and un-friendly, and the proposition could never be entertained for a moment by one of nature's gentlemen.

With traders or with outsiders it is different. Every man must have a chopper to cut down his coconuts, and these are the Burmese *dahs* supplied by the shops, which also provide such luxuries as rice and tobacco, cloth, nickel tablespoons [1] and forks, (used as ornaments and in certain ceremonies) besides ordinary trade-goods.

These are all bought for nuts counted in pairs and tied together by a strip of the husk. One or two pairs will buy matches, salt, fish hooks or rice ; for a gramophone the price will run into thou-sands (of pairs). The most important objects which have to be exchanged between the islanders are pots and racing canoes, which, owing partly to local production and partly to local taboo, are obtained from one particular island.

Temple tells how the people of Mus, Car Nicobar, bought a large racing canoe valued at 35,000 (pairs of) coconuts, from the island of Chowra (Chaura) (1899, p. 290). There was no intention of collecting 35,000 coconuts and transporting them over to the other island. That would have been far too onerous a task. The canoe was paid for by a number of other articles all valued in coconuts, until the total reached 35,000 (pairs). The list included domestic animals, utensils, implements, cloth, beads, ' silver ' spoons and even British money but they were all estimated in their worth in coconuts.

There are some obvious advantages and disadvantages in a coconut currency. The awkwardness of bulk and the inconvenience of having to wait until the money was ripe, would suggest that the Government order—that it was illegal to refuse to give (or accept one pice for one nut, i.e. 64 to the rupee—would be a boon. But it is unpopular both with the traders and with the Nicobarese The traders believe that they can make double profit on goods and on nuts, and moreover there is no danger of their till being rifled

---

[1] These ' silver ' spoons may almost be called a currency, as they ar an accepted standard of value, and enter into all the more important tradin transactions. Soup ladles are valued at 500 pairs of coconuts, down t mustard spoons at 200 pairs. These are amassed as wealth and destroye at death (Temple, 1896, p. 284 ; Kloss, 1903, p. 81).

While on the native side the Nicobarese have no use for money as money, though rupees and spoons are used as decoration, especially by wizards ; and the only conspicuous display of rupees that White-head saw was when they were buried in the coffin of the wife of a rich man, so that she should be gratified and be less inclined to annoy her relations afterwards (1924, pp. 78-9).

In these islands where the folk are peaceable, friendly, generous, honest and truthful ; where women are treated as the equals of men and even dogs are never beaten ; where, though they are keen on sport, there is no rivalry and no gambling ; where there is no worry about rent and taxes, and where all importation of drink is officially prohibited, the ideal of the simple life appears to be attained [1]—a life without money.   There is probably some truth in the remark of the working-class woman in England, when she was told about the life and conditions of the Nicobarese, ' They will soon learn to steal if they begin to get money ' (Whitehead, G., 1924, p. 211).

B. ASSAM AND BURMA

Turning from the outlying islands to the mainland of Further India, we can watch the successive stages in the evolution of money. Hodson, Political Agent in Manipur early in the century, tells how he was visiting a village off the beaten track, and exhibiting the wonders of Western culture in the forms of magic lantern, galvanic battery and repeating pistol.   When the show was over, and there was general conversation round the camp-fire, comparing modern times with the ' bad old days ', the villagers were asked to decide what was the strangest thing that the *Sahib log* had brought to Manipur.   The verdict was—coined money.   Not only because it was in itself an innovation, but also because the coins were so marvellously uniform, native handiwork being unable to achieve such regularity (Hodson, 1911, p. 123).

Even in the wealthy native states of Assam and Burma there was little indigenous money in early times, save in silver ingots or in punch-marked coins, and these were seldom seen among the less-advanced communities.   In the remoter hills coined money is still a rarity and across the frontier even a useless curiosity.

In this complex area, the meeting-place of so many streams of culture, it is difficult for an account to steer between unscientific generalizations and niggling detail.   Barter is the usual method of

[1] Hutton remarks that much of the simplicity and of the ideal aspect is only on the surface.   Chinese traders and Japanese shell-fishers bring distilled liquor in great jars which they hide by burying them in the sand. Also the existence of too many wizards (who have to be thrown into the sea with broken limbs) rather complicates the simple life for some individuals.

trading, *mithun*, cattle, rice, salt,[1] iron and other local products are used in exchanges ; gongs are an expression of wealth ; cowries may be found in one district, conch shell in another and beads elsewhere, taking the place of money ; while in the Wā country heads have a commercial value fixed on strictly business principles with a definite tariff (Scott and Hardiman, 1900, I, 1, pp. 497, 502).

Cowries, as has been seen, travelled along the trade-routes of India, but off the trade-routes they are seldom more than ornaments

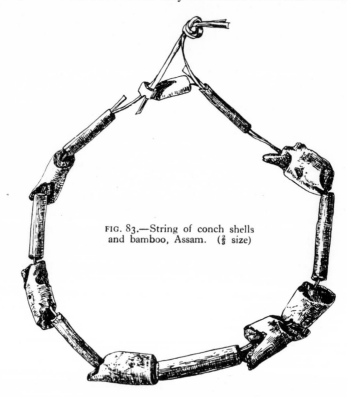

FIG. 83.—String of conch shells
and bamboo, Assam. (⅔ size)

or amulets.   In the hills they are worn more by the men than by the women, and although they are used in divorce (among the Khasia), have special significance (among the Angami and Sema Nagas) and are used in divination (among the Mikir), they have little share in native trading and it is doubtful if they were ever in popular use in Burma (*cf.* Steel, 1869, p. 308 ; Temple, 1897, p. 290 ; Stack, 1908, p. 35 ; Hutton, 1921 (i), pp. 24–5, (ii), p. 178).

[1] *Cf.* Temple, 1897, pp. 264 *ff.*, 281–2.   Salt in small flat cakes was currency among the Sema Nagas and still is in the Yachumi country to the east of them (Hutton, 1921 (ii), p. 58).

To a limited extent the conch shell takes the place of cowries; formerly a piece 8 fingers broad was worth a cow, and small beads made of it were used as money. Among the Yimtsungr (Yachumi) of the Naga Hills conch shell is still in use. Rough strings made of irregular bits of perforated shell and short lengths of bamboo (Fig. 83) have a token value of 2 to 4 annas, whichever is the local equivalent of a day's labour. The string is the unit, though it may be variously composed. Apparently anyone can make one of materials to hand, and a rich man will keep basketfuls ready, to be used for wages, or for buying cattle and wives (Hutton, 1921 (i), pp. 71-2).

Throughout the hilly areas of Burma and Assam in the last century cattle were the standard of wealth, and are still used as a standard in official payments and fines, and sometimes for the actual payments themselves. As Temple said

a man's revenue would be assessed by Government, not at so many rupees, but at a big buffalo; a fine would not be so many rupees but a cock and two small hens. So among the Chins, a fine would not be 10 rupees, but a full-grown hog (1899, p. 103).

Livestock, especially *mithun*; grain, especially rice; tools, especially daos; and family treasures, especially gongs; all these are valuable property and are used in presentations, 'bride-price', fines, exchanges and payments, commonly taking the place of money for certain formal transactions.

The most important unit of this kind in Assam is the *gayal* or *mithun* (*bos frontalis*), the domesticated form of the so-called 'bison' or *gaur* (*bos gaurus*). Fines, 'bride-price', 'bone-price' [1] or compensations for injuries are all assessed in *mithun*, though they are nowadays commonly paid in coin, the standard taken being 1 *mithun* = 35 rupees or thereabouts. Cattle are often used instead, when a man cannot afford *mithun*.

Among the Naga, wealth is in rice. There are rich men who boast of granaries full of rice, black with age, and who live on the high interest obtained from loans (Mills, 1926, p. 106). 'Bride-price' is here in rice, the amount varying between 5 and 60 basketsful, sometime a leathern shield or one or more daos may be added, though all have to be returned if the wife leaves within the year; 10 to 20 baskets of rice and 'a good dao' make the average payment among the Mongsen. Rupees are now taking the place of goods for 'bride-price', and among the Lhota Naga money is often paid by the bridegroom in place of the labour formerly given to the parents-in-law. But the final 'marriage price proper' is in rice, 250 basketsful,

[1] 'Bone-price' is the payment on the death of a married woman or her children, made by the husband or his representatives to the woman's clan (Shaw, 1929, p. 56).

though this may also be estimated in rupees, and paid in instalments, taking a generation to pay off. A man may be hampered all his life by debts incurred at the marriage of his mother, grandmother, or even his great-great-grandmother or great-great-aunt.

Among the Kabuis of Manipur in the middle of last century, the ' bride-price ' would include 7 buffalo, 2 daos, 2 spears, 2 strings of beads made of conch shell, 2 ear ornaments, 2 black cloths, 2 eating vessels, 2 hoes. Fifty years later, buffalo being scarce, the price did not exceed 100 baskets of rice, with a dao, hoe and cloth for the girl's parents. Among the Marings to the East, the regulated payment for a wife in 1859 was 3 gongs or 2 buffalo. Accidental homicide was compensated by payment of cows, from 1 to 10 according to circumstances and locality (Hodson, 1911, pp. 90, 92, 106).

Many more examples might be given, but these are enough to show that in isolated regions where there is no native money, and where wealth consists in cattle and grain, certain articles are recognized as conventional units in presentations and exchange, ' bride-price ' or wergeld. The most conspicuous of these are iron tools or weapons—daos, hoes and spears—ornaments, usually beads, and the famous gongs. None of these, with the exception of the daos, ever developed into token-money. Just as in Africa spear- or axe-heads swell into objects of parade or diminish into conventional tokens, so the daos of Assam occur in both exaggerated and miniature varieties, both, though otherwise useless, being used as currency.

These Naga daos are of interest for many reasons. First, they may claim to be linked both in name, in prototype and in function with the Chinese *tao* or knife-money, with a distinguished ancestry stretching back many hundreds of years (p. 238). Next, the currency dao (Fig. 84) is already becoming token-money. It is less often the ordinary working tool than a worn-out blade which can be used to make a new one, a degeneration which has progressed so far in the miniature dao or *chabili* (Fig. 85), that its prototype has been forgotten. Just as in Africa the Fan *bikei* have been called axes, spears or throwing-knives, so the *chabili* are called knives, spears or keys, the latter being the literal translation of their name.[1]

We have seen above some of the uses of the dao in ceremonial presentations or exchanges. The *chabili* perform the same functions. They are used in distributions at feasts ; they are offered by the ' medicine man ' to avert illness, 6 for a man and 5 for a woman ; and the bride takes one or more to her new home. All well-to-do men (among the Ao Nagas) keep a few bundles of them ready for such uses (Mills, 1926, pp. 103, 236).

[1] Mills (1926, p. 102) shows that the *chabili* are imitations of the old long-tanged dao now extinct, *cf.* ill., p. 60.

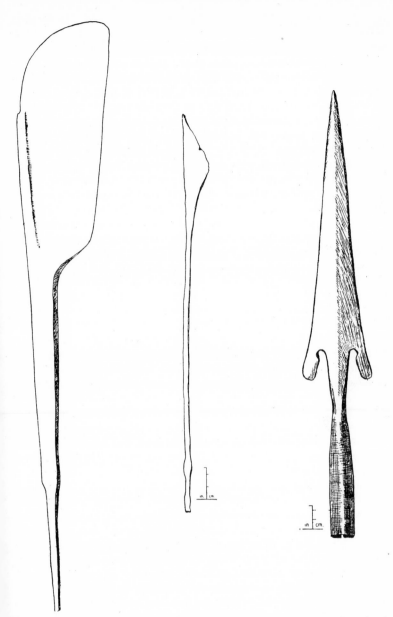

FIG. 84.—*Dao*, Assam.
(⅙ size)

FIG. 85.—*Chabili*, mini-
ature *dao*, Assam

FIG. 86.—Spearhead,
Assam

The spear often shares the functions of the dao. It plays an important part in presentations and figures in the Angami ' bride-price ', besides being used in fines and compensations for adultery. As a present it takes the form of an ornamental spear-shaft only ; if given with the head it indicates respect or homage, and is offered as tribute due from an inferior to a superior, paid by one village to another for services rendered, or sent as a token of submission after receiving a challenge (Hutton, 1921 (i), p. 220 *fn.*). A Naga spearhead is illustrated in Fig. 86. A complete Kachin spear ' formerly currency ' is in the Pitt Rivers Collection at Oxford.

Among the hill tribes of the Akyab district South of the Arakan Hills in Burma the presents given by the bridegroom include a wild bull, a white buffalo, 7 gongs and 5 spears, to be distributed between the father, uncle and elder brother of the girl. A pig and liquor for the feast have to be provided, and a gift—usually 30 rupees—for the girl's mother. In the case of the re-marriage of a widow, to quote the Census of India Report, ' It is permitted to collect widows, but only by unmarried relatives ', and the father only gets a spear and 2 gongs. Compensation for adultery is very heavy, approxi-mately a buffalo, a gun, and 7 or 8 gongs, but there is only a small fine for misconduct with ' uncollected widows ' (1931, Vol. XI, ' Burma ', Part i, pp. 264–5, 293).

There remains one class of currency objects peculiar to this part of the world. This includes the famous metal gongs, often called ' drums ', that are a form of currency not only among the hill tribes of Assam and Burma, but also in Siam and Annam, in Borneo, and the Philippines, and the Dutch East Indies.

If these are not, strictly speaking, money, they are the nearest approach to it. They are the most valued of possessions, and are the form in which wealth is stored, estimated, and exhibited. They are customary, if not essential, in ' bride-price ', in wergeld, in ceremonial presentations and in peace-makings.

The Burmese have a folk tale which tells how, when God was distributing the good things of this world, they went, by mistake, on the wrong day, and so received *nāts* instead of blessings. And their whole lives are spent in propitiating these often unfriendly spirits. The gongs were beaten to placate them and avert evil, and the Karens believed that the echoing of the sound was the voice of approving *nāts* (O'Riley, 1862, p. 164).

The best-known of these forms of visible wealth are the gongs of Manipur, of the Naga Hills to the north and the Lushai Hills to the south (with many native names in different districts) ; the bells, *deoganta*, of the Miri Hills on the Tibetan border ; the ' currency bowls ' of the Abor, their neighbours to the east ; the gongs of the Kachin in Northern Burma, still farther to the east ;

and the best known of all, the *kyee-zee* of the Karen in the mountains of Eastern Burma, between the Shan States and Siam.

The gongs are very varied in material, size, shape, character and value, and each kind has its native name.

The Konyaks have a gong of Burmese pattern with a central boss. The Kuki have a big gong, *dapi*, and a set of three small gongs, half a tone apart, and the value depends, like that of the Chinese *ch'ing*, on size and tone. The Chang Naga gongs, *laya*, are flattish, convex disks about a foot across, formerly of bell metal worth 4 or 5 rupees, but nowadays, being made of Assam brass, they have dropped to about 8 annas. These are not used as gongs, and would crack if beaten hard.

Parry (1932, pp. 200–2) drew up a list of the values of cattle, gongs, brass pots, daos, axes, hoes and other items commonly used in payment of marriage prices among the Lakhers and Maras of the Lushai Hills to the south of Manipur.

Livestock ranged from a good cow worth 60 rupees to a piglet, worth one. Gongs were priced according to their span and also according to their tone. One of 10 span, measured round the outside edge, if with a true sound, was valued at 70 rupees ; smaller ones came down to 20 rupees ; daos 2 rupees ; axes 1 rupee ; hoes 4 annas each.

He adds this significant passage.

They have no currency of their own. All transactions were carried out by barter and all goods paid for in kind. Even now there is little money in the country, but as they came to realize the value of money the objects generally given in payment of marriage prices gradually acquired a formal value in rupees. This formal value does not necessaily correspond with the market value of the article outside the Lakher country but holds good for all transactions among Lakhers.

Of the Hill Miris of Lakimpur on the borders of Tibet, Hunter wrote (1879, i, p. 347).

Their valuables consist chiefly in large dishes and cooking vessels of metal, and of great collections of Thibetan metal bells called *deogantes* [god bells] which appear to be prized as holy things and are sometimes used as money. The Miris pretend that they cannot now obtain these bells and that those they possess are heirlooms. They are valued at from 4 annas to 12 rupees (6*d*. to £1 4*s*.) each according to shape, size and ornaments. Those with inscriptions inside and out are most highly prized. Those without inscriptions are little valued, and as these inscriptions are nothing more than repetitions of the shibboleth ' *Om Mani Padmi Om* ' of the Thibetans it is easy to see that the Miris must have been inspired by that people to treat them with veneration.

The bell illustrated on Pl. 19 was obtained from the Dufflas (Daflas) of Northern Lakimpur to the west of the Miri. The bronze

' currency bowls ' of the Abor, to the East of the Miri, on the Tibetan border, are of Chinese manufacture, and their value corresponds to about £30 of English money. They are decorated externally with wings, with four small lugs, and in the interior with the conch, fish, &c., representing the 8 Buddhist emblems. Their local name is *danki*. They can scarcely be called money, but they are largely used for ceremonial presentation. Much the same can be said of the gongs so highly prized by the Kachin of Northern Burma. Money has no attraction for the Kachin nor indeed for the Burman in general, but he will give all his possessions, and more, for gongs. They are essential for ' bride-price ', together with cattle and cloth, but as they are scarce they have to be borrowed and passed on, leaving a wake of debt behind them.

Enriquez (1923, pp. 152–3) describes his complicity in a native elopement, which entailed his

doing the dirty work of baffling both Church and State. . . . By Kachin tribal law, you can compound for murder for a pig or two, but for eloping with your girl, you go to jail.

So the young pair decided to turn Christian in a hurry and be married in church, which necessitated delicate negotiations with the clergy and involved ' a maze of bishops, registers, catechisms, god-fathers and giving aways '. Baptism and marriage were speedily completed according to Christian rites, and it is interesting to note that a year later, after a general reconciliation, the man paid for his abducted wife with two magnificent gongs. ' All I got out of it ', says Enriquez, ' was a tarnished reputation with the Government of Burma.'

The famous *kyee-zee* gongs (Pl. 19) of the Karen of the mountains of Eastern Burma are also tokens of wealth, rather than currency, but they also have definite monetary value, according to size and sound, ranging between £5 and £50. They are treasured tribal heirlooms, and only change hands on important occasions, passing from family to family, or from village to village like the stone-money of Yap.

The *kyee-zee* is a thick copper or spelter cylinder about 2 feet long and somewhat greater in diameter at one end, which is closed with a disk of the metal, the other end being open. They are made by the Shans, and H. I. Marshall (1922, pp. 91, 124–5) gives an account of their manufacture.

Mason described them in 1869 :

On the outer circle are four raised frogs, as the figure of the cat some-times surmounted the ancient sistrum. Whether the sound of the instru-ment is intended to emulate the voice of the frog or not, must be left to

conjecture, for no one can give any reason for the frog being there.[1] . . .
In the settlement of their quarrels, and in the redemption of captives, the
indemnification always takes the shape of a *kyee-zee* or more, with perhaps
a few buffaloes or pigs thrown in as make-weights, just as in more civilized
countries a concession of territory and perhaps some men-of-war is insisted
on (*J.A.S.B:*, 1869, Vol. XXXVII, II, p. 128).

The earlier ones have single frogs, elephants, or other creatures ;
in the later ones there are two or more, one on the top of the other.
There are also ' hot ' or ' sad ' gongs, used on occasions of death or
calamity ; and ' cool ' ones for festivals, differentiated, in the Pegu
Hills, by the numbers of frogs (H. I. Marshall, 1922, Chap. XIII).

The Karens attach a fabulous value to these gongs and pay
absurd prices for those that have good tones. They have distinctive
names for 10 different classes distinguished by sound, the poorest
of which sells for 100 rupees and the best for a 1,000. Inferior
kinds range from 30 to 100 rupees. The Karens say that when a
good *kyee-zee* is struck it softens the heart, and the women weep for
their friends they have lost or from whom they are separated. They
can be used to ransom a village, or to obtain a wife, and a man
with 1 *kyee-zee* is worth more than a man with 7 elephants.

No Karen, however well supplied with other goods, is considered
rich unless he owns *kyee-zees*, and the passion for possessing them
leads to interminable quarrelling. A man will barter children or
relatives for them. If a youth wants to marry, he must somehow
obtain one or two, either by loan, which means trouble, or by theft,
which is worse.

A village which has many ' gongs ' is the envy of one without,
and wars are undertaken to carry them off. O'Riley regards the love
of *kyee-zees* as the root of all evil, for they are the original cause of
all intertribal feuds ; revenge for their loss is nursed from generation
to generation and is only satisfied by more *kyee-zees* or more lives
(1864, p. 216).

Where trading has developed a more regulated currency, metal
lumps or bars of silver form a transition stage between primitive
money and coins, and the various shapes of .Further India find a
place in orthodox coin collections. The best-known examples are
the ' shell '- or ' boat '-money of Burma ; Siamese ' shells ', ' leaves ',
' bracelets ', *k'a k'im*, *ticals*, ' bullets ' and ' canoes ' ; and the stamped
silver bars, which are real coins, of Annam.

Chinese travellers of the 7th to the 9th centuries brought back
tales of trading with the Southern Barbarians, buying rhinoceros
horn for cowries ' which form their currency '. They reported that

[1] Conjectures include rain-making and fertility rites, connected with the
frog. See also the frog on *mokko* ' drums ' (p. 268). *Cf.* Rydh, I, 1929,
p. 107. But other animals, such as elephants, monkeys and dogs, also
occur.

gold and silver were also found, and were used by the Pyu of Prome
(Pegu) as money 'the shape of which is crescent-like' (Harvey,
1925, pp. 10, 13). This may be recognized in the 'bracelets' of
Siam (p. 216) but in Burma the ingots are often called 'shells' or
'boats' according to their outline.[1]

It was formerly assumed that as cowry-currencies were imitated
in metal (in Europe, Egypt, India and China), so these shell-like
forms are imitations of earlier shell-currencies, but Temple attributes
the shell shape rather to accident than design, being due to the
natural efflorescence of silver under certain methods of extraction.
His evidence is illustrated in the Pitt Rivers Museum at Oxford, with
samples of *baw* or pure silver, as extracted from the crucible, used
as currency by weight; and *shan baw* producing 'shell-money'
with shapes of incipient shells (Temple, 1890, p. 323). The chief
use of these 'shells' was not as currency, but in customary presents
of Shan chiefs to the Burmese king.

Anderson described (1876, p. 44) ingot-making in Burma :

> To 6 *tikals* (1 tikal equals rather more than half an ounce Troy) of pure
> silver, 1 *tikal* 8 annas of copper wire are added and melted with alloy of
> as much lead as brings the whole to 10 *tikals* weight. The operation is
> conducted in saucers of sun-dried clay bedded in paddy husk, and covered
> over with charcoal. The bellows are vigorously plied and as soon as the
> mass is at red heat, the charcoal is removed and a round flat brick button,
> previously covered with a layer of moist clay, is placed on the amalgam,
> which forms a thick ring round the edge, to which lead is freely added to
> make up the weight. As it cools there results a white disc of silver encircled
> by a brownish ring. The silver is cleaned and dotted with cutch [to show
> the approximate weight, and degree of alloy] and is then weighed and ready
> to be cut up.

In the early trading days [2] goods were sometimes weighed against
ganza, an alloy of lead and brass which passed as money in Pegu,
either in odd lumps or in bars of specified weight 'stamped by
merchants of repute, but usually false' (Harvey, 1925, p. 122).

De Carné (1872, p. 177) travelling from Siam into Burma
describes the importance of the blacksmith, who is at the same time
goldsmith and manufacturer of money.

> The *tickal* and its subdivisions ceasing to have the current price, we
> were compelled to have our Siamese silver melted in a crucible which gives
> it the form of a macaroon. For daily transactions of small importance they
> cut off at hazard pieces of unequal value, which are appraised at a glance by
> the interested parties. They make use of scales in more serious transactions,
> for, in default of a uniform money, the standard of value is fixed by weight
> in silver.

---

[1] A 'shell' and a 'boat' (from the British Museum) are illustrated by
Ling Roth (1901, Fig. 16).

[2] Alexander Hamilton remarked that '*Ganze* passeth all over the Pegu
dominion for money', 1727, II, p. 41.

Chinese sycee silver found its way along the trade-routes, and is met with both in Burma and in Siam, often in the form of ' saddle-money ' (Fig. 109), brought probably from South China, by pack caravan (le May, 1932, pp. 8–9, Pl. II, Fig. 7 ; *cf.* Ling Roth, 1901, Fig. 4, pp. 16–17).

All these irregular and lumpy forms give way before the more convenient round coins, and it is interesting to note how these coins occasionally preserve the memory of earlier shells or seeds.

Temple quotes Brown's description of the *sel* of Manipur, worth about $\frac{1}{400}$ of a rupee.

> The only coin proper to the country is of bell metal and small in size, weighing about 16 grains. This is coined by the Raja as required, goods and money being taken in exchange. The metal is obtained chiefly from Burma and consists of old gongs &c. . . . The market value of the *sel* as it is called varies. When rupees are plentiful then *sel* are cheap, when scarce, the opposite.

Temple pointed out that the ratio of 400 *sel* to the rupee showed that it was based on the cowry ratio of 400 to the anna, i.e. the people though using *sel*, still counted them in terms of cowries. Moreover, the Manipuri *sel* are counted like cowries in quartettes, the quickest way of dealing with large quantities, when separating them with fingers or sticks (Temple, 1914, p. 27).[1]

The rupee of the present day thus preserves a faint memory of the earlier cowry currency. It also preserves the memory of equally primitive money in the seeds (' crab's eyes ') of the scarlet black-spotted pea, *rati gunja*, *Abrus precatorius*.[2] These were used as currency in West Africa (p. 83) and in Burma (*cf.* Pitt Rivers Museum). But their main claim to fame in monetary transactions is their use as weights both in Africa and in Asia.[3] In India the *rati* (1·75 gr. Troy) was the unit of weight (*cf.* p. 191). A hundred *ratis* (175 gr.) made the *sata-raktika*, a weight of metal ' which on the one hand can be traced back almost to the Vedic period, whilst in modern times it has developed into the rupee of the British Government ' (Chalmers, 1893, p. 336).

---

[1] This process can be seen to this day when cowries are used in gambling.

[2] Both in Africa and in Asia *Abrus precatorius* (*rati*, crab's eye, Indian liquorice, King Charles' tears, &c.) is often confused with *Adenanthera pavonina* (candareen, *kenderi*, saga, redwood, &c.). Both are often called by the same name (as *ywe* in Burma) and often the names are reversed (*cf.* p. 91 *n.*). Temple described both, discussing their relative weights (1897, pp. 312–18), but the confusion persists (*cf.* Wilkinson, *Malay-English Dictionary*, 1932).

[3] In Sumatra, 24 of these seeds = a *mas*, and 16 *mas* (mace) = a *tael*, equivalent to the Chinese *liang*, and more or less (but usually a little more than) the ounce (Ridgeway, 1892, pp. 127, 172).

C. SIAM AND INDO-CHINA

The riches of Siam and Indo-China consist in rice—some of the finest rice in the world is produced here—and buffaloes are described as ' the basic coin of the realm '. .And the contrast between the rich alluvial plains and the barren upland country must have encouraged exchange from early days.

The buffalo standard still survives, or survived until lately among the tribes of Annam.

In Annam the buffalo often serves as the general unit of value for the more valuable articles. Thus a large chaldron is worth 3 buffaloes, a handsome gong 2 buffaloes, a small gong 1 buffalo, 6 copper dishes 1 buffalo, 2 lances 1 buffalo, a rhinoceros horn 8 buffaloes, a large pair of elephant tusks 6 buffaloes, a small pair 3 buffaloes.

Ridgeway, from whose book that quotation from Aymonier is taken (p. 165), adds

Thus the buffalo which takes the place of the ox in China and South-East Asia is used as the commercial unit in like fashion as we found the ox employed among the Homeric Greeks, the ancient Italians, the ancient Irish and the modern Ossetes. But the Annamites themselves employ as currency the silver bar and string of cash. . . . Accordingly when the hill tribes have dealings with the people of the plain, the full-grown buffalo is reckoned at a bar of silver or its equivalent, a hundred strings of cash, while the small buffalo is set at 50 strings.

Taxes are paid in buffalo, one for each house, or a village may compound by a payment of 10 buffaloes, whose horns are at least as long as their ears.

The Bahnars of Annam who dwell on the borders of Northern Siam have as their highest unit the head, i.e. a male slave, who is estimated according to his strength, age and skill, at 5, 6 or 7 buffaloes or the same number of kettles, for the average value is the same. A full-grown buffalo or a large kettle is worth 7 large glazed Chinese jars. One jar is worth 4 *muks*.[1] Each *muk* is worth 10 *mats* or iron hoes, the sole agricultural implement of the wild tribes of all these regions. The hoe is the smallest monetary unit used by all the Bahnars, and is worth about a penny in European goods. This *mat* or hoe serves them as small currency and all petty transactions are carried on by it. A large bamboo hat costs 2 hoes, a Bahnar knife 2 hoes, ordinary arrows are sold at 30 for a hoe. A large elephant is worth from 10 to 15 heads or slaves, a horse costs 3 or 4 kettles or buffaloes.

Ridgeway's comment is as follows :—

When we read of such a state of human society we seem to be transported back into that far away Homeric time, and as we hear of slaves and kine,

---

[1] The *muk* was originally a special article, now only a unit of account (Aymonier, 1877, pp. 296–8).

chaldrons and kettles, we think of the old Epics with their tale of slaves valued in beeves and ' crumple-horned shambling kine and tripods ', and ' shining chaldrons '. In the light of such analogies we can at last understand the significance of the 10 axes and 10 half-axes which formed the first and second prizes in the *Iliad*. Who can doubt that these axes and half-axes played much the same part in the Homeric system of currency as the hoes do at this present moment in that of the Bahnars of Annam (1892, p. 166).

Hoes have already been seen as currency in Assam, though of less value there than the dao. The dao (*dakh*) is found as currency in Northern Siam also, but as an iron bar, not yet made into a tool. Aymonier describes these bars or lozenge-shaped pieces, about 5 to 6 inches (14 cm.) long, 1 inch (3 cm.) wide and rather less than ½ inch (1 cm.) thick, weighing some 200 grammes. They are measured from the base of the thumb to the tip of the first finger, two fingers for the width and one for the thickness in the middle, thinning off to the ends ; 10 or 12 go to the *tical*, 15 to the piastre, and they are also reckoned in bags of 50. Fifteen bagfuls or 300 bars go to the *nēn* or bar of silver. This is the usual money on both sides of the Mekong (Aymonier, 1895, I, p. 22).

It may constantly be seen how a bad or unregulated currency drives people back to barter and the use of primitive forms of money. Buffalo, rice and hoes persist in Annam, not because there are no coins, but because they have been introduced too freely. In the province of Binh Thuan on the South-East Coast of Annam the Mexican piastre in the middle of last century was worth some 6 to 10 strings of good sapeks (cash) or up to 20 strings of bad ones. The King had been in the habit of issuing copper or zinc sapeks of varying values, but about 1872 this privilege was sold to the Chinese, and the coins became smaller and smaller and of worse and worse metal. There was also an inundation of counterfeit piastres, with the result that the people were thoroughly suspicious of coins and in some parts refused to take them altogether.

Transactions there are made in padi, the true money of the country. Rice is bartered for tobacco, fish, cloth, &c. A basket of rice for a bunch of bananas, a glass of wine, 6 cakes or 5 eggs (Aymonier, 1885, pp. 45-6, 61-2).

Mouhot, travelling in the mountains of Cambodia in 1858-60, found beads still acceptable.

Glass ornaments and brass wire passed everywhere for money. A buffalo or an ox is valued at 6 armfuls of thick brass wire ; a pig is almost as dear ; but for a small piece of fine wire or a bead necklace, you can purchase a pheasant or a hundred ears of maize (p. 253).

Young Louis de Carné, exploring up the Mekong among the Laos (1872, pp. 183, 185), tells of his money difficulties. The Chinese ingot *te* and the Burmese ingot, also *te*, contained different quantities of silver, but both were in use. ' So the rogues offer you one when they are your debtors, and require the other when they are your creditors.' He found red cotton cloth the best ' currency ', but when supplies ran out he was reduced to desperate straits,

a pair of pantaloons for a duck, and—God forgive me such simony !—we exchanged the medallions and religious images which were destined for the Christians of the missions. . . . St. Antony of Padua went for a pumpkin ; St. Pancras for a basket of potatoes, and St. Gertrude for a cucumber.

The earliest form of money in general use consisted of cowries, which are frequently mentioned in the accounts of early travellers (Schneider, 1905, pp. 107–8 ; Ferrand, 1922, p. 50). They were carried as ballast in ships from the Laccadives, Borneo and the Philippines, and at the end of the 17th century, and up to the middle of the 18th, cowries (there called *bia*) were the usual small change of Siam, 800 to the *fuang*, ⅛ of a *tical*. In 1744 Siamese history records a shortage of cowries, and small red clay seals, called *prakab*, were stamped with various designs and issued as substitutes (le May, 1932, p. 125, Pl. XXXII, Figs. 11–14). That was merely a temporary setback. They became plentiful again and dropped in value. Bastian (1863, III, p. 213) noted that for large payments they were not counted, but measured in plaited baskets or coconut shells, 1,000 to 1,200 to the *fuang*. During the reign of King Mongkut of the Bangkok dynasty (1851–68) the value was fixed at 800 to the *fuang*, but with his introduction of tin and copper coinage in 1862 cowries were finally abandoned in commercial centres. They continued as gambling counters in towns, and are used by the croupiers in fan-tan, while among the peasants of the country districts they are still reckoned at some 600 to 1,200 to the *tical*.[1]

In an area so rich in metals as South-Eastern Asia, a currency in gold, silver, iron or mixed metal of different weights is to be expected, and these develop in the form of bars or lumps, taking different characteristic shapes in different districts.

It is strange [says le May, 1932, p. 7] that an Empire . . . which lasted for at least six centuries, and which could produce such a wonder of civilized culture as the great temple at Angkor still never found it necessary to employ any standard system of gold and silver coinage, as distinct from weights, throughout its territories. And yet perhaps not so strange when we consider that China until quite recently stood in almost the same position numismatically.

Payments in Cambodia were made in slaves, cattle, rice and other cereals, metal vessels and weights of gold and silver. The weights

[1] Le May (1932) describes on pp. 97–8 and illustrates on Pl. II, Figs. 1–4 and XXIII, 1–6, 6 of the 8 varieties of cowries (*C. annulus* and *C. moneta* among them) all having the same current value. ' Pig's mouth money ', p. 123, Pl. XXXI, Fig. 1, may represent, he thinks, a large cowry shell. *Cf.* Ling Roth, 1901, p. 16, Fig. 14, No. 2.

themselves were traditionally based on rice grains, 96 to the *fuang*.
Wergeld was in silver, by weight, 30 *once* (= 37·5 gr.) for a sound
man to 25 for a woman. Accidental killing (*homicide par imprudence*)
was compensated by a third of the price of the victim if a freeman,
or a third of his sale value if a slave (Aymonier, 1900, I, p. 89).

The lumps or weights of silver which pass for coins in this part
of the world are very varied, and most of them are familiar in currency
collections. Such are the ' snailshells ', ' shells ' and ' boats ' of
Burma already noticed (p. 216), and the ' shoes ' of China (p. 246).
The ingots or bars of Annam stamped with the name of the reigning
king are a nearer approach to coins. The silver bar illustrated in
Fig. 87 is inscribed with the name of Gia Long, founder of the
dynasty, who made a treaty with Louis XVI in 1787. There were
much larger and heavier bars, as well as bricks,
in gold, weighing up to 10 taels (385 grammes)
and in silver, up to 100 taels (Babelon, 1897,
p. 42).

In Siam there is more variety, including the
' canoe-money ' of the Mekong Valley, the ' leaf-
money ' of the Nan district, and the ' shell-money '
(*ngön hôi*), used in ' bride-price ' in the North.
But the most characteristic form, which lasted down
to the present day, is that commonly known as
' bullet-money ' or *tical*, though the Siamese name
is *bāt*.

The *bāt* or *tical* has been used to illustrate
obvious stages in the evolution of money, starting
from a bar of metal, estimated by weight, bent
double, gradually compressed into a ' bullet' and
finishing up as a stamped coin. But things are not always what they
seem, and the evolution of the *tical* is still obscure.

FIG. 87.—Silver
bar, Annam

The name is derived from the Indian word *tanka* or *tanga*
(originally the weight of a seed), applied to coins in India, Persia
and Turkestan, and still surviving in little silver or copper coins in
South-West India, at Goa and along the Malabar Coast (N.E.D.) [1]
(Temple, 1897, pp. 235–45, 253–6). The Portuguese carried the
word with their trade to Further India where the *tanka* became *tical*.
The *tical* roughly equalled the rupee, varying in weight from a little
over to a little under ½ ounce Troy, and in value from 1s. 2d.
to 2s. 6d., fixed in 1902 at 17 and 1925 at 11 to the pound
sterling.

There were smaller sizes, equal to about ½, ¼ and ⅛ of a rupee,

---

[1] *Tical* is pronounced *ticál* in Siam and *tic'l* in Burma. Le May derives
the word from the Arabic *thaqal*, Hebrew *shekel*. Cunningham believes
that our slang word ' tanner ' is a gypsy corruption of *tanka* (1891, p. 24).

the *song salung*, the *salung*, and the *fuang* (Graham 1912, p. 264). *Ticals* were stamped on their convex sides with marks of different patterns.[1]

'A student of the early coinage of Siam is faced with almost insuperable difficulties,' says le May, and we gratefully follow his guidance given in the *Coinage of Siam*, 1932, quoted largely in the preceding and following paragraphs.

The evidence of the coins themselves shows that there was a standardized coinage in use in Central Siam from the pre-Ayudhyan era (i.e. before 1350).

The shape of this standardized coin is peculiar : it consists of a short elliptical bar of silver, with both its ends pressed inwards so that they practically meet. This is called locally *p'ot duang*, where *duang* means 'worm' and p'ot means 'twisted' or 'curled'. This is the so-called 'bullet-coin' which continued to be minted up to the reign of King Mongkut, 1851–68. But there was another, and a different type of money in use in the North, probably contemporary with the 'bullet' coins of the central area ; this is the 'bracelet' type (Pl. 20, Figs. 5–7). This appears to be the earliest form of silver currency and may have been introduced by the Thai, who arrived about the 9th century A.D. The 'bracelet' may, in its turn, have been derived from Lower Burma where 'crescent-like shapes in gold and silver' are recorded by Chinese chroniclers of the T'ang period (*c.* A.D. 600–900) as the money of the Southern Barbarians (Pyu). Later the 'bracelet' took the standardized form known locally as *k'a k'im*, which was common to all the northern principalities for some centuries (Pl. 20, Figs. 1–4). The script found on these is not earlier than the beginning of the 14th century, and the coins persisted down to the 18th. The average weight of these *k'a k'im* is usually about 4 *bāt*, or a little over, and le May accepts them as representing the Thai *tael*, 'with a little weight thrown in for luck'. If it can be proved that the 'bracelet' type and its later development the *k'a k'im* were contemporaneous with the 'bullets', the evolution of the latter from either of the former (and no intermediate stages can be discovered) fails to be established.[2] It has been suggested that the origin of them all was Chinese sycee silver but that the northern folk adopted the 'bracelet' and later the *k'a k'im* type of money because they traded almost entirely on land and through hilly country, and found this type of coinage convenient to carry about strung together. On the other hand, the southern folk used the great river system as their means of communication and it was

---

[1] For explanations of the marks see le May, 1932, pp. 24 *ff.*, 53–4, &c., with 87 illustrations.

[2] For further discussion *cf.* Knowles, W. H., 1936, and le May's reply.

convenient for them to carry about coins of the 'bullet' shape in bags, which could be easily accommodated in their boats (le May, 1932, p. 12).

There is one characteristic which is shared alike by 'bracelet', k'a k'im, and the earlier of the bullet-coins, that is the 'cut' or 'nick'. This may be a cake-like slice, taken out of the metal, but becomes smaller and smaller, down to the 'padi-seed nick' (met k'ao san) of later Ayudhyan times. The 'nick' was made by the Chinese when the coins were sent to China for trading purposes, to test the quality of the silver; the 'cuts' were made in Siam, probably by authority, as they are so uniform, to 'lay the body bare to a suspicious world' (le May, 1932, p. 47).[1]

When the bullet-coins first came into use is entirely obscure. The earliest and most archaic forms may date from the 11th century or even earlier, but the general adoption and standardization date from the Thai Kings in the 13th and 14th centuries.

Le May illustrates nearly 100 bullet-coins (including some for-geries on Pl. XVIII) with 87 diagrams of marks. He also describes and illustrates the method of manufacture. In 1931 there was still one old man who had been a pupil of the coin craftsmen in his youth, who knew how to make the coins, and he gave a demonstration at the Royal Mint. The process was mediaeval, and the description is picturesque (1932, pp. 63–5, Pls. XV–XVII). The silver was weighed out, placed in an earthenware crucible, fused in the furnace, and poured into a mould submerged in water, producing a short elliptical bar 'rather like an elongated burnt almond sweet' curved below and flatter above. ·It was nicked across the middle on the flatter side, and then, set up on end, was hammered first on one side then on the other—an expert would take only five blows—until the shape was satisfactory. The stamping was done on an elephant bone.

The ticals become progressively more and more bullet-like down to the middle of the 19th century, and gold 'bullets' were also issued. But a little later, under the 4th sovereign of the Bangkok dynasty, though gold 'bullets' were still being issued, gold, silver, tin and copper coins in conventional flat shape were minted at the same time and became legal tender.

A further problem has been presented by the 'bullets' which are made not of silver but of a mixture of tin, copper and nickel in varying proportions. Tin is plentiful in the South, and the copper and nickel alloy is found on the borders of Siam and the French Lao states in the Nān region. These are marked with the same marks as the silver 'bullets' and probably belong to the same period, but they are much larger and heavier than the coins and le May thinks that they were more probably weights than currency. This

[1] The larins of Ceylon show similar cuts, p. 194, Fig. 81.

is curious, as they have no connexion with the *tael* or its derivatives.[1]

The ' bullets ' were not the only form of metal currency, and other types are the ' canoe-money ' or *lāts* of the Mekong Valley, the ' leaf-money ' of Nān in the Lao states, and the ' shell-money ' or *ngön hôi* used in marriage payments in the North. The *lāts* or ' canoes ' are very varied in shape and in composition, some being of silver, some of copper, some of alloy ; some having the appearance of model canoes, some no likeness whatever. They all come from the Mekong Valley. Four types are illustrated on Pl. 21, Figs. 1–4. The largest is sometimes called an ' ant-coin ', the irregular markings round the edge being attributed to the struggles of ants, dropped alive on to the molten metal [2] (Loehr, 1935, p. 22).

FIG. 88.—' Leaf-money ', Siam   FIG. 89.—*Ngön hôi*, Siam

The ' model canoe ' type (Fig. 2) was collected in the Ngum valley and is of copper, the smaller rougher one (Fig. 1) is from the Province of Ubon in the North-East, and amorphous types of silver come from the Province of Son Tong. The value was very variable from time to time and from place to place. Aymonier (1895, I, p. 60) quotes 24 to the *tical* at Bassak in 1866, falling to 40 in his day.

From the Nān region of one of the Lao States of Northern Siam comes the so-called ' leaf-money ' (Fig. 88). This consists of solid heavy disks of copper or debased silver, concave and convex, the latter face usually having a leaf-rib pattern on it, hence the name, but sometimes they are plain both sides. Some have perforations, which may be for suspension ; suggesting that they may be tokens

---

[1] Le May (1932) illustrates 7 of these on Pl. VI, Figs. 1–7, and describes them (pp. 17–18). They may be compared with the Burmese *ganza* (p. 210 above) which ' passed for money ' in Pegu in the 18th century (Harvey, 1925, p. 122).

[2] Mosher (1936, Pl. X, p. 32) calls them ' tiger tongues '.

or amulets rather than coins (le May, 1902, p. 124, Pl. XXXI, Figs. 5–6).

'Shell-money' or 'Pig's-mouth-money' are names given to the irregular inflated discs, often quite thin, from the borders of Siam and Burma, Pl. 21, Fig. 12 (*cf.* Ling Roth, 1901, Fig. 14, No. 2, and le May, 1902, Pl. XXXI, 1).

The *ngön hôi*, or 'silver shell-money' (Pl. 21, Figs. 10–11) are made of silver alloy in the shape of flat or almost flat shells, the flatter side covered with a yellowish-red substance made of the burnt yolk of a chicken's egg. The other side, slightly convex, is black and ribbed (Fig. 89). The sizes vary from ¼ inch to nearly 3 inches (2 to 7 cm.) across. Le May was told that these tokens were made solely for use in the ceremonies of marriage and divorce in Northern Siam.[1] The betrothal is simple. The bridegroom and bride bring clusters of about 100 areca nuts, as symbols that the families are united together. The man deposits 2 *ngön hôi*, about 12 *ticals* in value, as the marriage-price. The girl pre-

FIG. 90.—Leaves from the silver tree, Siam. (⅓ size)

sents a dish of flowers and wax candles. Divorce is equally simple. If a couple wish to part the man must once more pay the sum of 2 *ngön hôi* and the act is complete (le May, 1926, p. 191).

These silver pieces are sometimes called Trengganu token-money, in the belief that they date from the time when Trengganu was subject to Siam, and paid tribute in gold flowers. Trade was then in the hands of Chinese merchants, who issued their own tokens which became the trading-currency of Bangkok. The connexion between these *ngön hôi* and Trengganu (or even Bangkok) seems doubtful, as they are found in the North of Siam and do not appear to be known elsewhere.

The gold and silver flowers and leaves paid as tribute by the princes of the North or the rajahs of the South to the King at Bangkok are sometimes included in currency collections. The trees were often 8 feet high, with trunk, branches, flowers and leaves in gold or silver. A gold tree would be worth over 1,000 *ticals* (Temple, 1897, p. 289). The silver leaves illustrated in Fig. 90 were among contributions paid in tribute by the Lao States, representing ceremonial gifts rather than money.

---

[1] The *ngön hôi* given by a missionary to the Chase National Bank Collection in New York were used as fines, especially in atonement for certain sins, 'made by Government and sold at 3 rupees each'.

iv. CHINA

It is difficult to generalize about China. It is a vast land of infinite variety, cut up by nature and man into isolated communities which for centuries had little contact with the outer world. Like India, it is predominantly an agricultural country, with more cultivation to the acre and more intensive cultivators than are to be found elsewhere. Among these each family group tends to be self-contained and self-supporting ; payments are still made in kind, and by the mass of the people money is rarely needed.

In earlier times traders ranked low in the social scale, below artisans and far below farmers. Trade was not one of the honourable professions. Merchants and artisans were forbidden to occupy any official post at the beginning of the Han dynasty, two centuries B.C., though when they acquired great wealth, and the salt magnates and the iron workers were ' richer than the princes ', they were allowed by the Emperor Wu (124 B.C.) to purchase titles.

The configuration of the country gave no encouragement to trade either by sea or by land. Natural harbours are few, especially in the North. There were no profitably trading neighbours within easy reach to foster commercial enterprise and develop a race of adventurous seafarers. Barriers of mountains and deserts discouraged travel, and trade-routes were few and difficult. Travel was also discouraged by society. The duty of sons was to stay at home for the support of the ageing parents and grandparents, and for a man to leave his family was the equivalent of social banishment ; generation after generation lived, died and were buried, on the same plot of land.

But the land did not produce the superfluities which kindle trade. Subsistence crops were the rule (silk mulberry and tea were exceptions, both providing ' currencies '), and the incessant toil required by mere subsistence crops left room for little else. Trade was not stimulated either by surplus production or by the demand for luxuries in the mass of the frugal tillers of the soil.

Barter in commodities suffices for such simple societies and there are many references to grain as the standard of value and medium of exchange from the earliest times down to the present day. But there were three trade products which claim to be classed with currencies. These are salt, silk and tea. Salt is often mentioned in Chinese Annals. In the 7th century B.C. the State of Ch'i (modern Shantung) acquired great wealth through trade in salt, increased by the expedient of forcing tributaries to pay for it in metal currency. Marco Polo refers frequently to the use of salt as a medium of exchange, and, in Tibet in the form of cakes as ' money '.

The money or currency they make use of is thus prepared. Their gold is formed into small rods, and passes according to its weight without any stamp. This is their greater money. The smaller is of the following description. In this country there are salt-springs, from which they manufacture salt by boiling it in small pans. When the water has boiled for an hour it becomes a kind of paste, which is formed into cakes of the value of 2d. each. These, which are flat on the lower and convex on the upper side, are placed upon hot tiles near a fire in order to dry and harden. On this latter species of money the stamp of the Great Khan is impressed, and it cannot be prepared by any other than his own officers. Eighty of the cakes are made to pass for a *saggio* of gold [? = a gold florin]. But when these are carried by the traders amongst the inhabitants of the mountains and other parts little frequented, they obtain a *saggio* of gold for 60, 50 or even 40 of the salt cakes in proportion as they find the natives less civilized, further removed from the towns and more accustomed to remain on the same spot (Marco Polo, 1926, Book II, chap. 47).

The salt revenue from the kingdom of Manji (South China) brought the Great Khan a sum of 16,800,000 ducats a year, as Marco Polo noted, seeing the account being made up in his presence (*ibid.*, Chap. 78). On the borders of Yunnan, where Polo describes the salt currency in the 13th century, the cakes continued in use down to modern times, and travellers in these hilly inland regions find salt eagerly welcomed in exchange for food, or as payment of carriers at the present day.

Sericulture in China, the land of its origin, started long before history. Tradition ascribes its encouragement to the Lady of Hsi Ling, the wife of Huang Ti the Yellow Emperor, himself a patron of commerce, whose date is usually given as somewhere in the 3rd millennium B.C. But there was little trade with the Western World before the Christian era, when silk was literally worth its weight in gold in Roman estimation. It formed a medium of exchange between the Chinese and the neighbouring Mongol tribes to the west, and in Polo's time silk in skeins is mentioned as the only form of currency.

Ogodai Khan, in the 13th century, collected tribute and taxes in silk (Yule, 1903, p. 430 *n.*) and in a good year the Imperial Treasury would receive, besides silver and notes and cowries, over 1,000,000 catties [1] of raw silk and 350 rolls of woven silk (Morse, 1913, p. 135).

It is possible that the use of silk as money has left its imprint on metal.

The much-disputed Chinese terms *pu* and *pi*, given to tool-coins other than knives, have both been translated by Chalfant as ' silk ' (1913, p. 4). And the puzzling complexities of ' corrugated cash ',

[1] The Chinese catty weighs 16 taels or a third over the pound. Ridgeway connects it with the coconut used for the measure of rice in Cambodia and elsewhere (Ridgeway, 1892, pp. 159 *ff.*, 174-5).

also called 'lotus-root' or 'key-coins', &c. (see Fig. 96), have been interpreted as attempts to represent rolls of silk.[1]

Tea, like salt, was an imperial monopoly, and it still forms the currency between China and Tibet. Sulayman, the Arab merchant of the 9th century, wrote concerning it:

> Among the things that China produces in abundance the King reserves the monopoly of salt and of a herb dried that the Chinese drink in hot water. The dried herb is sold in all the towns for enormous sums. It is called *sah.* It has more leaves than the trefoil, it is a little more scented than that, but has a bitter taste. Water is boiled and poured over this herb, the infusion makes an antidote against all indisposition (Ferrand, 1922, p. 58).

Rockhill, who explored Eastern Tibet in 1889, was impressed by the magnitude of the tea-trade at Ta chien lu (Tibetan Darchendo) at the junction of two streams on their way down to the Yang tse kiang. He describes (1891, pp. 278–80) the 400 porters coming and going daily, laden with bricks of tea, 10 to 13 million being sent out annually into Tibet by this route alone. He quotes Father Desgodins' description of the 5 standards of bricks, some of which are used for currency, some not, though discrimination in museum collections is rare.

The standards differ according to the fermentation, colour, weight and proportion of wood to leaf; price depends on the distance and accessibility of the market.

The highest standard brick contains no wood, and only the best fermented leaves; it is dark brown, weighs about $5\frac{1}{2}$ pounds, and has values from 1·4 rupees at Ta chien lu, 2 rupees at Batang, up to 3 or 4 at Lhasa.

But it is the third standard which is generally used in trade and constitutes the current money of traders (Pl. 27, Fig. 2). This is made of leaves and a few tops of small branches well fermented, and is of a dark yellow colour. Each brick weighs $2\frac{1}{2}$ pounds, and is sold for 10 annas at Ta chien lu, 1 rupee at Batang, and 2 or more at Lhasa. Wages of workmen and servants are paid with these, and they are used for ordinary trading. Men bargain by stipulating so many bricks or packets (of 4 bricks), saying 'This sword has cost 3 bricks; this horse is worth 20 packets', and so on. When bricks or packets of tea are mentioned as money it is always this third standard which is understood, and these bricks are counted, not weighed.

The fifth standard is also used as currency. This is made almost exclusively of prunings mixed with a few leaves, sometimes with

---

[1] The Hobson-Jobson name 'sycee' used for Chinese silver-money is translated 'fine silk' (*hsi ssŭ*) and may have reference to earlier silk-currency, but is more probably derived from the silk-like lines on the metal (*cf.* p. 246).

no leaves at all. For that reason it is called *shing ja* (wood tea) by the Tibetans. Each brick weighs nearly 5 pounds and is sold at 12 annas 6 pies at Ta chien lu or 1 rupee at Batang. This tea, after being pounded in a mortar, is drunk, and it is also used as current money. Being composed largely of wood, it is of inferior quality and weighs twice as much as the third standard. When used in exchange these bricks are weighed, not counted.

Baber and Gill had met these inferior-quality tea bricks some years before at Ta chien lu. Baber saw the coolies bringing in the long scrubby straggly branches of uncared-for trees, and thought they were fuel. The manufacture is simple. The branches, twigs, leaves or sweepings are dried in the sun, broken up by beating with sticks on hot plates, sifted, steamed over boiling water, and put into moulds and pressed. To give a richer colour a little soot may be added to the poorer quality. After a day or so the cakes (*pao*) or bricks (*ch'uan*) are taken out and packed for transport. This was the method of manufacture in the Russian factory at Hankow for the Mongolian market, and that of the Chinese at Ya-Chou for Tibet was much the same (Gill, 1880, I, pp. 176–8).

Brick tea in spite of its weight and inconvenience is still the ordinary currency of traders and travellers. A brick of tea is not merely worth a rupee but in a certain sense it *is* a rupee, being accepted like a silver coin as legal tender.

When Peter Fleming and Mlle Maillart were leaving Chinese territory in 1935, and 'rather incredulously' turned their horses' heads in the direction of India, transport of money presented a difficult problem for the unknown journey. Coins are heavy and dangerous possessions in a lawless land, so they bought a 12-ounce bar of gold for 1,000 dollars, easily concealed and negotiable anywhere where a file and scales were available, and in addition bricks of tea, which together with coloured cloth were used for wages, for buying camels, provisions, &c., and were always legal tender in remote communities with no use for dollars (Fleming, 1936, pp. 109, 156, 223).

This preference for a full-bodied rather than a token currency is fostered by the experiences of the peoples of the hills in dealing with the wily Chinese traders, to whom all intricacies of adulteration of silver and manipulation of scales are familiar. They will therefore accept payments in brick tea, and can be bribed with turquoise beads or coral,[1] of which they are passionately fond, but the only coin that is welcomed is the Indian rupee.

After all his troubles with the weary process of cutting up and weighing out lumps of silver, and interminable disputing over the scales and the quality of the metal, Gill also welcomed the sight of

[1] Turquoise and coral beads are still used for purchases in Tibet.

rupees, and 'it was somewhat flattering to our national vanity to see the portrait of our Sovereign Lady Queen Victoria on the money we used' (1880, II, p. 77). It would not have seemed so flattering to the vanity of Queen Victoria had she known that she was called 'vagabond lama', her crown being mistaken by the Tibetans for the headgear of a religious mendicant (*ibid.*, p. 86).

Chinese traditions and early records mention tortoiseshell in their lists of objects used as money of high value, being obtained, so a writer of the 2nd century B.C. tells us, only from the coasts of what are now called Cochin China and Annam.[1] Lacouperie recognizes an echo of this early use in the expression *kuei-huo* ('tortoise-coin') which is an elegant term for a coin (1892, p. 193).

Of imported currencies the cowry stands alone (Fig. 91). Schneider suggests that China and Japan were possibly the first countries in which cowries were used as tokens of value and media

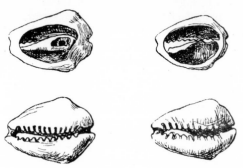

FIG. 91.—Chinese cowries

of exchange, Japan obtaining the shells from the islands between her and Formosa (though it is doubtful if they ever formed a real currency in Japan), while China was supplied from the East Indies (1905, p. 103).

There are abundant references to the money value of cowries in early Chinese writings. In the *I Ching*, one of the earliest books of the Chinese, 100,000 dead shell-fish are given as the equivalent of 'riches'. The famous dictionary of the Emperor K'ang Hsi (1662-1723) based on the *Shuo Wên* of Hsü Shin, who died about A.D. 120, says *pei* denotes sea creatures which live in shells. The

---

[1] If this was really tortoiseshell and obtained from Annam, its use as currency both in China and in Micronesia (*cf.* p. 141) forms another early cultural link between the two areas. But Jackson suggests that the 'great shells' usually interpreted as tortoiseshell were the large cowry *Cypraea testudinaria*, so named by Linnaeus on account of its tortoise-like appearance, and that the 4 degrees of shells mentioned as currency of different values were all cowries of different sizes (1917, pp. 178 *ff.*).

North Chinese name for cowry is *pei*, Canton *puei*, Korean *p'ae*, which the Japanese would pronounce *hai*, but this name has been supplanted by *takaragai*. This *pei* character enters into the composition of over 100 signs in the Emperor's national dictionary, indicating the important rôle of cowries in the earliest days when they denoted trade and barter. Later, this same sign is equivalent to money. Who has much has riches ; who has little is poor ; it enters into the composition of words such as buying and selling, tribute, miserly, dear, cheap, hoarding, spending and many others.

The sign for precious or valuable, *pao*, consists of a roof, beneath which are the signs for jade (nephrite), pots and strings of cowries, the three most highly valued possessions, which constitute wealth (*cf.* Schneider, 1905, *Textfigur*, p. 106).

Mere literary evidence is often suspect, but in the case of the cowry archaeological finds support its claim to antiquity. Cowries are found, sometimes already fossilized, in Stone Age deposits far inland as at Ling Chi, Hsien, the earlier capital of Ch'i (Shantung)

FIG. 92.—Imitation cowry in mother of pearl

and in the province of Chin (Honan) ; while a hoard of 200 were found in the old centre of Chinese civilization Cheng (Andersson, 1934, p. 323, Fig. 140). These were obviously highly valued treasures if not actual money, and there were imitations in stone, bone, mother of pearl (*cf.* Fig. 92) and horn, later in copper and bronze (Schlösser, 1935, Pl. 12, Figs. 38–40, p. 43).

Among the metal imitations the *pei huo* or ' cowry exchange coins ' traditionally ascribed to the 6th or 7th century B.C.,[1] are of particular interest. These are small, oval or pear-shaped, flat on one surface and curved on the other, usually pierced at one end (either top or bottom indifferently) with markings which can scarcely be meaningless, and which look like inscriptions.

Schlösser illustrates 8 types reproduced in Fig. 93. I and II are the commonest, the former usually called *kuei t'ou ch'ien* or ' ghost's head money ' and the latter *i pi ch'ien*, ' ants' noses' money '. The former name has reference to the appearance of the markings which have some human or superhuman resemblance. These markings have been interpreted as an inscription reading *pan liang*

[1] The British Museum dates the ' ghost's head ' coins 612–589 B.C., and records that they were issued by order of the Prime Minister of the King of Tsu (*cf.* Lacouperie, 1892, p. 196).

(or half tael), which would form a link with the later coins ; but others read ' oath ' or ' exorcism ' and connect them with the custom of placing such coins in graves, especially in the nostrils of the corpse, to prevent the entrance of spirits in the form of ants. This custom explains the nickname of the second type, ' ants' noses' money ', the inscription on which has been read as ' each 6 *Shu* '[1] (Lockhart, 1915, Fig. 102, and p. 4 ; Schlösser, 1935, Pl. 12, Fig. 4 and *fn.* p. 43).

The fourth type is interesting as showing the same inscription as on the *pu* coins, *chin* = unit of value or metal tool (Lacouperie, 1888, pp. 428–39).

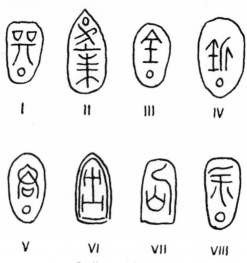

I   II   III   IV

V   VI   VII   VIII

FIG. 93.—Outlines of ' metallic cowries '
(From Schlösser's *Chinas Münzen*)

These metallic cowries, as numismatists call them, are of particular and controversial significance in a study of primitive money. Were they ' borrowed ' from bean-shaped coins of Aegina and Lydia already in existence (Lacouperie, 1892, p. xi) ? Or does their similarity illustrate ' convergence ' ? Do they represent a step in the evolutionary sequence from shells to metal coins ? Are they coins at all ?

If traders from the Indian Ocean established a colony in the Gulf of Kiao-chou (South Shantung) in 675–670 B.C. the introduction of Greek coins as models is easily explained (Lane-Poole, 1894, pp. 204–5). If, on the other hand, there was no contact with the Western World before the Christian era, borrowing would seem

[1] A *Shu* = grain was $\frac{1}{24}$ of an ounce or *liang*.

improbable (Andersson, 1934, p. 187). And if round coins in China were already in existence in the 12th century B.C. (Lockhart, 1915, pp. vi, 4) was there need for Greek models in the 6th or 7th? Illustrations may favour a theory of convergence, but actual comparison between the solid Aeginetan or Lydian dumps or blobs and the fragile little bronze slips, two of which weigh less than a farthing, gives little support to the argument. It is tempting to regard them as an obvious transition from shell-currency to metal coinage, a transition which can be traced in other parts of Asia, but the evidence is slight, their dates, inscriptions and purpose being uncertain and disputed. Their inclusion in most of the collections of Chinese coins cannot prove their right to be there, and it may be that they are merely charms after all.

Whether metallic cowries formed the stepping-stones or no, in due course cowries, here as elsewhere, were superseded by metal coins.

In other parts of the world where shell-currencies were in use their decadence seems to have been due to inflation and overproduction. In China it was from an opposite cause, the failure of supplies.

At the time of the Han dynasty (200 B.C.)

the cowry-currency was . . . fading away. It had received a great blow a long while previously from Hwei Wan, the Prince of Ts'in,[1] who in his second year, i.e. 335 B.C., recognizing the difficulties of finding a proper supply of shells and cowries and the rapidly increasing demand for a convenient currency, altogether suppressed it. The inland position of Ts'in, far away from the sources of supply, combined with the fact that metallic coins of various shapes and sizes had begun to be recognized as a more practicable medium of exchange in the other states of the Chinese agglomeration, were the two main reasons which led this ancestor of the founder of the Chinese Empire to abolish the cumbrous system of shell-currency and to adopt the more perfect system of metallic coins already put into practice by private persons in several of the neighbouring states. He issued then the round copper coin, with a central square hole, and the legend *pan liang* (= half-ounce) indicating its value, which was afterwards imitated by the rulers of the Han dynasty, and is, in fact, the direct and uninterrupted ancestor of the Chinese coins of the present day (Lacouperie, 1892, pp. 195–6).

Cowries survived however to be officially abolished again a century later, and to be revived by Wang Mang the Usurper two centuries after that. As late as the 14th century taxes were still being paid in cowries in China, although coins had been in existence for about two millennia : in a good year the Imperial Treasury would receive over a million (Morse, 1913, p. 135). And until recently, in China as in India, cowries could still be used for small change in out-of-the-way parts.

[1] = Hui Wan of Ch'in.

With the advent of a recognized metallic currency the study of primitive money normally comes to an end, but not in China. For the Chinese, although they may be credited with producing the earliest round coins, still for many centuries preserved a series of primitive forms.

In discussing these a writer who is neither a sinologue nor a numismatist must needs walk warily, relying to an unusual extent on authorities acknowledged in parentheses or preface.[1]

The difficulties of the currency problems are largely due to the incoherence of China, permitting innumerable series to flourish side by side, to the scarcity of archaeological evidence and the unreliability of historical records, and to linguistic difficulties. The recognized authority on Chinese coinage, the *Ku Ch'üan Hui* (= *Collection of old coins*) published in 1864 with the supplement (*Hsü Ch'üan Hui*) in 1875, is of little use to those unable to read the text.

Chinese money differs from that of any other part of the world in date, in material, in production and in form and imprint (Schlösser, 1935, pp. 11–14).

First, in date. Chinese coins claim to be the earliest of all, with round coins dating from the earlier half of the Chou dynasty (1122–249 B.C.) and other forms such as spade, hoe, knife, &c. (*Gerätemünzen*) earlier still. This is a moderate estimate. There are distinguished authorities in Europe as well as in China, who, relying chiefly on literary evidence, would shift the date some thousand years farther back. The testimony of the *Shu Ching*, the earliest historical work in China (much of which is undoubtedly later interpolation), assigns the origin of currency to the very beginning of the Shang dynasty in the 18th century B.C. This tells how Ch'eng T'ang, the founder of the line (1766 B.C.), issued the first coins at a time when there was a grievous famine in the land, partly for the relief of the people, partly as a means whereby parents who had been forced to pawn their children might redeem them.

The *Shih Chi* or *Historical Records* of Ssu-ma Ch'ien, written between 163–85 B.C., states that media of exchange were in existence in the Hsia dynasty which preceded the Shang dynasty, and even in

---

[1] The pitfalls are many, and authorities themselves flounder. The Museum of Archaeology and Ethnology at Cambridge contains a fairly representative collection of the main types of early Chinese currency, arranged and labelled under expert supervision. Yet a visitor with any special knowledge of the subject rarely fails to point out some error in chronology or transliteration, to cast doubts on the genuineness of individual specimens or to suggest some alteration in their arrangement. The Honorary Keeper of the Collection makes notes of all criticisms, which usually cancel each other out in course of time.

the time of the Emperors Shun and Yü [1] in the 3rd millennium.   A circumstantial list is given, including three kinds of metal, yellow, white and red (presumably gold, silver and copper), *chien pu, tao* (tool-coins), tortoiseshell, *kuei* (jade batons or tablets) and cowries.

Metal by weight was regulated for the payment of redeemable crimes even before the time of Yü (Lacouperie, 1892, pp. viii–ix), and there is no inherent improbability in the establishment of a tool-currency during this period (Lockhart, 1915, p. v).   There is general agreement, however, that little confidence can be placed in Chinese dates before the 8th century B.C., so unless this early money is inscribed, and unless the inscriptions can be correctly interpreted, and unless there is confirmatory archaeological evidence, any attempt at closer dating than ' the earlier half of the Chou dynasty ' must be merely tentative.[2]

Secondly, the material.

It is noteworthy that Chinese coins are, and have always been, almost exclusively of bronze, that is of a metal containing copper, mixed with tin, lead, more recently iron, and still more recently zinc, in varying proportions.

Gold and silver, the usual metals for coins elsewhere, were not current in China.

Possibly the preference for bronze may be explained by the early date of the currency here, which developed during the Chinese Bronze Age, when the metal was most highly valued by a people only just emerging from the Stone Age.   It persisted, possibly owing to another characteristic, not peculiar to China—forgery. Forgers were at work in the earliest days, as historians frequently lament, and their trade would have been fostered, and its consequences aggravated, by the issue of coins of higher intrinsic value. At the same time, as Vissering points out (1877, p. 11), had the metal been of higher intrinsic value, the costs of production could have been raised, and the processes of manufacture improved, thus lessening the risk of imitation.

The Emperor Wu Ti, one of the most famous of the Han line (140–86 B.C.), did indeed issue silver and tin pieces.   These were of three values : round, stamped with a dragon, 8 *liang*, worth 3,000

---

[1] Yü, founder of the Hsia dynasty (2205 B.C.), is reputed to have cast *pi* (valuables, metal implements or commodities easy to barter) for the relief of his people in distress (Lacouperie, 1892, p. ix).

[2] Lacouperie places uninscribed currency such as spade or *ching* between the 20th and the 7th century B.C.   He gives approximate dates for inscribed coins, placing knife-money first, 670–221 B.C. ;   spade-money 660–350 ; and hoe- or *pu*-money 665–221 ;   with the first inscribed round coins 660 B.C. (1892, pp. xlix, 1–3).   Lockhart attributed the ' first inscribed round coins to the time of Ch'eng Wang, 1115–1079 B.C.' (1915, p. vi).   These are the *Pao Huo* coins which he illustrates, Fig. 94, p. 32.

pieces of money. Square, with a horse, 6 *liang*, worth 500 ; and oblong with a tortoise, 4 *liang*, worth 300 pieces. But they were counterfeited on such a scale, not only by the forgers but by state officials, that they did not even circulate for a year.[1]

The practical advantage of a copper coinage before the days of banks and safes, was observed by Sulayman, the Arab merchant, in the 9th century.

If a thief enters the house of an Arab who traffics with gold and silver he can carry off on his back, 10,000 pieces of gold, or an equal amount of silver, and the trader is ruined. But if a thief steals into a Chinaman's house he cannot carry off more than 10,000 pieces of copper, which represents no more than 10 *mithkal* (about 20 francs). The Chinese therefore avoid merchants who use gold or silver (Ferrand, 1922, p. 81).

Thirdly Chinese coins are distinguished by being cast and not struck.[2]

From the earliest times down almost to the present century the same process was used. In the West the earliest coins, whether of Greece or of Asia Minor, were struck or stamped ; and though the Roman *aes grave* was cast, these pieces were only rude forerunners of stamped coins. The metal casting of the Chinese had reached a high perfection of technique as early as the Shang dynasty, and some archaeologists recognize and admire their skill in the preceding millennium. This early date, if accepted, would make the production of bronze coins at the beginning of the Shang dynasty less improbable (Schlösser, 1935, p. 13).

The most striking contrast is in the form.

From the ubiquity of round coins it might be assumed that a well-established currency among a civilized metal-using people would naturally take this convenient shape. Yet in China a currency representing tools or other objects was in use for centuries ; and these, the so-called 'tool-coins'[3] or irregular and awkward shapes, persisted side by side with round coins for several centuries. Archaeological evidence shows how metal imitates and finally supersedes stone as the Bronze Age succeeds the Neolithic, and one has but to watch the eager bartering of native goods for metal axes or other tools in less-civilized lands today to see how readily the latter can become a recognized currency. The bronze spade, hoe, knife

---

[1] Lacouperie says that no specimens of this fanciful mintage appear to be still in existence ; the representations of it which appear in some native books of numismatics (*cf.* Vissering, 1877, pp. 40–1) were drawn from the written description, and the false specimens which appear sometimes in collections were made from the drawings, for sale to collectors (1892, pp. 211–12).

[2] They have therefore no right, strictly speaking, to be called *coins*.

[3] 'Tool-coins' (*Gerätemünzen*) are all classed by the Chinese as *pu*, though the latter term is usually restricted by Western writers to the 'hoe' class (p. 236).

or other implement which superseded the stone one was at first a tool, later a token of value, growing smaller and thinner and lighter in the process, but still more or less recognizable as a ' tool-coin '. Spade-, hoe- or *pu*- and knife-coins are well known.   To these may be doubtfully added *ch'ing*-, bell- and key-coins.[1]

The variety in form adds to the complexity of Chinese currency, and the complexity is increased by the multiplicity of mints.   Although the currency under consideration was confined to a relatively small area in Northern China, yet the number of separate mints must have been very large to provide such a variety of issues.   Each city or trading centre or even trading guild had its own mint, and issued its own series of coins.   This characteristic persists down to our own times.

In England there is something infinitely respectable about the word mint. It is otherwise in China.   In the civil wars of that country the first sign that a protagonist has arrived (though not necessarily come to stay) is his acquisition or construction of a mint, and also, if possible, of an arsenal, but the mint is much the more important of the two (Fleming, 1936, pp. 301–2).   It is not surprising, therefore, that the total number of Chinese issues is reckoned at some 10,000.

Lastly, Chinese coins are peculiar in the absence of the imprint of the head, symbol or even name of the sovereign.   As the Emperor was sacred, neither his image, his symbols nor his name might appear on coins that passed from hand to hand, unworthy and unwashed hands too.   Such a desecration was unthinkable.   This lack adds enormously to the difficulty of dating, or even of sequence-dating Chinese coins.   It also precludes them from playing their part in illustrating the political history of China.   When we see how brilliantly a study of its coinage can illuminate and elucidate the history of Greece,[2] it is tantalizing to find that the far more abundant issues from Chinese mints throw so little light on Chinese history.

The more questionable of the tool-coins will be dealt with first. *Ch'ing* (or ' bridge '), bell- and key- (' lily-root ' or ' lotus-root heart ') coins are those most commonly accepted by Chinese numismatists, and, like the ' ghosts' heads ' and ' ants' noses ' already mentioned, they totter on the borderland between coins and charms. If they may be included in the former they present an interesting analogy with the iron currencies of West Africa, where almost any metal object has its exchange value.   The form is of less importance than the metal composing it, although some conventional shapes persist longer than others.

It must be acknowledged, however, that there is no proof that

---

[1] Still more doubtfully grater-, grid- and comb-coins (Schlösser, 1935, p. 15).

[2] *Cf*. Seltman's *Greek Coins*, 1933, in this series.

these objects are money. Very few of them can claim a high antiquity and many appear to be copies, and copies of copies. A standard of weight of copper underlies all Chinese metal currencies and it is the lack of this which shows that the bells, at any rate, did not have their origin from a central authority. Their essential ' prettiness ' also militates against them in contrast with the severe but uniform lines of the spade, ' hoe ' and knife issues. Still, as *ch'ing* are found in most, and bell and key in several well-authenticated collections of Chinese currency (even if their admission is partly due to their ' prettiness '), they deserve some consideration here.

The *ch'ing* money (Fig. 94) has a variety of names as well as a variety of shapes (*cf.* Schlösser's illustrations, 1928, pp. 99–106 ; 1935, pp. 24–5, Pl. 5, Figs. 3–5). It is called ' bridge ', ' yoke ',

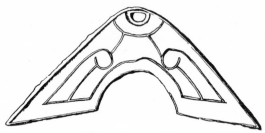

FIG. 94.—*Ch'ing* or ' bridge-money '. (⅔ size)

' moon ' and ' tingle-dangle ' money and has also been claimed as an attenuated agricultural implement, representing the curved metal blade, *ssŭ*, of the earliest type of plough (Hopkins, 1935, p. 713).

The similarity to the willow-plate pattern bridge suggested the first of these alternative names, but the asymmetry, a fairly constant factor, supports the claim to descent from a type of gong or sounding-stone. The Chinese name is *ch'ing shih pi*, which though elaborated by Lacouperie into ' coin in the form of a hanging piece fastened above which is rhythmically beaten by a stick in the right hand ' may be exactly transliterated ' sounding-stone ' or ' gong '.[1]

There is some evidence for believing that the earliest *ch'ing* were in stone or jade, for these have been found among Shang objects at Honan (Pope-Hennessy, 1923, p. 89).

Jade was valued for its aesthetic, symbolic and magical virtues and placed far above precious metals or gems, and enters into all estimates of wealth. Local supplies were scarce and soon exhausted, so it was imported, or extorted, mainly from Turkestan and Burma,

[1] *Ch'ing*, originally something like *king* or *köng*, is probably an imitative word, as is the Malay *gong*.

and according to the ancient books, fifteen walled cities would be ransomed with a single piece of jade ' the subtle essence of the rainbow incorporate in stone '. From the Son of Heaven down to the hereditary princes and high officers, all carried or wore jade in the form of *kuei, chang, huan, pi* and the like, not primarily for ornament but as badges of rank, or signs of imperial favour. The *kuei* are usually interpreted ' batons ' or ' tablets ', *chang* were half-tablets, *huan*, rings and *pi*, disks pierced with a central hole. We meet the latter again later on.

On account of its sonorousness when struck, jade sounding-stones or gongs were among special treasures. These under the name of *ch'ing*, are mentioned as forming part of the tribute provided by certain provinces in early records. Confucius speaks of the virtues which are symbolized in a ade *ch'ing* : ' When suspended, it hangs gracefully, like politeness. When struck it gives out a pure far-reaching sound, vibrating long, but stopping abruptly, like music ' (Bishop, 1906, p. 46).

Large sounding-stones were mounted singly like gongs, and struck ; others were mounted in series giving different notes.

The little bronze *ch'ing* are very varied in size, but usually range between 2 or 3 to 6 inches (6–15 cm.) across. Their shape is still more varied ; the commonest is that of a carpenter's square with obtuse-angled arms, one arm being longer than the other, but they also develop fishy or dragon-like outlines (colour plate facing p. 184). They are very thin and light, and the backs are usually flat and plain (like most of the Chinese currency up to the beginning of the Han dynasty). The metal is bronze with a high content of tin producing a slightly iridescent effect, similar to that of other early bronzes. All the earlier ones have a loop for suspension ; later ones a hole.

Schlösser (1928, p. 102) illustrates the successive types, with the decorative and dragon-like elaborations. He says that the place and period of their origin is unknown, though the negative clue of the absence of any inscription suggests that they are of early date. Chinese numismatists are, as a rule, silent on the subject [1] (*cf.* Lacouperie, 1892, p. 3). *Ch'ing*, sounding-stone, is a homonym of *ch'ing*, good fortune, and ' to strike the musical stone ' is equal to ' May blessings attend you '. This makes these objects especially appropriate for presents and they still form part of the bride's dowry in Pekin (Laufer, 1912, p. 329 ; Pope-Hennessy, 1923, p. 88).

[1] ' Fish-money ' is found in company with the *ch'ings* in collections of primitive currency or of coins. These may also be derived from earlier jade, as jade fishes were burial and temple offerings as well as girdle orna-ments in early times (Nott, 1936, pp. 101–2). On account of their symboliz-ing good fortune, wealth and abundance pairs of fish were always popular as amulets, and especially appropriate as bridal gifts. ' Tortoise ' and more shapeless ' coins ' also occur in this series (*cf.* Mosher, 1936, Pl. VI).

The little bronze bells are known in Chinese as *chung ch'ien* or 'bell cash' (Fig. 95). They are very varied (Schlösser records about 50 different types),[1] some shaped like temple bells, some like wind bells, some like cattle bells ; some are merely fantastic and most have no tongues. The only clues to their place of origin suggest an old culture centre in the bend of the Hoang Ho ; one inscribed bell belongs to the Han period (two centuries before and after Christ) but the majority are obviously much older.

There is no doubt that the special value attached to both gongs and bells in China, as in Africa, and as also in Further India, Borneo,

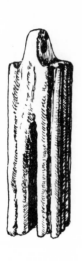

FIG. 95.—*Chung ch'ien*, or 'bell cash'   FIG. 96.—'Key coin'

the Philippines and beyond, is as much concerned with their magical as with their monetary content. This makes them especially suitable for gifts and particularly for marriage gifts.

The 'key-coins' or 'corrugated cash' (Fig. 96) are still more problematic and the Chinese name *ou hsin ch'ien*, translated 'lotus-root-heart-coin', is not helpful. Lacouperie says it was probably applied to them when their original significance was already forgotten (1892, p. xxxi). They have been thought to represent rolls of silk, and so to be metallic successors of the silk currency (*cf.* pp. 221–2). But Schlösser, who figures 9 of these from the Dorsten Collection in Westphalia, is clear that they were keys for padlocks,

[1] Schlösser illustrates 13 of these *Klanggerät-Münzen* in *Sinica*, 1928, p. 106 ; and 3 more in *Chinas Münzen*, 1935, Pl. 5, Figs. 6–8.

to be classed with the rest of the *Gerätemünzen* (1935, p. 27, Pl. 6, Figs. 9–17). They are quadrilateral in form with a hole or loop for suspension and complicated interior intricacies, not unsuitable to fit as a key into a lock. Few have any inscriptions, but some, probably not the earlier ones, belong, like the bells, to the Han dynasty.

Spades, *pu-* or ' hoe- ' and knife-money lead on to firmer though still uncertain ground. They are accepted as money; they were

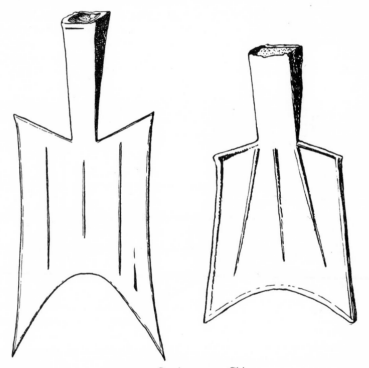

FIG. 97.—Spade-money, China

tokens representing definite values, used as media of exchange; but their dating and places of issue are obscure. The most archaic-looking, usually placed earliest in the series, are the *k'ung shu ch'an pi*, or ' spade-coins with hollow head '. They may be classified in three groups, those with level shoulders; [1] those, probably later, with upward-, and those with downward-sloping shoulders; the lower edge is curved with more or less projecting points (Fig. 97). They usually have three lines, either parallel or slightly radiating from the

[1] Lacouperie, 1892, p. 4, regards these as survivals of the shouldered celts.

handle; occasionally there are inscriptions referring to the place of origin. The words *sh'ao pi*, meaning 'little (or reduced) spade-coin', make their purpose clear, but their date is a matter of dispute save that they are placed in the Chou dynasty. General opinion (*cf.* British Museum) places the uninscribed hollow-headed type between the 11th and 8th centuries B.C. and the first inscribed examples in the 7th century (*cf.* Lacouperie, 1892, pp. 1, 4–16; Schlösser, 1935, pp. 29–30).

Chinese spade-money shows some resemblance to early Chinese spades. But the various names given to the next class of coins, usually called *pu*, indicate the different suggestions for their origin. They have been called 'hoe-', 'axe-', 'adze-', 'plane-', 'wedge-', 'cloth-', 'shirt-' and 'trouser-' money; also 'weight-money', 'leaf-money' and 'saddle-money' (Lacouperie, 1892, p. 18 and 1894, pp. 203, 206). The outline suggests some implement such as a hoe, but the term *pu* may be translated 'cloth' or 'silk' (Chalfant, 1913, p. 4), turning the same outline into shirt or trousers.[1] *Pu* may also mean 'to spread', which supports the agricultural-implement ancestry. From the evidence of the Honan finds and of the ancient bronzes Hopkins traces the origin of the plough, *lei*, to bifurcated branches of a tree cut into the fashion of a tuning-fork, which developed into the double-bladed implement from which the *pu* are derived (1935, p. 713). Shên Nung, of the mythical period, who preceded the Yellow Emperor Huang Ti, is credited with the invention of agricultural implements and the tilling of the soil. He is represented in a bas-relief of the Han Period using this queer two-pronged instrument which can be recognized as an ancestral type of *pu* (Schlösser, 1935, Pl. 9, pp. 31–6).

The *pu*- or 'hoe-' coins may be classified according to the rounded or angular shape of the 'shoulders', 'feet' and 'head' and of the space between the 'feet'. The hole, if present, is assumed to be for suspension, and thus to indicate the upper end of the coin, but it probably represents the hole for the nail originally fastening the implement to its handle. Only an inscription, and often there is none, can show which is the right way up, and many of the *pu*-coins stand on their 'heads'.

The extraordinary diversity of these coins—the *Ku Ch'üan Hui* illustrates over 600 and Lacouperie over 700 variations—suggests that they spread over many centuries but there is rarely an inscription, and when there is, it is usually the name of a place, such as An I, Ping Yang, An Yang, &c., no longer in existence, and rarely recognizable, so any dating must be largely guesswork.

[1] There is another theory, that the *pu*-coins represent the seal form of the character *ch'uan*, one of the oldest terms for money. *Ch'uan*-shaped coins are abundant, but mostly forgeries (Lockhart, 1915, p. vi, Figs. 23–5).

The An I specimen illustrated (Fig. 98A) is an angular-headed, round-shouldered, square-footed coin weighing 1 ounce. These usually show the value as ½, 1 or 2 *chin*. An I was a state at the bend of the Hoang Ho, and a chief centre of Chinese culture in the Hsia dynasty (2205–1766 B.C.) but that any *pu*-coins can date back to such an early time is improbable, and their connexion with the issue of the Emperor Yü himself is purely fabulous. They may belong to the beginning of the Chou dynasty, more than 1,000 years later, or, more probably, to the Feudal period between the 8th and 5th centuries B.C. (Lacouperie, 1892, p. l, and pp. 18–21).

The other *pu*-coin illustrated (Fig. 98B) is inscribed Ping Yang. One place of this name was the capital of the State of Han in the Province of Shansi, but there was also another in Shantung, and

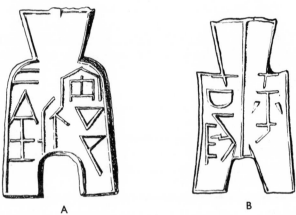

A   B

FIG. 98.—*Pu* or 'hoe-money', China

there may have been others. The great variety of Ping Yang coins suggests that they issued from different centres (Lockhart, 1915, pp. 2, 30). All these coins came to an end about 221 B.C. by the edict of Shih Hiang Ti, the first of the Ch'in emperors, who abolished all the forms of money then in existence and established a new and uniform coinage in place of the varied tool and round coins.

Two centuries later there was a revival of the *pu*-coins by the usurper Wang Mang.[1] He issued 10 coins in values from 100 to 1,000, all square-footed, with square level shoulders. They are inscribed according to their official value as Wee, Small, Young, Next, Almost, Middle, Mature, Approximate, Second-best and Largest. A later issue was inscribed *huo pu* = 'exchange *pu*'. These must have been issued in large, and forged in still larger,

---

[1] For Wang Mang's history see below, p. 245.

numbers as they are still abundant, and are collected by travellers as curios if not as coins (Chalfant, 1913, pp. 6, 21, Figs. 55–7; Schlösser, 1935, pp. 61–70, Pl. 14, Figs. 77–83).

Knife-money used to be a favourite illustration of the evolution of money. First a real knife, the base of the handle pierced with a hole for suspension, used in *barter* ; then, shrinking in size, with its edges blunted, useless as a knife but more convenient for *currency* ; lastly, the handle absorbing the blade as a tadpole its tail, we have the ' cash ' remaining as *money*. But no such degeneration can be traced. Knife-money was abolished, with the *pu*-coins about 221 B.C., but the various types current down to that time were all recognizably knives, with blade, handle and ring with *round* hole. The Yale-key-like type (Fig. 101), with blade in process of absorption, and ring with *square* hole (in imitation of cash) is the revived issue of Wang Mang the Usurper in the early years of the present era.

The origin of the currency knives is traditionally attributed to Ssu Shang Fu, or Grand Elder Shang, in the 12th century B.C., though no knives now in existence claim such an early date. According to the *Shih Chi*, the *Historical Records* of Ssu-ma Ch'ien (163–85 B.C.), Ssu Shang Fu received his name on account of the help he gave to King Wu of Chou in overcoming the Shang dynasty in 1122 B.C. As a reward he was given the fief of Yanchow in Ch'i (present Shangtung Province). He is stated to have made money in the shape of a knife known as *Ch'i tao chien*, inscribed with 6 characters, *Ch'i chien pang chiu ch'u huo* = money made at the beginning of the state of Ch'i.

The state of Ch'i is just where a recognized metal currency might be expected to develop. It was a grain, though not a rice-growing area, and had important trade in salt, a source of enormous wealth. It grew from small beginnings to absorb most of Shantung, and part of Chili province, with the enclosed Gulf of Pe chih li and the harbour of Kiauchou, which possibly attracted traders from overseas. It was always a go-ahead state, one of the most powerful during the Feudal period, and one of the last to submit to the Ch'in domination.

There are several varieties of knife-money,[1] the two commonest being the large curved scooped-ended Ch'i *tao*, and the lighter Ming *tao*, with straight-angled tip to the blade.

The Ch'i knives are solid and heavy, weighing about 2 ounces with a ridge all round the edge. The handle has 2 or 3 incised lines ; the blade has characters, often indecipherable, on the face and signs taken to indicate value on the back. The earliest ones

[1] *Cf.* Schlösser, 1935, where 7 types are outlined and described (pp. 37–41).

have 6, later reduced to 4, and later still (the most familiar type) to 3 characters. Many are altogether blank. The earliest are attributed to the 9th century B.C. and the three-character ones to between 500 and 220 B.C. (Lacouperie, 1892, p. 213).

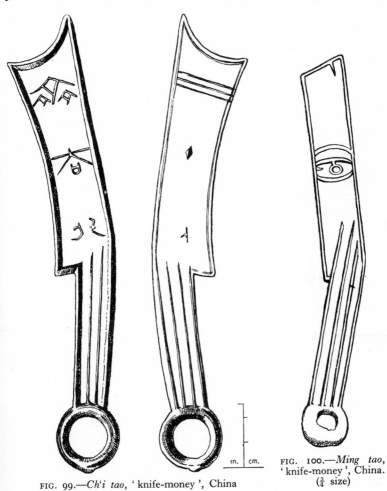

FIG. 99.—*Ch'i tao*, ' knife-money ', China

FIG. 100.—*Ming tao*, ' knife-money ', China. (¾ size)

The one illustrated (Fig. 99) is a three-character Ch'i knife read as *Ch'i ch'u huo* or ' Ch'i current coin ' [1]

The Ming *tao* (Fig. 100) are still more variable and abundant.

[1] There are other interpretations : *cf.* Lacouperie, 1892, pp. 234 *ff.* ; Chalfant, 1913, p. 15 ; Lockhart, 1915, Figs. 34–41 ; Schlösser, 1935, p. 41, Pl. 10, Fig. 32.

They are smaller and lighter, weighing only ½ ounce. The outline is slightly curved, or shows an angle at the junction of the blade and handle. They have raised rims all round, and straight lines up the handle. They have characters on the face of doubtful interpretation, and are distinguished by the sign of the city of Ming, the capital of the state of Chao (Shansi or Chili) on the back. The doubtful characters fall into four groups, which have been interpreted to mean *Right* (= West), *Left* (= East), *Public* (?) and *Outside*.[1]

The varieties of spade-, *pu*- and knife-currencies doubtless reflect the partition of· Chinese territory under rival princes (770–470 B.C.), and types multiplied during the Period of the Contending States (400–250 B.C.). With the supremacy of the state of Ch'in (249 B.C.) all local issues were officially abolished, though knife-money probably persisted in out-of-the-way parts on the borders of the Empire.

Though we have no intermediary proof of its continued existence for lack of information, we cannot help connecting with it . . . the practice still surviving in the present century among the Khamti and Sing-po tribes on the south-west borders of China, of using small square iron *dhas* or knives as currency. The very name of these *dhas* is obviously connected with the Chinese *tao* or knife-money, and speaks for itself (Lacouperie, 1894, pp. 205–6).[2]

FIG. 101.—Wang Mang *tao*, 'knife-money', China

The artificial revival of knife-money by Wang Mang the Usurper (A.D. 9–23) affords an interesting proof of the popularity of these queer coins in China. But his issue is very different from those of Ch'i and Ming.

The Wang Mang *tao* is of the Yale-key type, the original ring of the handle replaced by a cash-like coin. In the example illustrated (Fig. 101) the two characters on the handle are read *Ch'i tao* or 'graving knife' and those on the blade *wu pai*, or 500. The highest value inscribed ' equals 5,000 ' has the characters inlaid with gold.[3]

Chinese cash are so modern in appearance that they seem out of

---

[1] Chalfant, 1913, pp. 15–16. He illustrates the series (Figs. 22–5), and adds ' there are hundreds of varieties '. *Cf.* Lacouperie, 1892, pp. 265–98 ; Lockhart, 1915, p. 3 ; Schlösser, 1935, p. 39, Pl. II, Figs. 33–4.

[2] The Naga *daos* and *chabili*, and the *dakhs* of Northern Siam, show a further extension of knife-money (*cf.* pp. 204, 213).

[3] *Cf.* Lacouperie, 1892, pp. 311–18 ; Chalfant, 1913, p. 21, Fig. 51 ; Lockhart, 1915, pp. 146–53, No. 152 ; Schlösser, 1935, p. 58, No. 75.

place among the archaic-looking spades and hoes and other queer coins. But round-shaped coins were in existence quite as early as the others and some are probably considerably older. For Chinese cash constitute the longest unbroken numismatic series in the world, and can claim an ancestry traced back to the Stone Age. Round metal disks with round holes are attributed to the earlier half of the Chou dynasty (1122–249 B.C.) ; [1] and the first typical cash—' without, round as the heavens : within, square as the earth '—appear in the middle of the Chou dynasty (7th or 6th century B.C.). But as the square-holed cash may be traced back to the round-holed, so these may be traced back to bronze rings, and these to rings of baked clay, jade and stone.

Stone rings are not uncommon in the Stone Age excavations at Honan, and a beautiful jade ring from the Kansu district, farther west, of the *yüan* type, was associated with prehistoric deposits. At Sha Kuo T'un in Manchuria were found thin stone rings and numerous rings of mussel shell. These are of very graceful form and of unusual delicacy, and though, without further evidence, they cannot be claimed as currency, they are far too fragile for use as ornaments. Andersson interprets them as symbols to be used in cult ceremonies and as substitutes for the expensive stone rings found in the same area, and indeed in the same cave. If this suggestion be accepted ' there would be much the same relation between the stone- and mussel-shell rings as between the " sycee " of silver paper and the paper cash which is nowadays used at Chinese funerals instead of the genuine silver " sycee " and the copper coins which they imitate ' (Andersson, 1934, p. 199).

Jade rings, *huan*, or disks, *pi*, were symbols of rank or office, and therefore highly treasured, and they often occur in lists of presents or tribute in early Chinese annals (Lacouperie, 1894, pp. 32 *ff.*). In the 3rd century B.C. it is recorded that Wu Ti of the Ch'in dynasty received 1,000 strings of jade-money carved into rings, each ring weighing 10 *liang* (ounces) engraved with 4 characters, Celestial, Longevity, Everlasting, Prosperity (Bishop, 1906, p. 50).

Rings of bronze succeed to rings of stone, and appear to have been in use very early. It was during the latter part of the Shang dynasty (1766–1122 B.C.) that the Chancellor of Hsi Pai Hou, later famous as Chou Wen Wang (father of the founder of the Chou dynasty), is said to have issued the first bronze ring-money. This consisted in small flat bronze rings, about 1 inch (25–30 mm.) in diameter, with a round hole in the middle and no inscription.

Ring-money was officially recognized, for it is recorded in the *Shu Ching* that about 947 B.C., during the reign of King Mu of the

---

[1] Though many deny that any *round*-holed specimens are coins, and class them all as charms, badges, &c.

Chou dynasty, enactments were made for the optional redemption by mulcts and fines of penalties such as branding, mutilation or death.   The culprit was allowed to exonerate himself by paying 100, 200, 500 or 1,000 *huan* or pieces of ring-money in copper.   Similar ring-money was in use about the 5th century B.C. (Lacouperie, 1892, p. 48, and 1894, p. 35, n. 172, and 1894, p. 199 ; Schlösser, 1935, pp. 46–7).

To us in the West, rings and coins may appear quite distinct. Not so to the Chinese.   The ring form was classified according to its proportion of plane surface or ' flesh ' to hole (Fig. 102).   *Yüan*, with flesh narrower than the diameter of the hole ; *huan*, with flesh and hole equal in width ; and *pi*, with more flesh than hole.   Hence the transition is a natural one from rings to round coins with a hole in the centre which are classified as *pi*.   They were called *t'ien ch'ien*, or ' heavenly coins ', because they were believed to have fallen from heaven ; or because they enshrined the heavenly symbol of the jade *pi*.   Later on they were inscribed with value, weight or the name

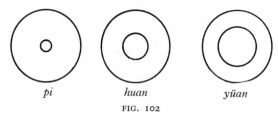

pi   huan   yüan

FIG. 102

of the place of issue, but there is no indication of date.   Schlösser illustrates 7 out of the 20 pieces in the Dorsten Collection and places them in the earlier half of the Chou dynasty (1935, pp. 48–9, Pl. 12, Nos. 44–50).   One of the commonest types—though genuine coins are rare—is illustrated in Fig. 103.   It has the inscription *Yüan*, the name of an old city on the borders between Chou and Chao in the state of Wei, probably Shansi.[1]

The same uncertainty of date obscures the origin of the typical Chinese cash with the square hole in the centre.[2]   History records that Ching Wang of the Chou dynasty ' continued to issue ' round

[1] Lockhart (1915) dates this type (No. 97) between 480 and 255 B.C.

[2] The Chinese call these coins *li* and *ch'ien*.   The non-Chinese name, cash, is modern, having been introduced by the Portuguese, probably from India (Tamil, *kasu*, Skt. *karsha* (*cf.* p. 191 *n.*)), and applied by Europeans to many small coins or weights of money in the East.   One thousand cash went to the *tael* (a Malay form, Hindu *tola* derived from Skt. *tula*, a balance, (*cf.* Chalmers, 1893, p. 373)) which was the Chinese *liang*, rather more than 1 ounce avoirdupois.   In theory 1,000 bronze cash equalled 10 silver or 1 gold coin, but theory and practice seldom agreed.   Moreover, there were rarely any silver coins and still more rarely gold.

coins with square holes, and his reign is placed between 544 and
519 B.C. As these were not apparently the first cash to be issued, the
earliest are attributed to about 600 B.C. which gives modern Chinese
cash an unbroken ancestry of more than two and a half millennia.[1]
These earliest coins are inscribed *pao huo*, 'exchange coin' or
'valuable exchange' (Fig. 104), and are the first to show the sign
pao which includes the sign *pei* (cowry) and so links modern cash
with that early world-wide currency. The earliest coins of this
period are smooth, but later issues show the 'walls' outlining the
border of the coin and the edges of the hole, introduced to prevent
clipping.

The Chou dynasty came to an end with the Period of the Contending States, when the Empire was the battlefield of warring
princes, all struggling for supremacy. The currency was in inex-

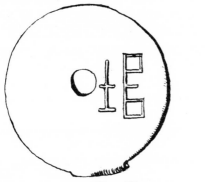

FIG. 103.—*T'ien ch'ien*   FIG. 104.—*Pao huo*

pressible confusion. The thin light coins issued at this time were
derisively called 'doves' eyes', 'hens' eyes' and 'unsinkable lads'
from the belief that they would not sink, even in water. 'One
thousand of these pieces piled together had only a height of 3 inches,
10 myriads of them was no more than a handful, and a *tou* (about
10 pints) of rice cost a myriad of such pieces' (Lacouperie, 1892,
p. 418).

A new era starts with the triumph of Ch'êng Wang of Ch'in,
'the Napoleon of China' who took the name of Shih Huang Ti,
the first sublime Emperor in 221 B.C. Much of the uncertainty of
earlier Chinese history is due to him, as, in his desire for progress,
he determined to break all links with the past. He destroyed the
old books, instituting a new script; he abolished the earlier forms

[1] Lockhart (1915, p. vi, No. 94) following the *Ku Ch'üan Hui* attributes the earliest *pao huo* coins to the beginning of the Chou dynasty
(1115–1079 B.C.), giving them a still longer life.

of currency (cowries and (?) tortoiseshell, silk and grain, spade-, *pu-* and knife-, as well as round-coins are mentioned) and issued a new coinage.[1] His dynasty, founded for 10,000 years, lasted 15, but his famous *Pan-Liang* coins (Fig. 105A) survived for nearly a century. In time, however, they became so debased, adulterated, shrunken in size, weight and value that they were in their turn abolished, and superseded by the *Wu Shu* coins (Fig. 105B) first issued by Wu Ti (140–87 B.C.).

The *Pan Liang* coins were supposed to weigh ½ ounce, or 4 *Shu*, 1 *Shu* being equal to 30 grains of corn. New coins of 5 *Shu* were issued by the State and became even more popular than the *Pan Liang*, and continued in innumerable forms, with only one important break, for more than 700 years.

The vicissitudes of Chinese cash lead beyond the bounds of primitive currency, but one point may be noted. As the coins were cast, forgery was only too easy, and references to this practice are

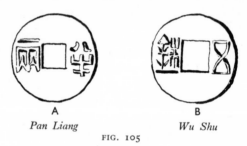

A   B

Pan Liang   *Wu Shu*

FIG. 105

frequent. In spite of punishments such as branding, imprisonment, confiscation, exile or even death, one of the Emperor's ministers complained (*c.* 40 B.C.) that 100,000 forgers were discovered in one year. (Large bribes were offered for their detection.) Coining appears to have been a home industry practised throughout the country, and it was no more possible then than it is now, to distinguish the true from the false. One result was the constant effort made by the successive emperors to restore the currency by new issues, leading to a bewildering variety of coins unmatched anywhere else in the world. Another result was the despairing return to more primitive forms, and even to barter in kind, providing a curious parallel to the return to barter in kind which resulted from the monetary chaos of recent years in Europe and America. This reaction may explain the popularity of such awkward coins as the knife- and ' hoe- ' money which persisted or were revived long after round copper coins were in general use. Recourse was even had to shell-money once more.

[1] His experiment in ' white stag notes ' is described below (p. 248).

All was of no avail against the counterfeiters, who issued such quantities of debased coin that the genuine money nearly disappeared in some parts of the Empire, where pieces of cloth had to be used again as a medium of exchange (Lacouperie, 1892, p. 211).

In the reign of the Emperor Yüan Ti (48–32 B.C.) it was proposed by the councillors of the Crown to abolish metallic currency altogether and to substitute grain, silk, cloth and shells, but there were difficulties in carrying out the suggestion.

Wang Mang the Usurper was more drastic.

Wang Mang had a brief but sensational reign, ostensibly from A.D. 9 to 23, during which time the currency, with its well-established copper coins of modern appearance, was utterly upset, and the whole financial system thrown into confusion.

The iconoclast Shih Huang Ti in the 3rd century B.C. had attempted to strengthen his position by breaking all links with the previous dynasty of Chou. Wang Mang hoped to gain favour by a return to the customs of the past. He abolished all the existing types of coins including the popular *wu shu*, and, besides re-establishing a currency in cowries and other shells he reintroduced, as we have seen, knife- and *pu*-money which had been out of use for over 200 years. Wang Mang was murdered in A.D. 23 and the currency was in such disorder and the people were so distrustful of it, that rice, cloth and silk were all used instead, every trader making what he could.

Four hundred years of monetary troubles and disorders had not convinced the rulers of the necessity of a sound currency. After the fall of the Han dynasty (A.D. 220) the King of Wei in the North thought that the best means of avoiding all these difficulties was to suppress the metallic currency altogether. Accordingly he abolished the *wu shu* pieces and ordered the people to use as currency only grain and silk. It was only opening another door to the counterfeiters, who, instead of casting bad metal, put moist grain into bags, and wove thin and fleecy silk so that after 40 years it was necessary to return to the metal currency and pieces of the time-honoured *wu shu* pattern were cast again and put into circulation (Lacouperie, 1892, p. 216).

The popularity and unparalleled longevity of Chinese cash are not hard to explain as they obviously satisfy to an unusual degree the needs of ancient and modern, of civilized and uncivilized alike. In the first place the coins probably retained some religious significance, thus combining magical with pecuniary profit; they were ornamental, and could be strung and worn like beads; they were easy to handle, to count and to carry; they were sufficiently solid to represent wealth, yet too solid to make theft easy. With the early invention of paper money and the use of silver for larger financial transactions, copper cash was sufficient for all needs and triumphed over all rivals, spreading with trade round the world. And even

though golden Persian darics and silver Athenian owls may look
scornfully down on them in the coin cabinet, these copper cash can
claim an historic lineage unique in the realm of numismatics.

Only gold and copper or bronze are mentioned in accounts of
early Chinese money. Gold was current by weight, cut into pieces
as wanted, from the time of Ch'eng, King of Chou, more than 1,000
B.C. down to the present day, but it was not cast into coins. Silver
was much later. This was also issued in lumps and bars, which
could be cut up as needed, and a piece, roughly scored for partition,
which was found on the body of a dead Boxer during the uprising
of 1900 is illustrated in Fig. 106. For trading, the well-known *yuan
pao*, 'shoe-money' or 'sycee taels' (Fig. 107) described by the
Chinese as *wan yin*, meaning 'fine silver', have been in circulation

FIG. 106.—Silver bar, China   FIG. 107.—Sycee tael 'shoe-
                                       money', China

for some centuries. The lump was impressed with a stamp, which
gave it its likeness to a shoe, and the term sycee, in Cantonese
hsi-ssu or 'fine silk', is thus explained :

> When the Shansi bankers melt silver into ingots, after it has been liqui-
> fied and poured into the mould and before it has again solidified, the mould
> is lightly tapped, when there appear on the surface of the silver fine silk-
> like circular lines. The higher the 'touch' of the metal, the more like fine
> silk are these 'circlings' on the surface of the silver. Hence ingots of full
> quality are classified as sycee (Lockhart, 1915, XI).

These ingots are of varying weights, the one from Honan (ill.,
Fig. 108) weighs over 4 pounds, but the 'sycee tael' reckoned at
1 ounce (though actually rather more) was the popular unit. It
played a vital rôle in Chinese economic life for many centuries and
it was only in 1933 that it was officially abolished.

The 'saddle-money' illustrated in Fig. 109 is a common form of
silver ingot, which finds its way over the Chinese borders into Burma
and Siam. The Chinese inscriptions in the panels (the three are
identical) read as *Hong Küng Tang Kee* (the name of the banking
house) and *Kong Ngee Bun Ngön* or 'genuine first-quality silver'.
Each of the two columns guarding the central panel also has the

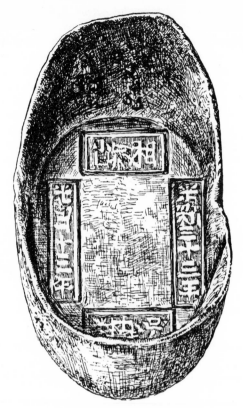

FIG. 108.—Sycee tael 'shoe-money', China

FIG. 109.—'Saddle-money', China

same lettering, which runs *Kong Ngee Kong Koh Tong Pao*, ' Genuine and negotiable for free circulation '.[1]

   China was the first country to issue bank-notes, and the founder of the Ch'in dynasty, Shih Huang Ti (249–202 B.C.) was the first to experiment with this form of currency. Continual wars had ravaged the land for many centuries, and the currency was totally discredited ; illicit minting and adulteration of coinage caused violent fluctuations of prices, adding to the miseries of the poor, embarrassing the Government and enriching speculators at no profit to the State. There are many accounts of the Emperor's attempts to grapple with the crisis, one of which was as follows :

> In the Imperial Park at Ch'ang An, the Emperor had a white stag, a very rare beast, which had no fellow in the Empire. On the advice of a Minister the Emperor had this animal killed and made a kind of treasury note out of its skin, which he believed could not be copied. These pieces of skin were a foot square and were made with a fringed border and decorated with a pattern. Each piece was assigned the arbitrary value of 400,000 copper coins. The princes when they came to pay their respects to the throne, were compelled to buy one of these pieces of skin for cash, and present their gifts to the Emperor upon it. This precaution insured the circulation of the ' White Stag Notes '. The limited amount of skin prevented this from being more than a temporary expedient (Fitzgerald, 1935, p. 164).[2]

   Authentic bank-notes in paper are mentioned in the time of the Emperor Hsien Tsung (*c.* A.D. 800) whose issue had the name of *fei hsien* (ch'ien) or ' flying money '. The best account of the Mongol issue is the familiar one given by Marco Polo concerning the paper-money of Kublai Khan.

> The Emperor's mint there is in this same city of Cambulac [Peiping]. For he makes his money after this fashion. He makes them take of the bark of a certain tree, in fact of the mulberry tree the leaves of which are the food of the silkworms [3]—these trees being so numerous that whole districts are full of them. What they take is a certain fine white bast or skin which lies between the wood of the tree and the thick outer bark, and this they make into something resembling sheets of paper, but black. When these sheets have been prepared they are cut up into pieces of different sizes. The smallest of these is worth a half *tornesel* ; the next, a little larger, one *tornesel* ; one, a little larger still, is worth half a silver groat of Venice ;

---

[1] *Cf.* le May, 1932, pp. 8–9, Pl. II, Fig. 7. Ling Roth (1901, Fig. 4, pp. 16–17) illustrates a similar coin which he calls ' shoe-money ' of the Jung Feng Steng Bank.

[2] These notes can scarcely be included in ordinary currency, but they are quoted as anticipating the leathern money issued in Italy in the 13th and in England in the 16th century. *Cf.* Yule's note to Marco Polo, 1903, I, p. 429.

[3] This was a misunderstanding, it is not the silkworm mulberry, *Morus alba*, but the ' paper mulberry ', *Broussonetia papyrifera*, the same tree that provided the tapa of Fiji and Samoa.

another a whole groat ; others yet 2 groats, 5 groats and 10 groats. There is also a kind worth one Bezant of gold and others of 2 Bezants, and so up to 10. All these pieces of paper are issued with as much solemnity and authority as if they were of pure gold or silver ; and on every piece a variety of officials, whose duty it is, have to write their names and to put their seals. And when all is prepared duly the chief officer deputed by the Kaan smears the seal entrusted to him with vermilion, and impresses it on the paper, so that the form of the seal remains printed upon it in red, the Money is then authentic.

With these pieces of paper, made as I have described, he causes all payments on his own account to be made ; and he makes them to pass current universally over all his kingdom and provinces and territories and whithersoever his power and sovereignty extends (1903, Book II, Chap. 24).

v. JAPAN

Japan is the last of all the civilized or semi-civilized countries of the world in which to expect to find primitive forms of money, and the space allotted to it in a geographical arrangement is filled, if filled at all, with beads, *kudatama* (Pl. 22, Figs. 1–4) ; with hypothetical ' ring-money ', *kin-kwan* and *gin-kwan* (Figs. 9–11) ; with enigmatic *magatama* (Figs. 5–8) [1] ; with *cho gin* or ' long silver ' good service badges (Figs. 14–15) ; with *mame gin* or ' bean-money ' for gifts (Figs. 12–13) and with *obans* and *kobans* (Figs. 16–17). Even the cowry seems to fail us here, for the only evidence for its former use is derived from its Japanese name. This is *takaragai*, *takara* meaning wealth or riches, and *gai* or *kai*, shells (Schneider, 1905, p. 108).

In Japan, even more than in China, agriculture was the foundation of economic life, and the agricultural class alone was honoured as the creator of wealth. Rice was the principal food of the people, the most important medium of exchange, and served as the standard of value. The position of a lord was estimated by rice-production, according to the *koku* or measures of rice which his land provided.

[1] As *magatama* are often included in collections of Japanese currency, though without historical support, Munro's note on them may be quoted here :

' There has been much discussion as to the nature and significance of these *magatama*. It has been suggested that they are embryonic forms, but it is more likely that they were shaped after the claw of some animal, possibly a tiger. This is supported by the existence of claw-shaped stones, closely resembling the talon of the tiger, one in my collection being almost an exact model. The tiger's claw is the strongest of amulets even to this day in Corea. Lastly, the word *magatama*, which is supposed to come from *naga*, curved, and *tama*, a gem, may with equal propriety, as it seems to me, derive its latter portion from the archaic form of *tsume*, namely *tume*, a talon or nail. The character in which it was written was given to it long after its coming into favour and about two centuries before the end of the dolmen period ' (1904, p. 5).

External trade was unnecessary, as the islands were self-supporting ; it was undeveloped, because there were no materials to foster it ; and it was ' not done '. Merchants were discouraged, and money was considered degrading. In the Tokugawa period (1600–1853) it was contrary to etiquette for the *samurai* to think or talk about money, and a disgrace to handle it. A *samurai* was proud to show his friends that he did not even know how to count money. To offer it was an insult. And it was the *samurai*, who permitted no luxury in dress or food, who set the fashion for all Japan.

This ideal of the simple life was no new development. In the 7th century sumptuary laws were minutely detailed and strictly enforced, and these were augmented and reinforced in the Tokugawa period. From the size and shape of a man's house, the material, quality and colour of his clothes, to his expenditure at his daughter's wedding, and the presents he might give his grandchildren, every detail was rigidly determined. The use of ivory and tortoiseshell was forbidden to farmers whose incomes were below a certain amount, their wives might not wear sandals nor bind their hair with silk. With such restrictions it is no wonder that present-giving was discouraged, that trade was reduced to a minimum, and that money was seldom seen. There was not even a native word for competition, the idea being foreign to classical ethical teaching (Chamberlain, 1938, p. 250, *fn.*). ' All wise rulers in all ages have valued cereals and despised money,' ran the proverb, with the explanation ' No matter how much gold and silver one may possess, one cannot live for a single day on these. Rice is the one thing needful for life.'

Money is first mentioned in the time of the Emperor Kenso towards the end of the 5th century, when Japanese history is still vague ; and both silver and copper coins are mentioned in the time of the Emperor Temmu, A.D. 674. In the following century copper mines were worked, silver coins were prohibited and copper coins issued, under the Emperor Gemmei. His era was therefore named *Wado*, meaning ' Japanese copper ', and the earliest Japanese copper coins date from the beginning of the 8th century. The copper was used more for gigantic images of Buddha than for coining, and the coins of the period were commonly melted down to make the smaller images for each household. From the end of the 10th to the end of the 16th century, and the advent of Europeans, copper coining was prohibited by imperial order. Gold dust, gold grains or gold and silver ingots, cut to various weights, were used in official exchange, and all the copper coins of this period (958–1587) are Chinese. The coming of the Dutch in 1600 broke in upon Japanese isolation, and during the 17th century powerful clans owning copper mines made their own coins, and the discovery of gold and silver gave an impetus to coin production. Under Tokugawa Iyeyasu first of the line of regents, gold, silver and copper coins were issued, but they were very rarely circulated.   Rice was still used for barter and there was as much excitement at the sight of a gold coin as of a precious jewel.   Traders were still regarded with disdain and stood lowest in the social scale, only just above outcasts who slaughtered animals and executed criminals.   And although in the 17th century copper and rice appear to have been used indiscriminately in small transactions, taxation in money was discouraged, in the belief that agriculture alone was of national importance.   It was not before the end of the 17th or beginning of the 18th century that rice was giving way before the advent of money, because economic life could no longer do without it (Matsuyo Takizawa, 1927, p. 49).

However rich a man might be in rice, this would not suffice for travelling expenses, for payments to artisans or to traders, and a merchant class, *chonin*, grew up, amassing riches and gaining power in the land.   ' Notwithstanding the fact that the *samurai* ought to be the rulers and the merchants the ruled, it appears that the *chonin* have now become virtual rulers ' is the lament at the beginning of the 19th century (Eijiro Honjo, 1938, pp. 11–13).

It seems probable that rice is responsible for the shapes of the *oban* and *koban*, the best-known coins of Japan (illustrated Pl. 22, Figs. 16, 17).   (The *oban* (great division) equals 10 *koban* (little divisions).)   The *koku* or measure of rice was an oval-shaped bag made of straw, and the oval gold coins with rounded corners are believed to represent the bag of rice : on old coins many parallel lines are found, indicating the lines on the plaited straw.

Hamilton has an observation on trading with these coins at the beginning of the 18th century :

> The Japanese are strict Observers of moral Rules, and particularly in Commerce, in so much that a Merchant of Reputation, in his Payment, puts up 5, 10 or any decimal Number of *Cupangs*, which is a broad oblong thin Piece of Gold (of 20s. value there) into a Silk Bag, and putting his Seal on the Bag, passes current for what the Seal mentions for several Generations, without so much as once looking what is in the Bag, and Gold is so plentiful and cheap that a *Cupang* of 20s. in Japan, passes current at Batavia or 32s., and when the mark is stamped on it by the Company it passes for 10s. Sterling (1727, II, p. 305).

vi. MALAY PENINSULA

Travelling down into the Malay Peninsula and East Indian Archipelago we enter one of the earliest and most famous trading areas of the world, for the spice trade was in full swing some centuries b.c. and it has shaped the history of the islands down to recent times.

Barter with beads was doubtless as profitable here, as on the coasts of Africa, possibly with the same type of beads, and these relics of early trade are found in the hoarded or buried treasures of natives who know nothing of their history.

Cowries were still in use ' among the meaner sort of people ' in the middle of the 17th century (Tavernier, 1678, I, II, p. 6); 50 cowries went to the *kepeng, pitis* or cash [1]; 3 cash to the sou or cent; and 100 sous or cents, or 15,000 cowries to the dollar. Skeat collected some on the East Coast, where 100 were said to make one *pitis* or cash. But the value varied a good deal with the locality (Temple, 1914, p. 153). They are nowadays valued as a medicine, being grated and drunk, recalling the use of aggry beads or holed stones on the West Coast of Africa.

The Malays, who spread into this region about 1,000 years ago, were maritime invaders, pirates rather than traders, but there must always have been a certain amount of trade with the primitive people of the interior. Down to last century this was carried on with the non-Malay folk by the system of ' silent trade ', described by Skeat and Blagden (1906, p. 227).

The Malays, wishing to exchange goods with the Semang, would take certain commodities, consisting chiefly of coarse cloths, tobacco and knives, and place them in any open space in the neighbourhood of the known Semang camping ground, and then retire to a convenient distance. The Semang would next approach, and having selected such articles as they fancied, bear them off, leaving in their place whatever they might deem a fair equivalent this latter consisted chiefly of elephants' teeth, eagle-wood, resin, canes and so forth.

In a tin-producing area such as the Peninsula, it is natural that a metal currency in tin should evolve as need arose, and here the transition follows the usual line of evolution from lumps or ingots these taking characteristic and easily recognizable shapes, ultimately settling into coins, which in some instances recall the history of their predecessors.

Chinese chroniclers of the 15th century report that

tin is found in two places in the mountains of Malacca, and the king ha appointed officers to control the mines. People are sent to wash it, and after it has been melted it is cast into small blocks weighing 1 *kati* 8 *tahils* c 1 *kati* 4 *tahils* official weight; 10 pieces are bound together with rattan an form a small bundle, whilst 40 pieces make a large bundle. In all thei trading transactions they use the pieces of tin instead of money (Winsted 1925, II, p. 43).

---

[1] *Kepeng, pitis* or *pichis* are names for small tin coins minted in imitatio of Chinese cash. They were estimated at $\frac{1}{15}$ of a *keneri* (= candaree: *Abrus precatorius* or ' saga pea '), $\frac{1}{16}$ of a *mas* in weight, or that weight gold, but they varied not only locally but also periodically, with the pric of tin.

The characteristic forms in which tin ingots were made were the *tampang* in sugar-loaf, ' pagoda ' or ' hat ' shapes ; and the *gambars* or models of animals, birds or insects.[1] Temple described this obsolete tin currency in 1914, basing his descriptions largely on the specimens given by Skeat to the Cambridge Museum, and the information which he supplied by letter. The pieces are well and fully illustrated in Temple's articles, but, as these are not easily found, some of the different forms are reproduced here (Pl. 23).

Dakers (1938, p. 31) traces the historical sequence of the *tampang* of Pahang. The ' sugar-loaf ' or truncated pyramid comes first ; next the pyramid or ' pagoda ' with the plinth ; then the pyramid becomes smaller and hollow, with its plinth wider, with room for inscriptions underneath ; this is the typical ' tin hat ' (though some have recognized an inverted rice husker here). These usually have a hole for stringing, and they fit one inside the other in nests (Fig. 110).

Temple wrote (1913, pp. 119–20) :

The regulated solid tin ingots constituted a currency made out of the customary forms of native tin castings, to meet the necessities of an external trade carried on by means of barter and currency, and to conform in weight and size to the weight-standards of that trade. Tin was adopted for the purposes of currency as being the staple metal product of the peninsula, and the system of tin currency devised by the Malays has not materially varied in historical times.

Tin mining is a simple, almost domestic industry, undertaken by men, their wives and children when not needed in the rice fields. The metal is run into sand moulds (sometimes soft stone or brass) hence the variety of shapes, among which the sugar-loaf is the easiest to withdraw from the mould (Winstedt, 1925, I, p. 29).

Solid tin lumps (*tampang jongkong*) of varying sizes, some 1 foot or more across, and looking as if turned out of a pudding basin, were in use in Selangor until recently. These are the firstlings of the smelting house,[2] to which a superstitious value was attached, and these first fruits were handed down as family heirlooms.

The solid ' sugar-loaves ' are varied. Some are quite plain : some have the *tampok manggin* or mangosteen rosette at the top of the truncated pyramid (Pl. 23) ; and some have a shallow receding step two-thirds up from the base. They weigh round about 100 ounces, and were used in Selangor for paying duty on tin and also passed as currency for general merchandise. Their value was low, only 25 cents, as the price of tin was only 15 dollars a *picul*. For

---

[1] *Tampang* means block or cake ; *tampang jongkong* is a large, and *tampang roman* a small, casting. Many museums still consider the animal shapes to be no more than toys.

[2] *Cf.* the specimen in the Pitt Rivers Collection and also Temple, 1913, Pl. II.

trading purposes the ' hats ' adapted to different weights fitting one inside the other were an advantage. These varied in shapes and in weights, but the weights corresponded roughly to a monetary scale, the price fluctuating with the price of the tin. They ceased to be legal tender in 1893 when they were paid in to the Treasury of Singapore (Dakers, 1938, p. 31).

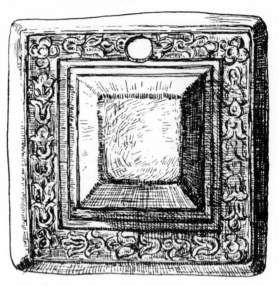

FIG. 110.—' Hat-money ', Malay Peninsula

Tin ingots also developed in different and more picturesque forms. Until recently the tin animals and birds of the Peninsula were regarded as toys or ornaments. All memory of their use as money had died out even among the traders of the ' bad old times ' and was not suspected by collectors. The history of their discovery deserves to be placed on record, and the following story is given by Skeat :

I had long been familiar with the singular fact that in the coastal districts of Selangor a certain fixed number of cents (2½ to be exact) was called locally a ' crocodile '. And one day I read in a Malay-Dutch dictionary under the word *buaya* (in Dutch *boewaja*) that the State of Selangor had a tin coin shaped like a crocodile. This first put me on the track, but although I was continually on the lookout for tin currency and succeeded in collecting some specimens they were all of the usual square *tampang* shape, even when solid. When the late George Muir Laidlaw obtained a cadetship in the Peninsula he came to me for preliminary training in Malay, and asked what he could do in the way of investigation. I told him about the *buaya* currency and asked him to look out for it. This he did, taking endless pains and making unceasing inquiries, and eventually *he* found the first specimen, followed by others, in Perak (W. W. Skeat).

The animals represented are crocodile, *buaya*, cock, *ayam*, elephant, *gajah*, tortoise, *kurakura* and mantis, *belalang*.[1] The frequency of the names *buaya* (crocodile), *gajah* (elephant) and *ayam*

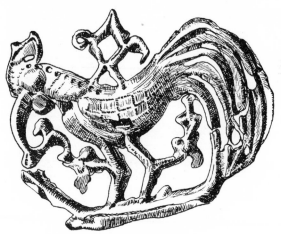

FIG. 111.—Malay cock

(cock) in Malay weights and coins led Temple (again basing his conclusions on specimens and information given by Skeat) to sum up as follows :

The solid ' animal ' ingot tin currency (*gambar*) arose out of an attempt to improve the regulation of the ingot currency by giving it readily recognizable forms, which could be made to conform to definite standards ; while the forms themselves were copied from those in use—with a very long history behind them—by the neighbouring countries carrying on the external trade, which were mainly Burma [2] and China (directly or through Siam) (Temple, 1913, p. 120).

---

[1] The British Museum which has provided the illustrations of cock, elephant and crocodile on Pl. 23 has also models of peacock, locust and fish.

[2] In Burma metal weights took the form of animals such as lion, deer, elephant, bull, &c. For the connexion between weights and currency *cf.* Temple, 1913, p. 117 *fn.*

There are larger- and smaller-sized animals, some being merely rough lumps, with projections bent down into bandy legs ; some are carefully modelled ; some are little more than outlined. But their weights correspond sufficiently exactly with those of the accepted currency ingots for Temple to have concluded that they served the same purpose. He believed that the Malays were influenced in this by the Indian ingots of various forms which include that of the tortoise. Solid lumps of tin need very little skill or imagination to turn them into tortoises, elephants or crocodiles. This has, in fact, been done in many cases merely by a little modelling and the addition of rather clumsy stiff legs.

Skeat wrote (in 1904) :

> The tortoise exactly resembles an ordinary piece of smelted tin with the addition of head and flappers. At first one would naturally expect that the ' animal ' currency would represent only animals that had a distinct barterable value, e.g. fowl, goat, cattle, &c. But the introduction of the crocodile—of which as currency there is (at least in Selangor and Perak) more ample evidence than in the case of any of the others—shows that this was not the underlying motive ; or, at least, not the sole one. Whatever the motive was, there is ample evidence to prove the use of the ' animal ' as currency and this evidence receives the most practical corroboration from the arrangements for stringing these coins together like cash. See the hole at the top of the ' cock- ' coins and over the nose of several of the crocodiles.

The names of crocodile, *buaya*, elephant, *gajah*, tortoise, *kurakura* and cock, *ayam*, are often found in the chaotically complicated system of weights and currency described by Temple, and the ' cock-coins ', *duit ayam* (*duit* = cent), with the figure of a cock, and the legend *Tanah Malayu*, or Malay Land, are found all over Malaysia.[1] These were made in Birmingham, and imported by private speculators. But there was an earlier issue of ' cock-coins ' or tokens, made by the British East India Co. in Sumatra. Specimens in the British Museum date

FIG. 112.—Currency kris, Java

---

[1] These *duit ayam*, though of small value (10 went to the *pitis* or cash) were not perforated for stringing. The *pitis* or cash, 1,000 to the dollar were the common currency. In Kelantan, Kedah and Trengganu they were cast in sets of varying numbers in a mould in the shape of a tree, and these *pokok pitis* or ' cash trees ' suggested to Skeat that the phrase ' shaking the pagoda tree ' was no mere metaphor. Temple illustrates on Pl. VII Fig. 2, the ' tree ' with 13 *pitis* in the Cambridge Collection. The date is A.H. 1314, i.e. A.D. 1896.

from 1797 onwards (Temple, p. 38 *fn.* ; Hanitsch, 1903, p. 199).
The Sumatra cocks preserve the memory of the cocks of Kedah,
but the neat little Birmingham coppers which succeeded them ' soon
swept the menagerie away completely ' [1] (Dakers, 1938, p. 32).

The kris (*kěris*) sometimes figures in currency collections and
one from Java in the Pitt Rivers Collection is illustrated in Fig. 112.

The kris of Indonesia has much in common with the ceremonial
axe or *couteau de parade* of the Congo.   The metal has a certain
sacredness in both areas.   In the Malay Peninsula iron is regarded
with special awe, a lump is part of the traditional regalia of more
than one sultan, and an oath taken on it is irrevocable.   The kris
is (or was) [2] part of the ceremonial or court dress, and could not be
carried without the permission of the sultan, just as in Africa, the
decorative axe or knife was the prerogative of the chief, his digni-
taries or favourites.   ' Their greatest bravery is in their crizes,' wrote
Sir Thomas Herbert in 1665, and adds ponderously, ' they ask their
idol on their crest pardon after they have perpetrated a homicide.'
A superstitious reverence for the *kěris* still obtains, and folk are
readier to dispose of its gold sheath than of a rusted blade, which
may bring good luck to house and crops (Winstedt, 1925, II, p. 43).
In Borneo the kris forms part of the ' bride-price ', and in Java it
may impersonate the bridegroom himself (*B.M. Handbook*, 1910,
p. 100).

vii. BORNEO

Islands are usually more conservative than the mainland, and
there were special conditions in Borneo which encouraged the
continuance of primitive forms of money.   Until recently the
currency was in a chaotic state and every sort of coin appears to have
been accepted.   Government accounts were kept in rupees, but
fines were paid in *reals*.   Trading was carried on in dollars, which
fluctuated between something under 5*s.* down to 1*s.* 4*d.*   Copper
coins of smaller denominations were as varied as cash in China, but
usually accepted if approximately of normal size.   With all this
instability it is not surprising to find a preference for solid valuables
such as slaves, buffaloes, jars, together with metal objects estimated
by weight in the form of gongs, bells and cannon, persisting down to
the present day.   Throughout the greater part of Borneo barter was
and still is the rule but a great many items may be classed as currency.

Hose gave the following list from the Baram district of Sarawak
alone : The Kalabits who inhabit the eastern portion of the district
use salt, tobacco and buffaloes as currency ; the Kenyahs of the

---

[1] A trace of the crocodile may be found in Borneo (*cf.* p. 261 *n.*).
[2] The kris is no longer in fashion, and the art of making them has died out.

southern portion use gongs; the Kayans of the central area use iron swords (*maleat*) [1] and beads; the Punans, a wandering tribe, use *libangs* [1] of camphor; the Miris, Dalli and Naroms, who inhabit the Coast to the north and west of the district, use buffaloes. Brunei Malays and Kadayans formerly used small pieces of iron (*blanja*) about 1 inch long and ¼ inch wide, valued at 1 cent. The Dyaks use old jars.

To this list may be added the cowries formerly used as small change, the beeswax and edible bird's-nests among jungle products, the brass cannon, inlaid caskets, buffalo bells and krisses, the plaited rings of the Iban and Kayan and the shell-money and bead strings of the Dusun. Some of these, especially the larger objects, represent wealth rather than money; many have long been out of use; but some are still the usual medium of commercial bargaining and essential items in *berian* ('bride-price' or 'bride-gift') and in wergeld.

I. H. N. Evans described the *berian* of a Dusun maiden of Tuaran. It consisted of two gongs, a kris, a necklace, one brass cannon and one cow.

The *berian* or bride-gift in Melano society is by weight, consisting of either 3, 5 or 7 *piculs*,[2] according to the class of the bride. A *picul* was worth some 25 to 30 dollars and the amount would be made up partly in brass gongs, bells or cannon and Chinese pottery, and might include household goods and a piece of gold. A certain type of basket called a Rejang basket from the river where the best are made, with a specially fine weave and a special pattern *salad timon*, (Pl. 24) was an essential part of the *berian*. These Rejang baskets were always acceptable in place of money in everyday trading with a value formerly of 4, now 2, to the dollar (J. C. Swayne).

The *unus*, rings of very finely plaited palm fibres (Fig. 113), could also be used instead of money, a ring being worth a cent. These are commonly worn by the men in considerable numbers on the arm below the elbow and on the leg below the knee. There may be as many as 300 of them on one leg, a handy way of carrying small change, and the Kayan say that they feel quite naked without them (*cf.* Ling Roth, 1896, I, pp. 5, 14, 15, 23).

Rice, salt, tobacco, beeswax and camphor suggest barter rather

---

[1] The *maleat* is interesting as affording comparison with our 'currency bars' (pp. 288-9). The Kayan were the chief workers in iron before it was introduced by the Malay and Chinese traders, and the *maleat* was merely an iron sword, forged and tempered but without handle or ornament. The value was about a dollar or 2s., but the best sort might go up to 10s. *Libang* is not a definite weight but the amount collected from one tree, mixed with chips of wood and put into a bamboo, exchange value about 3 dollars (C. Hose).

[2] A *picul* is a weight of about 133 pounds, representing a man's load

han money, but in Borneo they claim admission into the ranks of
urrency.   The salt is made up into hard tile-like cakes (*keping*) of
lifferent sizes, the smallest being worth 5 cents or 1*d*. and the largest
o cents or 1*s*.   The tobacco is plaited and measured in lengths,
rom the *buhak*, the span from the thumb to the second finger, to
he *siko*, from the first finger round the elbow and back to the finger
again.   Two *siko* are worth one large salt cake.   There is a regular
ystem of exchange between Brunei and the interior, a brass tobacco
oox (Fig. 114) being given for 10 span of tobacco.

The inconvenience of barter is often illustrated by Rajah Brooke's
oicture of the Dyak wandering for days in the bazaars of Borneo

FIG. 113.—*Unus*, Borneo   FIG. 114.—Tobacco box, Borneo

unable to find anyone who will take his beeswax for the particular
thing he wants in exchange (*cf*. p. 5), but beeswax is something
more than a mere object of barter.

Beeswax is the current cash in that country.   It is melted but not refined
and cast into Moulds of an oblong Square, the Breadth about two Thirds
of the Length, and the Thickness Half of the Breadth and a Rattan Withy
to lift them by cast in the Wax.   A Piece weighs a Quarter of a Pecul which
comes to an English Weight, Thirty-four Pound, and a Pecul is valued in
Payment at ten Masscies or Forty Shillings Sterling (Hamilton, 1727, II,
p. 149).

Hamilton adds: 'For smaller money they have Cowries.'
Cowries are abundant on some of the coasts of Borneo and though
they are no longer valued save for ornament they were formerly
exported to China in vast quantities.   Among the highly prized
articles which China supplied in exchange are the large jars (*tajow*)
which most Dyaks possess and keep stored as their greatest treasures.
There are several varieties of these jars, some having fabulous prices.

10 *

The most highly valued are the *gusi*, of a green colour, standing about 18 inches high. One of these, although it only looks like an ordinary water-jar, may be worth up to £400, payable in kind, with the debt lasting for years and years.[1]

The *rusa*, decorated with what native artists recognize as deer, are valued at from £15 to £16, but the *naga*, large handsome jars, some 2 feet high, with Chinese dragons, are less valued. These jars are collected, like old masters, for their antiquity and rarity rather than for their beauty. The many-coloured jars which in our eyes are really beautiful, have their exchange value, but are of small worth. Jars are often met with in folk tales, each with its own personality and sometimes with the gift of speech. A Dyak legend tells how at the death of a giant a tree springs from his head, its flowers turn into beads, its leaves into cloth and the ripe fruit into jars. Beads, cloth and jars all represent acceptable forms of money or storable wealth (Ling Roth, 1896, I p. 372 ; Cole, 1915). In recent times jars appear to be losing favour, probably due to inflation ; large numbers have been imported and many are now made in the island. Even the *gusi* are said to have depreciated, save those with genuine pedigrees, of which there are probably not more than a score in Sarawak. As small change the Iban use cups and plates reckoned at about 10 cents apiece and these are in common use for payment of local fines. Wages for a man to howl all night in a Kayan house (if the man had no friends and had to hire a professional) would be about 2 plates.

FIG. 115.—Buffalo bell, Borneo

Brass gongs found, like the jars, in all proper houses, are a recognized standard of value and may be included in currency. There are several varieties, their value calculated by span, by weight, by tone or by age and reputation. The cheapest, *gong kretas*, or ' paper gongs ', are worth about 2 dollars. These are used in fines and in marriage gifts. The *gong gilan* is a very old kind with beautiful notes and may be up to 150 dollars which is the highest price for a good male slave. A female slave would be only worth a *tawak*. The *tawak* gongs are measured by the span and valued by weight at about 74 dollars a *picul*. These are used in various ceremonies and their use as currency links them with the gong currencies of Assam and Burma (Hose and McDougall, I, p. 62 ; Ling Roth, II, p. 284).

The value attached to metal is due in great part to its production

[1] Twenty thousand dollars were offered (and refused) for a particularly renowned jar (Cole, 1915, p. 11).

of gongs, and this accounts for the curious acceptance of bells (Fig. 115), and of models of Portuguese cannon (Fig. 116) as money. The cannon are solid and heavy and are estimated, like the ordinary gongs, by weight, at 25 to 30 dollars a *picul*. They are used in 'bride-price' and in the purchase of slaves, a slave being valued in *piculs* of brass guns.[1] The buffalo bells, formerly currency in Brunei, were valued at 30 cents a *catty* ($= \frac{1}{100}$ *picul*).

The bead currencies of Borneo are of special interest, and although found now in the possession of the later invaders of the island, such as the Iban (Sea Dyak), this is probably the result of looting as they are connected with the culture of the earlier peoples, especially with the Kayan or the Dusun. Formerly these old beads were one of the principal forms of currency and they still constitute an important part of the wealth of many families. Some of the Kayan women are remarkably expert in recognizing genuine old specimens ; each variety has its definite name and its definite value. Single beads are valued in dollars, from 1 dollar for the pale yellow or blue *labang*, 10 for a special *lukut*, up to 100 for a *lukut sekala* (Hose and McDougall, 1912, I, p. 226, Pl. VIII, p. 34 ; Furness, 1902, p. 118).

The importance of beads in archaeological research is only beginning to prove fruitful with modern methods of analysis (Chap. IV, ii), but Borneo and the Federated Malay States have already provided links with Pemba, Zanzibar, Rhodesia and South India to the west and with Java, the Philippine Islands and Korea to the east. One of the Borneo beads, a white one with a purple manganese stripe, resembles Eastern Mediterranean products of the 4th or 3rd century B.C. (Beck, 1930, Pl. K, Fig. 15) and a cylinder bead with blue and red zones is similar to La Tène beads from Corsica (*ibid.*, Fig. 16).

Chevron beads are not uncommon in Sarawak hoards but the one described by Beck and illustrated (*ibid.*, Fig. 17) is of unusual interest. It is apparently an imitation of the old cane beads found in Europe (and called 'druid's beads') or in Africa (where they are called 'aggries') and their Bornean name is *kelam batang umar*, meaning 'bead worth part of a house'.

The true chevron bead, says Beck (*ibid.*, p. 179), is made from an elaborate cane with a radiating pattern in it, so arranged that when the cane is chamfered at the ends or is ground spherical, it forms a series of chevrons. In

---

[1] W. W. Skeat recognizes a trace of the Malayan crocodile currency in the Borneo cannon. In many of them the slow match, cast as if lying lengthwise on the top of the cannon, has a crocodilian form, while the cannon mouth is sometimes enlarged into crocodile jaws. But the local explanation is that these beasts are meant to represent the *naga* or dragon, familiar in mythology and a popular subject in metal-work as well as in wood carving and tattooing.

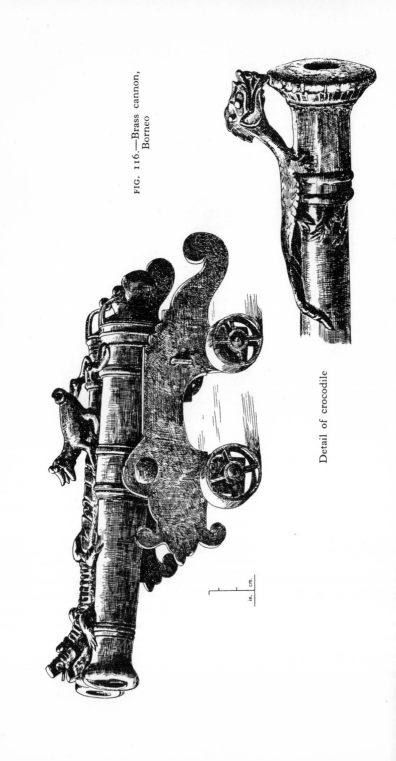

FIG. 116.—Brass cannon, Borneo

Detail of crocodile

these Sarawak beads a very similar effect is got by taking a blue base with a small white centre and then elaborately producing the red and white chevrons by applying threads of red and white glass. In some cases this is so skilfully done that a casual observer could easily mistake it for a cane chevron bead. The place of origin of these and other elaborate types remains a mystery.

Strings of shell-disks of the ordinary South Sea pattern are found among the possessions of the Dusun, who say that they are very old and they do not know when they were made; no one knows how to make them now. They have a currency value, 3 or 4 double strings are measured from the fork of the thumb to the elbow and equal a dollar. Many of these strings are stained with blue dye; some are curiously threaded with the shell-disks strung in zigzag lines on three or more parallel strings, others have the edge-to-edge stringing especially characteristic of the New Ireland ' pig-money' (Pl. 24).

Human heads have been called a form of currency in Borneo, or at least an essential item in the ' bride-price '. Among the Iban or Sea Dyak, a youth who had taken a head might have a better chance of success in courtship than one who had not, as he has thereby proved his valour; or the mother of a marriageable maiden, seeing a man hanging around may say, ' When you have something inside and outside your house [jars within and heads in the gallery outside] you can ask for my child.' But the possession of a head is not an essential qualification in marriage negotiations (Hose and McDougall, 1912, I, p. 76 *fn.*).

viii. THE PHILIPPINES

The coasts of the Philippine Islands, as of Borneo, abound in cowry shells, and they have been exported to neighbouring lands, probably even to India and Africa.

Da Morga, writing in the 16th century, said :

In any of these islands on the coasts a quantity of small white snails are found, which they call ' siguey ' ; the natives collect them and sell them by measure to the Siamese, Cambodians, Pantan men and other nations of the mainland where they serve as coin, and they trade with them as they do in New Spain with cacaos (1868, p. 285).

In exchange for cowries here as in Borneo the most highly valued articles, which became recognized as evidence of wealth, and partook of the nature of currency, were the porcelain jars and the metal gongs.

Magellan and Pigafetta noticed the jars and gongs in all the chief households, and there are many references to them in the accounts of early trade with the islands, though the importation of earthen-ware and common glazed pottery appears to have ceased about 1600 (Cole, 1912, p. 6). By this time not only the coastal peoples but the tribes of the interior had acquired a number of the old jars, and, when the supply ceased, they began to mount in value until a man's wealth was, and still is, largely reckoned by the number of old jars in his possession. As they were handed down from genera-tion to generation they began to gather to themselves stories of wondrous origin and deeds, until today certain jars have reputations which extend far beyond the limit of the tribes by which they may be owned. Cole saw a famous jar called Magsawi, a talking jar of supernatural origin (which he illustrates in Pls. III and IV, 1912). In the Philippines as in Borneo the jars turn into animals, and back again, and are credited with magical virtues.

Great prices are offered and sometimes accepted for the more renowned jars, and successful war parties are accustomed to return home with numbers of such trophies. All the wild tribes of the interior of the islands possess some and they enter intimately into the life of the people. Among some tribes the price paid by the bridegroom for his bride is wholly, among others, in part, in jars. A Tinguian youth goes to the house of his chosen bride at night carrying with him a Chinese jar, which he presents to his father-in-law, and thereafter he may never address his parents-in-law by name. These jars are sometimes used to contain the rice wine served out at ceremonies and festivals. In districts where head-hunting is still going on a Chinese jar is readily accepted as payment in full for a head, and many feuds are settled on this basis. Cole (1915, p. 15) describes how he accompanied a war party to a hostile village in 1907, and peace was arranged on the payment of one jar for each head that the one village held in excess of the other. Eleven jars were handed over.

Gongs are a common medium of exchange, but far less valuable. Da Morga (p. 302) described the Chinese gongs in the 16th century as ' like large pans, and very sonorous, they strike on them at their feasts and carry them in their vessels to the wars instead of drums '. An ordinary brass gong is about equal in value to a buffalo. Gold neck ornaments, and strings of amber-coloured glass beads are also used in exchange, and are also worth a buffalo. Jars are worth at least 4 buffaloes and often 4 times 4 buffaloes.

Among the pagans of the interior, buffaloes, pigs, fowls and rice suffice in place of money for exchange, as standard of value and evidence of wealth, and rice may almost be called their currency. ' Bride-price ', wergeld, fines and indemnities for injuries are all priced in carabao, pigs and rice, together with tools, such as axes, knives and spearheads. A man sells himself into slavery for a hog (worth 20 *peso*) [1] and 500 bundles of rice (worth 16·8 *peso*) (Barton, 1938, p. 56). An able-bodied slave in the lowlands was worth 5 carabao, and a carabao may be anything between 50 and 100 *peso*. (With the stamping out of rinderpest, buffaloes increased and the price dropped considerably.) Indemnity for adultery might consist of one woven shroud, one pig, one kettle, one blanket and some chicken ; for breach of promise (from the kin of the girl) a Chinese kettle-skillet (worth 3 *peso*), a woman's skirt (worth 2 *peso*), a chicken (worth less than a *peso*), axes and spearheads (worth $\frac{1}{2}$ or $\frac{1}{4}$ *peso*). For personal injuries to a woman the kin of the aggressor agreed not long ago to pay a long list, including kettles, pigs, chicken, a gong, a jar and a gold bead, but when a more valuable jar was also demanded, they refused. Whereupon her kinsmen killed a carabao belonging to the man's kin, injured its owner, and made sorcery until he died, and so squared the matter (*ibid.*, p. 181). Murder, however, admits of no indemnity, save a life for a life, expressed in heads, or, under Government supervision, jars.

Barton (1922) describes how rice is the ' currency ' of the Ifugao, of the mountainous interior of Luzon, among whom everything can be calculated in terms of bundles of rice. Rice keeps indefinitely in the granary, without damage or deterioration, and though cumbersome, yet for the small purchases of the Ifugao, this is no objection. For large transactions, such as the buying of land, pigs and buffaloes are the media of exchange, but these all have their values in rice, from a very small suckling, ' the size of a bamboo ' at $2\frac{1}{2}$ *peso* to a very large one at 30 ; 15 *peso* is the worth of a medium size pig or *pikat*, and the carabao is about 5 or 6 *pikat*, i.e. 75 to 90 *peso*. A rice field would be described as ' 5 *pikat* and 1 *kinlum* (suckling) ' or ' three carabaos and 4 *pikat* ' which equals 300 *peso*.

Rice has this serious disadvantage, from which pigs and buffaloes are free, that it fluctuates in value, its price at harvest being only half that during the growing season. But this disadvantage is more apparent than real, as the price does not rise gradually, but jumps suddenly with the season, and there is no fluctuation from one year to another. The harvest price is always the same, and does not vary from year to year or with supply and demand.

The Ifugao's monetary system was based on rice. Rice was his one universal medium of exchange. It suited the purposes of his crude civilization most admirably and he could even today get along with it almost as well as with money so far as his domestic trade is concerned (Barton, 1922, p. 430).

---

[1] *Peso*, originally a weight, *pensum*, equals a dollar.

ix. DUTCH EAST INDIES

Human skulls have been described as 'currency' or 'money' in New Guinea, Borneo and the Philippines because they are highly valued, are hoarded as treasures, are used in negotiations for 'bride-price' and are accepted as indemnities in head-hunting societies unfettered by Government interference.

Sulayman, the Arab merchant of the 9th century, in his enter-taining descriptions, partly from observation, partly travellers' tales, of the East Indies, reports that at Nias, off the West Coast of Sumatra, when a man wants to marry he cannot do it, unless he possesses the head of a man from among the enemies of his tribe. If he has killed 2 enemies, he marries 2 wives ; if he has killed 50 enemies, he marries 50 wives (Ferrand, 1922, p. 34).

Nicolo de' Conti gave a sensational account of the 'currency in heads '[1] of the Batak of the mainland of Sumatra 6 centuries later.

In one part of the island called Battech, the inhabitants eat human flesh and are in a state of constant warfare with their neighbours. They keep human heads as valuable property, for when they have captured an enemy they cut off his head and, having eaten the flesh, store up the skull and use it for money. When they desired to purchase any article, they give one or more heads in exchange for it according to its value, and he who has most heads in his house is considered to be most wealthy (1857, p. 9).

Money even now is seldom used by the natives in Northern Sumatra. Wealth is in buffalo and trading is by exchange of definite measures of rice and salt. Both are scooped up in a half-coconut, and this measure, the *gantang*, constitutes the unit for bargaining. Five *gantang* of rice will buy an axe or 4 packets of tobacco ; 12 will buy a sarong or a pot. One *gantang* of salt is worth 7 or 8 of *padi*, and 25 of *padi* will buy 30 of maize. Two and a half *gantang* of salt buys 4 lengths [fathoms] of native cloth or 1,400 betel nuts (Fischer, 1914, pp. 86-7).

Ring-money was not unknown in Sumatra. Millies describes and illustrates (1871, p. 117, Pl. XIX, Figs. 210, 211) a singular means of exchange among a tribe (the Korintji) in the interior of Palembang who formerly made use of yellow copper rings 'exactly like our ordinary curtain rings, but of rather cruder make'. Many have very small buttons or bosses on the outer surface. Their local value was very low, 15,360 to the gold *tahil*.

Brass arm-rings used as currency on the island of Bali may be seen in the Vienna Currency Collection (Loehr, 1935, p. 20) and the copper wire, *loloe amas* (meaning chain-money), in the Leiden museum

---

[1] Wiener thinks there is confusion here between Latin *testa* potsherd, porcelain and Italian *testa*, head (1920, I, 14 *ff.*).

may be included here. This is a hollow rope of four-strand plaited copper wire said to be used in Sumbawa and Sumba Islands for presents, for marriage gifts or in ratification of a contract, though not in ordinary exchanges.

Buffalo and rice are the standards of value in Java as in Sumatra. Trade beads, Chinese jars and metal gongs are used in important transactions and represent wealth; the kris was used here, as in Borneo, in presentations, and a decorative one from the Pitt Rivers Museum Collection is illustrated in Fig. 112. In both islands gold and silver bars or lumps were introduced with Indian dominion (Millies, 1871, pp. 8, 12–14, Pl. I) and the little silver ' buttons ' with archaic and enigmatic lettering, which date from the same period, were in use in Central and Eastern Java for several centuries (pp. 14–19, Pl. I, Figs. 13–24). Short pieces of doubled copper or pewter wire (*tang*) were issued by the Dutch, in imitation of the *larins* which they found in use on their arrival (Bucknill, 1931, pp. 55–6).

The Arab merchant, Sulayman, already quoted, gives a picturesque description of the gold ingots of the Maharajah of Java, and his royal treasury.

There was a lake or rather an enclosed estuary in front of the royal palace, and each morning the chief steward came before his sovereign with a golden ingot of a certain weight [unknown to the narrator]. Then, in the presence of the rajah, he threw the ingot into the lake. When the tide came up, it covered the ingots : when it receded, the ingots glittered in the sun. The rajah kept an eye on them as he sat in his great hall overlooking the lake. But no one touched them as long as he lived. When he died, his successor fished them all out, save one, and they were apportioned among the royal family, men, women and children, generals and slaves of the royal household, and distributed to the poor and needy. The longer the reign the larger the number of ingots, and the greater amount of wealth to be distributed (Ferrand, 1922, p. 97).

Celebes, notorious for its adventurous traders, appears to have developed a token currency in cloth, which has been collected as far afield as Borneo. This is in small fringed cotton mats, 3 to 5 inches (8–12 cm.) across, usually white, with fine coloured lines in warp and weft forming the border. They are used as currency in Central Celebes but appear to be derived from the island of Buton off the South-East end of the island—whence their name of ' the Sultan of Buton's bank-notes ' (*cf.* Loehr, 1935, p. 15).

Metal gongs (often called ' drums ') have been recorded as currency in Burma and Siam, in Borneo, the Philippine Islands, Java and Celebes (Heger, 1902). The *mokko* of the smaller islands, Solor, Pantar and Allor, to the east of Flores, probably belong to the same cultural influence, but their history is somewhat obscure.

In 1851, the Resident of Timor described ' a sort of copper drum called *moko*, in the shape of a spittoon with a cover '. Colf's description

30 years later is both more elegant and more accurate. 'J'ai vu
ces fameux *moko* . . . ils ressemblent à des supports à fleurs en
cuivre et rehaussés d'ornaments, tous les mêmes, et avec quatre anses.
Ils sont conservés commes d'anciennes reliques et ils ont jusqu'a
une valeur de mille florins' (Huyser, 1931, p. 225). They are waisted
'drums', of hour-glass shape (Pl. 25, and Fig. 117) with projecting
handles, decorated with various patterns of lines, human faces and
figures, animals and stylized flowers. They were the currency down
to 1914, in which year the Government withdrew them from commercial use. 'More than thirteen hundred *mokko*, Heaven knows
what beautiful specimens among them, were simply hammered down
and sold as old metal' (*ibid.*, pp. 227–8), and they are now difficult
to obtain. Their local price is said to have been some 5 or 6 gulden
(florins), though museums would even then gladly pay up to 50 or
60 for good pieces, and more than double that now. There have
been various theories as to their origin. The shape suggests Tibet,
but no 'drums' like this are found in Tibet, and there is nothing
Tibetan in their decoration. Neither is their derivation from the
ancient kingdom of Cambodia supported by any valid evidence.
Their local manufacture is unlikely, as no other objects of bronze
or copper are produced on the islands. Nieuwenkamp, 'the *mokko*
expert' as Huyser calls him, is of opinion that the oldest *mokko*
were made in East Java, after the model, not in size, but in form and
decoration of the famous drum of Pedjeng. There are not many of
these *mokko* 'drums' in museum collections, so Cambridge is
fortunate in having two. The larger one, illustrated in Pl. 25, has
a plain lower part, and conventional heads and festoons above the
handles. Though not identical, it is similar in design to many of
those illustrated by Huyser (1931, Figs. 31–3).

The smaller one (Fig. 117a) is of even greater interest, as it was
collected by I. H. N. Evans in the Tempassuk district in Borneo,
though the villagers could tell him nothing about it. It is a small
specimen, 14½ inches (36·7 cm.) high, and 8 inches (20·4 cm.) across
the top. He noted the similarity of the designs to those on silver
and brass ware of the Malay Peninsula, as well as of Chinese pottery.
The squatting or dancing human figure (Fig. 117b) has the ends of
the clothes turned up on the thighs in a way that is reminiscent of
that seen in reproductions of mythical characters of Burmese
legendry, and of the figures used in Siamese and Malay shadow
shows (*cf. Man.*, 1918, 11).

A *mokko* in the Leiden Museum shows the same little squatting
or dancing figures. Professor Kern, commenting on these, suggests
a 14th- or 15th-century date and that the designer of the figures may
have had a frog [1] in his mind. Huyser (p. 283, Fig. 4, iii) considers

---

[1] *Cf.* the frogs on the Karen *kyee-zees* in Burma (p. 209).

FIG. 117(*a*).—*Mokko*, Dutch East Indies. (⅛ size)

FIG. 117(*b*).—Details of *Mokko*

the inspiration to be derived rather from the squatting dwarfs, *gana*, with upraised hands, familiar in Hindu-Javanese architecture, whose relatives can be recognized on objects from Geelvink Bay, Timor and Soemba (Sumbawa).

Dr. Rassers, Director of the Leiden Museum, doubts both frog and *gana* derivation, and while recognizing the affinities between the squatting figures and those of Sumbawa, especially those of the textiles, thinks that they represent a divine initiator, and that the *mokko* were venerated in association with a local cult.

Chapter VIII

EUROPE

How pleasant it is to have money, heigh-ho !
How pleasant it is to have money !

CLOUGH

ALTHOUGH this chapter is headed Europe, and an earlier one Asia, there can be no definite division. Europe and Asia may be separated on a political map, but racial and cultural boundaries are ill-defined. Geographically Europe is a peninsular appendage of Asia, and Eastern Europe and Western Asia have been too often united by races and by cultures to be anthropo-geographically separable.

This linkage is illustrated in the history of the evolution of money, for the earliest coins appear in Asia Minor and the Greek islands, and there has been much discussion as to whether Europe or Asia can claim credit for the innovation.

' Money ', says the *O.E.D.*, ' = *moneta*, originally the name of a goddess (in classical times regarded as identical with Juno) in whose temple at Rome money was coined.' ' Money ' in common parlance, suggests coins. So we turn with special interest to the Eastern Mediterranean where, according to tradition, upheld by literary and archaeological evidence, the first coins were minted ; those of electrum by the Lydians and Ionians of Asia Minor, and those of silver, perhaps a little later, on the Greek island of Aegina.

These have been fully dealt with in a former issue of this series (Seltman, 1933) and are the province of the numismatist, who can read in them a history far more convincing than that of any ancient text. Here we are concerned with the earlier stages of currency, which are aptly summarized by Seltman in his opening chapter, part of which may be quoted here.

With the dawn of the Late Bronze Age, about 1600 B.C., the great nations round the Eastern Mediterranean entered into more peaceful relations with each other.

The age of internationalism had begun. It was about this time that the peoples of the south began to come into contact with the races whose standard of value was other than a gold standard. There were in Europe, as well as in the highlands and pasturelands of Western Asia, many races whose wealth lay not in metals but in flocks and herds, and among such backward peoples the natural and obvious unit of value was the ox or cow. This in Greece proper, as well as in the Italian peninsula, was the earliest measure of value, for, to cite but a few instances, at Delos in early times, at Athens under the code of Draco, and in the early laws of Rome, payments and fines were reckoned in cattle, while the ox was the standard of value to Homer's Achaeans in the 12th century B.C.

While the northerners and highlanders reckoned in cattle the Egyptians and the peoples of Mesopotamia were using gold, silver, electrum (a natural amalgam of silver and gold) and bronze which they had learnt to weigh in the balance for the purpose of estimating its value. Such a state of affairs existed when, about the beginning of the 16th century B.C., the peoples of the great rivers came into frequent contact with the rest of the ancient world. Traders from the Nile and from Babylonia began to meet with the traders of the Hittites, with Phoenician Semites, Cretans, islanders and rude tribes hailing from the northern shores of the Aegean Sea, and it was generally in the islands—very frequently in Cyprus and in Crete—that they met. Besides manufactured goods, linen and dyed wool, Egyptians and Semites brought their commercial rings of gold and electrum, Hittite subjects their silver and cattle, Cypriotes their ingots of copper ; and for many decades the bartering and bargaining of vociferous merchants, whose standards were so diverse, must have rent the air (pp. 4–5).

These diverse standards were adjusted to a common unit, that of the ox, and the ox had its equivalent in gold or in copper talents ; the gold talent (weighing some 8·5 grammes) was in the form of bars, which could be cut up into sections like Chinese silver (Fig. 106) ; in rings of various shapes, and in dumps, the forerunners of stamped coins; the copper talent, beaten out into a flattish plate, weighed some 25·5 kilo or about 60 pounds.

The copper ingots are, as might be expected, more commonly found than the gold coins-to-be, and they are recorded not only in Cyprus and Crete but as far west as Sardinia, as well as on the mainland of Greece and in the islands. Déchelette (1910, II, 1, pp. 399–40, 406) recognized in the outline a representation of the double-axe, which constituted a widespread currency percolating from Crete and Cyprus into Europe in the Bronze Age. Seltman, who illustrates an example from the Palace of Mycenae (14th century B.C.), points out how these heavy pieces represent not only the value but also the outline of the ox (Fig. 118a).

The ingots were cast in the shape of oxhides from which head and tail had been cut away ; one side of the ingot mimicked the hairy cowhide, the other side resembled the raw inside with its edges curling inwards (p. 7).

Sometimes the cruciform character is exaggerated until the ingot takes the form of a saltire ; sometimes the outline shows little more than the slight concavities that naturally result from the shrinkage of the cooling metal. This latter cause may well have been the origin of the outline which suggested the double-axe or the ox-hide according to the cultural bias or the imagination of Bronze Age or modern times. The concavities when exaggerated were functionally useful for transport, as may be seen in the Falmouth tin ingot of the Bronze Age (Fig. 118b) or in the Katanga copper crosses of the present day (Fig. 118c).

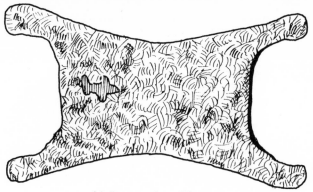

(*a*) Bronze talent, Mycenae

(*b*) Tin ingot, Falmouth

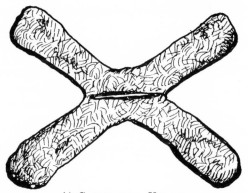

(*c*) Copper cross, Katanga

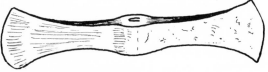

(*d*) Bronze axe-head, Germany

FIG. 118.—Metal ingots

In Central and Western Europe there were copper ingots in the form of lumps and bars, which show, as a rule, no distinguishing

FIG. 119.—Broken bits of *Aes formatum*

features. They might pass for money in parts of Africa today Ridgeway illustrates from roughly quadrilateral bits of bronze in the British Museum how these bars were broken up and argues that

the primitive *as* of Italy must certainly have been nothing more than a plain rod or bar of copper, which passed from hand to hand as the obols in Greece and the bars of iron and copper pass at the present among savages of Africa and Asia. This is what was called by the ancient writers the *raw copper* (*aes rude*) as distinguished from the *stamped copper* (*aes signatum*) of a later date.

It might seem an obvious process of logical evolution from the irregular bits of bronze (*aes rude*) to the cast ingots or bars (*aes signatum*), and from these to the circular *aes grave* and civilized coinage, an evolution which recalls that of the silver currencies of Eastern Asia already described. But there are doubts about the meaning of *aes rude*, which term appears to include any broken up bits of bronze, cast or otherwise, and about the place of the cast ingots (*aes signatum*) in the series.[1] Probably the earliest form of currency was

FIG. 120.—Broken bits of *Aes signatum* or *Aes rude*

[1] For discussion of the meaning of *aes signatum* and the doubt as to their use as currency, *cf.* Mattingly, 1928 pp. 8–9 ; Sydenham, 1926, pp. 12 *ff.* and for the dating, *cf.* Mattingly and Robinson, 1932, pp. 223, 253.

es formatum, shaped like a bun or a biscuit (Fig. 119). Next the
ronze was cast in long bars with simple designs upon them (Fig. 120).
Lastly the bronze was cast in true coins *aes grave*, either circular or
rectangular. One of the latter bearing the figure of an ox, is shown
in Fig. 121.

Ingots appear, here and there, to have developed into a ' tool
currency ' comparable with the various axe- and hoe-currencies of
more backward lands, and with the more advanced knife- and hoe-
currencies of China. And here we meet the double-axe again
Fig. 118*d*). Crete and Cyprus were both associated with the cult
of the double-axe ; both were rich sources of copper ; both were
active in maritime trade. So it is presumed that it was from either
Crete or Cyprus that these ingots came, axe-head shaped at both
ends, which have been found in Germany, Switzerland and as far
west as France.[1] They vary in length from 11 to 16 inches or more

FIG. 121.—*Aes grave*

(28–42 cm.) ; they vary very much in shape (though always more
slender than the typical Cretan double-axe) ; and they vary so much
in weight (from under 600 to over 3,000 grammes) that their relation
to a fixed standard has been disputed. They are certainly not
ordinary tools, as, although they are perforated in the centre, the
hole is not large enough for a working handle, and can only be for
stringing, while the majority are too light to suggest any serviceable
use. There seems no reason to doubt that they were a form of
currency, or at least were intended for gifts or offerings (Cook, 1925,
II, pp. 614*ff*.).[2] These ' tool ' forms are not confined to the Bronze

[1] Déchelette, 1910, p. 403, Fig. 163 ; Thilenius, 1921, pp. 15–16 ; but
cf. also Regling, 1926, in Ebert's *Reallexikon*, § ' Metal-Gerätgeld '.
[2] The ' pick ' shape presents the same problems, though not the same
symbolism, and here too it is suggested that the small holes are for threading
several pieces on a cord (*British Museum Guide ; Bronze Age*, 1904, p. 98,
Fig. 100).

Age or to copper.   Double-axes occur in silver as late as the Roman
period, and as far apart as Serbia and the British Isles.   These, being
associated with burials or sanctuaries, are usually called votive, not
currency, but, as Déchelette (1910, 405 *fn.*) points out, the former
hypothesis does not exclude the latter, since in classical times money
was placed in graves as well as being offered to the gods, a custom
which is still lively in China as in Africa at the present day.

That the double-axes were valued as a form of
currency is illustrated in the Homeric poems.   The
prizes offered in the funeral games of Patroclus
included slave women and oxen, kettles and tripods,
besides talents of gold.   ' But Achilles set for the
archers dark iron, and he set down 10 axes and 10
half-axes.'   The axe is taken to mean the double-axe,
and the ' half-axe ' a single-headed one ; the former
being the first and the latter the second prize.

FIG. 122.—
Coin, Tenedos

The double-axe on the silver coins of Tenedos (Fig. 122) may
preserve the memory of the earlier currency as well as the religious
beliefs associated with the symbol, thus endowing it with votive
as well as monetary value (*cf.* Ridgeway, 1892, pp. 318–19 ; Cook,
1925, II, pp. 655 *ff.* ; Laum, 1924, pp. 120 *ff.*).

There are some small socketed axes of the Late Bronze Age
(Fig. 123), especially abundant in Normandy and Brittany, which
carry on the tale.   They are too small or too fragile for use, and

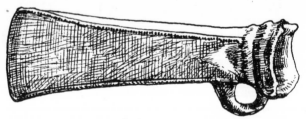

FIG. 123.—Socketed axe, Bronze Age

yet are found in huge hoards.   Some are even of lead, and obviously
useless as tools.   They may be talismans ; they may be votive
offerings ; they may be currency ; and they may have been useful,
like double-axes and Argive spits in commercial transactions [1]
as well as in religious rites (Déchelette, 1910, p. 254).

The frequent references to Ridgeway's work throughout this
book show how he blazed the trail by drawing attention to the many

---

[1] The same may be said of the ' wheel-money ' or spoked circles of Gaul,
exhibited in many collections of primitive money, which were primarily
amulets (de Widranges, 1861, pp. 213–30 with six plates of illustration ;
Déchelette, 1913, pp. 885 *ff.*).

parallels between ancient currencies and their modern survivals or analogies among backward peoples, and many of those who are unable to accept his conclusions are glad to draw from his rich store of facts. The inclusion of Europe in the cattle-currency-complex has been noted above (p. 187). Ridgeway showed that in the regions of Asia, Europe and Africa, where the system of weight standards which has given birth to all the systems of modern Europe had its origin, the cow was universally the chief object of barter (1892, p. 387).

Cattle were the standard of wealth and unit of value ; they had a sacred character and were offered to the gods as well as presented to potentates ; they were exchanged for slaves and extorted as tribute. The ' bride-price ' of a woman and the wergeld of a man were calculated in cattle.

Evidence of the cattle standard can be found in the Rig Veda of India and the Zend Avesta of Persia (as seen above), in the Brehon Laws of Ireland and the Ancient Laws of Wales. We have seen it actively at work in Eastern Asia and in Eastern Africa, and though it has vanished from more progressive Europe, traces are still obvious. There is the familiar literary evidence in the equation of cattle and money, *pecus* and *pecunia*. Ulfilas translates *pecunia* by the Gothic *faihu*, cattle, whence our word ' fee ', which meant cattle, wealth or money in King Alfred's day. Gothic *skatts*, meaning cattle, tribute or coin, becomes the O.E. coin *sceat*, or the ' scat ', still known as a tax in the North.

Ridgeway notes (1892, p. 4) how accounts were kept in cows a generation or so ago in the Caucasus, as they were also in Scotland ; in Hungary the prospective bridegroom's conventional opening is ' Pray tell me if you have a cow to sell ? ' (Kovalensky, 1891, p. 27) and ' bride-price ' is still paid in cattle in Albania (Hasluck, 1933).

Where a cattle standard exists, this is adequate, and discourages the growth of primitive currencies, as has been already seen. It is noteworthy that the largest and most varied collections of primitive money come from cattle-less areas.

A traveller once asked a patriarch [in Mongolia] owner of several thousand horses why he did not sell some every year. He replied, ' Why sell what I delight in ? I do not need money. If I had any I would shut it up in a box where no one would see it. But when my horses run over the plain everyone sees them and knows that they are mine and is reminded that I am rich ' (Bureau, 1888, p. 71).

Cattle cannot, however, provide all the requisites for money. They set the standard of value, they are less often units of exchange, and never sufficiently portable or divisible. Barter and the ox suffice on land. Barter has to find other aids in seaborne trade.

The scanty evidence of a cowry currency in Europe has been reviewed already (p. 29) and it is tempting to recognize in the bronze cowries found in Etruscan tombs or the gold cowries in Cyprus and elsewhere a parallel to the ' metallic cowries ' of China. But there is no proof that these scattered examples are more than ornaments or amulets. The earliest recognizable form of money here is in metal bars and lumps (as seen above) or in gold and silver in the shape of rings.

The great gold-producing land in prehistoric, as in historic times, was Africa, where in the 15th century B.C. gold was ' as common as dust '. Egypt was well supplied from the earliest ages, as her treasure houses prove ; and those of Assyria and the Indus Valley

FIG. 124.—Weighing gold rings, Egypt

illustrate the high estimate in which this ' giver of life ' was held. Both in Egypt and in Mesopotamia gold was treasured long before the Age of Metals had begun, but it was as ornament, it was not yet currency. And though ornaments here as everywhere else, might be used in barter, it is in the ring form that we first recognize a convenient form of money.

Egyptian wall-paintings illustrate the weighing of gold rings in a balance, against weights in the form of animals (Fig. 124). Ridgeway, when discussing the origin of the weight system of Egypt, argued that the unit of value was the ox, and adds (1892, p. 242) :

The fact that weights formed in the shape of cows and cows' heads are represented in Egyptian paintings as employed in the weighing of rings, indicates that in the mind of the first manufacturer of such weights there was a distinct connexion between the shape given to the weight and the object whose value in gold (or silver) it expressed.

The gold rings of the wall paintings which are taken to represent the ox-unit or talent might be classed by the Chinese either as *pi* or as *yüan* (*cf.* Fig. 102), of armlet or anklet size. Far more common and more widely spread are the small rings with a fairly constant weight of half a talent made of a bar of gold bent into a circle, with ends sometimes meeting, sometimes apart, or of finer wire coiled spirally. Most of these rings could not be worn on the finger, and although they might be strung like beads, if securely ring-like, and classed with personal ornaments, they are generally accepted as the earliest type of ' ring-money ', anticipating coined money in the Western World, as in the Orient. Rings have been found in gold, in silver, in bronze or in iron, from Scandinavia and Ireland in the

FIG. 125.—Mycenaean rings

West, Minoan Crete, ancient Greece (Fig. 125) and Rome, to India and Japan in the East,[1] often of sizes or shapes unsuitable for wearing as ornaments, and often appearing to fit into a graduated scale of weights ; this suggests that they were a form of currency, and their use in present-giving is abundantly seen in literature. Gold and silver ornaments were frankly estimated at their current value in metal calculated either by weight or in actual coins, when these were already in use. Ridgeway quotes examples (pp. 35–9) and more are added below.

[1] In China jade took a higher place than gold, and jade rings were used in present-giving, tribute and fines (*cf.* p. 241). In Mexico also jade was more highly valued than gold, but rings are curiously lacking in the New World, and there is nothing that can even be remotely claimed as ' ring money ' save the copper bangles of Vancouver (p. 302, Fig. 136).

It is difficult enough to discriminate between ornamental and currency rings in recent or contemporary material ; with prehistoric or early historic examples it is impossible. Bronze or Iron Age rings, though often admitted into currency collections, must necessarily lack proof.

Many writers are chary of admitting ring-money as currency at all, and enclose the word in inverted commas, to imply, like ' bride-price ', that it is a misnomer. But this is to ignore some important considerations.

First, one of the essential functions of money is that it is a sign of wealth. And how can wealth be exhibited more clearly to the world than in the form of possessions and personal adornment. This aim can be seen in the expensively bedecked women of all nations, from the Bongo, weighed down with her copper rings, the Crow squaw with her dress spangled with ' elk ' teeth, and the Indian women strung round with actual silver coins.

A further consideration is the absence of banks. Mesopotamia may have had its treasury-banks 2000 B.C. Greece may have had some such institution about 400 B.C. But banks were still rare in Eastern Europe in the Middle Ages and are distrusted in backward parts of the Continent and of our own islands at the present day. Among bank-less societies wealth is therefore best stored as well as displayed either in large and solid forms, such as the extreme examples of the Yap stone-money, the abnormal or supernormal iron tools of Africa, the North American ' coppers ', the bowls, gongs or ' drums ' of Eastern Asia and the East Indies. Or it is exhibited on the person in the almost universally distributed ring form, which may be remotely linked with the holed stones of the Neolithic Age.

Finally, though the ring form may owe much to religious, magical or symbolic significance, common sense shows its practical value. When clothing is scanty and pockets are not provided, an easily portable form of money is wanted, which accounts for the popularity of cowry, shell-disk and bead strings, of the anklets or armlets (*manillas* and *mitakos*) or necklets of West Africa and the holed cash for stringing in Eastern Asia.

' Are we opossums ; have we natural pouches like the Kangaroo ? Or how without Clothes could we possess the master-organ, soul's seat, and true pineal gland of the Body Social ; I mean a PURSE,' asked Carlyle.

Early Man (or Woman) solved the problem by means of the *Sammelringe* or ' Lake Dwellers' purses ' of Central Europe, often classed as bracelets or earrings in archaeological finds. These consist of a number of small rings dependent from a larger one which is usually of armlet size. The smaller ones are often in pairs of fixed

veights and constitute the typical ' ring-money ' of the Bronze Age.
Pl. 28, Fig. 1, illustrates a fine gold bracelet with ' ring-money ' dug
up in Grunty Fen, Cambridgeshire, in 1850, together with a bronze
rapier and a gold ' armilla ' so called from the spiral form in which
it was coiled.[1]

Currency rings do not form such an essential item in ' bride-
price ' as might be expected. But in early days the payments were
the perquisite of the father, uncle or other male guardian of the girl,
so although rings figure in lists in Africa or Melanesia where these
are male ornaments, livestock, spears or iron tools were more generally popular in Europe. When payment for the wife merges in
dowry, rings take a more conspicuous place, and the survival of the
custom of the wedding-ring worn by the bride suggests the flagrant
misappropriation of the earlier ' bride-price '.

The ' ingot torques ' of the Early Bronze Age may be included in
' ring money '. These are penannular neck-rings of thick wire with
flat-hammered ends rolled back into loops (Hawkes, 1939, Fig. 24, 3),
which were traded as bulk merchandise round the eastern end of the
Mediterranean and across the mainland of Europe, serving either for
ornament or for currency as did the *manillas* of Africa down to
modern times.

A silver neck-ring or torque served the same double purpose in
Russia. The ' divisibility ' of metal has been one of the chief reasons
for its popularity as money, for a rod or bar can be broken into small
pieces, so providing a transition between ingots and coins, as has been
illustrated by the *aes rude* (p. 274). Just as our word ' shilling ' is
popularly taken to refer to the cutting off of a piece of metal, hence
called a *scillinga*,[2] so in Russia the *grivenik* (a small coin) is derived
from the *grivna*, or neck-ring. This was cut up into segments, which
were later stamped with the same stamps that were used for coins.
Both torques and segments have been found together in graves in
the Government of Kiev (Pl. 26, Fig. 3).

Ring-money, bars, dumps or drops of metal are among the many
forms that bridge the transition from ingots to coins. The final
step is taken in the Eastern Mediterranean.

[1] Both are illustrated on Pl. V of the *Victoria County History of Cambridgeshire*, 1939.
The *Sammelringe* idea is seen again in the widespread *mitako* of the
Middle Congo, where the wire is coiled spirally, and several smaller rings
hang from a larger one (Mahieu, p. 30). It may be added that spiral ornaments similar to the Bronze Age gold ' armilla ' in copper, brass or iron form
a currency in the Congo (p. 80). The enormously heavy *minkata* of the
Sankuru which Mahieu illustrates (p. 33) is in the Tervueren Collection,
Brussels.
[2] The derivation of shilling is uncertain. *Cf.* Chadwick, 1905, pp. 12 *ff.* ;
Schröder, 1918, p. 273.

That coined money should have been evolved here is not surprising, for it was an area of intense commercial activity, encouraged and
fostered by natural advantages. The Lydians, 'the first shop-
keepers' as Herodotus called them, as well as the neighbouring
Ionians, received goods from the caravan routes and river communications across Asia. They had access to safe and sheltered
harbours for easy coastwise trade. They exported their famous
Chian wines, their purple dye which gave its name to Erythrae
and their Samian pots, but above all they were renowned for their
gold, which provided the fabulous wealth of Croesus, and still more
fabulous wealth of Midas (Seltman, 1933, pp. 18-19). Here, it
seems, coin of the realm was born ; and our study of primitive money
comes to an end. But before it ends, there are a few examples of
primitive types to be noted, before the universal use of coins obliter-
ates their memory.

Greek tradition represents Pheidon of Argos as the first to coin
money in Greece, and to have done so at the island of Aegina.
There may be doubt as to the part played by Pheidon. There is none
as to the part played by Aegina.

Aegina, 'the eyesore of the Piraeus', as Herodotus called it
later, when intercepting the trade both of Athens and of Corinth,
owed its greatness to its position in the Gulf, in full sight of the
mainland. It was comparatively barren, so had not much to offer
in the way of natural produce, but it was here that traders coming
from Egypt or from Asia met with those from the Peloponnese or
from Northern Greece. There was no gold or copper in the
Peloponnese, but it was rich in iron, so it was but natural that
when currency developed it should be in iron, heavy and cumbersome though it must have been. Plutarch's complaint that 10 minas
worth required a large room for storing and a yoke of oxen for
transport, may be compared with the description of Torday's trials
in the Congo, where iron-currency alone was accepted (p. 58).
The passage describing the abrupt transition from iron rods to coins
is well known :

> First of all men Pheidon of Argos struck money in Aegina ; and having
> given them [his subjects] coin and abolished the spits (obols) he dedicated
> them to Hera in Argos. But since at this time the spits used to fill the hand,
> that is, the grasp, we, although we do not fill our hand with the six obols,
> call it a grasp full [drachma] owing to the grasping of them (Ridgeway
> 1892, p. 214).

There have been various conjectures as to the actual form of the
'spits' but the question was settled in 1895 by the discovery in the
ruins of the Temple of Hera at Argos of a bundle of iron rods
originally 180 of them, about 40 inches (1 m. 20 cm.) long. With
them was a heavy rectangular bar of iron of about the same length

ammered out towards one end.[1] The bundle of ' spits ' is very
agmentary, but together they weigh almost the same as the iron
ar, i.e. 73,000 grammes, which was obviously a fixed standard.
eltman (1933, p. 35) has calculated that a ' drax ' or handful of
of the best-preserved specimens weighs 2,418 grammes, and a single
obelos ' 403 gr., and that ' Pheidon fixed the silver drachm at its
iven standard because in his day the ratio of iron to silver was as
o to 1. He intended his new silver obolos and silver drachma to
ave the same purchasing power which the now discarded *obelos*
nd " drax " of iron had possessed.'

The translation of *obol* by ' spit ' is perhaps unfortunate. The
ord ' spit ' is so closely associated with the special implement used
or roasting as to overshadow its more general use for any pointed
ar or rod, or indeed anything pointed, as a spit of land or sandbank.[2]
he Argive spits are what would elsewhere be called iron rods or
ven ' currency bars ', which take different shapes in Etruria, Central
urope, Gaul, Spain, and Britain, West Africa or Eastern Asia.
heir latest European descendants may be recognized in the osmunds
r ' Northmen's iron ' of the Middle Ages which were ' commonly
sed as currency ' (Åkerman, II, 2, 7, 1898).

In certain Greek coins, traces of earlier currencies have been
ecognized. The ox on Athenian coins has been claimed as a
nk with the cattle-currency, but it may have been merely a civic
r family device or that of the magistrate responsible for the mint.
Cities often adopted as their device the export for which they were
amous, such as the amphora of oil for Athens, or of wine for Terone,
nd the silphium, possibly a royal monopoly, for Cyrene (Seltman,
933, pp. 44, 67, 182).

There is more doubt about the ' tunny fish.' of Olbia (Pl. 28).
Olbia was an important Milesian trading settlement in the Black Sea,
shing being the chief industry, supplemented by trade in furs,
laves and amber, and later, corn. The fish-shaped bronze pieces
ssued in the 5th century have been regarded as metal tunny fishes,
llustrating, like the metal cowries of China, a transition between
urrency and coinage. Cyzicus on the southern shores of the Bay
f Marmora certainly issued coins with the device of a tunny fish,
heir city badge ; but the Olbian ' fishes ' are now recognized to be

[1] These are illustrated in Fig. 6, p. 34, of Seltman's *Greek Coins*, 1933,
n this series. Mahieu (1924, p. 7) suggests that the bar is a spearhead,
nd compares it with the Congolese *liganda*.

[2] It is, however, possible, as Laum argues (1924, pp. 106 *ff*.) that ' roast-
ng spits ' is the more exact translation, and that these were the actual
mplements used in sacrifices at the temple. If so their dedication to Hera
nds modern illustration in the dedication of the spits used at festivals for
acrifice to the gods in Lapland or of the spears used in the sacrifice of cattle
t Shilluk and Dinka shrines.

II

dolphins not tunny ; the fishing wealth there was not in either tunny
or dolphin but in sturgeon ; and the issue of round coins also with
dolphins attributed to the same period weakens the belief in their
transitional character and leaves their origin unexplained. 'The
smaller dolphins, mostly so perished that we cannot establish their
true weight, may very likely have been mere tokens . . . but from
the way in which they are held in the hands of the dead . . . they
seem to correspond to the coins for Charon found elsewhere'
(Minns, E. H., 1913, p. 482, Pl. II).

The inscriptions if read as θγ, an abbreviation of 'tunny' on the
smaller, and APIXO for ἄῤῥιχος, 'basket' on the larger-sized piece
suggested that the one was the price of a fish, and the other of a
basketful. But the slight difference in size does not warrant such a
distinction, and, as Ridgeway pointed out, you do not usually see
fish 4 or more feet long, by the basketful (1892, p. 317 fn.). Moreover, these are not the only inscriptions. There are others, which
appear, like APIXO to be personal names, probably those of governors.
No satisfactory explanation of the fishy forms, which were apparently contemporary with conventional coinage, has yet proved
acceptable. They may have been votive offerings, but it is safe
to regard them as minimized ingots rather than as coins, as *saumon*
rather than as dolphins.[1]

It is in the outlying parts of Europe that culture lag preserves
relics obliterated elsewhere, and traces of earlier or antiquated
currencies can be discovered in the North and West, Iceland and
Britain.

The Icelandic sagas preserve the record of an age when the
currency was in cloth, *wadmal*, and in silver (commonly in the form
of rings estimated by weight). Blood feuds were paid off in rings
trading was regulated by the *wadmal* standard. Barter sufficed for
trade down to the 15th century at least, as may be judged from the
trade regulations of that date. The chief products of the island were
the *wadmal*, spun from the fleece of the sheep, and fish. The cloth

[1] The abnormal shape of the 'ham-money' of Nîmes has suggested
comparison with the Olbian fishes. These are conventional round coins
of Octavius and Agrippa, with a crocodile on the reverse commemorative
of the conquest of Egypt, but there is a curious projecting leg, nearly as long
as the diameter of the coin, familiarly called 'pig's trotter' but more
elegantly '*patte de sanglier*'. They have a hole in the centre, so placed
that the leg hangs downwards, and as they have been found only in the
basin of the famous fountain at Nîmes, it is assumed that they are votive
offerings connecting a boar cult with the cult of the nymph of the fountain
and that they were worn as charms, hung up as offerings, and thrown into
the fountain itself (La Saussaye, 1842, p. 173, ill., Pl. XX, Fig. 36, and
Pl. XXI, Fig. 46 ; cf. interpretations of Babelon, 1901, p. 675 ; Thilenius
1921, p. 23, who regards them as trade advertisements ; and Laum, 1924
p. 118).

as the standard for local exchange,[1] with silver for higher values ;
nd fish, ' stockfish ' or dried cod, was the unit for external trade
ith the English.[2] Imported cloth, flour, iron, timber and other
oods were all estimated in stockfish. Four tuns of flour or of beer
r one tun of butter for 120 stockfish. Wine was cheaper, a tun for
oo fish. A pair of women's shoes cost 3 fish, and a horseshoe one.

The silver, or occasional gold, used in more important trans-
ctions was in lumps, bars or rings estimated by weight. Rings and
ealth are almost synonymous in early literature. A chief or a hero
a ring-giver in Icelandic sagas as in Beowulf ; both Scyld and
Irothgar are praised as *beaga-bryttan*, distributors or givers of rings,
nd one who gives not rings is described as a bad ruler. King
astmere (in Percy's *Reliques*) gives rings of gold or talents of gold
ndiscriminately. Frithiof breaks his ring in pieces and distributes
to his followers, so that they shall not be impecunious in the
nderworld. Rings were used in marriage payments and in wergeld,
ne latter being estimated by *baugatal* or ring tale ; a silver ring
eighing 12 ounces was the compensation for the loss of a thrall ;
oo rings or 100 head of cattle for a freeman (Dasent, 1861, pp. 397 *ff*.;
hadwick, 1905, pp. 392 *ff*., 1912, p. 352).

Coined money came late into the out-lying islands and even to
ne mainland of Western Europe. Sweden can boast a magnificent
eries of 'coins', a series so primitive in form that they recall the
x-hide ingots of the Bronze Age. These, however, are not
urvivals but ingenious money of necessity. The large flat sheets
f copper called plate-money (Pl. 26, Fig. 1) were produced during
ne 17th and 18th centuries for the purpose of compensating for
ne drain of silver needed to pay the Danish war indemnity (for the
)anes insisted on silver), of exploiting the copper mines and en-
iching the royal treasury. The 8-daler piece of 1659, measuring
bout 2 ft. long by 1 ft. broad, and weighing over 32 pounds, is
ne of the largest coins in the world. Still heavier coins were
ssued. One of the 10-daler pieces of 1644 weighing 45 pounds
though no larger than the 8-dalers) is in the Kungliga Myntkabinett
t Stockholm.[3]

[1] Taxes were paid in *wadmal* in Orkney and Shetland, down to the
7th century; and in Iceland in Dasent's time, a cow was still reckoned at
s value in *wadmal*.

[2] See the Proclamation for the regulation of English trade with Iceland,
etween 1413 and 1426, quoted by Ridgeway, 1892, pp. 18–20. Stockfish
an still be used in place of money in Northern Europe. In 1937 the Bergen
teamship Company paid an Italian firm over 7,000 tons of dried cod, as
art of the purchase price of a steamer (*The Times*, 1.1.37).

[3] Only three of these 10-daler pieces are recorded as being still in exist-
nce (*cf.* A. Wahlstedt, 1930). The illustration, Pl. 26, Fig. 2, of an 8-daler
iece in the Göteborg Museum was kindly supplied by the Director.

We are accustomed to the picture of our savage woad-decorated ancestors first being lured into bartering with Phoenician traders some centuries before our islands were linked on to the mainland by Roman overlords :

> Some grave Tyrian trader . . . unbent sails
> There, where down cloudy cliffs, through sheets of foam
> Shy traffickers, the dark Iberians come—
> And on the beach, undid his corded bales.

But if we turn from historians to archaeologists we get an impression of early trade long before the Phoenicians visited this out-of-the-way part of the world.

The Stone Ages afford evidence of exotic objects which have found their way into the country, for even if amber and jet may be attributed to local sources, jadeite or callais or Egyptian beads may not ; while megaliths and beakers are proofs of culture contact before the end of the Neolithic period.

A claim has indeed been made that the squared blocks of flint found in some numbers in Palaeolithic sites near Woldingham, were the first steps in the evolution of money (L. Mann). It is not unreasonable to believe that flint, so valuable and so unevenly distributed in the British Isles, should early form an article of barter or exchange, comparable with the honey-coloured flints of Pressigny or the obsidian round the Mediterranean. East Anglian flints are found in Somerset, and the quantities of semi-prepared flints from Antrim found in Wigtownshire suggest trading on a larger scale.

We are on safer ground in the Bronze Age, and turn naturally to Ireland as the main source of gold not only in England, but in Western Europe as well.

The Cuchulain Saga, with paganism breaking through its Christian veneer, gives a good idea of what was considered wealth in Ireland. In the boasting match between the King and Queen of Connaught, Medh begins by proclaiming her fame in dividing gifts and giving wages. Ailell retorts ' As for giving of wages and dividing gifts, you are no better than myself '. The argument leads to comparison of their wealth, displayed for all to see, beginning humbly with the vats and iron vessels of their households (recalling the cauldrons of the Greeks and of the Annamese) next their ring chains, brooches and clothing, then their sheep, horses, swine and lastly cattle. Slaves were not mentioned in the calculation, but higher valuables were always reckoned in slaves, a slave being nominally worth three cows. A ' chariot worth three times seven serving maids ' is offered, together with lands, and ' my own close friendship along with that ' for the Brown Bull of Cuailgne. The tribute paid by the King of Leinster in A.D. 106 is recorded as consisting of 150 cows, 150 swine, 150 couples of men and women in servitude

50 girls and the King's daughter in like servitude, 150 cauldrons, with 2 passing large ones of the breadth and depth of 5 fists (*Annals of the Four Masters*, O'Donovan; *cf.* Ridgeway, 1892, pp. 31–2).

Medh's brooch, with its exact weight in *ungas* (*uncia* = ounce) and her enumeration of her rings and her thumb-rings, illustrate the forms in which gifts were bestowed and debts were calculated. The evidence of the use of ornaments as money in Teutonic lands has been referred to above (p. 285). The custom continued in England as late as the 10th century and even later as is recorded in legacies. Arm-rings (*beagas*) of 30, 50, 80 or 120 mancuses [1] were bequeathed in Anglo-Saxon wills, and in one bequest the gold

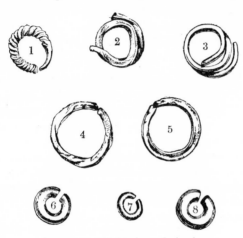

FIG. 126.—Gold rings, Ireland

off a wooden cup is given to be added to a ring, or 16 mancuses of red gold instead, that amount of gold having been put on the cup (Whitelock, 1930, pp. 12 *ff.*).

The wealth of gold and of bronze rings in the Museum of the Royal Irish Academy bears testimony to their popularity in Ireland, and if they fit into a definite weight scale, the belief in their use as money as well as ornament is supported (Fig. 126).[2] There are abundant references in Irish literature to the giving of gold ornaments, and rings for ' bride-price ' and wergeld are mentioned in history or legend. The wealthy ladies had their arms covered with rings, ready to bestow on poets, musicians or story-tellers, whom they

[1] The mancus was the name of a coin (from the Arabic *man-kush*, meaning ' stamped '), traditionally weighing 70 barleycorns, equal to the Roman *solidus* and of the value of an ox (*cf.* Chadwick, 1905, pp. 10, 23, 47).

[2] The Irish rings are usually accepted as currency, but their weight standard is disputed (*cf.* G. Coffey, 1913, p. 70).

wished to reward, and provincial kings attending
the meeting summoned by their superior had to
bring a ring of red gold with them, and leave it
behind or get into trouble (Joyce, 1903, II, pp
224–5 ; O'Curry, p. 169). Fand (in the Cuchulain
story) says ' When Manannan the Great married
me . . . he gave a bracelet of heavy gold as the
price of my beauty '. And St. Finnian of Clonard
(who died about A.D. 550) liberates a serf by means
of the gold ring that St. Brigid had given him
which weighed an *unga* (ounce).[1]

Many of the Irish penannular rings have slightly
expanding and flattened or cup-shaped ends, and
this is the pattern of the *manillas* of the West Coast
of Africa, the close resemblance (shown in the
illustration on p. 89) linking together cultures
separated by three or four thousand years (*cf.* Evans
1881, pp. 382, 387 ; Ridgeway, 1892, p. 42).

Before leaving the subject of rings reference may
here be made to the disks of shale, nearly as hard as
jet, pierced in the centre, often classed as currency
and labelled ' Coal-money '. It is believed by
some, though evidence is lacking, that these disks,
which have been found in large hoards, were used
by the unsophisticated British as money (*cf.* Mosher
1936, pp. 45–6, Pl. XV), but they are more generally
regarded as the ' chucks ' left over after making the
armlets or bracelets which were such popular ornaments in Roman or Romano-British times.

The use by the Britons of bars of iron or bronze
as money has better support. Caesar's statement
(*B.G.*, v.12.4) about the currency of the ancient
Britons has often been quoted, but we are still in
doubt, owing to variant MSS. readings as to whether
he really wrote ' iron rods ' or ' iron rings ', ' iron
spearheads ' or something else. The orthodox reading is : *utuntur aut aere aut nummo aureo aut taleis
ferreis ad certum pondus examinatis pro nummo*, which
literally translated gives : ' They use either bronze or
gold coinage or iron *cuttings* weighed to a definite
weight by way of money.' *Taleis*, or ' something
cut off ' (which has provided our word tally)

FIG. 127.—Iron
currency bar
from Glou-
cestershire

[1] Ridgeway (1892, App. C, p. 395) argues that as the
silver *unga* (ounce) was the price of a cow, so the gold
unga was the price of a male slave.

dmits the interpretation of 'rods' or 'bars'; the substitute of *nulis* provides 'rings'; that of *lanceis* 'spearheads'; and *alliis*, other forms'. And as rods, bars, rings and doubtless also spear-eads and other forms of iron could all be used 'by way of money' 'e can generously accept all the variant readings.

'How the idea of using iron bars as currency reached this country at present a mystery,' wrote Reginald Smith in 1912 (p. 442), ut they occur in considerable numbers in South-West Britain and attered along trading routes to North and East (see Childe's map, *rehistoric Communities*, 1947, p. 226). They are of varying length, sually round about 2 feet (60 cm.) long and of graduated weights, pparently in an ascending scale of a $\frac{1}{4}$, $\frac{1}{2}$, 1, 2, 4, though this is isputable. They are typical of the La Tène culture which reached 'ritain, probably through Brittany, some 4 centuries B.C.

The 'currency-bar' theory is too well established to be easily pset, though doubts have been raised as to whether these 'sword-haped bars, with rudimentary socket handles' (Fig. 127),[1] should eserve the name of money, or whether they are merely moods, e. swords which have been moulded or forged, but not yet finished y the smith.[2] Whether currency or not they provide an excellent lustration of the recurring difficulty of attempting a rigid severance f objects used (i) in barter, (ii) as a medium of exchange, or (iii) s tokens of value. It seems probable that these 'currency bars', vhich have been found in hoards of hundreds, can, like so much of \frican 'currency', claim a place in each section of the tripartite lassification.

Copper bars are just as debatable as iron ones. The illustration, 'ig. 128, shows 2 of the bars found in a Bronze Age barrow near \oyston, Herts, in 1861; 13 of these were found all together 'as in nest'. They are almost pure copper, hammered square, and cut nto short lengths of a few inches. There is no evidence to prove hat these were more than the stock in trade of an ancient bronze-ounder, providing him with the raw material for making his im-lements; and one of the bits, not found with the others, was indeed ashioned into a roughly chisel-like shape. But they may have erved as currency, too, and are by many accepted as such. The nest' was at the base of a barrow called Money Hill, on the track f the Icknield Way, one of the earliest trade-routes of the country, nd the bars may represent a form of *aes rude* which never developed

[1] One of a hoard of 140 from Bourton on the water, Glos.

[2] When iron 'currency bars' were found at the foot of one of the standing tones of Wayland's Smithy in Berkshire, it was a happy coincidence with he legend, according to which payment for shoeing a horse was left on hese stones for the invisible smith—one of the last echoes of 'silent trade' England. On closer examination the bars are unlikely to be older than he 18th century. (*cf.* Fox, 1940, Note 9, p. 433).

into *aes signatum* (Fox, 1923, pp. 36, 63, Pl. XVIII, Fig. 10). I
is worth while drawing attention to this hiatus, before reaching
final summary of conclusions.

It is commonly assumed that as trading develops a need for
convenient medium of exchange, the evolution of money progresse
in three successive stages, of *tool, ingot, coin* ; from bartered good
to metal, which is first estimated by weight, and finally stamped an
becomes coinage. ' Mankind learnt first to value, next to weigl
and last of all to stamp metal.'

It may be conceded that ' Mankind ' progressed by these thre
successive steps in the Eastern Mediterranean, though, as has bee
seen, the literary evidence is uncertain and confused, and the tangibl
evidence is fragmentary.

But ' Mankind ' is not confined to the Mediterranean, and thes
successive steps, obvious and logical though they may appear, ar

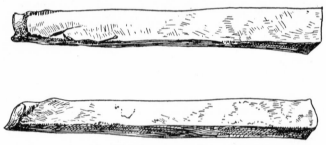

FIG. 128.—Copper currency bars. (¾ size)

seldom to be detected elsewhere. Apart from the Mediterranea
(and a few sporadic examples) a native coinage in metal has bee
evolved only in India and China, in both of which countries Gree
influence has been claimed, and in more recent times, in Furthe
India and the Malay Peninsula ; and seldom do we find convincin
evidence of this sequence.

In India the punch-marked coins are not a primitive form, bu
as yet there is no trace of their development from an earlier weighec
ingot stage.   Nor in China is there evidence of progressive evolution
Cowries, bronze tools and cash jostle each other through the centurie
side by side, with silver as a later commercial addition.

The *larins* of the Persian Gulf probably provide the best exampl
of an evolutionary process if we could accept their origin in fisl
hooks or in nose-clips, which is difficult ; and even with the hel
of Russian *grivna* or Siamese *ticals*, Annamese stamped ingots o
Malay *tampangs* there is inadequate support for a universal theory
When the final stage, that of coined money used in commercia

transactions, is reached, this is in most cases an entirely foreign introduction, brought in by trade or conquest, and has no roots in native economic development.

The early coins of Europe show that they were all borrowings, not native growth, and Britain may provide a typical and final example. The local currency had advanced, we may presume, beyond the barter stage to the use of metal estimated by weight, in gold, silver, bronze or iron. But none of these developed into stamped coins. The first coins found in Britain are Roman ones brought over by trade, and the first British coinage is that of the conquering Belgae.

This universal introduction of coined money by trade or conquest explains a further point. It has been argued above that ' bride-price ' played an important part in the early evolution of money. It also plays an important part in the retention of primitive forms.

We have seen that besides Aristotle's four points, there are two more essential qualities in money : a religious or magical tinge, and ' acceptability '. It is obvious that when coins and conquerors come over together, the question of acceptability does not arise, and the tinge of magic or religion usually vanishes. So coins are unsuitable in an important ceremony such as marriage in which gods or ancestors as well as the family are concerned ; the use of cowries and hoes in Africa, shell-money in Oceania, daos and gongs in Burma—in short the whole museum full of primitive money—was first necessitated and is still essential for ' bride-price '.

If, as many believe, money is the root of all evil, Eve is once more marked out for blame.

Chapter IX

AMERICA AND THE WEST INDIES

Wealth is power

i. West Coast. ii. Eastern maize area. iii. Northern caribou and Central-Southern bison area. iv. Area of intensive agriculture. v. West Indies.

THE evolution of money and the systems of exchange and barter in which it expands, are so intimately bound up with culture, and culture is so dependent on environment, that a geographical and cultural grouping of the American Indians provides a convenient framework for the consideration of the scanty evidence of their currency. The literature is abundant. Holmes complained more than 50 years ago that the references to wampum alone would fill a volume. Much has been written since that time, and archaeology has confirmed or confuted earlier speculations. Great interest is taken in America in primitive currencies, as is shown in such fine displays as the Knox Collection at Buffalo and the Chase Collection in New York. But what is still lacking is evidence as to how these objects were used, and, in many cases, what right they have to be called money at all. That the objects were used in ceremonies, in ostentatious displays, in presentations, in ' bride-price ', in fines and compensations and in exchanges, is sufficiently recorded, but it is difficult to prove that more than a few of them were used as currency before the coming of European traders, who adopted native objects of value to serve as money.

Swanton's article, ' Media of Exchange ', in the *Handbook of American Indians*, 1910, gives a comprehensive survey and a full bibliography. His material, supplemented by the collections of currency in American museums, can be distributed anthrogeographically in the following scheme, based on Wissler's map of the food areas of the New World.[1] This map divides the American Indians into culture groups with occupations dependent on the main food supply, and, slightly simplified, can be used to group the types of currency which are equally dependent on local material and local needs.

For this purpose the areas may be described as :

1. The West Coast from Alaska to California, with salmon to the north and wild seeds to the south. Slaves and coppers were standards of value and exchangeable goods in the North, even after

[1] *The American Indian*, 2nd ed., 1922, Fig. 1.

the adoption of the blanket as currency, and there were various kinds of shell-money.

2. The Eastern maize area from New Brunswick to Louisiana. Wampum, made on the East Coast, spread throughout the region and across the continent.

3. The Northern caribou and Central-Southern bison area from Alaska and Labrador in the North narrowing down to the Gulf of Mexico. Here there was no native money, though teeth and skins had barter values and are included in collections of currency. Shell-money came in from both East and West.

4. The area of intensive agriculture, stretching for 5,000 miles from the South of California across Central America and down the coast of Chile in South America, including both Mexico and Peru. Beads and disks of shell, stone or clay are often exhibited as Aztec ' money ', forerunners of the authentic trade beads which were still in use in Mexico in recent years.

There may have been a tool-currency in Mexico, and cacao beans were used for small change and, packed in bags, for large purchases.

There is no mention of currency or even of markets in the early histories of Peru, though coca was used in exchanges, and although there are a few sporadic specimens of ' primitive currency ' from farther south in museum collections, the manioc and guanaco areas of South America are blank.

After the Discovery the coming of the colonists opens a new page and the West Indies are linked on to the mainland of America. It is instructive to note their early struggles to cope with financial difficulties and the return to barter necessitated by the absence of coins.

i. WEST COAST

' Before the arrival of Europeans,' says Swanton

inter-tribal trade had resulted almost everywhere in America in the adoption of certain standards of value, the most important being shell, beads and skins.

All down the Western Coasts, both in the northern salmon area and the acorn and other wild seed districts to the south, there were shell-currencies with definite values, which were used both for gifts and for exchange. The best known of these are the *Dentalium* strings, the clam disks, the *Olivella* apices and pieces of abalone (*Haliotis*) shell.[1]

Dentalium or ' tusk shells ' occur along the sea coast, especially in the neighbourhood of Vancouver and Queen Charlotte Islands,

[1] Schneider, 1905, figures strings of *Dentalium*, Pl. 15, Fig. 1, *hawock* clam disks, Pl. 14, Fig. 5 ; and *abalone* (*Haliotis*), Pl. 16, Fig. 1.

and are collected by the Indians.   The live shells which have to be
dredged are better coloured than the dead ones which are washed up

They let down long poles to which are attached pieces of wood fitted
with spikes or teeth, between which the shells become fixed.   The squaw
string them neatly.   A small bit of dried sinew taken from the caribou i
passed through the shell lengthwise, there being a hole at each end.   The
string is generally ornamented with fragments of *Haliotis* shell and tufts o
dry wool of the mountain goat (Stearns, 1887, p. 315).

A string of 25 fair-sized shells equals about a fathom.   Such a
string was called *hiaqua* (variously spelt) in
the Chinook trading jargon of the Coast, or
allikochik (Fig. 129), a corruption of *otl we-tsik*
' human beings their shell-money ', the name
given to it by the Indians in Northern California, to distinguish it from the money of the
whites (Kroeber, 1925, p. 25).   This represented the highest standard of currency, which
would purchase one or two slaves.   *Kop kop*
was a name for inferior strings made of smaller
or broken shells in various lengths.   While the
hiaqua represented pounds, one string fetching
40 to 50 dollars, *kop kop* represented shillings
and pence.

Although there are *dentalium* shells on the
Californian Coast the Indians did not collect
them there, but obtained their supplies, with
added prestige, from the far north.   Hence
they had high values, and the importance of
allikochik among the Yurok suggests a comparison with that of *diwarra* among the natives
of New Britain.

FIG. 129.—*Dentalium*
shell-money, Cali-
fornia

' The persistence with which the Yurok
desire wealth is extraordinary,' says Kroeber
(1925, p. 41) :

They are firmly convinced that persistent thinking about money will
bring it.   Particularly is this believed to be true while one is engaged in any
sweat-house occupation.   As a man climbs the hill to gather sweat-house
wood—always a meritorious practice, . . . he puts his mind on *dentalia*.
He makes himself see them along the trail or hanging from fir trees eating
the leaves. . . .   In the sweat-house he looks until he sees more money-
shells perhaps peering at him through the door.   When he goes down to
the river he stares into it and at last may discern a shell as large as a salmon,
with gills working like those of a fish. . . .   Saying a thing with sufficient
intensity and frequency was a means towards bringing it about.   A
man often kept calling ' I want to be rich ' or ' I wish *dentalia* ' perhaps
weeping at the same time. . . .   The practical efficacy of the custom is
unquestionable.

In California strings were not measured by the fathom, but from the thumb-tip to the shoulder, about $27\frac{1}{2}$ inches (70 cm.) ; 11 of the largest shells filled such a string, 12 of the next largest, down to 15 of the smallest that were strung in this way to form a count.

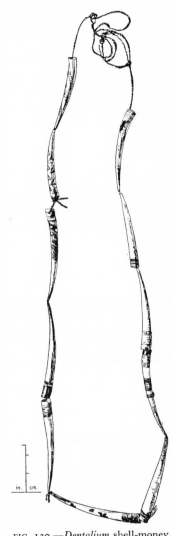

Single shells were measured by the creases on the left hand. The longest shells known were about $2\frac{1}{2}$ inches (65 mm.) long and one of these would reach from the crease of the last joint of the little finger to the crease on the palm opposite the knuckle of the same finger. The value of such a shell in early days was about 5 dollars.

As all hands and arms are not of the same length it was necessary for the man on reaching maturity to establish the values of the creases on his hand by comparison with money of known length. He had a set of lines tattooed on the inside of the forearm. These lines indicated the length of 5 shells of the several standards. This was the principal means of estimating money. The first 5 on the string were measured by holding the tip of the first shell at the thumbnail and drawing the string along the arm and noting the tattooed mark reached by the butt of the fifth shell (Goddard, 1903, p. 446).

Kroeber (1925, Pl. II) illustrates a Hupa measuring a string in this way. If a string of 5 shells reached from the thumbnail to the first tattoo mark, it would be worth 25 dollars, but only 1 in 10,000 would achieve this (Ingersoll, 1883, p. 477). A man owning a pair of such strings would be renowned far and wide, and, even for a high-born wife, he would not part with more than one.

FIG. 130.—*Dentalium* shell-money, California

In North-Western California, the Yurok, Karuk and other tribes decorated the shells (Fig. 130) by scratching patterns on them. They also wound strips of garter snake-skin round them, and tied on little tufts of tiny scarlet woodpecker feathers. But the value still depended on size, not on decoration. Only the larger shells were thus treated, and only the larger shells counted as money. The small shells, more than 15 to the count, were strung as necklaces, and had no currency value except among the inland tribes.

The function of shell-money is most clearly illustrated among the Yurok of the North-West, who regard every possession and every privilege as personal; every injury and offence is against an individual, not the community, and can be exactly valued in terms of property; hence every invasion of privilege or property and every offence must be exactly compensated. This was the idea behind wife purchase, which was compensation to the kinsmen of the woman for her loss. There was no fixed price, for that depended on the rank and wealth of the individual, and social status depended on the amount paid. The higher the price, the higher the standing, not only of husband and wife, but also of their children. Even when two men traded sisters as wives the full amount of money must be paid, as this (among the Yurok) was indispensable (Kroeber, 1925, pp. 21–2). For a wife from a wealthy family 10 strings seem to have been expected, perhaps one of them of 11 or 12 shells, together with headbands of woodpecker scalps, an obsidian blade [1] and other treasures. The average Shasta bride-price is 15 to 20 full-sized *dentalium* strings, 10 to 15 of clam disk strings, 20 to 30 woodpecker scalps, with perhaps deer skins added (*ib.*, p. 298).

Wergeld was calculated and negotiated in the same way. For the killing of a (Yurok) man, 15 strings, obsidian, woodpecker scalps and other property would be exacted, perhaps including a daughter (*ib.*, p. 28). Both marriage and wergeld were definite, commercial, negotiated transactions; all property possessed a value fixed by custom, or by previous changes of ownership, but negotiations were a cause of much dispute, each side claiming as much as it dared, and usually ending in compromise.

Among the Shasta injuries of all sorts, from loss of property and petty theft, to murder and killing in avowed warfare, were settled by payments. The blood-money payable for every individual was exactly the same as the amount paid for his or her mother by her husband, so 'bride-price' and wergeld were easily computed.

Strings of *dentalium* shells were not the only form of money in California. They were predominant in the North-West, but the Pomo farther south and the still more southern Chumash, were centres for the distribution of what are generally called 'clam disks' or *hawock* (ill. Schneider, Pl. 14, Fig. 5). The Pomo made them

---

[1] Obsidian blades had standard values. Those of half a foot to a foot were worth a dollar an inch; a 20-inch piece would be worth 50 dollars, but a giant of 30 inches or over would be beyond price (Kroeber, 1925, pp. 26–7 and Pl. 2).

of *Saxidomus aratus* or *gracilis*, farther south they were made of *Pachydesma*. *Dentalium* and clam disks were used side by side over much of California, but to the south, *dentalium* petered out and was scarcely counted as money.

The large shells are found along the Coast;

these were collected, broken up, ground approximately round on sandstone, bored, strung and finished by being rolled on a slab. The value varied according to the diameter of the disks, and the thickness of the shell, and the degree of polish. The handling of a lifetime imparted a gloss unattainable in any other way, and was appreciated as fully by the natives as by any ethnographic collector (Kroeber, 1925, pp. 248–9).

These strings were a popular form of ornament over much of the West Coast area, penetrating inland on to the Plains. The disks are found in early graves and prehistoric sites, which proves their antiquity, though there is no evidence that they were used as money.[1]

The value of the clam disks, which might be used singly or in strings, varied very much from tribe to tribe. Among the Pomo it seems to have been low, about 1 dollar a yard, or $2\frac{1}{2}$ dollars for 400 beads. Among the Wintun, inland from the Pomo, the beads were counted, not measured, the largest being 5 to the dollar; 20 beads was the fee for each ceremonial initiation. Among the Maidu, still farther inland, the largest beads nearly 1 inch across were valued half a century ago at 4 to the dollar, smaller ones, less than $\frac{1}{3}$ inch across, 5 to the dollar, down to smaller still at 20 to the dollar. Among the Chumash in the South the measurement was, as is usual for Southern and Central California, by the circumference of the hand, half the circumference being equal to a Spanish *real* or American 'bit' or eighth of a dollar (Kroeber, 1925, pp. 249, 359, 421, 565).

Ingersoll, writing in 1883 (p. 478), said that the shells were bored with a flint-tipped bow drill, and were, 10 years earlier, still used by the Indians as the equivalent of silver, the Pomo stone beads being 'gold money'. When the metal drill was introduced the value of the beads decreased.

Similar shell-disks were made also on the Atlantic Coast and traded inland, being very popular as ornaments among the Iroquois. These were made from *Busycon perversum* and other shells and, like wampum, were used and imitated by traders.

[1] Drake is believed to be referring to these strings when in 1579 he was repairing the *Golden Hind* on the Californian Coast. He speaks of the 'Chains' (which he thought were of bone) worn as ornaments 'the Links being in one Chain . . . almost innumerable' and says that the 'Links of these Chains' were also hung on the feather baskets characteristic of the Pomo. But the description of 'chains' and 'links' are more applicable to the edge-to-edge dangles with tiny *Haliotis* pendants (which he also admired) that still decorate the finest baskets.

Olivella shells also counted as money in California, but were little valued, and appear to have been more used for funeral offerings than as currency. The shells are fairly common along the coasts, and, after rubbing off the tip, they were strung, like the *dentalium*, mouth to mouth, and called *kol kol*. Among the Maidu, and other inland tribes, the value was 1 dollar a yard (Kroeber, 1925, pp. 421, 448).

More valuable than the shell-money was the 'gold-money' consisting of cylindrical stone beads, made by the Pomo and traded by them from tribe to tribe at least as far as the mountain barrier of the Sierra Nevada (Pl. 29, top row).

FIG. 131.—Abalone (*Haliotis*) shell pendant,   FIG. 132.—Buttons, St.
California   John's River

These are cylindrical beads, from 1 to 3 inches in length of a variety of magnesite found at White Buttes, near Cache Creek in the territory of the South-Eastern Pomo. These were ground down, perforated, baked and polished. The heating changes the colour of the stone from a dull white or streaked grey to a lustrous buff, salmon or red, often beautifully banded or shaded. These cylinders, which the Indians often call their 'gold' as compared to the more numerous 'silver' disks of clam shell, were too valuable to be sold by the string, and were negotiated for individually or inserted like jewels as finishing pendants in lengths of the shell-beads. The material seems quite similar to the meerschaum of our pipes (Kroeber, 1925, p. 249).

These reached very high values inland, the Maidu estimating one 1-inch long at 5 dollars. But 'their individual variability in size and quality, and consequently in value, was too great to allow them to be reckoned as ordinary money', though 'they were too precious to be properly classifiable as ornaments'. 'They rank rather with the obsidian blades [1] of North-Western California, as an equivalent of precious stones among ourselves' (Kroeber, 1925, p. 825).

There are many other valued ornaments which are often called money though it is difficult to establish their claim to the name. Conspicuous among these are the long cylindrical white beads made of the columella of a univalve or the hinge of a bivalve, used in decoration both in California and on the Plains, as well as forming the 'wampum sticks' to the East.

Abalone (*Haliotis*) shell occupies the same intermediate position between ornament and money; it is primarily decoration, but as it had a trading value it is included in collections of American currency. The shells themselves were treasured on account of their iridescent beauty, and the estimation may have been heightened by magical concepts (*cf.* Jackson, 1917, p. xii). Whole shells were used in barter and bits were cut out into rectangular shapes 1 inch to 2 inches long and about half as broad, perforated and strung together with *dentalium* shells, or shell-disks (Pl. 32 and Fig. 131) as necklaces or ear pendants and stitched on to clothing. As *hawock* represented silver, so *ullo* (*uhl lo*) or abalone represented gold; each of the rectangular pieces was worth 1 dollar and a necklace of 10 pendants, 10 dollars (Stearns, 1869, p. 326; Schneider, 1905, Pl. 15, Fig. 1).

These shells were traded all down the West Coast from Alaska to Mexico. Even at the end of last century the Indians of New Mexico were as glad to receive shells as money in horse-dealing, and 6 dollars or a good abalone shell was a fair price (Ingersoll, 1883, p. 479).

Buttons and thimbles were popular in trading with the Indians who wore them as decorations, the buttons stitched on to clothing and the thimbles as dangles on skin fringes. So strings of buttons came to have a definite exchange value, and were passed from hand to hand like wampum (Fig. 132) and bits of abalone and other shells were rounded and perforated with holes in the centre in imitation of European buttons (Pl. 29).

Scalps of the red-headed woodpecker have already been mentioned as items in the 'bride-price' and wergeld of Californian tribes and they were a form of currency among the Karok of the Klamath River district (Fig. 133). They were valued according to size, from a dollar to half a dollar. A 'large' scalp was one in which the scarlet reached to the bill (though the bill was seldom left to

[1] See *fn.*, p. 296.

measure by) ; this was worth a third-sized *dentalium* shell or a hatful of tobacco, ' but the old men kept a small-sized hat for measuring ' (Harrington, 1932, p. 162).

FIG. 133.—Woodpecker scalp, California

Shell-money was in use all down the West Coast from the Alaskan coasts to Southern California. But there were two classes of objects which are usually recognized as assuming the rôle of money that are peculiar to the culture of the North-West ; the ' coppers ' (Pl. 30) and the ' property celts ' (Fig. 137). The former were associated with the coast tribes, the Kwakiutl, the Haida, the Tsimshian and the Tlinkit ; the latter with the Salish of the interior.

The coppers, consisting of beaten-out sheets of conventional shape some 2 or 3 feet high, were more a sign of wealth and position than a medium of exchange, and they played an extraordinarily important part in tribal ceremonies. They were used for presentation on occasions of great parade, for cementing alliances, and for ' bride-price '. They might be exchanged for slaves or broken up and distributed at a potlatch to show power and disregard of property. They were displayed beside the dead or nailed to the mortuary column of the house. Originally made of native copper, found in abundance in this region, they continued to be made of copper obtained from the whites. They are now rare, but some queer specimens which find their way into store-rooms of American museums suggest that recent counterfeiting may have been profitable. Boas (1895, pp. 344 *ff.*) whose account of the potlatch has been quoted on pp. 14–15, describes the coppers of the Kwakiutl and the ceremony connected with their purchase or presentation.

The upper part is called the ' face '. This part is covered with black lead in which a face, representing the crest animal of the owner, is graven. These coppers have the same function which bank notes of high denomination

have with us. The actual value of the piece of copper is small but it
is made to represent a large number of blankets and can always be sold for
blankets, some of the more famous, which have been often sold, being rated
at six to seven thousand blankets. . . . Coppers are always sold to rivals
and often a man will offer his copper for sale to the rival tribe. If it is not
accepted it is an acknowledgement that nobody in the tribe has money
enough to buy it, and the name of the tribe or clan would consequently
lose in weight.

Boas describes (with illustrations, Pls. 6–10) the elaborate
ceremony of buying a copper, the piles of blankets, the rivalry and
the boasting. Each copper has a name [1] and the one whose sale is
described was *Maxtsolem*, meaning ' all other coppers are ashamed
to look at it '. The price ultimately paid was 7,500 blankets.
With the blanket at 50 cents this would be 3,750 dollars or some
£940.

Rivalry between chiefs and clans finds its strongest expression
in the destruction of property. A chief will burn blankets, or a
canoe or even break up a copper, thus indicating his disregard of
the amount of property destroyed, and showing that his mind is
stronger, his power greater than that of his rival. If the latter is
not able to destroy an equal amount of property without much delay,
his name is ' broken '.[2]

' The origin of these coppers and of their peculiar form and
use is not known ' (Swanton, 1907, p. 346). The shape has suggested a shield, and many writers describe them as ' shields ' or
' shield-shaped ', a description which is not only tendentious, but
ambiguous, shields being of various shapes and, in America, mainly
circular. Confirmation of the shield origin has been detected in
wood carvings of the North-West Coast. In the Provincial Museum,
Victoria, B.C., there is a carving showing the first man to bring
copper to the Indians. But as he is holding the object before him
in both hands it is less suggestive of a shield than of an offering.
On a house post now in the Museum of Natural History in New
York (Fig. 134)[3] there is the figure of a man with a copper, but the
unwarriorlike attitude in which he is clasping it to his body does

[1] The importance both of names and of coppers was pointed out by
Ridgeway in a MS. note. The male name of highest rank among the Nass
River Indians is *Wucinxpeltk*, which means ' dividing copper into 10 pieces '
this being the indication of the chief's generosity. This may be compared
with the old Scandinavian term of praise, ' Ring-breaker ', applied to a
liberal man.

[2] Owing to the reckless rivalry exhibited at the potlatch the celebration
was forbidden by the Canadian Government, and the owners of coppers
were invited to hand over their treasures and receive compensation. One
famous copper was valued at $20,000.

[3] The drawing was kindly made by Miss Helen Cabot, Museum of
Natural History, New York.

not indicate its use as defensive armour. The explanation seems to be that as the actual coppers that a man possessed were placed on his grave to indicate his wealth and position, so the same coppers, each one of which would be known by name, were carved in wood on his mortuary column or on his ' totem pole '. Coppers of abnormal size, standing some 6 feet high, were placed one on either side of mortuary columns or ' totem poles ' at Alert Bay, and figures clasping similar but smaller coppers were carved on the columns.

There is the same uncertainty, though far less literature, on the subject of the miniature coppers (Fig. 135). They may be small models of the larger coppers ; they may be derived from the broken pieces ; they may be the original type, the later ones representing the enlargements (*Wücherformen*) characteristic of material wealth in the other continents ; they may be money ; they may be merely ornaments. These diverse interpretations are not totally irreconcilable. They are classed by Emmons [1] together with the larger coppers as ' used as medium of exchange before the coast was visited by Europeans ', and some, though this is rare, have the totem animal engraved on them. But all are pierced at the upper edge for suspension, and a Tlinkit one in the Dresden Museum is described as a forehead ornament worn in a dance, also used as money.

Among copper quasi-currencies of the North-West Coast must be included the Nimkish (Kwakiutl) bangles illustrated (Fig. 136). These were described by Temple (1899, p. 118) and are now in the Pitt Rivers Collection. They were kept in tens on sticks and used as wedding dower, each married woman having hundreds of

FIG. 134.—House post, Museum of Natural History, New York

[1] Several of his specimens ranging in height from 2 inches to 8 inches (5–20 cm.) are in the Museum of Natural History, New York.

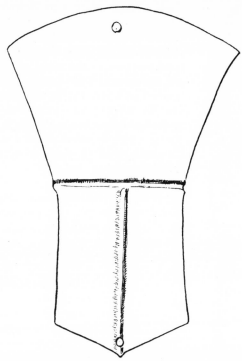

FIG. 135.—Miniature copper, British Columbia. (¾ size)

them. Nowadays they are still worn as ornaments, though silver is preferred, and they have no currency value. They are the nearest approach to 'ring-money' in the whole of the continent, and the only link with that popular form which stretched from Asia to Ireland and continued in use as money from the Bronze Age in Europe to Africa at the present day.

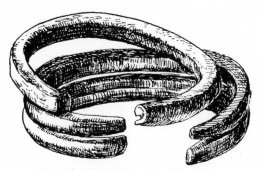

FIG. 136.—Copper Bangles, Vancouver

FIG. 137.—Jade 'property celt', British Columbia

The 'property celts' are very long narrow chisel-like pieces of green stone—jadeite or nephrite—which rarely show any signs of having been used. The one illustrated (Fig. 137) is 16½ inches (42 cm.) long and 1¼ inches (3·5 cm.) thick, of a deep green, mottled and flaked in lighter green.[1] It was obtained by Emmons from an old living site at the mouth of Steen Creek, on the Fraser River, sóme 8 miles above Lytton, British Columbia, and the natives called it a war implement.

Emmons (1923, pp. 26–7) quotes the information given him concerning these tools.

The long celt was not hafted as a common adze, and it seems that at least most of them were not used as tools at all. . . . According to the old Indians these long celts were 'property' and good ones were exchanged for considerable value.

The rock is found abundantly in boulders brought down by the Fraser River and its tributaries, but only for a stretch of about 30 miles above its junction with the Thompson River. It was the best material available for native tools before the coming of the Europeans with iron, so it was as precious and as widely traded as good flint in Britain. But it was even harder to work, and these long 'celts' must necessarily have been rare. The high value, and acceptance as a medium of exchange, may be due to their beauty or their rarity, but those who are looking for alien influences along the North-West Coast are struck by their similarity to the pieces of Chinese jade of the same shape which may have been tools (unused) but were recognized badges of rank and used for investiture and for presentations (cf. p. 233).

Smaller pieces were made into the axes, adzes, chisels and knives characteristic of the Fraser River territory and traded by the Salish as far as Vancouver Island. The coast tribes such as the Kwakiutl, Tsimshian, Haida

[1] Cf. the coloured illustration, which Emmons describes as 'a perfect specimen', 1923, Pl. VI, Fig. a.

nd Tlinkit were dependent on stone tools, among which jade was
ore-eminent, for their house-building, their wood-carving, their
otem poles or mortuary posts and their canoes.   Among the Tlinkit
he value of a jade axe-blade 2 or 3 inches (5-8 cm.) long was
rom 1 to 3 slaves.   When its owner used it his wife should refrain
rom all frivolity, for should she be guilty of misconduct, and should
iis blade break, the Tlinkit Adam threw the blame on his Eve
Emmons, 1923, p. 18).

ii. EASTERN MAIZE AREA

The eastern maize area is distinguished by the most familiar of
ill American currencies, the one which explorers and settlers themselves used and so introduced the word wampum into our language.
Wampum is the shortened form of wampumpeag,[1] the Algonquian
name for the purple and white tubular or cylindrical beads made
from *Venus mercenaria* and other shells.   Strings of these were used
in ceremonial presentation, for fines and compensations ('blood-
money') for peace-making after hostilities, for conveying messages,
for recording tribal history, as ornaments and also as a medium of
exchange.

Unfortunately the early references to wampum are hopelessly
confused as the same names are used for the purple and white tubular
beads made of *Venus mercenaria*; for the long white tubular beads
made of the inner whorl of a conch shell (*Strombus gigas* and others,
Pl. 29) which were a medium of exchange; and for the strings of
disks of 'South-Sea' type,[2] made of various (usually white) shells,
worn, as were all the shell-strings, as ornament.   Few of the contemporary writers give sufficiently accurate descriptions and most of
them are second-hand.   Much has been written since their time,
but there is still no clear agreement as to when or where wampum
was first made, whether it was a native industry before the coming
of the white-faces or the result of European contact,[3] or whether
any strings now in museums are of purely native manufacture.

[1] *Wampumpeag.* *-ag* is the Algonquian plural ending, and the word is
not *wampum peag*, as mistakenly divided by the early writers, who made
peag into an abbreviation, and accepted it as a synonym for wampum.
Roanoke is the name for white or inferior strings in Powhatan or Virginian
dialects, but the name did not come into such general use.   Wampum
became the general name for all kinds of shells and ultimately a synonym,
for money in general.

[2] *Cf.* p. 115.

[3] The derivation of wampum belts from France, via Brazil to Canada
and New York by sea, and overland from the Gulf of Mexico to the Great
Lakes, is traced by Wiener, 1922, II, Chap. IV.

Beverley, writing of Virginia (1705, III, pp. 58 *ff.*) says:

The Indians had nothing which they reckoned Riches before the English went among them, except *Peak, Roenoke* and suchlike trifles made out of the *Cunk* shell. These past with them in stead of Gold and Silver and serv'd them both for Money and Ornament. It was the English alone that taught them first to put a value on their Skins and Furs and to make a Trade of them. *Peak* is of two sorts or rather of two colours, for both are made of one shell, tho of different parts. One is a dark Purple Cylinder and the other a white. They are both made in size and figure alike, and commonly much resembling the English *Buglas*,[1] but not so transparent nor so brittle. They are wrought as smooth as Glass, being one third of an inch long and about a quarter, diameter, strung by a hole drill'd thro the Centre. The dark colour is the dearest, and distinguished by the name of *Wampom Peak*. The English men that are called Indian Traders value the *Wampom Peak* at eighteen pence per yard, and the white *Peak* at nine pence.

The quahaug or 'hard clam', *Venus mercenaria* (Pl. 31, at top) is white inside, but has a purple rim and it is of this part that the purple beads are made, which vary between a deep rich colour, almost black, the most valued, and pale violet; some are merely streaked with purple. The size of the beads varies from the shortest (probably also the oldest) $\frac{1}{4}$ inch (6 mm.) long to $\frac{3}{4}$ inch (1 cm.). Six wampum beads were measured from the end of the thumbnail to the first thumb joint. The white beads are often much longer than the purple in the same string.

The shells are fairly common along the eastern coasts, especially in the neighbourhood of Long Island, which was a centre for manufacture and distribution.[2]

The contrast between the comparative rarity of the beads along the Coast and their abundance inland suggests that wampum was sent as tribute to the powerful Iroquois in Central New York and Pennsylvania. The Narragansetts are associated with wampum-making, and it is probable that the tribe called 'la Porcelaine' (? Rhode Island) were given that name on account of their shell industry, 'porcelaine' being the usual French name, as 'porcelan' the Dutch, for both shell and beads (Farabee, 1922, Eckstorm, 1934).

The Narragansetts (said Ogilby, 1671, p. 151) are the most numerous and rich

being the Storehouse of all such kind of wild Merchandize as is among them. These men are the most curious minters of their Wampompeage and Mowhakes, which they form out of the inmost Wreaths of Periwinkle-shells. The Northern, Eastern and Western Indians fetch all their Coyn from the Southern Mint Masters.

---

[1] i.e. Bugles, small tubular glass beads, then fashionable in Europe.

[2] The Indian name of Long Island was Si-wan-aki or Land of Shells, corrupted by the Dutch into Sewanhacky or 'Wampumland' (Tooker, 1901). But *cf.* Wiener's derivation (1922, Vol. II, p. 250).

He mentions the use of wampum in dowry, adding that a fathom worth 7 or 8 shillings had to be paid to the *Sagamore* or King for every marriage, and that it was also spent at funerals, being buried with the dead (p. 154).

It has been assumed, though proofs are difficult to obtain, that wampum beads were made by the Indians before the coming of the whites, and that the industry was due to the same causes that produced the shell-money of Melanesia ; that is the need of dwellers on small and comparatively barren islands to manufacture something exchangeable for goods on the mainland. Disk beads are found in ancient graves and other deposits and their antiquity is unquestioned. But it is difficult to believe that the fine cylindrical beads could be bored without a metal drill, for the diameter is rarely more than ⅛ inch (4–5 mm.). Roger Williams, writing in 1643, said that before the Indians obtained awls from the Europeans, ' they made shift to bore their shell-money with stones '. The old catalogue of the Sloane Collection in the British Museum has this entry which relates to 1700 or 1702.

A collar consisting of blue and white shells whereof four blue ones make a penny and six white ones. They drill the holes with the point of a sharp flint, and worle them round on a fine gritty stone (Bushnell, 1906).

Bushnell believes that some (though very few) of the bi-conical beads now existing were drilled with flint, but it is possible that metal was already available on the coast, along which ships and traders had been adventuring since early in the 16th century.

The Royal Society Catalogue (1681) recording the rarities preserved at Gresham College, describes ' Indian Money called wampum peage ', adding

Strings pass among the Indians, in their usual Commerse, as silver and gold amongst us. But being loose is not so current. The meanest is in single strings. Of which here is both the white and black. By measure, the former goes at five shillings the fathome ; the latter, at ten. By number the former at six a penny ; the latter at three.

After mentioning the bracelets which come next in value, it continues

The best is woven into *girdles* . . . these . . . are sometimes worn as their richest ornament ; but chiefly used in great payments, esteemed their noblest presents, and laid up as their treasure.

These wampum belts were a feature of the Iroquois and Algonquian tribes, and spread inland, as far as the Great Lakes (Sauk and Fox). Wampum in beads or strings spread farther. It was so useful in trading for furs with the Indians in a country where all commerce was by barter and coins were practically unknown that it was given the status of legal tender, the values being fixed by the

colonists in each district, and varying from state to state and from
time to time.

This extensive use of wampum led to its manufacture by the
colonists as well as the Indians and to its progressive deterioration
and depreciation. The Dutch in the neighbourhood of New York
with the help of steel drills and lathes, provided strings for trading
along the Coast and inland, and in 1760 or 1770 J. W. Campbell
started his factory (Pascack, Bergen County, New Jersey), which
worked for a century. An expert could make 15 to 20 strings about
1 foot long in a day. These were tied up in bundles and distributed
to the traders. European competition destroyed both the native
industry and the high value of wampum, and with the recession
of the fur trade, together with the Indians, the settling of the country
and the gradual incoming of coins, it ceased to have any currency
value.

iii. CARIBOU-BISON AREA

Between the salmon and wild seeds area of the West Coast, and
the agricultural woodlands of the East, lie the vast stretches of
country occupied only by wandering hunting tribes, mainly dependent on the caribou and the bison. Barter was the custom of the
Indians, as it was also of the colonists from 1580 down to the present
day. To the north fur-trading was encouraged and developed in
response to commercial demands, and the beaver skin became the
unit and standard of value. It was usually reckoned as worth about
2s., and it represented two marten skins, which were again divided
by skins of lesser value : 20 beaver skins would buy a gun, nominally
worth 40s. Moose skins were declared legal payment for debts in
1674, and an enactment five years earlier had fixed wheat as legal
tender at 4 francs the *minot* or 3 French bushels (Chalmers, 1893,
p. 175). When trading developed further, and barter proved inconvenient, tobacco and wampum were used in dealings with the
Indians, until the Hudson Bay blanket, graded according to quality,
established itself as the standard of value.

The blanket was also the standard of value on the Plains, as the
gradual extermination of the bison and the pressure of emigration
disintegrated native resources and native culture. But before the
coming of the white man there had been extensive exchanges between
the Coast and the interior, for sea-shells are found far inland,
increasing as usual in value the farther they went. Clam-shell
disks came in from the West, and wampum from the East. Copper
from the Great Lakes is found in mounds and graves west of Ohio
and Mississippi valleys and as far south as Florida, though there is
no record of its use. Pipes of catlinite from the borders of Minnesota

nd South Dakota have been found all over the States and far into
Canada, and, though mainly used as gifts with ceremonial significance,
had a certain trading value (see below). Red ochre, for face-
painting, was a medium of exchange in Arizona.[1] In America, as in
Africa, European beads were brought over by early traders and ousted
the shell or stone beads of native make ; and to continue the comparison, the part played by the length of calico in Africa is here
taken by the blanket, which served as a unit of currency, a standard
of value, and, in the mass, as a symbol of wealth.

' Beads ', said Richardson (1861, p. 391) who explored the country
between the Mackenzie and the Coppermine in 1825-6,

are the riches of the Kutchin and also the medium of exchange throughout
the country lying between the Mackenzie and the West Coast, other articles
being valued by the number of strings of beads they can procure. No such
near approach to money has been invented by the nations residing to the
eastward of the Rocky Mountains, though their intercourse with the fur-
traders has given them a standard of value in
the beaver's skin. . . . To be accounted a
chief among the Kutchin a man must possess
beads to the amount of 200 beavers. The
standard beads and the one of most value is
a large one of white enamel which is manufactured in Italy only and can with difficulty
be produced from thence in sufficient quantities.
Fancy beads, i.e. blue and red ones of various
sizes and the common white ones, are, however, in request for ornamenting their dresses.
Dentalium and *Arenicola* shells are transmitted
from the West Coast in traffic and are greatly
valued.

FIG. 138.—Wapiti teeth,
North America

The beads were strung in 7-foot lengths, which were joined
together at a distance of 1 foot, and the whole was called *naki eik*,
or bead clothing. Each string was worth one or more beaver skins
according to the value of the beads and the whole *naki eik* was equal
to 24 (Swanton, 1907).

Farther south teeth could be used for currency as well as for
ornament (Pl. 29 and Fig. 138).

This particular form of money [Balfour, 1890, p. 54] consists of the canine
or ' eye ' teeth of the wapiti (*Cervus canadensis*) which goes by the name of
' elk ' in those regions. The canines are alone used, and of these there are
but two in each animal. They pass as currency among the Shoshone and
Bannock tribes of Idaho and Montana and probably, no doubt, other tribes
also, passing as a substitute for coin amongst the natives themselves and
not between natives and whites. They represent at present a value of
25 cents of American money but with the increasing scarcity of wapiti it
is reasonable to suppose that the value will rise, if these teeth retain their
function as currency.

---

[1] *Cf.* Pitt Rivers Museum. This is worth recording on account of the
parallel in Australia, both possibly perpetuating a relic of Stone Age culture.

Elk teeth are conspicuous in the culture of the Crow of the Yellowstone. The larger the number displayed, the greater indication of a man's prowess in hunting, his wealth and importance, so they were strung in necklaces and stitched on to clothing and possessions. A wealthy woman's dress might have 1,000 teeth on it. This would be too heavy for comfortable wear, but was suitable for parade. The teeth were used for purchases; 100 would buy a good horse. The main purpose, however, was for presentation on marriage, for ' no Crow dared to think of marrying until he possessed enough elk teeth to decorate his bride's best dress' (Mason, 1926, p. 398).

Imitation elk teeth were manufactured for trading with the Indians, and, being rather larger than life size, were highly prized until familiarity bred contempt. They are still used as decorations and are still stitched on to dresses, but no longer used as money.[1]

The wapiti or ' elk' also provided the Indians with purses. The horn was hollowed out and slit, and was used for storing *dentalium*; the bladder was dried and also used as a purse, for storing porcupine quills. These quills sometimes figure in collections of currency, for, being a popular form of decoration on the Plains for belts, clothing, pouches and other possessions, they were bartered from tribe to tribe, spreading far beyond the range of the porcupine itself.

The bladder purse full of quills (a Sioux purse is illustrated in Pl. 31) was used in exchanges, and so ' passed for money'.

iv. AREA OF INTENSIVE AGRICULTURE

The area of intensive agriculture is the one in which money would be expected to develop, and it seems surprising that the advanced civilization of Mexico, with its organized government, its armies, its established priesthood and educational system, its schools (girls separate from boys), its remarkable skill in architecture and metallurgy, with advanced methods of smelting and casting copper, silver and gold, yet had no better money than cocoa beans.

Yet if one reviews the many queer forms of primitive money, cocoa beans are seen to be superior to many of them. The beans are as pleasant and convenient to handle as cowries, and as easy to count; and though not as durable, they more than compensate for that deficiency by their food value. In early times they were rare importations from the south, and were extorted as tribute from conquered states, thus establishing a currency value. And they

[1] Caribou teeth also had a certain trading value, and, mounted as ' money-belts', were accepted as trading units. One from Alaska in the Chase Coin Collection contains 134 teeth.

suffered the fate of all popular currencies at the hands of counter-feiters. 'Certain dishonest persons used to bore holes in the kernels through which they extracted the contents, filling the hollowed kernel up once more with earth.' They were also imitated in clay, dis-guised with a coating of varnish. The beans were used as currency 'all over Central America. Indeed, one early writer, not a cleric, tells us that in Nicaragua a lady's favours could be had at the price of 8 cocoa beans' (J. Thompson, 1933, p. 67). The use of cocoa bean currency persisted in Nicaragua down to 1875 and has survived into the present century in some of the remoter parts of Southern Mexico and Guatemala.

The scarcity of primitive money in Mexico, as in the rest of the area of intensive agriculture, is partly explained by the universal

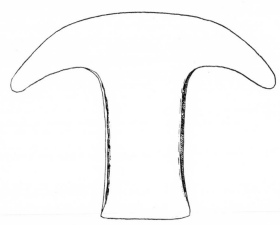

FIG. 139.—Copper 'axe', Mexico. (½ size)

system of slavery, for the slave, male or female, constituted the wealth of the owner, and provided a standard, if not a unit, of value. In slave-owning as in cattle-owning communities, there may be need for smaller change, but only as subdivisions of real wealth. The highest Aztec monetary unit was a sack containing approximately 24,000 cocoa beans, so the subdivisions were ample. When coins were introduced later, 8,000 went to the *xiqui*, a coin of varying values, current in Mexico and Yucatan down to the 17th century.

Brown (1937, p. 149) states that

pieces of cotton cloth served as a medium of exchange, and these were a little bit more valuable than cocoa beans. For extremely expensive purchases tiny nuggets or flakes of gold packed in perfectly transparent duck quills were used for money.

Such quills may be seen in the Knox Collection, Buffalo.

The existence of a token currency in Mexico in the form of 'axes' (Fig. 139) may be compared to the existence of axe-currencies of the Bronze Age in Europe, both in the amount of speculation involved, and the absence of conclusive evidence. Ridgeway's notes prepared for the 2nd edition of his *Origin of Currency* may be quoted here :

The Aztecs of Mexico were using axes of a well-known type at the time of the Spanish Conquest. These axes have a shank that varies in length, sometimes short, sometimes long. This flat shank widens out into a broad crescent-shaped blade. The shank is flat, but has each edge flanged especially near the blade. These axes are often very thin and light and seem ill-adapted for work. Hence it has been commonly held that they were used for money. It has been said that if they were merely monetary tokens the flanges would not have been put on, but experience shows that in the transition from the real implements of everyday life to mere models to be used as tokens, primitive peoples are very careful to reproduce the characteristics of the original. However, the small copper axe from Mitla [Fig. 140] shows that the Aztecs had certainly employed miniature axes fashioned exactly like the axes of real life, flanges and all complete. . . . We need not treat with incredulity the statement of the Indians that these axes were used as money, for it is beyond doubt that everywhere the axe is one of the most prized forms of money in early primitive communities. It is also quite possible that for a long time after the Spanish Conquest and the introduction of iron tools, the old copper axes, when discarded for practical purposes, may have continued in use as currency, as did wampum in the New England States and as at the present moment the stone axes of New Guinea, these being still highly valued as a medium of exchange although the English steel axe has displaced them from practical life.

FIG. 140.—Miniature copper ' axe ', Mexico

A considerable amount has been written about the ' axe-money ' or ' hoe-money ' of Mexico, ' the earliest American coins ' as they have been called. They were frequently referred to by early Spanish writers, and Pradeau (1934) summarizes the most important document written in 1548 by Tenorio, a Spaniard, resident in Oaxaca, then part of New Spain.

This is the form of copper coins that were in use in New Spain. The value placed and at which they were commonly accepted, was of 4 such pieces, if new, for 5 Spanish *reales*. If worn, many refused to accept them and then they were sold to be melted down and remade into coin at 10 pieces for our Spanish *real*.

These copper objects are found in tombs in large numbers. They are so common in some parts, that a farmer growing sugar cane found a sufficient quantity to make the cylinder of his sugar mill of them. Pradeau says that an explorer in the neighbourhood of

Mount Alban, near Oaxaca, found an urn containing more than a hundred of these pieces which, he was told, were brought into Oaxaca in great numbers to be melted down for bullets during Maximilian's reign.   He called them hide-scrapers, and added

> While this scraper-money is not coinage in the true sense of the word, it undoubtedly represented personal wealth, and being valuable, durable and portable, it stood in lieu of money among the Mixtec, Toltec and Zapotec tribes and was passed from hand to hand and buried with their dead. . . . It undoubtedly deserves a place in all collections of ancient money (Pradeau, 1934, p. 88).

These debatable objects have been identified as tools for varying purposes, as ornaments to be worn on the head, and also as religious

FIG. 141.—Copper ' axe ', Peru

symbols, besides being claimed as money.   Pradeau's own opinion is that they were pottery implements, *tajaderas*, of varying sizes, used to mould the revolving mass of clay.   The Zapotecs, not having money, used any article that had any practical or ornamental value as a medium of exchange.   He notes that no historian made any reference to this so-called axe- or hoe-money being in circulation before 1548, that is, 25 years after the Conquest, and 11 years after the establishment of the first mint in New Spain.

> I am inclined [he says] to think that the scarcity of coins of small denominations with which to carry on the meagre commercial transactions between the newly-rich Spaniards and the impoverished natives was responsible for the introduction of the *tajaderas* as medium of exchange (Pradeau, 1934, p. 89).

These objects are included in most, if not all collections of currency in the Old World, as in the New, but it is in the latter that special information is sought, and the varying labels are significant. The Knox Collection in Buffalo accepts not only these, but many other tools, as ' Money of the Aztecs in Ancient Mexico ' (Mosher, 1926, Fig. 26) ; Washington is more cautious, with the label, ' T-shaped object probably used as a medium of exchange ' ; and the Heye Foundation Museum is more cautious still, ' implement of copper, *tau*-shaped, perhaps intended for use as money '.

Farther south, and off the main trading routes in Central as in South America, money has little appeal to the natives, who live by barter, without any medium of exchange. The trader in Nicaragua may exchange handfuls of salt, or even empty food tins, for gold dust ; balls of rubber may be accounted a medium of exchange in the Amazon region, and accepted as fines or tithes, and tobacco approaches more nearly to a currency ; but south of Mexico, money (properly so described) cannot be said to exist.

Some thin ' axe-heads ' of copper or bronze (Fig. 141) similar to the enigmatic *tau*-shaped pieces of Mexico have been found in considerable numbers in Peru, in association with Inca burials, and it is possible that they have the same dubious claim to be classed with currency. A better claim can be made for coca, which is mentioned in all descriptions of primitive money in South America.

As early as 1675 Rice Vaughan in his *Discourse of Coins* wrote :

> In Aethiopia they use certain stones of Salt instead of Money, in Ginney, Shells, in New-Spain, Cacao, Coca in Peru, of one which is a fruit, the other an hearb (p. 6).

FIG. 142.—
Snail-shell
string, Gran
Chaco

Subsequent writers have repeated the statement without adding to the information.

The lack of any conception of money value in the vast hoards of Inca gold seems as strange to us as it did to the Spaniards four centuries ago. It was all dedicated to religious service and neither external trade nor money were included in the strictly regulated state. So although coca leaves, so highly prized and so widely distributed, and traded beyond the regions where they could be grown, were bartered and paid as tribute, they have small claim to inclusion in collections of primitive money.

There are a few claimants from farther south. The Pitt Rivers
Collection includes a hank of dyed wool from the Gran Chaco (ill.,
Ling Roth, 1908, Fig. 2, I, p. 9), and a long string of snail-shell
(*Bulimus*) disks from the same region, a part of which (the whole
is 16 feet long) is seen in Fig. 142.[1]

Geographically British Honduras should have been parenthetically
inserted between Mexico and Peru, and it must not be omitted, for
the logwood that served the colonists for currency down to 1784
is an instructive example of primitive money.

In this colony ' the local standard of value, within little over a
century from the present time [says Chalmers, 1893, p. 139] has in
succession been mahogany, the gold doubloon, the British shilling,
the fractional parts of dollars, and lastly the Guatemalan dollar '.
The determining motive in each case has been 'acceptability';
popular agreement being the dominant factor in colonial procedure.
The very first law of the first popular Convention in 1765, and the
first article in the law provided that ' whoever shall be found guilty
of profane cursing and swearing shall . . . forfeit and pay for every
such offence the sum of 2s. 6d. Jamaica currency or the same value
in merchantable unchipped logwood '.   Later (1766) it was provided
that ' all debts contracted in the Bay of Honduras shall be payable
in logwood, unless there shall be a special agreement made between
the parties in writing to the contrary '.   And penalties of ' 5 l.
logwood currency ' and ' 50 l. Bay currency ' show that the terms
were used indiscriminately.

In 1784 it was resolved that ' the established price of mahogany
shall be 15 l. per 1,000 feet ; that all wood under 15 inches shall be
deemed unmerchantable, and not admitted in payment for debts ;
that the established price of logwood shall be 6 l. per ton for chipped
and 4 l. per ton for unchipped logwood ; and that such price shall
continue in force until the 1st of June, 1785 '.   At the same time
the Colony was put on a metallic basis by the resolution ' that all
business in future shall be kept and transacted in Jamaica currency ',
the doubloon (16 dollars), the dollar (6s. 8d.), and the variable
' maccaroni ' (Chalmers, 1893, p. 140).

In Africa and Melanesia, where local currencies once flourished,
tobacco has assisted at their extinction, and whether this may be
regarded as a reversion to barter, or whether tobacco should be
included in primitive money, it is not easy to decide.

In the New World tobacco was almost universally cultivated
within its climatic limits and traded far beyond them, from Hudson

---

[1] Strings of pierced disks strung in the usual ' South Sea ' fashion and
looking like *pele* (p. 156) are worn as ornaments in Chile but there is no
suggestion of any use as money.

12

Bay in the North to Gran Chaco in the South, and no account of the early money of America would be complete without some mention of its use.

Chalmers in his general survey of colonial currency, records how in the West Indies and the ' Plantations ' on the mainland of America which were so closely linked together in colonial history, ' the early insufficiency of metallic currency led to the monetary use of tobacco corn, wampum, sugar, rum, cotton wool, mahogany [logwood] molasses, ginger, indigo, skins &c.'.

In Virginia tobacco *was* money, and one of the first laws passed by the General Assembly of the colony was an act (1618) fixing its price. It was declared a currency, and the treasurer of the colony was directed to accept it at a valuation. It was rated at 3s. per pound for the best quality ' and not more or less, on the penalty of three years servitude to the colony '.

Curious, adds Chalmers, as a detail in the history of prices is the statement from Holmes' *American Annals* quoted in Hankey's *History of Banking in America* that the hundred and fifty ' young and uncorrupt girls ' imported into Virginia in 1620 and 1621 as wives for the colonists were rated originally at 100 pounds of tobacco (£15), but subsequently at the increased rate of 150 pounds (£22 10s.).

The Rev. Mr. Weems, a Virginian, wrote, it would have done a man's heart good to see the gallant young Virginians hastening to the waterside when a vessel arrived from London, each carrying a bundle of the best tobacco under his arm and taking back with him a beautiful and virtuous young wife (Chalmers, 1893, p. 6 *fn.*).

They must have been stalwart, as well as gallant, to hasten with a roll of tobacco weighing 100 to 150 pounds under the arm.

So important was tobacco to the colonists that in 1642 a law was passed making it the sole currency. Contracts payable in money were forbidden.

But the act had an unexpected effect. Anyone could grow the weed, and soon ministers, clerks, laborers, carpenters and others were cultivating ' money ' in their own backyards. For a time everything went smoothly : tobacco had a ready sale and the price was fixed. Unrestricted production however brought about overproduction and the purchasing power of tobacco began to diminish, until by 1665 it had fallen to two cents a pound. A business depression settled over the colonies. . . . Many persons signed petitions asking the government to forbid planting of tobacco for one year. These requests were not granted. The people then took matters into their own hands and went about the country destroying crops and tobacco plants. The unruly element became at length so strong that it threatened to undermine the government, so in 1684 a law was passed adjudging as traitors any group to the number of eight or more persons who should go about destroying tobacco plants. The penalty was death (Mosher, 1936, pp. 62–3).

Ogilby, writing in 1671, says

he general trade of Maryland . . . depends chiefly on Tobacco, it being
he Planters greatest concern and study to store
imself betimes with this Commodity, wherewith he
uys and sells and after which Standard, all other
Commodities receive their price there (p. 188).

Even as late as 1705 it could be said of
Maryland

Tobacco is their Meat, Drink, Cloathing and
Money ; Not but that they have both Spanish and
English Money pretty plenty, which serves only for
Pocket-Expences and not for Trade, Tobacco being
he Standard of that as well with the Planters and
others as with the Merchants (Oldmixon, quoted by
Chalmers, 1893, p. 5).

'Wherever the trader has been he has left
tobacco and vice behind him' is as true of the
New World as of the Old, though it is popularly
believed that, in North America, tobacco was
there first.[1] Ritual smoking is of such importance in native ceremony that pipes which were
largely used in presentations are sometimes
included in objects used as currency.

The pipes were made of wood, horn, bone,
clay or stone, the most highly valued being those
of steatite (soapstone) or of catlinite (pipe-
stone), the latter only obtained from the quarries
of Dakota and Minnesota (McGuire, 1897).
Pipes were used for presentation and for native
barter in Northern Canada among tribes such
as the Bungay and the Cree of Northern Mani-
oba ; they were also media of exchange (Fig.
143). They were equally important in the East.
Ogilby (1671, p. 151) refers to large stone pipes
made by the Indians of New Netherlands imi-
ating the English pipes so well that, save for
he difference in material 'it were hard to dis-
inguish them'. These were bartered by the
ndians for trade goods and European pipes were
popular articles for exchange. Specimens of
early clay pipes of 17th- and 18th-century shapes,
together with trade beads, bits of pottery, combs,
himbles, &c., are seen in the collection of articles
raded to the Indians in the Peabody Museum at New Haven.

FIG. 143.—Cree pipe

[1] Cf. Wiener, Vol. II, Part II.

V. WEST INDIES

A brief review should be added here of the money substitute
adopted by the early colonists in the West Indies, where the incon
veniences of barter necessitated the selection of some commodit
desired by all, which was given a legal though fluctuating value
This ' primitive money ' differs from that of native developmen
heretofore discussed, for coins (*reals* and ' pieces of eight ') wer
already in existence, so the colonists had a nominal standard of value
but the coins themselves were so scarce that their task was to fin
some practical everyday substitute. It is instructive to compar
their efforts and the results with those of less civilized peoples
Chalmers (1893) from whose book much of the preceding and al
of the following information is drawn, says

> The three centuries of colonial currency have exhibited the phenomena
> singly or in combination, of barter, monometallism (gold, silver and eve
> copper), bimetallism, and paper currency of all grades of imperfection
> there are few experiments in currency which that history does not record
> and no blunders of which it does not indicate the punishment : the genera
> lesson which it enforces is that the ukases of governments are futile whe
> opposed to trade relations and the natural trend of commerce (pp. v–vi)

The list of substitutes starts with cotton and tobacco, and th
use of the latter has already been discussed in the Plantations o
the mainland. It was equally important in the islands ; up to 164
in Barbados, up to 1670 in the Leeward Islands, and still later in th
Bermudas.

The town officers were paid in tobacco, and so were the trades
men, who occasionally objected :

> in tobacco housewives reckoned their marketings, and tenants paid thei
> rents, and with tobacco fines, eked out with lashings, the Government battle
> against the social irregularities of the islanders (p. 151).

In the Bermudas in 1670 it was ordered ' that tobacco in all cases
be the payment [for accommodation of persons at the assizes] an
not to be refused for current payment ' and in 1698

> that all tobacco being merchantable . . . shall and may go and pass Curren
> Payment to pay and fully satisfie all Debts . . . at the Rate and Curren
> Value of Three Pence per Pound (p. 152).

After the middle of the 17th century tobacco was supplanted by
sugar in most of the islands. Oldmixon (1741) wrote :

> As to the product of the country [Nevis] and its trade, what has been
> said of Barbados, Antego and the other Charibbee Islands will also serv
> for this. Sugar is the staple commodity here as well as there, and serve
> for all the uses of money. For all the trade of the island is managed by

ugar. Pounds of sugar and not pounds of sterling is the balance of all
heir accounts ; and exchanging that commodity for others did the
nhabitants' business as well as if they had silver (Chalmers, 1893, p. 63 *fn.*).

In Barbados wages, fees and fines were computed, if not paid,
n Muscovado or brown sugar, rated at 10*s.* for 100 pounds, the
ating being raised and lowered by Act of Assembly. Merchants
artered the goods they imported for sugar, cotton and ginger, and
ften complained that the islanders had ' no money but brown sugar '.
The Act (? 1645) concerning morning and evening prayer in families
rovided that ' whosoever shall swear or curse, if a master or free-
nan he shall forfeit for every such offence 4 pounds of sugar ; if a
ervant, 2 pounds of sugar '.

In the Leeward Islands tobacco was the earliest currency. ' One
housand pound of good Marchantable tobacco in Role ' was the fine
or commerce with the heathen in Antigua in 1644, and a like fine
vas imposed by a Montserrat Act of 1668 for Sabbath-Breaking by
unlawful gaming, immoderate and uncivil drinking—or any other
prophane and illicious Labours of the Week-days, as digging,
houghing (hoeing), baking, crabbing, shooting and such like indecent
Actions '. In 1691 the Governor wrote that trade was almost wholly
by way of Truck, there was very little money and it was not the
standard of trade, the merchants keeping all their books and accounts
in sugar, and calculating all their debts in the same.

An ' able preaching Minister ' was maintained by 14,000 pounds
of sugar a year, or the value thereof in Tobacco, cotton wool or
Indigo ; and such Minister could not demand more than 100 pounds
of sugar for solemnizing a marriage.

In 1700 an Act was passed that money might be tendered instead
of goods, at the rate of 12*s.* 6*d.* for 100 pounds of Muscovado, 2*s.*
for 1 pound of Indigo, 9*d.* for 1 pound of ginned cotton, and 1½*d.*
for 1 pound of tobacco or ginger. Nevertheless, through the 18th
century sugar continued to be used as currency, and to be legal
tender for debts. In Antigua in 1756 taxes were to be paid one-
third in coin, and two-thirds in ' good Marchantable Muscovado
Sugar ' ; as late as 1779 sugar could still be paid as a fine for not
keeping the full quota of white servants required by law ; and in
1784, on St. Kitts, it was permitted to pay taxes in cash, sugar or
rum, at the option of the person or persons liable to pay the same.

Even in Jamaica, which, as the head-quarters of the military
and naval forces as well as of the buccaneers, abounded in coins,
notably the Spanish ' pieces of eight ', sugar was legal tender by
Act of 1751 ' where both parties agree for payment in sugar and
other produce of this island '.

It may be argued that these colonial currencies are *barter*, and
not *money* and have no place in this discussion. It must be admitted

that, to confine ourselves to the main commodities, tobacco and sugar, these are deficient in those qualities conventionally demanded of money. They are not sufficiently *durable*, as both deteriorate with age. They are not conveniently *portable* and although both are *divisible*, yet their *recognition* occasioned continually recurring dispute as to what was ' marchantable '. All these disabilities were, however, outweighed by the possession of the most important quality of all, that of *acceptability*. Tobacco and sugar were universally accepted in taxes, in wages, in rent, in fees, in fines, in legacies and in dowries. If this is not ' money ' it is something behaving as such, and so comes within our definition in the opening chapter.

SUMMARY

WRITERS on the origin of the use of money often start with a consideration of barter and its inconveniences. From ' silent trade ' (a primitive though abnormal form of barter) they trace the evolution of trading and money side by side, relying mainly on literary evidence for probing into the past.

This study relies mainly on the tangible evidence of the actual types of primitive money—or money-substitutes—used by ' unrisen ' people and others all over the world, and is concerned with the purposes, when discoverable, for which they were used. The evidence suggests that barter—in its usual sense of exchange of commodities—was not the main factor in the evolution of money. The objects commonly exchanged in barter do not develop naturally into money and the more important objects used as money seldom appear in ordinary everyday barter. Moreover, the inconveniences of barter do not disturb simple societies. The variety of material and the complexities of uncivilized attitudes towards money preclude generalizations, but the evidence appears to support the following line of argument.

In the beginning Man lived in self-supporting and self-contained groups. Except in an area where provisions are unlimited, a society depending on hunting and food-gathering for its subsistence is necessarily unsociable and ' has no truck ' with its neighbours. Early exchanges were in the way of *present-giving*, and were expressions of friendship with no ulterior economic purpose, although the latter—an expectation of an adequate or even improved return—cannot be excluded from human dealings. Present-giving or gift-exchange, seen in simple forms in the Andamans, Torres Straits or New Zealand, may develop into elaborate ceremonial as in Fiji or the North-West of America, but remain distinct from trading with money.

Barter develops between areas of contrasted produce, such as coastal and inland, forested and open country. We see the barter of fish or shells for vegetables, game for bananas, &c., in Melanesia or the Congo, and the establishment of regular markets. Trading voyages such as those of Torres Straits and New Guinea take us a stage further by the introduction of conventional presents. But so far there is no need for any medium of exchange such as is commonly described as money.

This is the state of affairs over about half the world at the present day. Barter suffices for most of the natives of Australia, New Zealand and the islands of the Pacific, and for the less-advanced peoples of Africa, Asia and the Americas, where native economy is not upset by the trader and the missionary.

321

The use of a conventional medium of exchange, originally 'full-bodied' but developing into 'token' money, is first noted in the almost universal customs of '*bride-price*' and *wergeld*. When sister-exchange is not practicable, some other value must be substituted; where life for life is not demanded, some equivalent must be found. The history of 'bride-price' and wergeld (which has yet to be written) shows how formal the customary gifts become, fitted to definite scales of value. It is not without significance that in any collection of primitive currency the majority of the items are described as 'used in bride-price'.

When once a system of conventional gifts or payments with a definite scale of values has been established (and this is necessary for 'bride-price' and for wergeld) the first steps are taken in the evolution of money. It develops thereafter in response to human needs into the accepted medium of exchange. *Nutzgeld* still remains *Nutzgeld*. Cattle may constitute wealth and form a standard of value. They cannot, strictly speaking, be called money. *Money*, to be generally acceptable, needs more convenient material and finds the four essential qualities (portable, divisible, durable, recognizable) in shells, beads or metals. Two further qualities have been shown to be necessary, one geographical and one more difficult to define. The objects that come to be used as money are mainly non-local, or if local are the product of a special area or a special class; and they have prestige or essential virtue, religious or magical. *Cowries* and *beads*, most universal of all forms of primitive money, have magical as well as monetary value and still hold their own over a large part of the world, though everywhere disappearing now with the advent of the trader and trade tobacco. *Metals* best illustrate the transition from 'full-bodied' to 'token-' money. The spears and hoes of Africa, the knives and spades of China, and the spits of Argos are familiar examples. The tools may become amorphous and valued according to their weight in metal, or survive as attenuated imitations of their former selves. Metal, whether gold, silver, copper, iron or tin, is everywhere useful and everywhere valued, and estimated by size, shape or weight. Ingots are preliminary stepping-stones to coins. Ingots, as lumps or bars, develop in response to local needs or whims in special forms, such as manillas, Katanga crosses and Kissi pennies, Malay hats and Siamese bullets, or our own currency bars and 'ring-money'.

To us, looking backward, the next step appears obvious and inevitable, but it was only in rare spots (possibly only in one rare spot) in the Old World that the final stage was reached, and definite weights of metal, rounded, flattened and stamped, can be called *coins*. Here the study of primitive money comes to an end.

BIBLIOGRAPHY

Abercrombie, J., ' Glass Beads and Associated Types in Britain ', *J.A.I.*, XXXV, 1905.
Acharya, G. V., and R. G. Gyani, ' Résumé of Numismatic Records in India ', *Numismatic Supplement*, No. XLVII. *J.R.A.S.B. Letters*, Vol. III, 1937.
Åkerman, J. Y., ' Remarks on . . . Some Ancient Beads ', *Archaeologia*, **34,** 1851
Alexander, B., *From the Niger to the Nile*, 1907.
Allan, J., ' The Coinage of the Maldive Islands ', *Num. Chr.*, IV, Vol. 12, 1912.
—— *Catalogue of the Coins of Ancient India*, 1936.
Anderson, J., *Mandalay to Momein*, 1876.
Andersson, J. G., *Children of the Yellow Earth*, 1934.
Andree, R., ' Aggriperlen ', *Z.f.E.*, XVII, 1885.
Ankermann, B., *Ostafrica. Das Eingeborenrecht*, 1929.
Annevoie, D. M. de M. d', *Deux ans au Katanga*, 1921.
Arkell, A. J., ' Agate Beads ', *Antiquity*, 1936.
—— ' An Extinct Dafur Hoe ', *Sudan Notes and Queries*, XX, 1937.
Armstrong, W. E., ' Rossel Island Money ', *Economic Journal*, XXXIV, 1924.
—— *Rossel Island*, 1928.
Arnot, F. S., *Garenganze*, 1889.
Aymonier, E., *Notes sur l'Annam*, 1885.
—— *Voyage dans le Laos*, 1895.
—— *Le Gamboge*, 1900.

Babelon, E., *Les origines de la monnaie*, 1897.
—— *Traité des monnaies grecques et romaines*, 1901.
Balfour, H., ' Note on the Use of " Elk " Teeth as money ', *J.A.I*, XIX, 1890.
Banerji-Sastri, A., ' Punch-marked Copper Band from Patna ', *Journ. Bihar and Orissa Res. Soc.*, XXIV, 1938.
Barbot. *See* Churchill.
Barret, W. *See* Hakluyt's *Principal Navigations*, Vol. VI, 1904.
Bartels, M., ' Proben d. kostbaren Perlen d. Basutho ', *Z.f.E.*, XXIII, 1891, *Z.f.E.*, XXV, 1893.
Barth, H., *Travels and Discoveries, 1857-8*, 1858.
Barton, R. F., ' Ifugao Economics ', *U. Cal. Pub. Am. Arch. and Eth.*, Vol. 15, No. 5, 1922.
—— *Philippine Pagans*, 1938.
Basden, G. T., *Among the Ibos of Nigeria*, 1921.
Bastian, A., *Reise in Siam im Jahre 1863*, 1863.
Battell, A., *Strange Adventures*, Hakluyt Soc., 1901.
Beasley, H. G., ' Notes on the Red Feather Money of Santa Cruz ', *J.R.A.I.*, LXVI, 1936.
Beck, H. C., ' Classification and Nomenclature of Beads and Pendants ', *Archaeologia*, LXVII, 1928.
—— *Man*, **134,** 1930.
—— ' Use of the Microscope in the Study of Ancient Beads ', *Journ. Roy. Mic. Soc.*, LIV, 1934.
Benedict, R., *Patterns of Culture*, 1935.

Bennison, J. J. (ed.), *Census of India, 1931*, Vol. XI.
—— *Burma*, Pt. I, 1933.
Bentley, W. H., *Pioneering on the Congo*, 1900.
Betham, W., *R. Ir. Acad. Trans.*, XVII.
Beverley, R., *History and Present State of Virginia*, 1705.
Binger, L. G., *Du Niger au Golfe de Quineé*, 1892.
Bishop, H. R., *Investigations and Studies in Jade*, 1906.
Blackwood, B., *Both Sides of Buka Passage*, 1935.
Boas, F., ' Social Organization and Secret Societies of the Kwakiutl Indians ',
    Rep. U.S. Nat. Mus., 1895 (1897), 1895.
—— ' Ethnology of the Kwakiutl ', *35th An. Rep. Amer. Eth.*, 1914.
Bosman, W., *New and Accurate Description of the Coast of Guinea*, 1705.
Bowdich, J., *Mission to Ashanti*, 1819.
Bowrey, T., *Geographical Account of Countries round the Bay of Bengal,
    1669-1679*, 1905.
Brelsford, W. V., *Handbook of the Livingstone Memorial Museum*, 1937.
Brent, J., ' On Glass Beads with a Chevron Pattern ', *Archaeologia*, **45**, 1872.
Brewster, A. B., *Hill Tribes of Fiji*, 1922.
British Museum Guides. *Antiquities of the Bronze Age*, 1920.
—— *Antiquities of the Iron Age*, 1925.
—— *Antiquities of the Stone Age*, 1926.
Brown, F. M., *America's Yesterday*, 1937.
Brown, G., *Melanesians and Polynesians*, 1910.
Bucknill, J., *Coins of the Dutch East Indies*, 1931.
Bühler, A., ' Alter u. neues Geld im Bismarck-Archipel ', *Schw. Handels
    wissenschaftliche Zeitschrift*, 1934.
Bureau, P., ' Les Tartares-Khalkas ', *La Science Sociale*, VI, 1888.
Burger, F., *Küsten und Bergvolken d. Gazellehalbinseln*, 1913.
—— *Unter d. Kannibalen d. Südsee*, 1923.
Burns, A. R., *Money in Ancient Times*, 1927.
Burton, R. F., *Lands of Casembe*, 1883.
Burton, R. F., and V. L. Cameron, *To the Gold Coast for Gold*, 1883.
Bushnell, D. I., jr., ' Wampum ; Its Origin ', *J.A.I.*, Vol. XVII, 1906.

Cameron, V. L., *Across Africa*, 1877.
Candler, E., *Vagabond in Asia*, 1900.
Cardinall, A. W., ' Aggrey Beads of the Gold Coast ', *Journ. Af. Soc.*,
    XXIV, 1924-5.
—— *Natives of the Northern Territories of the Gold Coast*, 1921.
Carlile, W. W., *Monetary Economics*, 1912.
Carné, L. de, *Travels in Indo-China*, 1872.
Chadwick, H. M., *Studies on Anglo-Saxon Institutions*, 1905.
Chalfant, F. H., *Ancient Chinese Coinage*, 1913.
Chalmers, R., *Colonial Currency*, 1893.
Chamberlain, W. H., *Japan over Asia*, 1938.
Chase, S., *The Tyranny of Words*, 1936.
Chaudoir, S. Baron S. de, *Recueil de monnaies de la Chine*, 1842.
Cheeseman, E., *The Two Roads of Papua*, 1935.
Chinnery, E. W. P., *Anthropological Report, Territory of New Guinea*,
    No. 6, 1931.
Christian, F. W., *The Caroline Islands*, 1899.
—— *The Pacific Islands*, 1910.
Churchill, J., *Collection of Voyages*, 1704.
Codrington, O., ' Manual of Musalman Numismatics ', *As. Soc. Monog.*,
    VII, 1904.

Codrington, R. H., *The Melanesians*, 1891.

Coffey, G., *The Bronze Age in Ireland*, 1913.

Cole, Fay C., ' Chinese Pottery in the Philippines ', *Field Mus. Nat. Hist. Pub. 162* ; *Anthrop. Series*, Vol. XII, No. 1, 1912.

—— 'Traditions of the Tinguian', *Field Mus. Nat. Hist. Pub. 180*, Vol. XIV, No. 1, 1915.

Colle, le R. R., *Les Baluba*, 1913.

Conti, N. de', *India in the Fifteenth Century*, 1857.

—— *Discovery of the East Partes* (ed. Penzer), 1937.

Cook, A. B., *Zeus*, 1925.

Coombe, F., *Islands of Enchantment*, 1911.

Coote, W., *Western Pacific*, 1883.

Coushnir, I. S., ' Chinese Coins without Currency ', *China Journ.*, XVII, 1932.

Cowan, A. C., ' Early Trading Conditions in the Bight of Biafra ', *Journ. Roy. Af. Soc.*, XXXIV, 1935 and XXXV, 1936.

Culwick, A. T. and G. M., *Ubena of the Rivers*, 1935.

Cumming, R. Gordon, *Five Years' Adventures*, 1850.

Cunningham, A., *Coins of Ancient India*, 1891.

Dakers, C. H., ' Hat Money or Tampang of Pahang ', *Straits Times Annual*, 1938.

Danks, B., ' On the Shell Money of New Britain ', *J.A.I.*, XVIII, 1888.

Dapper, O. M., *Description de l'Afrique*, 1686.

Dasent, G. W., *The Story of Burnt Njal*, 1861.

Davids, Rhys, ' On the Ancient Coins . . . of Ceylon ', *Int. Num. Or.*, Vol. I, Part VI, 1877.

Déchelette, J., *Manuel d'archéologie préhistorique*, 1908.

—— *Celtique ou Protohistorique*, 1910–14.

Denham, D., and H. Clapperton, *Narrative of Travels and Discoveries in North and Central Africa, 1822–4*, 1826.

Dennett, R. E., *Nigerian Studies*, 1910.

Diamond, A. S., *Primitive Law*, 1935.

Dopsch, A., *The Economic and Social Foundations of European Civilization*, 1937.

Dundas, C., ' History of Kitui ', *J.R.A.I.*, XLIII, 1913.

Dupuy, W. A., ' The Geography of Money ', *Nat. Geog. Mag.*, Dec. 1927.

Earthy, E. D., *Valenge Women*, 1933.

—— ' Short Note on a Kisi Smith ', *Man*, **180**, 1934.

—— ' The Social Structure of a Gbande Town ', *Man*, **271**, 1936.

Eckstorm, F. H., ' The Attack on Norridgewock ', *New England Quarterly*, 1934.

Elton, F., ' Notes on the Solomon Islanders ', *J.A.I.*, 1888.

Emmons, G. T., ' Jade in British Columbia ', *I.N.M. Misc.*, **35**, 1923.

Enriquez, C. M. D., *A Burmese Arcady*, 1923.

Erdland, A., *Marshalinseln*, 1914.

Evans, I. H. N., *Among Primitive Peoples in Borneo*, 1922.

Evans, Sir J., *Ancient Bronze Implements*, 1881.

Fábri, C. L., ' Punch-marked Coins ', *Journ. Roy. As. Soc.*, 1934.

Farabee, W. C., ' Recent Discoveries of Ancient Wampum Belts ', *Mus. Journ. Penn.*, XIII, 1922.

Felkin, R. W., ' Notes on the Madi ', *Proc. Roy. Soc. Edin.*, XII, 1884.

Ferrand, G. (tr.), *Voyage du marchand arabe Sulayman (851)*, 1922.

Finsch, O., *Samoafahrten*, 1888.
—— ' Ethnolog. Erfahrungen ', *Ann. d.k.k. Hofmus. Wien*, 1888–93.
—— ' Südseearbeiten ', *Abh. d. Hamb. Kolonialinstituts*, XIV, 1914.
Firth, R., Art., ' Trade, Primitive ', *Ency. Brit.*, 1929.
—— *Primitive Economics of the New Zealand Maori*, 1929.
—— *We, the Tikopia*, 1936.
Fischer, H. W., ' Batakländer ', *Kat. de Ethnog. Reichs Mus.*, Bd. VIII, 1914.
Fitzgerald, C. P., *China*, 1935.
Fleming, P., *News from Tartary*, 1936.
Fox, C., *Archaeology of the Cambridge Region*, 1923.
—— ' Distribution of Currency Bars ', *Antiquity*, XLV, 1940.
Foy, W., ' Zur Geschichte der Muschelgeldschnüre in der Südsee ', *Ethnologica*, II, 1913.
Furness, W. H., *Home Life of Borneo Head-hunters*, 1902.
—— *The Island of Stone Money*, 1910.

Gardner, G. B., ' Ancient Beads from the Johore River ', *Journ. Roy. As. Soc.*, 1934.
Gibbons, A. St. H., *Exploration and Hunting in Central Africa*, 1895.
Gill, W., *River of Golden Sand*, 1880.
Goddard, P. E., ' Life and Culture of the Hupa ', *U. Cal. Pub. Am. Arch. and Eth.*, I, 1903.
Goodwin, A. L. H., *Communication Has Been Established*, 1937.
Gouldsbury, C., and H. Sheane, *The Great Plateau of Northern Rhodesia*, 1911.
Graham, A. W., *Handbook of Practical, Commercial and Political Information*, 1912.
Granet, M., *Chinese Civilization*, 1930.
Grant, J. A., *A Walk across Africa*, 1864.
Grierson, P. W. H., *The Silent Trade*, 1903.
Guinness, H. G., *New World of Central Africa*, 1890.

Haddon, A. C. (ed.), *Torres Straits Reports*, Vol. IV, 1912 ; Vol. V, 1904 ; Vol. VI, 1908.
—— ' Copper Rod Currency ', *Man*, **8**, 1908.
Hall, H. R., *Ancient History of the Near East*, 1913.
Halliday, W. M., *Potlatch and Totem*, 1935.
Hambruch, P., *Nauru*, 1915.
Hamilton, A., *New Account of the West Indies*, 1727.
Hamilton, W., *Hindostan*, 1820.
Hanitch, R., ' On a Collection of Coins from Malacca ', *J.R.A.S. Straits Branch*, No. 39, 1903.
Harrington, J. P., ' Tobacco among the Karuk Indians of California ', *U.S. Nat. Mus. Bull.*, **94**, 1932.
Harvey, G. E., *History of Burma*, 1925.
Hasluck, M., ' Bride-price in Albania ', *Man*, **203**, 1933.
Hatchett, G. W., ' Kibanga of Kigoma ', *Man*, **19**, 1928.
Hawkes, C. F. C., *Prehistoric Foundations of Europe*, 1939.
Head, B. V., *Historia numorum*, 1911.
Hedley, C. H., ' Ethnology of Funafuti ', *Mem. Aust. Mus.*, III, 1896–1900.
Heger, F. van, *Alte Metalltrommeln aus Südost Asien*, 1902.
Heine-Geldern, R. V. von, ' Polynesier und Indogermanen ', *Z.f. Rassenkunde*, 1935.
—— ' Urheimat und Wanderungen der Austronesier ', *Anthropos*, XXVII, 1932.

Herberstein, S. von, *Notes upon Russia*, 1851.
Herbert, T., *Some Years' Travels*, 1665.
Hill-Tout, C., *British North America*, 1907.
Hilton-Simpson, M. W., *Land and Peoples of the Kasai*, 1911.
Hobhouse, L. T., G. C. Wheeler and M. Ginsberg, *Material Culture and Social Institutions of the Simpler Peoples*, 1930.
Hobley, C. W., *Kenya : From Chartered Company to Crown Colony*, 1929.
Hocart, A. M., ' Cult of the Dead in Eddystone ', *J.R.A.I.*, LII, 1922.
—— *Progress of Man*, 1933.
Hodson, T. C., *The Meithis*, 1908.
—— *Naga Tribes of Manipur*, 1911.
Hofmayr, W., *Die Schilluk*, 1925.
Honjo Eijiro, ' Economic Ideas in Tokugawa Days ', *Kyoto University Review*, XIII, 1938.
Hopkins, A. I., *Isles of King Solomon*, 1928.
Hopkins, L. C., ' The Cas-chrom *v.* the Lei-ssu ', *Journ. Roy. As. Soc.*, 1935.
Hornell, J., 'Indonesian Influence on East African Culture ', *J.R.A.I.*, LXIV, 1934.
—— ' The Sacred Chank of India ', *Madras Fisheries Publication*, No. 7, 1914.
Hose, C., and W. McDougall, *The Pagan Tribes of Borneo*, 1912.
Hose, E. C., ' On the Twelve Tribes of Tanganyika ', *J.A.I.*, 1882.
Hudson, R. S., *Livingstone Memorial Museum Handbook*, 1936.
Hügel, A. von, *Proc. Camb. Antiq. Soc.*, XLVIII, 1908.
Humphreys, C. B., *The Southern New Hebrides*, 1926.
Hunter, W. W., *Statistical Account of Assam*, 1879.
Hutchinson, M. (tr.), *Report of the Kingdom of Congo . . . by Filippo Pigafetta, 1591*, 1881.
Hutton, J. H., (1) *The Angami Nagas*, 1921.
—— (2) *The Sema Nagas*, 1921.
Huyser, J. G., ' Mokkos ', *Nederlandsch-Indie Ond en Niew*, 1931.

Ibn Batuta, *Travels in Asia and Africa, 1325–54*, tr. H. A. R. Gibb, 1929.
Ingersoll, E., ' Wampum and its History ', *Am. Nat.*, XVII, 1883.
Ivens, W. G., *Melanesians of the S.E. Solomon Islands*, 1927.

Jackson, J. W., *Shells as Evidence of the Migrations of Early Culture*, 1917.
Jäger, F., ' Das Hochland der Riesenkrater ', *Mitt. a.d. deutsch Schutzgebieten*, 1913.
Jeffrey, M. D. W., ' The Cowry Shell ', *Nigeria*, **15**, 1938.
Jobson, R., *The Golden Trade*, 1933.
Johnston, H. H., *Grenfell and the Congo*, 1908.
—— *History of the Colonization of Africa*, 1905.
—— *The Opening up of Africa*, 1911.
—— ' Survey of the Ethnography of Africa ', *J.R.A.I.*, XLIII, 1913.
Johnstone, J. H., and J. B. Cleland, ' History of the Aboriginal Narcotic Pituri ', *Oceania*, 1933–4.
Jones, N., *Occasional Papers of the Rhodesian Museum*, No. 40, 1938.
Joyce, P. W., *Social History of Ancient Ireland*, 1903.
Junker, W., *Travels in Africa*, 1890.
Junod, H. A., *Life of a South African Tribe*, 1912.

Kann, E., ' Silver in China ', *Chinese Journ.*, 1934.
Keary, C. F., *Introduction to British Coins in the British Museum.*

Keary, C. F., *Guide to the Study of English Coins*, 1885.
—— *Catalogue of the English Coins in the British Museum* (ed. R. S. Poole), 1887–93.
—— *See* Lane-Poole, 1894.
Keate, G., *An Account of the Pelew Islands*, 1789.
Kendrick, T. D., and C. F. C. Hawkes, *Archaeology in England and Wales*, 1932.
Keppler, J., *Indian Notes*, VI, 2, 1929.
Kimble, G. H. T. (ed.), *Pacheco Pereira*, 1937.
Kingsley, M. H., *Travels in West Africa*, 1897. *West African Studies*, 1899.
Kirkman, J. S. *The Arab City of Gedi*, 1954.
Kloss, C. B., *In the Andamans and the Nicobars*, 1903.
Knowles, L. C. A., *Industrial and Commercial Revolutions*, 1922.
Knowles, W. H., *Siam Soc. Journ.*, XXXIX, i, 1936.
Knox, R., *Historical Relàtion of Ceylon*, 1679.
Kovalensky, M., *Modern customs and ancient laws of Russia*, 1891.
Krause, F., ' Zur Ethnographie d. Insel Nissan ', *Jahrbuch d.st. Mus. f. Völkerkunde*, Leipzig, 1906.
Kroeber, A. L., ' Handbook of the Indians of California ', *Bureau Amer. Ethn. Bull.*, **78**, 1925.
Kubary, J. S., *Bewohner der Mortlock Inseln*, 1878.
—— *Ethnographische Beiträge zur Kenntniss der Karolinen Archipels*, 1895.
Ku Ch'uan Hui, 1864. *Supplement. Hsu Ch'uan Hui*, 1875.

Lacouperie, A. Terrien de, ' Metallic Cowries of Ancient China ', *J.R.A.S.*, XX, 1888.
—— *Catalogue of Chinese Coins in the British Museum*, 1892.
—— *Western Origin of the Early Chinese Civilization*, 1894.
—— *See also* Lane-Poole, 1894.
Lambert, Père, *Moeurs et superstitions des Néo-Caledoniens*, 1900.
Landtman, G., *The Kiwai Papuans of British New Guinea*, 1927.
Lane-Poole, S. (ed.) *Coins and Medals*, 1894.
La Saussaye, L. de, *Numismatique de la Gaule Narbonnaise*, 1842.
Laufer, B., ' Jade ', *Field Mus. Nat. Hist. Anthrop. Series*, X, 1912.
Laum, B., *Heiliges Geld*, 1924.
Layard, J. W., *Stone Men of Malekula*, 1940.
Le May, R., *Asian Arcady*, 1926.
—— *Coinage of Siam*, 1932.
Lenormant, F., *La monnaie dans l'antiquité*, 1878.
Lewis, A. B., ' Melanesian Shell Money ', *Field Mus. Nat. Hist. Anthrop. Series*, XIX, No. 1, 1929.
Ling Roth, H., *Natives of Sarawak and North Borneo*, 1896.
—— *Great Benin*, 1903.
—— ' The Burmese Collection ', *Bankfield Mus. Notes*, 1, 2, 1901.
—— ' Trading in Early Days ', *Bankfield Mus. Notes*, 5, 1908.
Liorel, J., *Kabylie du Jurjura* [1892].
Livingstone, D., *Missionary Travels* (ed. Arnot), 1899.
Lockhart, J. H. Stewart, *Currency of the Farther East*, 1907.
—— ' Collection of Chinese Copper Coins ', *R.A.S.*, *N. China Branch* 1915.
Loehr, A., *Führer durch die Ausstellung der Bundessammlung von Medaillen, Münzen und Geldzeichen*, Wien, 1935.
Loir, H., ' Tissage des fibres de raphia au Congo belge ', *Ann. du Mus. du Congo*, 1935.
Lugard, F. J. D., *The Dual Mandate in British Tropical Africa*, 1929.

Lugard, F. L., *A Tropical Dependency*, 1905.

McCarthy, F. D., 'The Story of Money', *Aust. Mus. Mag.*, 1935.
—— 'Trade in Aboriginal Australia', *Oceania*, IX, 4, 1939–40.
Macdonald, G., *Coin Types*, 1905.
McGuire, J. D., ' Pipes and Smoking Customs of the American Aborigines ', *Rept. Am. U.S. Nat. Mus.*, 1897.
McMahon, A. R., *Karens of the Golden Chersonese*, 1876.
Maes, J., ' Les Mobenge ', *Revue congolaise*, 1910.
—— ' Les monnaies des Wania-Bungu ', *Revue congolaise*, 1911.
—— ' Le ngula au Congo belge ', *Congo*, 1920.
—— and O. Boone, ' Les peuplades du Congo belge ', *Pub. du bureau de documentation ethnographique. Mus. du Congo belge*, Series 2, Vol. I, 1935.
Mahieu, A., *Numismatique du Congo* [1924].
Maine, H. S., *Early History of Institutions*, 1875.
Malinowski, B., *Argonauts of the Western Pacific*, 1922.
Marshall, F. H., *Catalogue of Jewellery in the British Museum*, 1911.
Marshall, H. I., *The Karen People of Burma*, 1922.
Marshall, J. H., *Mohenjo-Daro*, 1931.
Mason, J. A., ' Collection from the Crow Indians ', *Mus. Journ. Univ. Penn.*, XVII, 1926.
Maspero, G., *Dawn of Civilization*, 1910.
Masudi, A. ul, *Les prairies d'or* (ed. B. de Meynard), 1861–77.
Mattingly, H., *Roman Coins*, 1928.
Mattingly, H., and E. S. G. Robinson, ' Date of Roman Denarius ', *Proc. Brit. Acad.*, XVIII, 1932.
Mead, M. (ed.), *Co-operation and competition among Primitive Peoples*, 1937.
—— *The Mountain Arapesh*, 1938.
Meek, C. K., *Northern Tribes of Nigeria*, 1925.
—— *A Sudanese Kingdom*, 1931.
Meinicke, K. E., *Inseln des Stillen Ozeans*, 1875.
Melville and Standon, *Journ. of Conchology*, IX, 1899.
Merensky, M., ' Schmuckkorallen d. Afrikanischen Völker ', *Z.f. Eth.*, XIV, 1882.
Meyer, E., and W. Foy, *Bronzepauken aus südost-Asien*, 1907.
Millies, H. C., *Recherches sur les monnaies des indigènes de l'archipel Indien et de la peninsule malaie*, 1871.
Mills, J. P., *The Ao Nagas*, 1926.
Minns, E. H., *Scythians and Greeks*, 1913.
Montandon, G., *Traité d'ethnologie culturelle*, 1934.
Monteiro, J. J., *Angola and the River Congo*, 1875.
Montpellier d'Annevoie, *Deux ans au Katanga*, 1921.
Morga, A. da, *The Philippine Islands*, 1868.
Morse, H. B., *Trade and Administration of China*, 1913.
Mosher, S., *The Story of Money*, 1936.
Moubray, J. M., *In South Central Africa*, 1912.
Mouhot, H., *Travels in the Central Parts of Indo-China, Cambodia and Laos, 1858–60*, 1864.
Müller-Wismar, ' Yap ', *Hamburg Wissensch. Stift.*, I, 1917.
Munro, N. G., *Coins of Japan*, 1904.

Nachtigal, G., *Reisen in der Sahara und im Sudan*, 1887.
Nadel, S. F., *Africa*, Vol. X, No. 4, 1937.
Nalder, L. F. (ed.), *Tribal Survey of Mongalla Province*, 1937.

Nevermann, H., *Bei Sumpfmenschen und Kopfjägern*, 1933.
Nieuwenhuis, A. W., ' Kunstperlen und ihre kulturelle Bedeutung ', *Int. Arch. f. Eth.*, XVI, 1903.
Norden, H., *Fresh Tracks in the Belgian Congo*, 1924.
Northcote, G. A. S., ' The Nilotic Kavirondo ', *J.R.A.I.*, XXXVII, 1907.
Nott, S. C., *Chinese Jade*, 1936.

Ogilby, J., *Asia*, 1673.
—— *Africa*, 1676.
—— *Description of the New World*, 1671.
Orde-Browne, G. St. J., ' An African Shell Ornament ', *Journ. Roy. Af. Soc.*, XXIX, 1929–30.
O'Riley, E., ' Journal of a Tour to Karen-ni ', *Journ. R.G. Soc.*, XXXII, 1862.
Overbergh, C. van, *Les Bangala*, 1907.
—— and de Jonghe, *Coll. de Monog. Eth.*, 1907.

Pacheco Pereira, ed. Dias, 1905 ; ed. Kimble, 1937.
Palgrave, W. G., *Journeys through Central and Eastern Arabia*, 1865.
Parkinson, R., *Dreissig Jahre in d. Südsee*, 1907.
Parry, N. E., *The Lakhars*, 1932.
Paulitschke, P., *Ethnographie Nord-Afrikas*, 1873.
Petri, H., ' Geldformen der Südsee ', *Anthropos.*, 1936.
Pfeil, J., *Studien und Beobachtungen aus der Südsee*, 1899.
Pickering C., *Races of Man*, 1863.
Pigafetta. *See* Hutchinson, 1881.
Polo, Marco, ed. Yule, 1903 ; ed Komroff, 1930 ; ed. Moule, 1938.
Pope-Hennessy, U., *Early Chinese Jades*, 1923.
Pradeau, A. F., ' Hoe Money of Mexico ', *Numismatist*, XLVII, 2, 1934.
Prasād, D., ' Classification and Significance of the Symbols on the Silver Punch-marked Coins of Ancient India ', *Numismatic Supplement*, XLV ; *Journ. and Proc. As. Soc. Bengal*, N.S., XXX, 1934.
—— ' Observations on Different Types of Silver Punch-marked Coins ', *Numismatic Supplement*, XLVII, *J.R.A.S. Bengal*, III, 2, 1937.
Purchas, S., *Hakluytus Posthumus or Purchas his Pilgrimes*, 1905.
Pyrard de Laval, F., *Voyage to the East Indies, etc.*, ed. Gray and Bell, 1887.

Radcliffe-Brown, A. R., *The Andaman Islanders*, 1922 ; *Man*, **96**, 1929.
Ratzel, F. (tr. Butler), *History of Mankind*, 1896–8.
Read, C. H., ' Beads from the Gold Coast ', *Man*, **1**, 1905.
Reeve, L., *Conchologica systematica*, 1842.
Reich, N., ' Marriage and Divorce in Ancient Egypt ', *Mus. Journ. Mus. Univ. Penn.*, XV, 1924.
Ribbe, C., *Ein Sammelaufenthalt in Neu-Langenburg*, 1912.
—— *Zwei Jahre unter den Kannibalen des Salomo-Inseln*, 1903.
Richardson, J., *Arctic Searching Expedition*, 1851.
—— *The Polar Regions*, 1861.
Richie, J., ' The Use of Alcyonarias as Money ', *Nature*, I, 5, 1913.
Ridgeway, W., *Origin of Metallic Currency*, 1892.
Rivers, W. H. R., ' Primitive Colour Vision ', *Pop. Sci. Monthly*, LIX, 1901.
—— *The Melanesians*, 1914.
Robertson, H. A., *Erromanga, The Martyr Island*, 1902.
Rockhill, W. W., *Land of the Lamas*, 1891.
Romilly, H. H., *Western Pacific and New Guinea*, 1886.
Roscher, W., *Principals of Political Economy*, 1878.

Roscoe, J., *The Baganda*, 1911.
Ross, W., ' Ethnological Notes on the Mt. Hagen Tribes ', *Anthropos.*, XXXI, 1936.
Roth, H. Ling. *See* Ling Roth.
Rydh, H., ' Symbolism in Mortuary Ceramics ', *Bull. Mus. Far Eastern Antiquities*, I, 1929.

Salvíac, P. M. de, ' Les Gallas ', *Geog. Journ.*, 1901.
—— *Un peuple antique au pays de Menelik, les Gallas*, 1902.
Sarazin, F., *Neukaledonien*, 1929.
Sarfert, H., ' Kusae ', *Hamb. Wissensch. Stift.*, Bd. IV, i, 1919.
Sayce, R. U., *Primitive Arts and Crafts*, 1933.
Schapera, I., *Handbook of Tswana Law and Custom*, 1938.
Schlösser, R., ' Klanggerätmünzen ', *Sinica*, 1928.
—— *China's Münzen*, 1935.
Schmeltz, J. D. E., and J. P. B. de J. de Jong, *Ethnog. Album, v.d. Stromgebiet v.d. Congo*, 1904–16.
Schmidt, M., *Kunst und Kultur in Peru*, 1929.
Schneider, O. (ed. C. Ribbe), *Muschelgeld-Studien*, 1905.
Schoff, W. H., *Arrianus, Periplus*, 1912.
Schoolcraft, H. R., *Indian Tribes of the United States*, 1851–7.
Schröder, ' Studien z.d. deutschen Münzname ', *Z.f. verg. Sprachforschung*, XLVIII, 1918.
Schurtz, H., ' Grundriss einer Entstehungsgeschichte des Geldes ', *Beiträge z. Volks-und Völkerkunde v. Weimar*, 1898.
Schweinfurth, G., *Heart of Africa*, 1873.
Scott, J. G., *Burma*, 1921.
—— and J. P. Hardiman, *Gazetteer of Upper Burma*, 1900.
Seligman, C. G., *The Melanesians of British New Guinea*, 1910.
Seltman, C., *Greek Coins*, 1933.
Shaw, W., *The Thadou Kukis*, 1929.
Skeat, W. W., and C. O. Blagden, *Pagan Races of the Malay Peninsula*, 1906.
Smith, E. W., and A. M. Dale, *The Ila-speaking Peoples of N. Rhodesia*, 1920.
Smith, H. S., *Yakusu*, n.d.
Smith, R., ' The Hunsbury Hill Finds ', *Arch. Journ.*, 1912.
Smith, W. C., *The Ao Naga Tribes of Assam*, 1925.
Speiser, F., *Südsee Urwald Kannibalen*, 1913.
—— ' Völkerkundliches v.d. Santa Cruz Inseln ', *Ethnologica*, II, 2, 1916.
—— *Neu Hebriden*, 1923.
Stack, E., *The Mikirs*, 1908.
Stanners, W. E. H., ' Ceremonial Economics of the Daly River District ', *Oceania*, 1934.
Stearns, R. E. C., ' Shell-money ', *Am. Nat.* III, 1869 ; VI, 1877.
—— ' Ethnoconchology ', *Rep. U.S. Nat. Mus.* (1887), 1889.
Steel, E. H., ' The Khasias ', *Journ. Eth. Soc.*, VII, 1869.
Stephan, E., and F. Graebner, *Neu-Mecklenburg*, 1907.
Stuhlman, F., *Mit Emin Pascha*, 1894.
—— *Handwerk und Industrie in Ostafrika*, 1910.
Sulayman. *See* Ferrand.
Swanton, J. R., Art. ' Exchange of Media ', *Handbook of American Indians*, ed. Hodge, 1907–10.
Swayne, J. C., ' Rejang Baskets ', *J.R.A. Soc. Malay Branch*, 1932.
Sydenham, E. A., *Aes grave*, 1926.

Takizawa, Matsuyo, ' Penetration of Money Economy in Japan ', *Columbia University Publications*, 1927.

Talbot, P. A., *In the Shadow of the Bush*, 1912.
—— *Peoples of Southern Nigeria*, 1926.
—— *Tribes of the Niger Delta*, 1932.

Tavernier, J. B., *Collections of Travels through Turkey into Persia and the East-Indies*, 1684 (tr. V. Ball), 1925.

Temple, R. C., ' Currency and Coinage among the Burmese ', *Indian Antiquary*, 1896–8.
—— ' Beginnings of Currency ', *J.A.I.*, XXIX, 1899.
—— *Census of India*, 1901.
—— *Nicobars*, 1903.
—— ' Obsolete Tin Currency and Money of the Federated Malay States ', *Indian Antiquary*, 1914.

Tennant, J. E., *Account of the Island*, 1857.

Terrien de Lacouperie. *See* Lacouperie.

Tessmann, G., *Die Pangwe*, 1913.

Thilenius, G., ' Primitives Geld ', *Arch. f. Anthr.*, XVIII, 1921.

Thomas, E. S., ' The African Throwing Knife ', *J.R.A.I.*, LV, 1925.

Thomas, H. B., and R. Scott, *Uganda*, 1935.

Thomas, N. W., *Reports : Edo-speaking Peoples*, 1910 ; *Ibo-speaking Peoples*, 1913.

Thompson, J. E., *Mexico before Cortez*, 1933.

Thompson, P. A., *Lotus Land*, 1906.

Thomson, B., *The Fijians*, 1908.

Thurnwald, R., *Economics in Primitive Communities*, 1932.
—— ' Im Bismarckarchipel und auf den Salomoinseln, 1906–9 ', *Z. f. Eth.*, I, 1910.
—— *Forschungen auf den Salomo-Inseln und dem Bismarck-Archipelago*, III, 1912.

Tooker, W. W., ' Indian names for Long Island ', *Algonquian Series*, 4, 1901.

Torday, E., *Causeries congolaises*, n.d.
—— and T. A. Joyce, ' Notes on the Ethnography of the South-Western Mbala ', *J.A.I.*, XXXV, 1905.
—— ' Notes on the Ethnography of the Ba-Huana ', *J.A.I.*, XXXVI, 1906.
—— ' Notes on the Southern Ba-Mbala ', *Man*, **52,** 1907.
—— ' On the Ethnology of the South-Western Congo Free State ', *J.R.A.I.*, 1907.
—— *Notes ethnographiques sur les populations habitants les bassins du Kasai et du Kwango oriental*, 1922.
—— ' Notes ethnographiques sur les . . . Bakuba : Les Bushongo ', *Ann. du Mus. du Congo belge*, III, Vol. II, Part I, 1911 ; Part II, 1922.

Tourneur, V., *Gazette numismatique*, 1910.

Viljoen, S., *Economics of Primitive Peoples*, 1936.

Vissering, W., *On Chinese Currency*, 1877.

Wahlstedt, A., *Svenska Numismatica Foreningen*, XXV, 1930.

Walker, C. H., *The Abyssinian at Home*, 1933.

Weeks, J. H., ' Bangala of the Upper Congo ', *J.R.A.I.*, XXXIX, 1909.
—— *Among Congo Cannibals*, 1913.

Westermarck, E., *History of Human Marriage*, 1891.

White, B., *Romance of Currency*, 1934.

Whitehead, G., *In the Nicobar Islands*, 1924.
Whitehead, R. B., Review of Allan's *Catalogue of Coins*, *J.R.A.S.*, 1938.
Whitelock, D., *Anglo-Saxon Wills*, 1930.
Widranges, de, ' Ancient Gaulish Money ', *Arch. Cambrensis*, 1861.
Wiener, L., *Africa and the Discovery of America*, 1920.
Wild, R. P., ' Stone Artefacts of the Gold Coast and Ashanti ', *Gold Coast*
—— 'Ashanti iron discs used as money' *Man*, **99,** 1936.
Williams, Roger, ' Key into the Language of the Indians, 1643 ', *Coll. R.I.
    Hist. Soc.*, 1827.
Winstedt, R. O., (*a*) ' Life and Customs ' ; (*b*) ' Malay Industries ', *Papers
    on Malay Subjects*, ed. Wilkinson, R. J., 1925.
Winterbottam, T., *News from Sierra Leone*, 1803.
Wirz, P., *Nova Guinea*, XVI, 1924.
Wissler, C., *The American Indian*, 1922.
Withers, H., *The Meaning of Money*, 5th ed., 1937.
Woodford, C. M., ' Notes on Malaita Shell Bead Money ', *Man*, **43,** 1908.
—— ' Report on the British Solomon Is.', *Colonial Reports*, 1897.
Woolley, G. C., ' Murut Basket Work ', *Journ. R. As. Soc. Malay Branch*,
    1929–32.

INDEX OF AUTHORS

335

PLATE 1

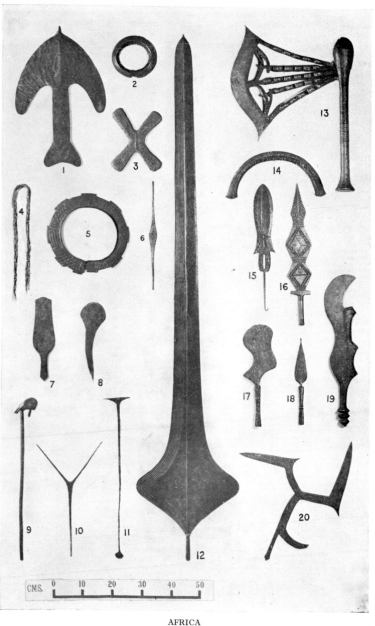

AFRICA

1. Marriage hoe, Uganda, p. 98
2. Anklet, Congo, p. 76
3. Katanga cross, p. 77
4. Copper wire, Nigeria, p. 76
5. Collar, Congo, p. 76
6. Iron bar, Nigeria, p. 87
7. *Shoka*, Congo, p. 66
8. Axehead, Nigeria, p. 89
9. Copper ingot, Transvaal, p. 107
10. Ogoja penny, Nigeria, p. 87
11. Kissi penny, Liberia, p. 87
12. Spearhead, Congo, p. 64
13. Zappozap, Congo, p. 64
14. King manilla, Nigeria, p. 90
15-19. Congolese knives, pp. 70-1
20. Throwing knife, Congo, p. 69

PLATE 2

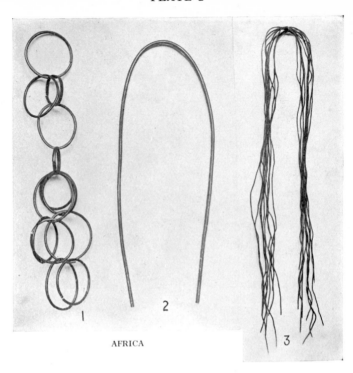

AFRICA

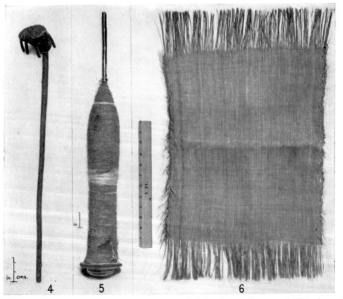

1. *Mitako*, Brass wire, Congo, p. 76   2. Calabar bar or brass rod, Nigeria, p. 87
3. Cheetems, Copper wire, Nigeria,   4. Copper ingot, Transvaal, p. 107
    p. 88
5. Cotton spool, Sierra Leone; *cf.*   6. Mat-money, Congo, p. 57
    p. 85

PLATE 3

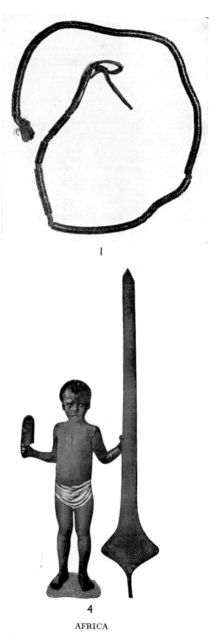

2

3

1

4

AFRICA

1. Brass rings strung on leather thong, S.E. Africa,
   p. 94
2. Native bead currency, Nigeria, p. 60
3. Holed stone, Togo, p. 60
4. Lokele boy with *shoka* and *ngbele*, Yakusu,
   p. 64
5. *Jibbu*, Bubi belt, Fernando Po, p. 50

5

PLATE 4

WHALE'S TOOTH USED IN PRESENTATION, FIJI

pp. 110, 129–30

PLATE 5

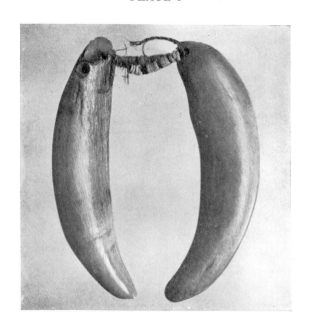

WHALES' TEETH AND ORANGE COWRIES, FIJI
pp. 110–11, 129–30

PLATE 6

MONEY-MAKING, SOLOMON ISLANDS
pp. 117–18

PLATE 7

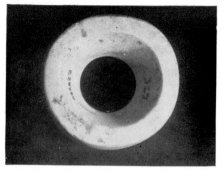

Limestone ring, Pelew Islands, p. 119

Clam shell ring, Rubiana, Solomon Islands, p. 123

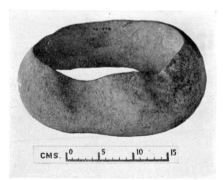

Stone *navela*, New Hebrides, pp. 125, 167–8

RINGS, MELANESIA

PLATE 8

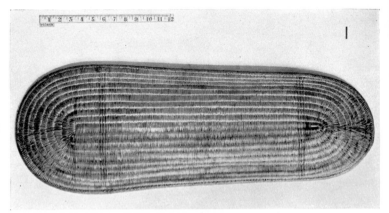

Gaudalcanar Shield, pp. 133, 162

St. Matthias Belt, p. 131

New Hebrides Mat, p. 133

MELANESIA

PLATE 9

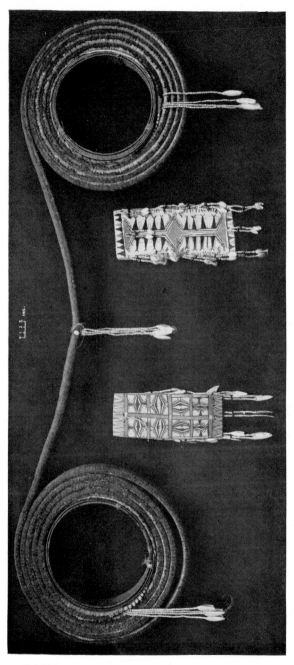

FEATHER-MONEY, SANTA CRUZ, MELANESIA, *p.* 135

PLATE 10

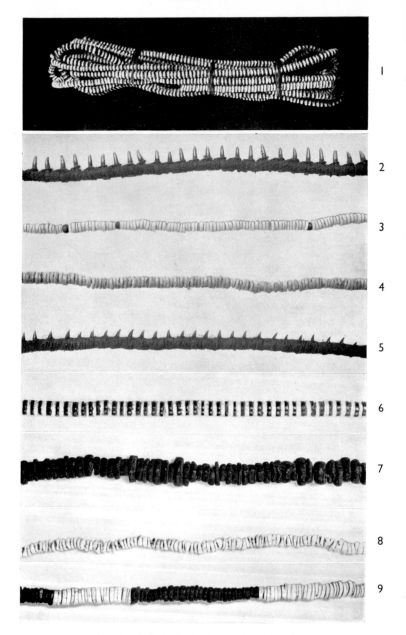

SHELL- AND TOOTH-MONEY, MELANESIA

1. New Britain, *diwarra*, p. 150

2–5. Solomon Is., porpoise teeth, white and a purple *beroan* and flying-fox teeth,
pp. 129, 161

6. Gilbert Is., *tekararo*, p. 140   7. Guadalcanar, p. 162

8. Banks Is., *som*, p. 165.   9. New Hebrides, p. 167

PLATE 11

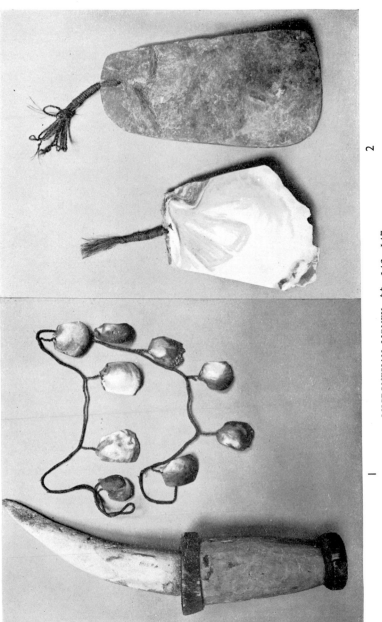

2

1

MICRONESIAN MONEY, *pp.* 142, 147

PLATE 12

1

2

MICRONESIA
Stone-money, Caroline Islands, p. 144

PLATE 13

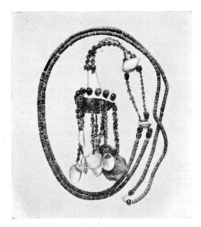

BAGI, NEW GUINEA, *p.* 172

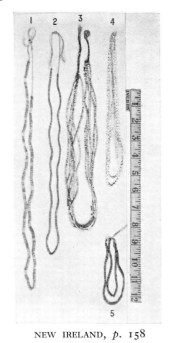

PELE, DUKE OF YORK ISLAND, FIGS. 6-15

6. *A mui*
7. *A pirr*
8. *A munbun*
9. *A mbui*
10. *A mbiubiu*
11. *A lillie*
12. *A kalakalung kambang*
13. *A bingam*
14. Drill
15. Pounder

NEW IRELAND, *p.* 158

FIGS. 1-5 NEW IRELAND

1. *Tapsoka*
2. *Arangit*
3. *Bau (tikutkut, titpele*
4. *Birok* or ' pig-money ?
5. *Mui tikutkut*

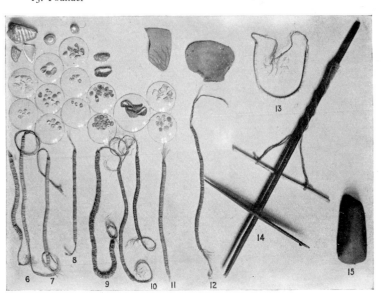

PELE, DUKE OF YORK ISLAND, *p.* 156

PLATE 14

SAMAKUPA AND ARM-RING, NEW GUINEA

pp. 172-4

PLATE 15

'PIG-MONEY', NEW IRELAND
p. 158

PLATE 16

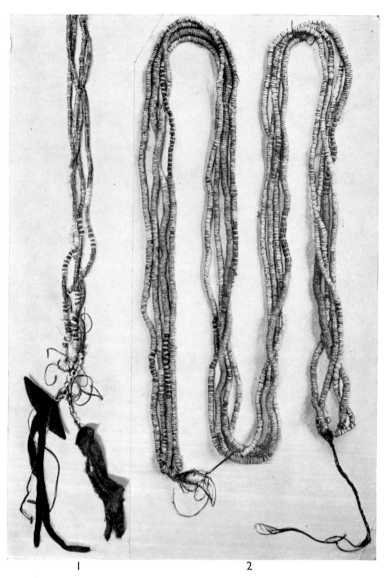

1   2

SHELL-MONEY, SOLOMON ISLANDS
p. 163

PLATE 17

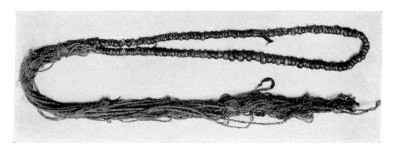

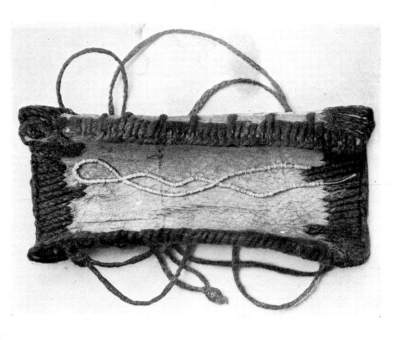

BEADS AND SHELL-MONEY IN PURSE, NEW CALEDONIA

pp. 170–1

PLATE 18

Ndap

Nkö

ROSSEL ISLAND MONEY
p. 184

PLATE 19

1. INGOTS, CEYLON, *p.* 189
2. *DEOGANTA*, ASSAM, *p.* 207
3. KAREN *KYEE-ZEE*, *p.* 208

PLATE 20

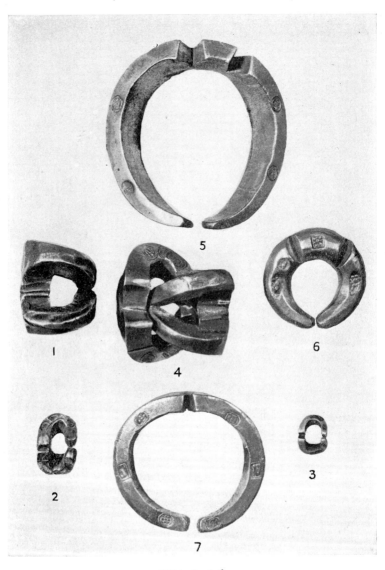

SIAM, *p.* 216

1-4. *K'a k'im*
5-7. ' Bracelets '

PLATE 21

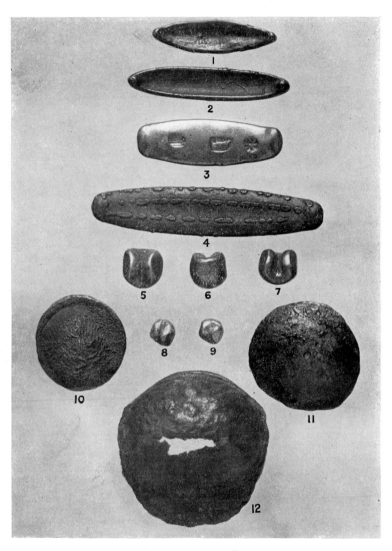

SIAM, *pp.* 215 *ff.*

1–4. *Lāts*, or ' canoe money '   10–11. *Ngön hôi.*
5–9. *Ticals*, or ' bullets '   12. ' Pig's mouth money '

PLATE 22

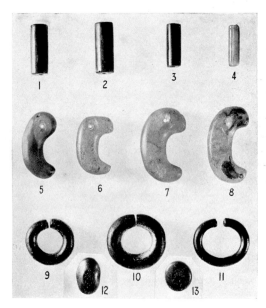

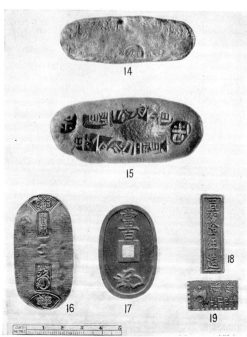

JAPAN, *p.* 249

1-4. Beds
5-8. *Magatama*
9-11. 'Ring-money'

12-13. 'Bean money'
14-15. Badges
16-19. Coins

PLATE 23

1

2

MALAY PENINSULA, *p.* 253
1. Tin ingots   2. *Gambars*

PLATE 24

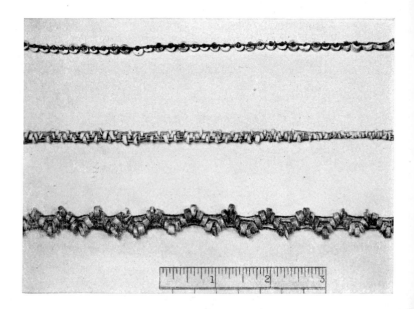

1

2

BORNEO

Shell-money, *p.* 263, and Baskets, *p.* 258

PLATE 25

MOKKO, DUTCH EAST INDIES, *p.* 268

PLATE 26

1

3

2

1, 2. PLATE MONEY, SWEDEN, *p.* 285

3. *GRIVNA*, RUSSIA, *p.* 281

PLATE 27

1

2

1. Squirrel Skin, *p.* 189
2. Brick Tea, *p.* 222

MONGOLIA

PLATE 28

1

2

1. RING-MONEY, BRITAIN, *p.* 281
2. OLBIAN DOLPHINS, *p.* 283

PLATE 29

STONE BEADS, SHELLS, TEETH, NORTH AMERICA, *Chap. IX*

PLATE 30

COPPER, NORTH-WEST COAST AMERICA, *p.* 300

PLATE 31

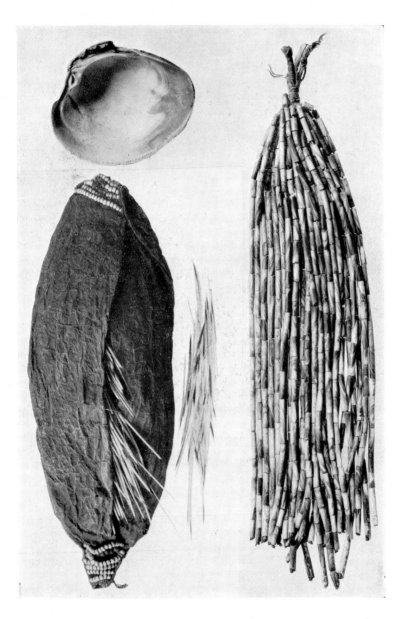

WAMPUM, PURSE AND PORCUPINE QUILLS, NORTH AMERICA, *p.* 306

PLATE 32

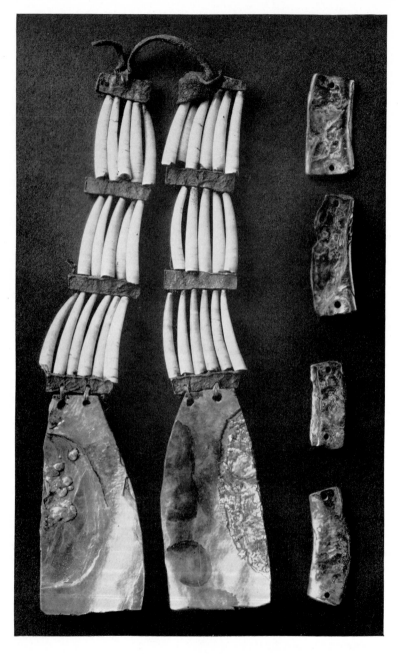

DENTALIUM, AND ABALONE ORNAMENTS, BRITISH COLUMBIA, *p.* 299